Intellectual Property Culture

Intellectual Property Culture

Strategies to Foster Successful Patent and Trade Secret Practices in Everyday Business

Eric M. Dobrusin

Ronald A. Krasnow

OXFORD
UNIVERSITY PRESS
2008

Oxford University Press, Inc., publishes works that further Oxford University's objective of excellence in research, scholarship, and education.

Oxford New York
Auckland Cape Town Dar es Salaam Hong Kong Karachi Kuala Lumpur Madrid Melbourne
Mexico City Nairobi New Delhi Shanghai Taipei Toronto

With offices in
Argentina Austria Brazil Chile Czech Republic France Greece Guatemala Hungary Italy
Japan Poland Portugal Singapore South Korea Switzerland Thailand Turkey Ukraine
Vietnam

Copyright © 2008 by Oxford University Press, Inc.

Published by Oxford University Press, Inc. 198 Madison Avenue, New York, New York 10016
www.oup.com

Oxford is a registered trademark of Oxford University Press
Oxford University Press is a registered trademark of Oxford University Press, Inc.

Library of Congress Cataloging-in-Publication Data
Dobrusin, Eric M.
  Intellectual property culture : strategies to foster successful patent and trade secret practices in everyday business / Eric M. Dobrusin, Ronald A. Krasnow.
    p. cm.
  Includes bibliographical references and index.
  ISBN: 978-0-19-533833-1 (pbk. : alk. paper) 1. Intellectual property--United States. 2. Patent practice--United States. 3. Trade secrets--United States. I. Krasnow, Ronald A. II. Title.
  KF2979.D63 2008
  346. 7304'8--dc22
                                                                                        2008009556

1 2 3 4 5 6 7 8 9

Printed in the United States of America
on acid-free paper

Note to Readers

This publication is designed to provide accurate and authoritative information in regard to the subject matter covered. It is sold with the understanding that the publisher is not engaged in rendering legal, accounting or other professional service. If legal advice or other expert assistance is required, the services of a competent professional person should be sought.

(From a Declaration of Principles, jointly adopted by a committee of the
American Bar Association and a Committee of Publishers and Associations.)

You may order this or any other Oxford University Press publication by
visiting the Oxford University Press website at www.oup.com

To Franklin, Jackson, Shari, Ellie, and Charlee

—Eric M. Dobrusin

To Ellen, Ben, and Jack

—Ronald A. Krasnow

Contents

Acknowledgments

Special thanks go to Shelley Erla, for going above and beyond the call of duty, once again. Thanks also to Dan Aleksynas, for his attention to detail and his editorial support, as well as Jeff Thennisch and the others at Dobrusin & Thennisch PC, and Rex Jackson and others at Symyx Technologies, Inc. and Relypsa, Inc. who have pitched in when it has mattered. Matt Gallaway and his team at Oxford University Press have been great in helping us navigate along the path to completion.

We were lucky along the way for the input and suggestions of Mark Fischer, Mike Fitzpatrick, Dominique Gimbert, Hal Sornson, Norm Sims, Peter Bawden, Martin Faehndrich, Paul Stone, Derek Minihane and all of our clients and colleagues for their collective wisdom and experience, which helped guide the teachings of this book.

Of course we could not have tackled this project without the support and love of our families and good friends, to whom we owe a big debt of gratitude. Thank you Shari, Franklin and Jackson and to Ellen, Ben and Jack. Thank you also, Mom, Dad, Nana Ruth, Stacey, Michael, Megan, Amanda, Sheila and Burt.

CHAPTER

1

The Intellectual Property Culture

culture n. 1 the arts and other manifestations of human intellectual achieve-ment regarded collectively. ▪ a refined understanding or appreciation of this. ▪ the customs, arts, social institutions, and achievements of a particular nation, people, or other social group. ▪[with adj.] the attitudes and behavior character-istic of a particular social group: *the drug culture* . . . .[1]

word history for "culture": Middle English (denoting a cultivated piece of land): the noun from French *culture* or directly from Latin *cultura* 'growing, cultiva-tion'; the verb from obsolete French *culterer* or medieval Latin *culturare*, both based on Latin *colere* 'tend, cultivate.' In late Middle English the sense was 'the cultivation of the soil' and from this, in the early 16th century, arose the sense 'cultivation (of the mind, faculties, or manners).'[2]

---

1. Oxford American College Dictionary at 333 (Oxford University Press, 2002).
2. *Ibid*. at 333.

The Knowledge Economy: Understanding the Culture of Intellectual Property

We all now care about intellectual property (IP). It is the only form of property that we can think up and then get a right to exclude others from what we just thought. That simple ability powers the knowledge economy. Interestingly, while the focus on the knowledge economy is new, its governing laws and concepts are not. What *is* new is that, as Thomas Friedman has urged, the world is "flattening."[3] In other words, as a result of technology, ideas and news pass around the globe faster than ever and resources become known and accounted for faster than ever. Thus, while one country may have more of one type of resource than another country, the one resource that all countries have is a population. Empowering that population to use its brains and ability creates powerful intellectual property. As such, as Jaffe and Trajtenberg[4] have observed "it is now 'knowledge'–not labor, machines, land or natural resources—that is the key economic asset that drives long-run economic performance."

Countries around the world have turned their attention to the active fostering of innovation and creativity. This theme permeated President George W. Bush's 2006 State of the Union address:

> to keep America competitive, one commitment is necessary above all: We must continue to lead the world in human talent and creativity. Our greatest advantage in the world has always been our educated, hardworking, ambitious people—and we're going to keep that edge.[5]

Ireland, another leading participant in the world's knowledge economy, has expressed for itself:

> Sustained investment in R&D is an essential foundation to maintain the competitiveness of the enterprise base and to develop Ireland as a knowledge-based society, so as to increase productivity growth, provide a source of opportunity in new growth areas and to develop a basis for creating knowledge driven competitive advantage across all sectors of the economy. It will benefit society by informing public policy and decision making across all sectors such as health and the environment.[6]

---

3. T. L. Friedman, *The World is Flat* (Farrar, Straus and Giroux, 2005)
4. A. B. Jaffe and M. Trajtenberg, Patents, Citations and Innovations—A Window on the Knowledge Economy at 1 (The MIT Press, 2002).
5. Hon. Pres. G.W. Bush, *State of the Union Address* (January 31, 2006); http://www. whitehouse. gov/stateoftheunion/2006 (accessed December 2, 2007).
6. *Ibid.*

In 2000, leaders of the European Union noted that: "a strategic goal for the next decade: to become the most dynamic and competitive knowledge based economy in the world. (Lisbon 2000 EU Council Strategy objective)."[7] The previous year another world leader in the knowledge economy New Zealand recognized how the knowledge economy would transform existing companies:[8]

> New Zealand companies need to better understand and use the concept of intellectual capital. They need to look at their products, processes, and people, and assess and augment the amount of knowledge they possess. They must unlock the value of their hidden assets, such as the talents of their employees, the loyalty of their customers, and the collective knowledge embodied in their systems, processes, and culture. They must learn how to turn their unmapped, untapped knowledge into a source of competitive advantage.

It is now clearer than ever that innovation and creativity lie at the heart of economy. The world will not stand still and suppress this knowledge. The World Bank now employs a "Knowledge Assessment Methodology" and maintains a "Knowledge Economy Index,"[9] which is used to rank individual countries, following "four pillars":

- Economic Incentive and Institutional Regime (EIR)
- Education and Training
- Innovation and Technological Adoption
- Information and Communications Technologies (ICT) Infrastructure.

In 2007, the top-ranked four Knowledge Economy Index countries were all Nordic countries: Sweden, Denmark, Norway, and Finland. Canada ranked 7th, ahead of the U.S. (10th); New Zealand (11th); Germany (15th); and Japan (17th).[10] Note that the classic "superpowers," the largest economies of the world, do not possess the most advanced knowledge economies. The future race for economic power will not necessarily be dictated by mere population and money, but by how knowledge is cultivated, harvested, and shared within and from the population.

Any organization that plans to invest in the knowledge economy needs to protect the fruits of its investment, and IP is the vehicle. In what can be seen as a cross-matrix to what governments are saying and doing, companies and

---

7. *Ibid.*
8. http://www.med. govt.nz/templates/MultipageDocumentPage_17263.aspx (accessed December 2, 2007).
9. *See* www.worldbank.org/kam (accessed December 2, 2007).
10. http://siteresources.worldbank.org/KFDLP/Resources/461197-1170257103854/KEI.pdf (accessed December 2, 2007).

organizations are thinking and acting globally. To thrive, organizations must seek to create, keep and use corporate knowledge, which is the collective understanding of the people in the organization no matter where those people reside. For example, research and development centers are opening or expanding in China and being linked to other centers in other parts of the world, including the U.S., Europe, and Japan. Thus, IP today can be seen as another form of land grab or arms race.

This book is designed to help organizations build and manage their own IP culture for competing in this race. Today, a number of organizations do not have a refined understanding or appreciation of the IP principles or how to apply them to their particular situation. It is one objective of this book to assist organizations to develop their attitudes and customs.

1-1

Organization managers and governments alike can routinely ask practical questions of their organizations and how they operate when it comes to IP, such as:

- What kinds of innovations does our organization produce?
- How do we protect our particular innovations with intellectual property?
- Where is the invention disclosure form to submit possibly patentable inventions to the organization?
- When do we file a patent application (e.g., the day before the big show, as the product first ships to a customer, when the technology is being developed or when the idea first occurs to us)?
- Do we gather new ideas from all parts of the organization (e.g., Does our CEO go around the company to see what's new and then contact patent counsel excited about the new technology being developed)?
- Do our CEOs know why they are free to market their products and services around the globe (e.g., are CEOs aware of at least one patent controlled by a competitor and explain why they free to market both inside and outside the United States)?
- What is the strategy for global IP protection for our technology?
- Are we organized to maximize our intellectual property (e.g., Who is assigned to monitor IP and who does that person report to? or How is our records kept or electronic data stored so we can show infringement? or Do new employees sign invention assignment agreements upon being hired and do candidate employees sign nondisclosure agreements when being interviewed?)?
- What is spent on patenting and how does it reflect our strategy?

- Is confidential information marked "CONFIDENTIAL" (including emails, corporate documents, etc.)?
- Are people in our organization responding to the IP culture (e.g., Do people in the organization sees a patent number marked on a competitor's product and goes online to read the patent? or Upon discovery of an infringement by a competitor, do the sales and project engineers associated with the targeted product become passionate about wanting to sue the competitor? or Do individuals in the organization start clipping and circulating patent-oriented articles in the Wall Street Journal and other business publications?)?

Intellectual Property (IP) Is the Currency of the Knowledge Economy

In its most simplistic sense, intellectual property is a form of property that governs products of the mind. As most people recognize it, IP generally encompasses patents, copyrights, trade secrets, and (to a certain extent) trademarks. However, to confine IP to such simplicity potentially disserves its importance in a knowledge economy. Viewed by the role IP plays in a knowledge economy, it has many aspects and characteristics, providing the legal framework that defines the rights and benefits that flow from knowledge.

Let us begin to define and explain intellectual property by examining the words that define its label. "Intellectual," of course, denotes a product of the mind—a manifestation of knowledge. That part is relatively easy for most people to grasp. However, the "property" part of the designation is less straightforward.

The "property" aspect of "intellectual property" is the cornerstone upon which ideas of the mind are converted into wealth-generating capital. Yet, "property" is a difficult concept to grasp. Notions of "property" vary from society to society. In the West, "property" is generally regarded as that which can be represented by documentation, possessed and transferred.[11]

In *The Mystery of Capital*, Peruvian economist Hernando De Soto explores the fundamental attributes of property and the institutional framework within which it exists.[12] Among his many rich theories and observations,

---

11. Within the broad meaning of "property," there are two major categories, tangible property and intangible property. Tangible property, of course, is that which can be touched or seen. It may be a machine, a computer, inventory, or a building. Unfortunately, intangible property can not be seen—it must be imagined. Intellectual property falls into the intangible category of property, and for that reason, it is especially difficult for even many of the most intelligent people to understand it.

12. Credit for the link of De Soto's work to IP belongs, at least in part, to Property Rights Alliance. *See, HORST Intellectual Property Rights Index (IPRI)*, published at www.intellectualproperty rightsindex.org (accessed December 6, 2007). Additional credit goes to Bryan P. Lord, of

De Soto explains that a system founded upon the documentary acknowledgment and representation of property as a transferable asset makes the asset visible to others, and effectively connects the asset to the economy.

De Soto identifies six "property effects" that have allowed citizens to generate capital:

1. Fixing the economic potential of assets
2. Integrating dispersed information into one system
3. Making people accountable;[13]
4. Making assets fungible
5. Networking people
6. Protecting Transactions.

In accordance with the De Soto property model, a healthy IP culture is one that recognizes and strives for the creation of intellectual property as transferable products of the mind that are susceptible to lasting representative documentary records, which are recognized and understood universally, and upon which action others may be held accountable for violations within a legal system that recognizes the property.[14]

In other words, intellectual property, including patents and copyrights, is the deed, the basis, the foundational right that is governmentally granted and can be transferred and enforced between private parties. It is another objective of this book, in other words, to help you develop an IP system at your organization that maximizes intellectual property value; for, consistent with de Soto teachings, it is one premise of this book that intellectual property value is maximized when it can be traded or shared so that others can add their knowledge, expertise or resources. This includes trading and sharing internally within an organization so that the organization has the option to trade and share externally.

AmberWave Systems Corporation, who testified on March 29, 2007, before the U.S. House of Representatives, Committee on Small Business. *See*, "The Mystery of (Intellectual) Capital" prepared Statement of AmberWave Systems Corporation. http://www.innovationalliance. net/files/AmberWave%20House%20SB%20Committee%20Testimony%20on%20Patent%20 Reform% 203_29_07a_0.pdf

13. Desoto, Hernando. *The Mystery of Capital: Why Capitalism Triumphs in the West and Fails Everywhere Else* (Basic Books 2000). DeSoto states at page 56: "People with nothing to lose are trapped in the grubby basement of the precapitalist world. "

14. *See also*, Lord statement supra at 3–4 (identifying a 6-prong "blueprint for a successful intellectual property system" addressing, *inter alia*, capturing and recording inventions, and use and accountability for use of inventions).

Patents, Trade Secrets, and Copyrights as IP

In the U.S., patents and copyrights[15] have their basis in the U.S. Constitution:

> The Congress shall have Power . . . To promote the Progress of Science and useful Arts, by securing for limited Times to Authors and Inventors the exclusive Right to their respective Writings and Discoveries. . . .[16]

Patents protect inventions, and specifically "any new and useful process, machine, manufacture, or composition of matter, or any new and useful improvement thereof. "[17] Copyrights protect original works of authorship, and specifically:

1. Literary works
2. Musical works, including any accompanying words
3. Dramatic works, including any accompanying music
4. Pantomimes and choreographic works
5. Pictorial, graphic, and sculptural works
6. Motion pictures and other audiovisual works
7. Sound recordings
8. Architectural works.[18]

Trade secrets, in contrast, are defined in Section 1(4) of the Uniform Trade Secrets Act as:

> information, including a formula, pattern, compilation, program device, method, technique, or process, that: (i) derives independent economic value, actual or potential, from not being generally known to, and not being readily ascertainable by proper means by, other persons who can obtain economic value from its disclosure or use, and (ii) is the subject of efforts that are reasonable under the circumstances to maintain its secrecy.

By their very nature, patents are published documents, and therefore cannot be trade secret. However, it is possible that trade secrets may exist in combination with a patented invention. Copyrighted subject matter may be trade secret or not. Some technologies can be the subject of patents, copyrights as well as trade secrets.

---

15. Trademarks are also a major type of IP, but because they tend to relate more to marketing and less to technology, they receive less attention in this book.
16. U.S. Const. art. I, § 8, cl. 8.
17. 35 U.S.C. § 101.
18. 17 U.S.C. § 102.

The "Exclusive" Nature of IP Rights

Essential to an understanding of the basic IP concepts treated in this book is the need to understand the exclusive nature of IP rights. The term "exclusive" is commonly misunderstood to mean that the party owning the IP right has an absolute **right to use** its IP to the exclusion of others. That is not the case.

Many IP professionals have heard their manager or client say, "we own that technology." Depending on the context that statement can represent a lack of understanding of IP.

The exclusivity conferred by IP rights is **not the right to use** IP, but rather the right to exclude others from its use. This subtle distinction between the "right to exclude" and the "right to use" has profound implications that are often misunderstood. An owner of IP may have the right to exclude others from use of the IP, but that right gives the owner no right to use the IP, particularly if someone else owns a dominant IP right. In later chapters, this concept is explored in greater detail, as to both how the right to use (referred to as "freedom to practice") is derived and how the right to exclude affects it.

Why Organizations Want a Healthy IP Culture

To thrive in the knowledge economy, organizations must cultivate attitudes and behaviors that recognize IP, respect IP, and trade upon the value of IP. This needs to be done organically, within each individual organization, and to meet the specific needs and characteristics of each such organization.

Whether an organization realizes it or not, it already has an IP culture. This may come from a history of innovation, influences of a key investor or the desire to display a scientific "coolness." The culture may simply be one of sophistication, avoidance, indifference, or even ignorance. Thus, another object of this book is to acquaint organizations with processes and ways of thinking that can foster a "healthy IP culture." It is hard to know precisely when the IP culture of an organization finally arrives at a healthy IP culture, but it is an object of this book to give practical measures of health that organizations can use.

Keeping a Perspective

So much of what the average person knows about IP is gained from the media, and particularly from news stories about extraordinary outcomes in closely fought infringement lawsuits. Many will recall that in 1990 Polaroid won a near $ 1 billion award against Kodak. More recently, NTP forced RIM (makers of Blackberry®) to pay hundreds of millions of dollars as part of a settlement. Alcatel-Lucent won a jury verdict of about $1.5 billion against Microsoft. To some, these cases are evidence of "extreme" IP, while to others it conjures up images of blatant technological theft that leads to billions of dollars in lost profits, which should be addressed with sufficient compensation.

What goes unreported, however, is the more typical award, which normally is well below $10 million.[19] What also goes unreported is the fact in 2004 and again in 2005 86 percent of cases filed in courts settled privately for undisclosed amounts.[20]

Clearly, the world of intellectual property is no less immune to media sensationalism. The press loved reporting how the Patent Office granted U.S. Patent No. 6,004,596 for a peanut butter and jelly sandwich;[21] however, if you search the internet for the most significant patent grants from the first week of April 2005 (the same week as the Court of Appeals for the Federal Circuit upheld the invalidation the peanut butter and jelly sandwich patent), no stories appear reporting that approximately 3,300 U. S. patents were granted on April 5, 2005, more than twenty of which were granted to Intel, nine to Motorola, a handful to Microsoft, and even three to Porsche.[22] There is no doubt, when an occasional patent "catastrophe" occurs, the consequences can be severe. However, the reality is that the frequency of such mistakes is statistically rare, and they can usually be spotted well before they occur.

It is important to remember that most patents that ultimately grant are for meaningful technological contributions, and will be respected by others. The boundaries for an occasional few patents will be unclear, and they will become the subject of a dispute. Yet, a vast majority of those patent disputes will get resolved with both the patent owner and the accused infringer carrying on with their respective businesses.

In the chapters to follow, there will be occasional illustrations of the "extreme" situation. This is necessary to help define the endpoints on the continuum of likelihoods. But the catastrophic extremes are not a good reference point upon which to develop an IP culture. Therefore, rather than dwell on these low-frequency occurrences, we will focus attention on the commonplace, the more typical, average, and, ultimately, productive situation.[23]

---

19. According to one resource, "Based on Federal Judicial Center data presented at the March IPO damages conference, the median patent damages award in 2005–2006 was just under $4 million and plaintiffs won 74% of the time." Ratliff, "Damages," 2007 AIPLA Annual Meeting; http://www.aipla. org/Content/ContentGroups/Speaker_Papers/Annual_Meeting_Speaker_Papers/200717/Ratliff-paper.pdf (accessed December 4, 2007).

20. http://www.patstats.org/HISTORICAL_DISPOSITION_MODES_FOR_PATENT_CASES. rev2.doc (accessed December 4, 2007).

21. *See, e.g.,* http://www.msnbc.msn.com/id/7432980/ (accessed December 4, 2007); http://online.wsj. com/article_email/SB111266108673297874-INjgYNolad4o5uoaXyGb6qGm5. html (accessed December 4, 2007).

22. In fact, of the patents granted on April 5, 2005, only eight made it on the list of silly patents http://www.patentlysilly.com/archives.php?date=2005–05.

23. In the Internet age, there are a wealth of accessible statistics pertaining to IP. They will be referenced frequently throughout this book, most containing web addresses.

Some Essential Terms of Art

Throughout the book, many efforts are made to define terms of art in the IP world. Some efforts will be better than others. Most of the terms are legal,[24] while most of the definitions are in lay terms; as a result, none of what we say should be regarded as legal authority.

The following is a list of the more commonly used terms, along with our definitions:

Infringement: The violation of an IP right; used mainly in the context of violations of patents and copyrights, with "misappropriation" being used to address violations of trade secrets.

Invention: A discovery of a uniquely different device, machine, process, composition, or article than what has previously been done. It usually involves a mental act (the "conception") and physical act of building and testing or preparing a patent application (the "reduction to practice"). Inventions (or innovations) may or may not be patentable.

Novelty: A concept used for determining patentability of an invention that requires a comparison between the invention and what has been previously done (as of a certain date) to identify at least one feature that is different.

Obvious: The standard applied in the U.S. to determine if a novel invention is patentable; the novel aspects of the created technology and the prior art are compared to see if the novel aspects would have been obvious to a person of ordinary skill in the art at the time of the invention or whether an "inventive step" has occurred.

Design Around: A technology that is developed to avoid infringing a known IP right of another party.

Person of ordinary skill in the art:[25] A hypothetical person who is used as the reference point for trying to objectively determine the level of knowledge in the art.

Prior art: What has previously been done; for example, it may be a prior public use, a prior invention, a prior commercial activity, a prior publication, or even a prior patent.

Prosecution: A communications process that patent applicants follow to obtain a patent, and it refers to the transactional and negotiation proceedings that occur before a Patent Office (either in the U.S. or abroad) to overcome any objections or rejections made by Patent Examiners.

---

24. If unsatisfied with the definition given, another resource to review might be *Black's Law Dictionary* (7th ed. 1999), regarded as one of the premier secondary resources for basic explanations of legal terms. Of course, when case law is cited, a review of those cases will help also.

25. "Art" is a funny word as it conjures images of Rembrandt, DaVinci or Van Gogh. But it is the word the founders used in the U.S. Constitution to define the purpose of patents. The easiest way to get past the awkwardness of regarding science and technology as "art" is to realize you already use the term regularly when you refer to an advanced technology as "state of the art."

Specification or Written Description: The written description of an invention that accompanies patent documents. It is typically long and verbose. Patent documents conclude with numbered paragraphs called patent "claims." It is the claims that define the boundary of a patent grant—they are the part of the patent that can be infringed.

USPTO: The U.S. Patent and Trademark Office, or the agency that grants patents for the U.S.

A Framework for IP Culture

The chapters that follow have been organized less as a conventional law treatise than a self-help reference. In some respects, the book is a straightforward discussion of the common issues encountered in building and operating an IP culture in the modern knowledge economy. In the early chapters, we will emphasize processes, practices, and training to help an organization establish the framework for a healthy IP culture. Various strategies and tools are next discussed to help establish and execute an IP program within an organization. For those readers who fear dissatisfaction with a law book that does not include significant legal analysis, a healthy dose of the underlying statutory and case law is also provided.

CHAPTER
2

Building the Culture

Training Generally

Developing a Strong IP Culture

Except in rare circumstances, a strong IP culture does not come naturally but must be built and maintained through a pattern of consistent and repetitive actions targeted at establishing in employees' minds the importance of IP to the organization. That importance is nothing less than the competitive advantage in the marketplace that IP has conferred upon the organization.

To establish and fortify an IP culture, an organization must possess several foundational building blocks, including training of personnel (including managers, sales and marketing personnel, scientists and engineers) to establish awareness of the needs for and benefits of IP; recruiting enthusiastic IP conscious managers who can lead by example; establishing organizational practices or policies aimed at protecting IP by agreement; and building an infrastructure that fosters sensitivity to the value that IP brings to the organization. Not appreciated by most organizations, many of these building blocks are already present (and establishing a healthy IP culture may be easier than you think). For those organizations, and organizations that have yet to establish any IP culture foundation, the following sections will provide the rough framing of the IP culture that will subsequently shelter their intellectual assets.

Key Ingredients: Everyday Work, Humor, and Images

Establishing or building a culture of innovation and IP starts with the company's employees. What they understand, how they behave, and what is important to them will dictate whether the company's culture is one of innovation supported by IP or not. First, preconceived notions that IP is grown and cultivated only from within research and development departments must be discarded. Innovation and IP can come from all groups, including sales, marketing, information technology (IT), supply chain as well as senior management or the shop floor. The competitive advantage that an organization possesses derives, not solely from the brainpower of research and development, but from the creativity and sensitivity of all members. Thus, employee training is critical for all groups.

This does not mean that training can be made uniformly applicable to all facets of the company. Each part of the company needs, and deserves, training individualized for that group's function. Though the basic principles that will be advanced in the training will share common links, training should attempt to identify scenarios that personnel will most frequently encounter and apply these basic principles to such scenarios.

Typically, the most successful forms of training will include some assembly of useful and useable written materials, ranging from explanations of the differences between patents, trade secrets, copyrights, and trademarks, to a review of standard forms and documents used by the organization in the administration of its IP functions. Perhaps as valuable to most organizations, but overlooked by many, is the need to accompany any written training materials with attention-grabbing, interactive roundtable discussions or workshops.

Three key ingredients help engage an audience's attention during this presentation, and most IP professionals miss them. The first is relating IP principles and concepts to employees' everyday work. The second is a healthy dose of humor. The third is images.

Relating innovation and IP concepts to their daily work basically requires showing employees—not only how they can spot inventions, become inventors, or both—but also how even the smallest things they do on a daily basis (e.g., escorting a guest through a facility in which sensitive company information is kept) can protect the IP of the organization, and reinforce its culture. For example, supply chain can invent methods critical to your organization's success.[26] Senior management can invent new business directions and a computer-implemented method for affecting its business. Additionally, employees should be shown the patenting activity of competitors, which will emphasize the importance of their own work to the company. In these instances, employees respond well to hypotheticals. They also respond well to post-hoc explanations of actual case studies with which they are familiar.

One sure-fire technique to inject humor in a presentation (apart from telling "tasteless" lawyer jokes) is to include a sample of a silly patent. An abundance of silly patents can be found to engage audience members at Web sites that keep track of these patents, including www.totallyabsurd.com, which lists patents such as a diaper for a bird.[27]

The use of images can be the key to a successful presentation, especially for presentations to the technical community. As a rule, engineers and many scientists process patent information better through the use of drawings or graphical depictions. A common breakdown in communications between lawyers and the technical community is caused by lawyers' inability to

---

26. For example, the computer company Dell, Inc., has patented its method of supplying parts to its manufacturing facility, monitoring its parts supply, and manufacturing according to customer orders. *See, e.g.*, U.S. Patents 6,816,746 (Method and system for monitoring resources within a manufacturing environment), 6,615,092 (Method, system and facility for controlling resource allocation within a manufacturing environment), and 6,711,798 (Method for manufacturing products according to customer orders). Dell's manufacturing method has been hailed as a hallmark of the company's success.

27. Examples of patents of general historic interest that also make for attention grabbers include the Wright Brothers' flying machine (U.S. Patent No. 821,393); Houdini's diver suit (U.S. Patent No. 1,370,316); Alexander Graham Bell's telephone (U.S. Patent No. 174,465); the Otis elevator (U.S. Patent No. 31,128); Edison's light bulb (U.S. Patent No. 223,898); Goodyear's vulcanized rubber (U.S. Patent No. 3,633). For other interesting patents, *See* http://www.ipmall.info/about/user11.asp (accessed November 17, 2007).

synthesize their words into images that can be processed more efficiently by technical personnel.

An important point to remember for any training is that there is no such thing as a perfect training presentation. Even the most sophisticated organizations continue to update and fine-tune their training materials to respond to ever-changing needs of the organization. Much time can and will be lost if training is delayed in a search for perfect training materials. The fact and frequency of training sessions can ultimately prove as important as the content of training materials or the manner in which they are presented. In practice, a series of sessions (e.g., four 2-hour sessions) will likely improve the chances of retention as compared with a single all-day session. Small groups rather than large will invite more active participation.

Also, it is important to start the training the day any new employee sets foot within an organization. While it would be nice to have a written manual or pamphlet that can be distributed to the new employee, it is not critical. It could prove likely as effective to merely walk the employee through the organization, pointing out various security measures that may have been taken by the organization (e.g., sign-in sheets, escorted guides, password-protected computers, and similar precautions). The purpose of these precautions should always be articulated: to protect the confidential information of the organization from which it derives a competitive advantage. Likewise, the existence of an IP culture can be demonstrated to the new employee at any orientation or through the required execution of employee nondisclosure and technology ownership assignment agreements.

2.1 The Little Touches that Reinforce

There are a host of ways that the principles taught during formal employee training can be reinforced with relatively little investment in resources. For example, some organizations display plaques commemorating important patents in conspicuous locations within their buildings. Others compile orientation materials, such as a brochure or even a video, which feature the roles certain patents owned by the organization have played in its success.

Training Senior Management

Senior management sets the tone for the IP culture in your organization, just as they set the tone for other parts of the organization. If IP is important to senior management, the importance will trickle down and be made important to the rest of the organization. Accordingly, one step on the path to assuring a healthy IP culture is through a strong sensitivity to IP issues within the senior ranks of an organization. In some organizations, this is not difficult, and it is almost an intrinsic trait that recruiters should seek to identify in the manager even before offering such a position within the organization. For example, it is almost always a given that in the pharmaceutical industry recognition of the need for patent protection will be ingrained in the minds of management because their businesses cannot survive without the exclusivity provided by strong patent protection. Indeed, the impact upon market share that occurs upon expiration of drug patents and its effect upon the market value of the organization is profound. However, where patents are not clearly being enforced to provide market exclusivity, there may be no universal measure for senior management to gauge whether the right culture is being formed and whether the necessary IP is being generated. In this context, it is important to set proper expectations for senior management, including metrics for measuring IP performance. In general, senior management should expect IP to perform like other parts of the business.

For senior management to sensitize others within an organization to the importance of IP, senior management itself must have adopted a strong belief system and understanding as to (1) why IP is important to their business and (2) how to determine if the right IP is being created. Senior management also should be trained appropriately so that they, as individuals within the organization, have a reasonably appropriate expectation of what IP can do, and what it cannot do. It is up to IP counsel, managers, and/or facilitators to demonstrate the aspects of IP relevance to senior management.

2.2 Right to Exclude v. Right to Practice

Ask most novices what rights a patent confers, and they will respond that a patent gives the right to the owner to make, sell, or otherwise use the patented technology. This does not capture the true nature of a patent grant. A patent is merely a right to exclude others from making, using, selling, or offering to sell a patented technology. A patent does not guarantee its owner any right to commercialize under the patent. For example, suppose that ACO patents a four-legged chair. While the ACO patent is still in force, BCORP patents a four-legged chair with a mesh seatback. The ACO patent could be used by ACO to keep BCORP from commercializing its chair with the mesh seatback. Likewise, the BCORP patent could be used to keep ACO from commercializing a version of its basic four-legged chair having a mesh seatback. Again, the right conferred by a patent is merely the right to exclude others from exploiting the patented technology. That right provides no guarantee to the patent owner of any right to exploit its own patented technology.

The sophistication level of senior management's IP knowledge can be measured any number of ways. Any measure invoked to test this sophistication should adequately test managers' working knowledge of the most basic foundational premises that will govern organizational conduct. For example, senior managers should show a demonstrated familiarity with sound answers to basic legal topics concerning IP, with advanced questions including:

1. What is the *eBay*[28] case and how would it impact the business of the organization if its principles were invoked in a contested infringement lawsuit?
2. Can an organization start a negotiation for an IP license without giving the other party the right to start a declaratory judgment action against it in view of the *SanDisk* [29]case? If so, how?
3. Upon becoming aware of a patent to a competitor that pertains to the business of an organization, what steps should an organization try to follow to reduce its potential exposure for a large damages claim?
4. What is the *KSR*[30] decision?

Each of these questions is answered in this book; however, only a detailed business analysis can start to deal with the training and metrics that senior management will need for an IP buy-in on importance to their overall business.

This book will illustrate why IP is important to business. IP can do a number of things, including causing competitors to design around, providing freedom to operate (avoid litigation or cross-licensing), provide exclusivity in a product or service, provide pricing power, cause collateral sales, and give a marketing benefit. However, IP typically is not the entire source of revenue. Thus, the personnel responsible for the IP function of an organization need to assess the impact that IP can have to an individual business on a case-by-case basis.

More specifically, what can be protected by patents as well as what cannot be protected by patents needs to be understood by senior management and placed in a context related to their organization's products and services. Trade secrets need to be kept secret, and this will affect behavior. Trademarks and copyrights need constant policing.

Diligent tracking and mapping of IP to the products and services of the organization provides the foundation for showing senior management the importance of IP. There are several ways to track and map IP to products and services. For patents, one popular way to track and map patents is a technique known as "claim charting."[31] As will be discussed in greater detail in later chapters, the patent

---

28. eBay, Inc., v. MercExchange, L.L.C., 126 S. Ct. 1837, 164 L. Ed. 2d. 641, 78 U.S.P.Q. 2d 1577 (2006).
29. SanDisk Corp. v. STMicroelectronics,Inc., 480 F. 3d 1372 (Fed. Cir. 2007).
30. KSR Int'l Co. v. Teleflex, Inc., 127 S. Ct. 1727, 167 L. Ed. 2d 705 82 U.S.P.Q. 2d 1385 (2007).
31. In claim charting each and every element of at least one independent claim in a patent is related directly or through equivalents to the features of the product or process under consideration. If the patent has extra or substantially different claim elements that are not in the product or service, either directly or through equivalents, then the patent cannot be said to

claims are the numbered paragraphs at the end of patents. The claims are to a patent as the description of a piece of land is to a real estate deed. It verbally defines the boundary of the patent. The patent claims are the only part of a patent that can be infringed. Thus, the claims of the patent define the right to exclude.

Too many managers are misled, by the disclosure of the patent specification or the publication of a patent application, into believing that all the technology that is disclosed is actually protected by the claims. In fact, much of the disclosed technology might have been in the prior art or critical embodiments might have been disclaimed or "dedicated to the public" during prosecution. In actuality, many (if not most) patents describe more than what is claimed. As a result, absent a solid understanding as to the true boundaries of a patent, it is possible for an organization to overestimate the breadth of a patent. In training senior management, it could prove valuable to adopt practices that rely upon claim charts and not merely the specification for assessing a patent's relevance to a product.

Claim charting is also an effective technique because it forces the person performing the analysis to focus on the words of the claims. If a specific feature was added to the claim to get the patent during prosecution proceedings, the task of claim charting will help to identify the feature. One caution to claim charting is that such charts, the product of an analysis that often involves advice of counsel, may contain attorney opinions or attorney-client privileged information, which should be carefully handled.

For large IP portfolios, claim charting also affords a benefit in that it can be used to provide explanatory summaries to others within the organization. In some cases, a value can be given to the relative importance of IP that will map to a product or service, with that relative value guiding enforcement, continuation, foreign protection and budget considerations.

2.3 Claim Charts

Claim charts have three common uses. A first use is to analyze whether and how a patent issued to a competitor bears any relation to a technology of an organization, a freedom to operate question. The elements of the competitor patent claim can be set forth in a table and corresponding features in the

---

"read on" the product or service. Unless a special claim format is used (i.e., "consisting of" or "consisting essentially of" claims), it will not matter that there are additional features in the product or process, so long as all the elements of the claim are in the product or process. Claim charting can even require three columns, one for the claim element, one for the specification's support for or interpretation of that claim element (or reference to a drawing) and one for the features of the product or process. Claim charting will also be discussed in this book under the topic of infringement. One easy way to get started on claim charting is using the free tools at www.pattools.com. This website provides a claim chart generator, which is the basic form that is needed. *See also* Appendix 6.

organization's technology (if any) can be identified. The second common use is to analyze whether and how a patent to an organization covers its own technology. Likewise, the elements of the patent claim can be set forth in a table and corresponding features in the organization's technology (if any) can be identified. The third common use is to analyze whether a patent claim is invalid in view of prior art. In this technique, the elements of the patent claim are set forth in a table and corresponding features in the organization's technology (if any) are identified.

As can be appreciated, the results of the analysis from the use of claim charts can be sensitive and potentially damning, inasmuch as they may reveal the existence of infringement. Therefore, it is important that claim charting activities are undertaken under supervision of counsel and reasonable measures taken to uphold whatever attorney-client privilege may exist, as discussed in greater detail in later chapters.

Finally, most senior managers can benefit from being taught certain tricks of the IP trade, including some of the special language that allows executives to engage in sensitive IP dialogue without inviting liability upon the company. As one example, frequently senior management personnel will engage in direct communications with legal counsel for purposes of seeking legal advice. This creates an attorney-client privileged communication that protects the communication from later disclosure. However, senior management might then mistakenly share the substance of the privileged communication (directly or indirectly) with a person outside the organization, resulting in the waiver of the privilege.[32] Training about attorney-client privilege could help ameliorate this risk.

As another example, it could prove valuable to train senior management in how to avoid causing a lawsuit by accusing someone of patent infringement at a meeting, which could lead to declaratory judgment jurisdiction and a lawsuit.[33] Some statements to avoid include: "our patent covers your product,"

---

32. Among the training organizations might consider offering to senior management is a prudent way to mark personal notes, memoranda, reports, meeting minutes, e-mails and other documents, to identify the document as a privileged communication. It also could prove prudent to train senior management and other personnel as well to avoid using certain terms in their notes and records. Documents from the files of an accused infringer that contain words like "infringe" or "copy" are the proverbial "smoking gun" documents in patent lawsuits.

33. Declaratory Judgment Act is at 28 U.S.C. § 2201, *et seq.* Recent case law applying to this act is *Teva Pharmaceuticals* USA, Inc. v. *Novartis Pharmaceuticals Corp.*, 482 F. 3d 1330 (Fed. Cir. 2007) which held that the only requirement standing for a declaratory judgment action is an Article III controversy, which only requires an injury-in-fact caused by the defendant that can be redressed in court. Another case to consider is *SanDisk Corp.* v. *STMicroelectronics, Inc.*, 480 F. 3d 1372 (Fed. Cir. 2007), which held that there was declaratory judgment jurisdiction where licensing discussions were occurring, despite an explicit pledge by the patentee not to sue the prospective licensee.

"you need a license under our patents to sell that product," and "we'll see you in court"! While these statements might seem fun to say, they can lead to significant attorney fees if not said differently or in the proper context.

The numerous topics presented above should provide sufficient background for senior management to understand the importance of IP to their business. Thus, another question to answer is that if IP is important to the business, what should senior management expect from IP?

Senior management should set expectations for the determination and assessment of the correct type of IP to seek for the organization. For this, senior management first must be able to recognize the major types of IP (e.g., patent, copyright, and trade secret) and to associate each with the particular needs of the organization. Senior management may also be schooled in the most appropriate metrics to address the particular IP needs of the organization. Selection of the appropriate metric, however, will be driven by the leaders of the organization in their decisions about the strategies and long-term business planning for the organization.

Important to choosing the correct IP metric for guiding management decisions is a coordination of the language of the metric with the language of the business to be served by the IP; that is, for an organization to be able to recognize the value that IP brings to its business, it is important to school senior management and their IP advisors in the organization's business language. For example, one approach is to express an IP metric by focusing on what the IP does and how it specifically relates to a facet of the business. An IP metric directed at a manufacturing operation might best focus on "make" language. An IP metric directed at a marketing and sales operation should focus on "sell" language. Research and development function IP might focus on "use" language.

2.4 IP Metrics

IP metrics can be put into the same language senior management uses on a daily basis, so that they better understand the value IP is bringing to the business.

The following includes examples of metrics identified by Williamson, *How Metrics Can Put IP at the Heart of Your Company's Agenda, Intellectual Asset Management*, (August/September 2004), at 35–39 reproduced at http://www.ipperform.com/Metrics-IAM-Mag-ARTICLE-ISSUE-7.pdf.

- Revenues attributed to IP
- Market share attributed to IP
- Royalty rates
- Tax benefits

- Market share or margins for protected versus un-protected products
- Time to market/product lifecycles
- Return on investment
- Damages from enforcement
- Research and development costs in relation to total patents and patent costs

Other metrics are also discussed in Chapter 8 in terms of assessing success of strategies.

Another approach that helps bridge the divide between the worlds of IP and traditional business is to school senior management to communicate IP issues in terms of the expected life cycle of a technology. Senior management needs to understand that with each stage in the life of a technology, there are corresponding stages in the life of potential IP for protecting that technology.

Assuming an organization engages in life-cycle planning for its products, one technique may be to superimpose on any planning document a corresponding IP life-cycle plan. One such plan might be structured to include the following successive stages:[34]

Stage 1: Product or technology is new, market size is unknown – life-cycle plan will identify dates when the business will prioritize its potential patent filings, make filing decisions, and file patent applications for capturing the inventions, taking into account (i) ranking of inventions according to well known criteria (such as ability to detect infringement, ability to design around and criticality of the technology to the business of the organization), and assessment of foreign markets and foreign patentability, (ii) number of applications; and (iii) research and development costs per invention or application.

Stage 2: Product or technology is introduced to the market, patent offices respond to filed applications. By this time, it is more likely that the commercial form of the technology will be established. Accordingly, the planning of the organization will be directed at assessing whether the claim coverage being sought in the patents will cover the commercial version of the technology, and whether supplemental protection ought to be sought through additional applications. Patents will start to grant and decisions to pursue additional patent coverage through a subsequent application filing (e.g., a "continuing" application) will need to be made. During this stage, the focus will also be on exploring abandonment of low-value IP and re-allocation of

---

34. *See also* the presentation given by Kent Richardson, Rambus, Inc. Kent Richardson, remarks at Strategic IP Leadership Conference, Valuing and Promoting IP in your Organization, Hosted by Kimberly-Clark Corporation, (April 12–13, 2007), "Patent Metrics for the Patent Life Cycle."

resources to protect those inventions or technologies that most directly impact the product. Considerations might include (i) market size and percent of market covered by IP, (ii) re-ranking of relative importance of inventions and reassessment of foreign markets and foreign patentability, (iii) number of patent filings (e.g., budget); and (iv) anticipated patenting success rate based upon examination results to date.

Stage 3: Product is starting to mature and competitors have entered the market. By this time, assuming the technology is being commercialized by the organization, the IP emphasis will likely shift toward securing the most benefit from the exclusive privileges that a patent confers. About this time, it is most likely that any competitive market entry will have occurred, and emphasis will start to shift, not merely toward assuring the commercially valuable features of the technology are protected from copying, but also toward assuring the broadest possible range of protection available from the patent filings. For instance, the filing of continuation patent applications to cover a competitor's product entry likely will be explored, as will the continued pursuit of foreign patent protection. Considerations will include the use of the IP (i) to help preserve or enhance differentiations as compared with technology of competitors (e.g., feature differences), (ii) whether any infringement suits are appropriate, which might lead to an award of an injunction, money damages, or both, and (iii) market share. Appendix 5 illustrates a life-cycle time line, and includes other examples of milestones that might be charted.

In addition, senior management will want some indication of efficiency and relevance of the patent portfolio, as well as the patent group. Again metrics can demonstrate these efforts. What can be measured, meaning what might be useful metrics, include:

- Number of patent applications filed (and/or as compared to R&D dollars)
- Number of patents granted (and/or as mapped to products on the market or competitive products on the market)
- Number of inventions disclosures submitted (again as compared to R&D dollars)
- Number of patents used by a business unit and estimate of value
- Incremental gross margin
- Lead time to market, market share, price premium
- In-licensing costs versus development costs
- Competitor IP spending
- Use of patents after ten years (or five years)
- Number of citations in competitor patents or articles
- Patent quality and importance (e.g., claim breadth and scope indices)

Any particular metric that is used by senior management to assess IP effectiveness will drive the IP process. Choice of the right metric is, therefore, important.

Training Sales and Marketing Personnel

Though not the prototypical source of the discovery of the means for solving a particular technological problem, sales and marketing personnel are primary market-facing teams for an organization. This places them in a unique position important to the success of IP for an organization. Typically, these personnel are the first to see competitive products or services, the first to hear an accusation of infringement (one way or the other) and the first to hear of a customer problem with a patent or third party. In addition, sales and marketing personnel are often the first persons in an organization to learn of customer needs or problems that require resolution. Thus, to establish a healthy IP culture, it is also important for sales and marketing to receive sufficient training to understand the implications of what they learn in the field, and when and how to pass that information along to others within the organization.

The training of sales and marketing personnel need not vary too much from training offered to other employees. Thus, they too should be schooled in the types of IP that exist, the nature of the IP right to exclusivity, IP jargon, the process of procuring IP rights and recordkeeping. In particular, IP jargon is important because it is common for sales or marketing personnel to hear that a competitor has "patented" a particular product or feature. This may mean a number of different things, including that a patent application has published (which is just a request for a patent) or that a patent has actually issued (which provides an actual right that must be examined by counsel). An education in IP jargon will give sales and marketing personnel the needed background to better understand what they hear in the marketplace.

It is also important for sales and marketing personnel to gain an understanding of laws surrounding inventorship. To the latter point, a common scenario that occurs in many industries is that a salesperson of an organization will be asked to attend a meeting with a customer, at which the customer expresses a problem it faces with one of its products, and requests the salesperson to have the organization solve the problem. In the course of solving the problem, an invention is made. It is important, in this instance, for any patent application to name the correct inventor. The salesperson being the direct conduit between the customer and the organization is in a unique position to know if the customer made any inventorship contribution to any application filed by the organization, or if the organization made an inventorship contribution to any application filed by the customer.

For sales and marketing personnel, training in one or more of the following areas could be of value to an organization:

1. Competitive intelligence (e.g., ask the sales and marketing people to gather evidence on what your competitors are showing at trade shows, and show them how that information would be used in a claim chart for

senior management; also, for example, show the sales and marketing people how marketing affects damages in a patent lawsuit, e.g., under lost sales);

2. Key product features (e.g., show sales and marketing people how market feedback can change your patenting strategy, including foreign filings or continuations or continuation-in-part applications);

3. Branding and product launch (e.g., coordinating branding and product launch activities with IP protection and trademark clearance[35]); or

4. Marking (e.g., making sure that products sold by the organization are marked with patent numbers to ensure that a full measure of damages can be obtained for infringement per 35 U.S.C. § 287; and reviewing products and literature of competitors to see if the competitor identifies any patents relevant to its products).

Training Potential Inventors

Everything just discussed about sales and marketing is good foundation for training the pool of all possible inventors in an organization, along with some additional topics. Specifically, potential inventors need to understand more about the patenting process used within the organization, and training might include answers to general invention and inventorship questions.

Potential inventors could be taught answers to general questions, including: Who is an inventor? How is inventorship determined? What is an invention? How do you get a patent? How much does it cost to get a patent? Does an inventor have any special obligation? What is "prosecution"? What is the difference between a trade secret and a patent? What is a defensive publication? Who owns the IP?

Successful training of potential inventors might also seek to answer questions that are specific to each individual organization, such as the following: **How does the organization select the order of people listed on the patent as inventors?** The law does not require listing inventors in any particular order or fashion, and does not distinguish between the inventive contributions

---

35. In the course of patent infringement disputes it is common for a defendant accused of infringement to try to extract from filings made before different government agencies information that could be harmful to a patent. For example, an accused infringer might look to derive some argument from a first use date supplied in a trademark application that may be inconsistent with a position taken under the "public use" bar to patentability of 35 U.S.C. § 102(b). *See, e.g., Bruno Indep. Living Aids, Inc. v. Acorn Mobility Servs., Ltd.*, 394 F. 3d 1348 (Fed. Cir. 2005)(U.S. Food and Drug Administration filing used to support charge of inequitable conduct in procurement of patent); and *Crystal Semiconductor Corp. v. TriTech Microelectronics Int'l Inc.*, 246 F. 3d 1336 (Fed. Cir. 2001).

of one inventor versus another.[36] Thus, a company standard operating procedure could be adopted and used to avoid confusion and hurt feelings among inventors. Generally, listing inventors alphabetically by their last name is common, with an exception for when the inventive entity agrees on an order. In preparing a patent application, an inventorship meeting or discussion should occur, and this is an ideal time for the attorney to address inventorship order.

When should an inventor disclose an invention to the individuals responsible for the IP function of the organization? There are clear bars to patentability (i.e., activities that stop or bar the validity of patent coverage), such as absolute novelty[37] (applicable in most commercially significant foreign countries), which require not only disclosure, but filing of a patent application prior to public disclosure. Thus, inventions need to be disclosed to the IP group prior to public disclosure. However, much earlier disclosure is typically warranted. For helping to avoid future problems, ideas and inventions desirably should be written up in some sort of an invention disclosure form and submitted at two earlier points of time. One attractive time for submission is prior to entering into discussions or disclosures to other companies (even if under a confidentiality agreement). This serves to document the work of one company relative to the other, and is extremely useful to resolving issues of inventorship and ownership between companies. Post-patent grant lawsuits to force the naming of inventors are provided for under 35 U.S.C. § 256, and costs of such suits can be saved by an early disclosure form. The second attractive time is at or even prior to when the invention has been actually reduced to practice. Actual reduction to practice (generally regarded as the time when an invention is built and tested to show it works for its intended purpose in its intended environment) is one factor that courts have adopted as determining that an invention is "ready for patenting" (albeit for purposes of 35 U.S.C. § 102(b)).[38] Nevertheless, it is an easy milestone that personnel can be trained to recognize.

When is the right time to file a patent application? As a general practice, it is desirable to file patent applications prior to market introduction or other acts of public disclosure or commercialization. This helps to avoid absolute novelty problems in many foreign countries, if foreign protection is desired.[39] But, for developmental technology, the answer to this question depends heavily on the technology, including the economic potential of the technology and

---

36. *See, e.g., Fina Technology, Inc. v. Ewen,* 265 F. 3d 1325 (Fed. Cir. 2001).
37. "Absolute novelty" generally refers to a system by which once a certain activity has occurred (typically public activity), the activity becomes "prior art." In contrast, the system in the United States affords a grace period before certain activities qualify as prior art.
38. *See generally, Pfaff v. Wells Elecs. Inc.,* 525 U.S.55 (1998).
39. The U.S. is unique in affording a one-year grace period for filing, pursuant to 35 U.S.C. § 102(b). *See also, Pfaff v. Wells Elecs. Inc.,* 525 U.S.55 (1998).

the ability for advances in the technology. For a breakthrough technology, patent application filing might be (1) delayed a bit to allow for full scoping of the limits of the technology or for the generation of key test data, (2) rushed if others are known to be working on a similar technology or the same problem or (3) coordinated as part of a comprehensive IP program including prior art searching. In technologies that are heavily competitive or in a crowded field, patent applications ideally should be filed promptly, and sometimes even immediately following conception of the idea for the invention. Prompt filings also can help secure market benefits for products that have short life cycles. It is often valuable to start the patent process early enough to help ensure a patent grant before the technology becomes obsolete.

How should an invention be disclosed internally within the organization to assure proper evaluation for filing? Organizations should consider the use of a document called an invention disclosure form that is easily accessible to personnel.[40] For example, it may be published on a computer network, or it may simply be a paper form that is available throughout a facility. An advantage of a form is that it poses a common set of questions to elicit the basic information needed by the organization to make informed filing decisions, and to facilitate the task of counsel in preparing the application.

2.5 **Mentoring**

For organizations with sufficient resources to do so, another valuable mechanism to facilitate training of personnel on IP issues, and for cultivating an IP culture, is the establishment of a mentoring program. As with any other company mentoring program, senior personnel who have IP experience can be assigned to one employee or a group of junior employees to whom he or she can communicate the IP values of the company and its practices.

Agreements

Another important ingredient for establishing a healthy IP culture is the establishment of sound organizational practices and policies to protect IP rights through the use of agreements. A variety of basic agreements are vital for optimizing IP protection, such as confidentiality agreements, or IP ownership agreements, and a number of good reasons for using them. For example, disclosure of an invention without a confidentiality agreement could possibly destroy patentability in most of the world under the absolute novelty standard. Also, the failure to employ confidentiality agreements when it is

---

40. There are other names to these forms, including "Record of Invention", "Patent Memorandum" or "Disclosure of Invention".

reasonable to do so could have the effect of forfeiting valuable trade secrets, an essential requirement of which is the employment of reasonable measures to protect the secrets from disclosure. As another example, the failure to define ownership of IP rights with certain individuals could result in the unintended result that personnel (e.g., an independent contractor) hired to help develop a valuable technology could end up jointly owning that technology with the hiring organization. Accordingly, from the outset of their employment within an organization, and throughout the period of employment, employees need to be taught that they are responsible for knowing when to get and use some of these agreements. A culture of IP views these agreements as essential to business.

Confidentiality Agreements

Confidentiality agreements, also called nondisclosure agreements (or even "secrecy agreements" in some contexts), are an important foundation for IP protection. The basic commitment is that one party agrees to keep secret the information disclosed by another party. The other basic part of the agreement is to limit the use of the information that is disclosed. Uses vary from the general—such as, to evaluate a business opportunity—to the specific—such as, to allow the recipient to fix a piece of equipment.

There are widely varying practices for confidentiality agreements. Some companies require all visitors to sign a confidentiality agreement as they enter the premises, and they make this easy by making it a form at the front desk or as part of a visitor badge or as part of a login at a computer terminal that registers all visitors. Others have a variety of forms, including one-way agreements, where one party is disclosing to another; two-way (or mutual) agreements, where both parties are disclosing to each other; vendor agreements, where a vendor agrees to keep everything confidential; or even recruit (or candidate) agreements, where a person hoping for a job or being recruited agrees to keep everything confidential.

Each circumstance calling for a confidentiality agreement may dictate different terms in the agreement. An IP culture will help those operating in the culture understand which clauses are needed. For example, sometimes an organization wants to make sure that it does not receive confidential information because it does not want to be restricted by how it may use information received from a party, i.e., the organization wants to avoid becoming "contaminated" with confidential information or a disclosing party. In that circumstance, it is useful to make it clear, before information is provided, that the information will not be treated in a confidential manner.

Confidentiality agreements tend to be relatively simple and can be condensed to a single- page document in many transactions. The agreements typically will spell out the restrictions on use of confidential information, how confidential information is to be designated as confidential information, and exclusions of certain classes of information from the definition of confidential information. Additional provisions beyond those are commonly within the discretion of the parties. For example, some parties may elect to include an express obligation to transfer ownership rights for inventions or other IP that may arise in the course of the confidential relationship.

The typical transaction in which confidential information is shared is often treated within organizations as a low-level transaction. Thus, the organization will often maintain a library of form agreements to which its employees have access. This is a common practice and works for many situations. However, the practice is not universally applicable. For instance, among the various logistical difficulties posed by form agreements is the lack of ability to change the form, and sometimes onerous or lopsided terms that are placed into a form, which may not be appropriate for the transaction at hand. Because many people are brought up in an environment that trains them to regard confidentiality agreements as common, mere formalities, parties tend to enter the agreements without fully understanding their full implications, let alone without the advice of counsel. Little do these individuals appreciate at the time of signing the potential for latent liability to which they have exposed their organization. It is, therefore, important for an organization that seeks a healthy IP culture to understand the nature of confidentiality agreements and some of the potential pitfalls.

To help illustrate, examples of confidentiality agreements are attached as Appendices 1–3. However, some important clauses are first addressed. Perhaps the most commonly negotiated provision in nondisclosure agreements pertains to marking disclosed information as confidential or requiring that any shared confidential information be provided solely in written form. Organizations large and small like the bright-line certainty that a requirement of a conspicuous "CONFIDENTIAL" marking provides. The sentiment is that if a document is shared and not marked confidential, then no obligation of confidentiality should attach to it. However, this has the potential to impose hardship for some organizations, such as those which may lack the discipline or training to recognize the need to mark something as confidential or those that innocently neglect to mark the confidential designation. One mechanism for breaking negotiation deadlocks on this issue is to compromise with language to the effect that "the obligation of confidentiality shall only apply to written information that is marked as confidential, oral information that is promptly summarized and designated as confidential, and information that reasonably is of the type that is customarily regarded in the industry as confidential"[41].

---

41. *See* Chapter 7 at 25.

Another important provision in confidentiality agreements pertains to a definition of the scope of information being disclosed and how such information can be used. Issues concerning scope of information often arise when one or both of the parties to the agreement are worried about contamination. The scope of the information being disclosed, thus, needs to be narrowly crafted. Contamination issues can be dealt with by precisely defining how confidential information shall not be used for certain expressly stated purposes, and by also explicitly elaborating upon the scope of the uses that *are* permitted uses.

Another provision that often receives little attention, but which can create nightmares for some organizations is the choice of forum provision. Although this may seem minor, most organizations will want to be careful of the locations in which they voluntarily agree that they can be hauled into court if a dispute should erupt.

Organization/Employee Agreements

As mentioned, one of the earliest opportunities an organization has to impress the role of intellectual property upon its personnel is during the hiring process. This is the new employee's first exposure to the importance that the organization places upon its IP. In establishing this culture, employee agreements are particularly useful tools, especially in the area of protecting trade secrets and in the avoidance of subsequent disputes over ownership of IP rights.

It is, therefore, advisable practice for all employees[42] (new and existing) to enter into employment agreements with the organization that attempt to protect confidential information and require its use only for the purposes of the company–with a broad definition of information, trade secret, and invention. In many circumstances, a clause requiring that employees shall not place themselves in the position of conflict of interest with the company can also be required. It is also recommended that a limitation on public disclosure of company information be placed in the agreement so that publications or presentations are reviewed by IP personnel prior to disclosure (to protect the absolute novelty standard).

Another common provision in these agreements is a covenant not to compete with the organization while employed and after employment. Post employment noncompetition is a state-by-state issue with some states allowing for fairly broad restrictions,[43] and others allowing only strict,

---

42. The text here refers to employees, but should also be regarded as encompassing independent contractors as well. The law of IP ownership can be particularly murky when it comes to these relationships. Many organizations that have not taken adequate precautions have found themselves as joint owners of IP rights with departed contractors as a result.

43. *See, e.g., Stoneworks, Inc. v. Empire Marble and Granite, Inc.*, 49 U.S.P.Q. 2d 1760 (S. D. Fla. 1998).

fair restrictions.[44] Most noncompete clauses that are reasonable with regard to technology, industry (or field), geography, and length of time on the restriction will be upheld. For example, clauses that restrict direct competition for one year or less in the same industry are typically considered reasonable. Detailed review of noncompete clauses is essential, but if your business depends on trade secret protection, you should consider using the most aggressive clause reasonably possible in your state.

Provisions that impose an obligation upon an employee (or contractor) to disclose and assign rights in any intellectual property generated during the employment are also common provisions. Such provisions may also require employees to cooperate with preparation and prosecution of patent applications for inventions or otherwise in the procurement of IP rights. This clause may also require employees to keep adequate records of such inventions.

Compensation for inventions should also be addressed in employee agreements, with the typical clause providing for the salary of the employee being compensation for inventions. Some companies prefer to award a nominal amount upon execution of an assignment for the patent application (for example, one dollar). As will be discussed in the context of German and Japanese invetions, the regional law may dictate certain compensation.

2.6 **Inventor Compensation**

Some countries have laws that mandate compensation to inventors for inventions. Japan and Germany are two significant examples. It is especially important to seek counsel when attempting to address the compensation of employees for inventions.

Employee agreements can also anticipate different categories of employees, such as (i) rank-and-file employees who simply need reminding of the IP culture and their obligation to operate within that culture, (ii) senior management who need to be reminded of the severe consequences of disclosure of trade secrets, and (iii) employees hired to invent (e.g., research and development personnel) who need to be taught the most information and behavior expectations. For simplicity, it is possible for some organizations, particularly smaller ones, to employ a single agreement designed to address all employee types. However, larger companies may use different agreements for different categories, as well as for employees in different countries, where the laws can be different.

---

44. *See, e.g., Metro Traffic Control, Inc. v. Shadow Traffic Network*, 22 Cal. App. 4th 853, 30 U.S.P.Q. 2d 1684 (Cal. Ct. App. 1994).

Independent Contractors and Temporary Employees

Companies also need agreements with independent contractors and temporary employees to protect confidential and proprietary information. For most situations, if contractors or temps refuse to sign these agreements, they should not be allowed on the premises. This agreement may typically be a cross between a confidentiality agreement and an employee agreement as well as standard practices that one would expect of full-time employees. Typical clauses in these agreements will reflect the nature of the work to be performed by the contractor or temp, and include the following:

Confidentiality restrictions, including all the standard requirements listed above for confidentiality agreements, as well as requiring the contractor to take reasonable steps to protect the confidential information of the company, protect the confidential information of third parties that the company may have, liquidated damages for breach of confidentiality, and return of confidential information.

There should be an agreement as to ownership by the company of all copyrightable material, trade secrets, and inventions made, conceived, or discovered by the contractor solely or in collaboration with others, all in the context of performing work for the company. In addition, the contractor should agree to disclose inventions, assist in prosecution, and keep records sufficient to show inventions were made (or reduced to practice).

Ideally, conflicting obligations should not exist, and contactors should be able to represent that they can perform the work without using the inventions, trade secrets, or otherwise of any third party. If such representation is not possible, then the reasons why should be understood and reasonable efforts made to address them otherwise.

Finally, it should generally be required that contractors not use subcontractors unless the subcontractors are bound by the same obligations as the

---

2.7 Introducing Employee Agreements Midstream in the Relationship

An organization will often seek to introduce or modify an employment agreement well past the time when the employment relationship commenced. Most employees have no problem agreeing to the modification. However, an occasional employee will hold out, usually asserting that the modification is not accompanied by proper consideration. Although chances are, this is not the only difficulty that has been encountered with this employee, most of these situations can be readily managed without impacting the employee's performance or tenure. Nevertheless, appropriate advice of counsel should be sought.

contractor on confidentiality (and they provide proof of the subcontractor being bound). This is needed for proper trade secret protection but can be controversial in some states.

Ownership or Other Rights by Operation of Law

In addition to agreements that assign ownership of intellectual property, sometimes there is a law or common law practice that transfers ownership, or at least some rights, from the inventor or author to the company without any agreement to the contrary. The employee practicing in a culture of intellectual property should understand when this may happen and how the organization wants to address the situation.

Hired to Invent (Employed Inventors)

There is a line of case law starting with Supreme Court cases from the 1800s that states that if an employee was hired to invent or work on a particular project, then the results of the effort belong to the company.[45] This is based on the implied contract that if the employee was hired to invent, then the company has already bought the invention. This applies typically only to inventions, but not to copyrights.

Under copyright law,[46] with only certain limited exceptions, if an organization hires a contractor to create a work for the company (such as an article or book or logo or drawing), then the actual author and copyright owner is the contractor.[47] On the other hand, as to any works made by an employee during the course of employment, they belong to the organization as employer, the work being deemed as a "work-made-for-hire".

---

45. *See Solomons* v. *U.S.,* 137 U.S.342, 346, 11 S. Ct. 88, 34 L. Ed. 667 (1890). A more modern case applying the hire-to-invent implied contract to assign is *Teets v. Chormalloy Gas Turbine Corp.,* 83 F. 3d 403 (Fed. Cir. 1996).

46. Pursuant to 17 U.S.C. § 106, a copyright confers upon its owner a "bundle" of rights because it provides the owner a list of rights that it has, such as the right to copy the work, distribute the work, display or broadcast the work, perform the work and prepare derivatives or modified versions of the work. A "work" under copyright law is different from an invention under patent law. An easy way to think of it is that a work under copyright law is a very specific expression of an idea, but an invention patented under patent will be all of the specific expressions put together. Also, many things can be copyrighted that generally cannot be patented, such as works of literature.

47. *See generally,* 17 U.S.C. § 101 ("work made for hire" definition), and *Community for Creative Non-Violence v. Reid,* 490 U.S.730 (1989).

Shop Rights

A shop right is effectively an implied license (*See* also Chapter 7) from an employee to a company to an invention that the employee made or perfected using the resources of the company.[48] This typically occurs when the employee was not one hired to invent or perform work outside of the scope of their employment. The resources of the company can be supplies, facilities, labor, or any other resource. Generally, the license is royalty-free, nonexclusive, and personal to the company (i.e., nontransferable as a sublicense). However, the license that the company gets is fairly narrow in that it is limited to use in the company's business.

Corporate Officers

Certain members of senior management, and particularly corporate officers, may have an additional implied or fiduciary duty to the company as a result of their position with the company.[49] Accordingly, even in the absence of an express agreement to assign IP ownership rights, such an obligation may be implied on the basis that due to the relationship with the organization it is not equitable for the officer to act for his or her own exclusive benefit in exercising dominion over such rights.

Inventor Compensation

Generally, employee agreements should handle inventor compensation. Without an agreement in place, state common law governs how inventors are compensated. Thus, while the common law may operate to give employers ownership of the inventive output of employees who are hired to invent, their compensation is not set necessarily by their salaries. For employees not hired to invent, the situation worsens for the employer because the invention may not be owned and the employee may demand substantial compensation. To establish a culture of IP in your organization, agreements are essential.

Nonetheless, once the rights are straightened out, incentives for the employees to disclose their inventions in a timely manner and for important patents can establish a culture of IP. Many companies have incentive programs.

---

48. *See McElmurry v. Arkansas Power & Light Co.*, 995 F. 2d 1576 (Fed. Cir. 1993).
49. *See generally Kennedy v. Wright*, 676 F. Supp. 888 (C. D. Ill. 1988) and cases cited therein.

Incentives or Awards to Employees

Establishing a culture of innovation is built on several building blocks, each of which can be used for an inventive or award program. The building blocks include the message from senior management, consistency (keep a program going), training, and recognition for innovation.

The most common award or incentive for employees is money. Companies may pay a set amount to each person named on an invention disclosure form, an additional amount for being a named inventor upon filing a patent application, and sometimes even additional amounts for granted patents and/or foreign filing of patent applications. Each of these steps in the process shows the additional value of the invention to the organization, i.e., the amount awarded for the invention disclosure is small, but if the disclosure form matures into a patent application, then it has more value and inventors are more richly rewarded. Similarly, if a patent application is foreign filed (which is expensive), then the invention is considered more valuable and the inventors are given an additional award. These monetary awards can become a significant budget item so some companies look for alternatives.

Alternatives include an inventors' lunch or dinner. Plaques can be given out. Newsletters, walls of fame, public recognition at company events are also common.

More unusual incentives may include time to invent, where inventors are given unstructured time in the lab and resources (e.g., capital items) to work on any technology or idea that excites them. Innovation measures can also be built into employee evaluations.

Foreign Inventors (Germany and Japan)

Many foreign countries provide for a company to automatically own the inventions of its employees. However, typically, these countries also provide for employees to be compensated for their inventions based on the commercial value of the invention.[50] If organizations have foreign inventors, then the compensation laws will change depending on the country. Today, inventions may be made with inventors working jointly in different parts of the globe. Corporate documents (such as invention disclosure forms) should be tailored to address this possibility, such as by including a specific question asking where the

---

50. Also, for example, the United Kingdom (UK) patents law that generally provides that where an invention is made by an employee in the course of his duties, the invention belongs to his employer. The law also contains provision for employee-inventors to claim compensation from their employers, where the patent or the invention or both has been of outstanding benefit. Patents Act 1977, Section 39, as amended in 2004.

invention activities occurred. Japan and Germany are examples of countries that have significant consequences from the answers to such questions.

In Japan, under Article 35 of the Japanese Patent Laws, the right to an employee invention (the right to obtain a patent) vests initially in the employee, with the employer granted a nonexclusive license. However, the employer is entitled to take ownership of an employee invention where there is an employment agreement. If this happens, the employee is entitled to receive "reasonable compensation" from the employer. Article 35 further provides that the "reasonable compensation" should be determined based on profits earned by the employer from the invention and the contribution ratio of the employer in the invention's development.

Perhaps the most publicized recent case to apply Article 35 of the Japanese Patent Laws is *Nakamura v. Nichia Corporation*.[51] In that case, the Tokyo District Court ordered Nichia to pay Nakaumura, a former employee, approximately $190 million in compensatory damages, much more than the $2,000 that was originally paid. Nakamura is the inventor of the blue light-emitting diode (LED) of high brightness, which is used in most white LED applications (like mobile phone screens). Nakamura assigned the rights in respect of his invention to Nichia under company rules. Nichia experienced exponential growth in sales. In *Yonezawa v. Hitachi Ltd*[52], the Tokyo High Court (an intermediate appellate court) ruled that employee-inventors have the right to compensation for their patented inventions no matter where the invention is exploited. The High Court awarded about $1.1 million in damages for patents covering optical disc technology, increasing the damages by nearly a factor of five to reflect revenue earned by Hitachi on foreign patents covering the invention.

In Germany, the law is similar. As a rule of thumb, under German law, copyrights, designs, trademarks, and other intellectual property rights are owned by the employer as long as the creation is related to, and can be considered as part of, the work done by the employee under his employment agreement. For inventions to be patented, however, there is a different rule that generally states that whenever an employee who is employed under German law makes an invention in the course of his employment, the invention falls within the scope of the German Employees' Inventions Act (Arbeit nehmererfindungsgesetz or AEG), which has very detailed rules for both the employer and the employee on notification and exploitation of the invention. For example, the AEG provides for strict deadlines that have to be met and that are crucial to establish ownership and the right of exploitation. In addition, if the employer claims the invention, the employee is entitled to compensation, with the amount set by "the economic usability of the invention, the employee's tasks and position within the firm, and the firm's share

---

51. Tokyo District Court Case No. Heisei 13 (WA) 17772.
52. Tokyo High Court, Case Hei 14(ne) No. 6451.

in the emergence of the invention" (Section 9 AEG). For example, the head of an R&D department will receive less than an inventor. In Germany, there is also a Compensation Directive, which is not legally binding, but is nonetheless widely followed so that there is compliance with this otherwise vague Section 9. If a company has inventors located in Germany, consultation with Germany attorneys is a necessity.

IP and IT Cooperation

In the context of IP disputes or otherwise, in establishing or in proving IP rights, evidence will be necessary to establish any of a number of different facts ranging from the time when and under what circumstances a technology is made, when it is commercialized, the extent it is commercialized, awareness of competitive technology, patenting activities, and other associated facts. Necessary to the success of implementing a healthy IP culture is the establishment of sound recordkeeping protocol that will help assure availability when records are needed, which for many patent disputes may be longer than the normal expected life of a document under traditional retention policies.[53] In the contemporary organization, the establishment of such protocol needs to address both traditional paper records and electronic records.

According to one University of California research study, 93 percent of all information generated during 1999 was generated in digital form on computers.[54] That number is increasing. An organization's ability to obtain and enforce any IP rights, and obtain remedies for any infringement thereof, or to be able to rely upon a suitable prior use type of defense in any action asserting infringement will depend upon what an organization can prove in court. Because the vast majority of the evidence supporting intellectual property and the damages from its infringement is in electronic format, it is critical that IP professionals have an understanding of how their information is stored and what retention policies are in place or should be in place. Thus, electronic information should be managed according to a corporate policy or

---

53. It can be seen immediately that competing tensions are created by the need for long-term record preservation for IP records and shorter-term preservation periods established in the record retention policies followed by large numbers of organizations. The effective balancing of these competing tensions and the adoption of a sound corporate retention policy will likely require a cross-organizational coordination of efforts, undertaken with close supervision of counsel. One approach advocated in later chapters calls for the creation of certain archive compilations of historical documents.

54. Kenneth J. Withers, Senior Judicial Education Attorney, *Electronic Discovery Disputes; Decisional Guidance, Civil Action*, Federal Judicial Center, at 7 (Summer 2004).

standard operating procedure, particularly with regard to the admissibility and authentication of the evidence in court.

In this section, we explore some of the more salient issues an organization needs to consider for establishing reliable corporate data and the state of its corporate knowledge at any given time. Given the growing significance of electronic information, the target audience of this section is not solely members of the intellectual property community within an organization, but also members of the information technology (IT) community. Those two groups must establish a coordinated and cooperative relationship to help assure the reliability of important evidence pertaining to IP.

Electronically Stored Information (ESI)

This section uses the phrase electronically stored information (ESI), which is the expression that has gained popular acceptance, largely due to its use in the recently adopted *U. S. Federal Rules of Civil Procedure.*[55] As background, consider that ESI records can be attacked in a variety of ways, and the IP professional has to prepare the organization to refute these attacks. Typically, the burden to show particular ESI inadmissible or unreliable rests on the party attacking the ESI; however, good practices are suggested to help assure that the ESI will:

1. Survive admissibility challenges that arise as a result of compliance with discovery rules; and
2. otherwise be admissible under the *Federal Rules of Evidence (FRE)*.

In general, ESI can be attacked as inadmissible or unreliable by attacking the hardware on which the ESI is found (e.g., hardware changes that might affect data integrity), the software used to read the ESI (e.g., version changes that are unsupported or flawed or faulty), the ESI's accuracy (e.g., failure to track who created which documents and when), the system security or lack thereof (e.g., who had access and what type of access), and/or the translation of the ESI records to human readable form. Today there are a variety of blogs that track the various attacks and the admissibility of electronic information, including www.ediscoverylaw.com, which tracks updates and provides case citations for particular topics and www. discoveryassist. com/Quotes.asp which has a variety of resources detailing how discovery is changing.

---

55. *See* Fed. R. Civ. Pro. 26, 34 and 37; *See also,* Eric Dobrusin and Katherine White, *Intellectual Property Litigation: Pretrial Practice* (Aspen 2d ed. 2007 supp).

To ensure the value of ESI in an IP culture, it is therefore desirable to address and adopt practices in accordance with the following topics:

RECORD RELIABILITY

- ESI is created and maintained in a controlled/organized environment under policy or standard operating procedures (SOP).
- Security restricts access, changes, witnessing, and commenting
- Regular submission of records to system
- Audit trail time stamps all events (record creation, source, changes, etc.)
- Archiving according to corporate retention policies and in appropriate format
- Activity log records all system changes (hardware and software)
- Training is documented

AUTHENTICATION

- User is identified
- Changes to records are retained

INTEGRITY

- Access to stored records is limited to identifiable personnel for authorized purposes
- Accessibility and readability is ensured for the lifetime of record

Recently, Magistrate Judge Grimm issued a decision of more than 100 pages detailing the evidentiary issues surrounding most types of ESI. *Lorraine v. Markel American Insurance Co.*[56] dealt with an insurance claim on a boat, and there were numerous electronic documents (email, contracts, etc.) that the parties submitted in connection with their respective motions of summary judgment. In detailing what the parties should have done to have their supposed evidence properly considered, Judge Grimm lays out the considerations for an attorney for ESI of all types, including:

- FRE 104(a) and (b)–judge/jury determines if admissible, and need to use admissible evidence to show admissibility of other evidence;
- FRE 401 and 402–only relevant evidence; and
- FRE 901 and 902–authentic evidence, ensures trustworthiness.

---

56. 241 F. R. D. 534 (D. Md. May 04, 2007).

As Judge Grimm candidly points out, "failure to authenticate . . . almost always is a self-inflicted injury."[57]

> Because it is so common for multiple versions of electronic documents to exist, it sometimes is difficult to establish that the version that is offered into evidence is the 'final' or legally operative version. This can plague a party seeking to introduce a favorable version of its own electronic records, when the adverse party objects that it is not the legally operative version, given the production in discovery of multiple versions.[58]

In this context, IP professionals might seek to work with IT professionals to implement policies that will be followed and which will assist the organization in the management of corporate ESI. Many of these policies may also be dictated by other laws, such as Sarbanes-Oxley.

Document Retention Policies

The Arthur Anderson demise taught, or should have taught, everyone that it is not good to have a policy that is only followed in times of trouble. In that case, documents at Arthur Anderson were shredded in accordance with company policy only after trouble at Enron started, by which time it was too late.[59]

Policies (if adopted) need to be followed or they may become useless, at best; at worst, they may set standards for behavior that will not be met. Also, when litigation, administrative actions or other proceedings start or are anticipated, a hold on document destruction needs to be enacted. This is emphasized in the newly enacted *Federal Rules of Civil Procedure*, which emphasize the duty of organizations to preserve, collect, and produce ESI. Electronic records should be stored or disposed of by following a policy and before litigation. Specifically, Fed. R. Civ. Pro. 37(f) deals with ESI and states that "[a]bsent exceptional circumstances, a court may not impose sanctions under these rules on a party for failing to provide electronically stored information lost as a result of the routine, good-faith operation of an electronic information system."[60]

Fundamental policies might include:

Prohibit unethical or fraudulent behavior While this may seem straightforward, it should not be forgotten that computer systems will have internal

---

57. *Ibid.*
58. *Ibid.*
59. *See* factual discussion in Arthur Andersen LLP v. U.S., 544 U.S.696 (2005).
60. Fed. R. Civ. Pro. 37(f). *See also,* The Sedona Conference Commentary on Legal Holds: The Trigger & The Process, August 2007, reproduced at http://www.thesedonaconference.org/content/smicFiles/Legal_holds.pdf accessed April 2, 2008.

clocks giving time and date stamps to most records (consider the word processing document that automatically gets a new date whenever it is opened). Backdating of documents (or the appearance of backdating) can be extremely risky. In the context of inventions, the usefulness of evidence may be discounted if not proved to have been made contemporaneously with an event or experiment. If stored as ESI, then a document that records events after the fact may have to be carefully drafted and stored against later alteration.

Provide for security of records and information This means that IT should have controls in place over who can access certain documents, data, or servers. It is common in both large and small organizations for IT rules to be nonexistent or ignored because they impose difficult working restrictions (e.g., shared servers are sometimes locked down). Policies should dictate against IT policies being ignored, but it should be recognized that *if* a policy is being ignored or circumvented that it may be a poor policy and should be changed.

Data backup Most people are aware that servers need to be backed up as part of the good faith effort (and corporate responsibility) to maintain information, but the policy should detail many aspects that might not be considered, such as whether backup tapes can be reused or not.

Accountability and responsibility for passwords/electronic signatures Employees should know that computers identify the user by the login password and that work performed on a computer with their login will be viewed as their work (for better or worse).

Validation and auditing When the organization is in a conflict, expect that the other side (who are not your friends) will have access to your computer system to check it out for flaws that might affect your evidence. Thus, written records showing that you audit your computer systems for bugs or flaws, as well as validating the ESI has integrity, can become important in fending off any attacks on this basis.

Additional policies that could relate specifically to intellectual property deal with data and long-term storage. With all that has been written since the introduction of the ESI rules within the *Federal Rules of Civil Procedure*, abundant guidance is available to help establish such policies.

CHAPTER
3

Making the Culture Contagious: Intellectual Property within an Organization

Processes and Basic Questions to Keep in Mind

Strong IP cultures tend to exist in organizations where leaders follow processes and motivate others to do the same. While the first and second chapters explained the overview and some basic tools to set up the intellectual property culture, this chapter focuses on the processes that can make an organization's IP culture "hum," by spreading IP values throughout the organization and implementing frameworks for decision making that enable an organization to prioritize, understand, and establish realistic goals for its IP. Such processes will not only shorten decisionmaking, which is especially critical to the success of many IP endeavors, but should also empower those making the decisions with an enhanced sense of control.

Open and candid communication within an organization—and sensitization of organization personnel to seek answers to the following general questions—will in most instances lead to sound and satisfying IP decisions. They will also lead to a consistency that enhances confidence in the processes within the organization.

The following basic questions will be posed in many contexts throughout our discussion:

1. To what extent is the subject technology, or will the subject technology be, commercialized by the organization or a competitor?
2. Is there, or will there be, any viable licensing interest in the subject technology or can it otherwise be deployed to generate revenues?
3. What realistic goals for the subject technology are sought by taking action according to the decision?
4. Is there other IP owned by the organization that can be used to achieve such goals?
5. Is there a reasonable means to attain such goals apart from the action sought to be taken according to the decision?
6. Will the action sought to be taken involve a reasonable deployment of the resources of the organization?

Communication Is Key

A culture of intellectual property demands that personnel have access to information about the organization's intellectual accomplishments. Unlike machinery or other capital resources that can be observed and operated on a shop floor, to most, IP is a mystery. It does not spit out parts every few seconds. It does not transport parts from one end of a plant to another. To the uninitiated organization, for instance, a patent is just a paper filled with legalese and with nice-looking drawings. The patent may not seem of much value to the organization because personnel do not understand it. Accordingly, one of the first steps toward establishing a healthy IP culture is to establish the IP as an important asset, especially to the leaders of the organization—and properly communicate the value of the IP. IP can have whatever face an organization puts on it. Communication about IP is important because it sets the tone for how seriously IP matters are taken by the organization.

Communication is important also to define those situations in which IP should be used or protected. Communication helps to establish a knowledge base that will guide inventors to know when to contact counsel. For example, frequent communication and training will help to induce the technical community to initiate contact with counsel to start the process of patenting a particular technology. Frequent communication on these types of issues will also help avoid the hard feelings that may fester with inventors who expect that the organization should actively be doing something about his or her work. Communication also sends an important unspoken message from senior management to inventors by demonstrating that the organization values the technical contributions inventors are making. The availability of counsel to listen to ideas of inventors and to share with inventors how inventions fit within the bigger picture of the organization can go a long way to enhance inventors' esteem. Needless to say, communication will also help assure that a quality patent application that serves the needs of the organization can be prepared and filed quickly.

Communication also is important to establish respective roles of members of the team that administers the organization's IP function. It humanizes what could otherwise be a cold and impersonal process. Communications from in-house counsel can also show personnel the role played by the in-house counsel, what his or her work produces, and why that work is important.

3.1 Keep Messages Simple and Understandable

Survey most clients, and they will express overall satisfaction or dissatisfaction with their counsel simply on the basis of whether the counsel communicates intelligibly with the client, in terms that the client will understand. For lawyers, this means non-lawyer-speak. It often requires the lawyer to adopt a "chameleonesque" vocabulary consistent with the audience. For example, the lawyer will speak intelligently in business terms for business persons, scientific terms for scientists, marketing terms for marketers, or sales terms for salespersons. It may even require the lawyer to confess ignorance and seek to have audience members elaborate about their respective roles in the organization.

What Information IP Counsel Communicates

Counsel needs to distinguish between two types of information, namely information that the entire company can and should see, and information that is restricted to a limited subset of people.[61] Opinions on this vary widely, but overall the information made available companywide sets the tone for the IP culture at your organization. Every organization must, therefore, determine for itself the extent that its IP information should be accessible. Clearly, in a controlled information culture, an us-and-them feeling can result. However, being too open may create disclosure problems or lack of control over company information.

Classes of Information

The following list helps to identify classes of information that IP counsel are commonly called upon to communicate in the course of fulfilling their roles in the organization, along with some possible approaches to handling such communications.

Publicly Available Information

As a baseline, publicly available information can be made available by counsel to the entire organization. This can be done by establishing databases, computer network files, or even old-fashioned bulletin boards.

Published Patents and Patent Applications

Published patents and patent applications can be listed in a directory or otherwise summarized so that personnel can readily access pertinent information. Each organization will have its own set of preferred information that will facilitate searching. For instance, some organizations maintain tabulated databases that include a representative image or summary of the patent document. Other information might include the number (e.g., patent number or publication number), names of some or all inventors, title, relevant filing dates, publication dates or patent grant dates, and possibly even a link to a copy of the patent document (e.g., a pdf file, a searchable text file, or both). It will take relatively little effort to create such a compilation and to train personnel of its existence and how to use it. Having the compilation in a format that is consistent with other files the organization keeps will make personnel

---

61. The discussion here assumes that appropriate measures will be taken to preserve the communications as confidential and subject to applicable attorney client privilege.

more comfortable using it. Bear in mind, as a general proposition, relatively few persons within an organization take the time to develop skills for searching patents on the Internet. Faced with the choice of finding it themselves or dialing the phone number of counsel to find it, most people will opt for the latter.[62] In a perfect world not only will this information be captured within the organization, but there will be a "go to" person (preferably other than counsel) familiar with it, who can assist with locating pertinent documents.

Published Papers or Conference Presentations

Like patent documents, there is relatively little down-side in making these types of documents available on a widespread basis (without commentary or editorializing). By their very nature, they are not confidential,[63] and it is often in the best interest of organizations that these documents be publicly disclosed for purposes of IP laws and practices.

3.2 Approve Papers and Presentations Before Making Them Public

In many industries, tremendous emphasis is placed on publishing, presenting at trade shows, or both. It is important that members of an organization communicate any possible publication to counsel in advance of publication for at least two significant reasons. First, the publication or presentation triggers a time period in the U.S. within which any patent application must be filed. Outside of the U.S., with only limited exceptions, the publication or presentation will foreclose any patent rights for what is published or presented. Second, counsel needs an opportunity to review the content to assure that the content and the subject of any patent application are consistent, to assure consistency in disclosure of prior art, and to avoid unnecessary statements that could be distorted by an adversary in the context of litigation. *See* Appendix 8.

---

62. This information can be found for free at freepatentsonline.com as well as google.com, uspto. gov.epo.org, and others.
63. It is important to distinguish between private presentations (e.g., presentations shown to a limited audience) and public presentations. This discussion does not advocate widespread dissemination of private presentations. Access to those should be addressed on a case-by-case basis.

These documents are publicly available and should be made available to the entire company for all to see. Presentations in particular are hard to find on the Web and, thus, the organization will appreciate seeing what others are presenting about the company or its technology.

A note of caution, as a precondition for publication, a publishing journal may demand transfer of copyrights to the journal. Work-made-for-hire contracts[64] may necessitate such transfers by the organization. Upon transfer of rights, unless certain rights are reserved, then technically the organization may have divested itself of the right to copy the article, even if limited to internal distribution.[65]

IP Resource and Training Materials

This particular class of information is valuable to circulate widely within an organization. The more people who access and review this information, the more your IP knowledge base grows. This class of information includes several categories.

Training Materials

To successfully cultivate an IP culture, training up and down the organization is valuable. Presentations made by counsel at internal training meetings can be made available as Webcasts or podcasts simply by recording the sessions and uploading them to an IP server. Training materials and information will then be available to employees around the globe for reference at the training session, to those who cannot attend a training session, as well as to those who simply want to refer to them at their own convenience.

Explanations of IP Processes

In a number of instances, specific explanations should be prepared to help personnel better understand the processes employed by the organization for its IP, or to otherwise contemplate and answer most frequently asked questions. For example, an organization chart can be made available to illustrate the persons through whom an IP decision must be processed. Another illustrative

---

64. 17 U.S.C. § 101 (1999).

65. Many companies use a license from the Copyright Clearance Center (www.copyright.com) for internal distribution of copyrighted articles and the like. Such licenses include most common scientific publications and are useful to avoid any liability for internal distribution of the type discussed here.

explanation might be one that tracks the process of patenting an invention, from the initial idea, to documenting the idea in an invention disclosure, to filing an application, and even through to the expiration of any patent. Appendix 5 illustrates how such events could be correlated with events in a product life cycle.

3.3 IP Disclosure: Frequently Asked Questions

The following are among the more common questions that members of an organization will ask. Developing and posting answers to these questions should help to conserve valuable resources.

1. How do I submit an invention disclosure?
2. To whom do I submit an invention disclosure?
3. How soon will I know if the disclosure is approved for patenting?
4. Will I receive any extra compensation if this idea is patented?
5. If the organization decides not to patent my idea, can I get the organization to waive its rights so I can patent on my own?
6. When do I mark patent numbers on patented products?
7. How do I properly notify others of any copyright I may have?
8. How should I mark confidential information before I give it to people outside the organization?
9. How do I submit a presentation or paper submitted for approval prior to presenting or publishing?
10. Does the company keep a list of trade secrets and how can I add to that list?
11. How do I contact the IP department to ask a question?
12. What should I do to report an infringement?
13. What should I do if someone outside the organization accuses the organization of infringement?
14. What should I do if I discover a patent belonging to someone else that looks relevant to my technology?
15. How can I search databases to see if someone else has IP rights that relate to what I am doing?

Although some of these questions appear to be general legal advice, most of them will be specific to each company. In addition, none of this information is, or should be, a secret inside acompany. There is a lot of information on intellectual property on the Web, much of it bad or inappropriate for a particular company. By providing the appropriate information in the correct format, personnel get the information that they should have.

Form Documents

Certain basic forms can be made available to personnel on an unrestricted basis. Examples may include the invention disclosure form (*See* Appendix 4), public disclosure request form (*See* Appendix 8, and contract or licensing request form. Each of these forms is used to request services. In addition, forms that might be provided by the IP group include laboratory notebook practices and procedures (*See* Appendix 7), standard nondisclosure agreements (*See* Appendices 1–3), standard copyright use agreements, and other standard agreements that protect or relate to IP.

Information about IP Counsel's Work

This category of information is borderline, as it often encompasses sensitive information, such as filing decisions and reasons for them, status reports, assessments of patentability or patents of others. Some organizations might elect to treat some or all of this information as sensitive and, consequently, restrict access to only those with a need to know. Others may regard the need to foster an open IP environment, with complete access to this information, as imperative to make all persons within the organization feel included in the culture.

There are also two key types of information that will help the organization understand what counsel is doing and that their requests are being handled (and not ignored).[66] First, counsel's pending workload and priorities can be explained. Paralegals or secretaries can handle task lists and predict when counsel will respond to requests. In addition, the pending patent docket and deadlines can be made available. Eighteen months after filing, most patent applications are published, so counsel's work is publicly available, in any event.[67] Second, internal organization action on IP requests can be made available. For example, if the organization is submitting many invention disclosures, but decisions on filing are not communicated (e.g., reasons not to file) then the pace of invention disclosures will almost surely drop.

---

66. One of the most common complaints, in general, by clients about counsel is their lack of responsiveness to requests for advice. Telephone messages that are not returned or emails that request an answer that are not returned for long periods of time (e.g., weeks) leads to a feeling of being ignored. If counsel is busy, that level of effort needs to be explained to people in the organization.

67. Empowering employees with training to search the Patent Application Information and Retrieval (PAIR) database of the USPTO to access the record of pending applications could save countless of administrative hours. *See,* http://www.uspto.gov/external/portal/pair (affording access to published application information; access to unpublished applications is also possible).

3.4 **Intra-Organization Communications**

The following table specifies a range of communications that organizations will commonly encounter in the course of establishing a healthy IP culture. *Active Communications* refer to those communications that are actively shared with and among personnel, such as face-to-face, by phone or video-conference, net meetings, or e-mail strings. *Passive Communications* refer to those communications that can be maintained in a preselected location (e.g., in a library or on a computer network) for retrieval by personnel at the convenience of such personnel. Due to their sensitivity, *Restricted Access* communications should be made to a smaller group of individuals within the organization on a "need to know" basis and with expectations that the communication is not shared outside the group. *Unrestricted Access* communications, in contrast, are less sensitive and can be shared throughout the organization with appropriate measures to safeguard privilege or confidentiality.

	Restricted Access	*Unrestricted Access*
Active Communications	–Drafts of patent applications	–Presentations
	–Opinions of counsel	–Workshops
	–License negotiations	–Award presentations
	–IP Strategies	–Patent grants
	–Budgets	–Patent/literature databases
Passive Communications	–Filing decisions	–Invention disclosure forms
	–IP meeting minutes	–Confidentiality agreement forms
		–Invention disclosures submitted for consideration
		–Status reports
		–Training materials
		–Newsletters
		–Policy manuals

What the Business Side Should Communicate

Successful communication in a healthy IP culture is a two-way proposition. While IP counsel desirably communicates certain information to help foster client confidence, there are several categories of information that the business side of the organization needs to actively communicate to counsel for them to do their jobs effectively. The specific type of information will vary from organization to organization and will depend upon the nature of the business of the organization and its intellectual property philosophy.

Examples of information to encourage the business side of an organization to communicate to counsel include invention activity information; critical deadlines for disclosures of ideas or samples to third parties; product development plans; product strategies; market information and key competitors for each relevant product; goals and objectives of the organization for its IP; specification of results that would be deemed a success; the status of any negotiations undertaken by the business independent of counsel; changes of personnel within the organization; notification or awareness of products or relevant patents to competitors; any scheduling constraints that might impair the ability to communicate with counsel; and the IP budget and how it fits into an overall organizational budget.

Information about Inventions

When considering processes for gathering and communicating information about inventions, many techniques exist. However, two basic approaches, the "top-down" approach and the "bottom-up" approach are commonly used to communicate invention information from the businesses to IP counsel. Both of these approaches will need to work within the underlying premise that there are typically three different categories of personnel who, by virtue of their duties, are best situated to recognize the occurrence of an invention and the need for communicating information about the invention to initiate the patenting process. The first category includes inventors or other members of the technology community (e.g., scientists, engineers, technicians, or the like). The second category generally will include mid-level and even some senior-level managers, who on a daily basis have knowledge of the organization's business plans and strategies and are positioned to recognize how best to position the invention for fulfilling the organization's overall strategic objectives. The third category includes personnel having responsibility for administrating some IP function. This could be counsel or a paralegal, a patent liaison, an intellectual asset manager, or another IP advisor as will be discussed in a later chapter.

The bottom-up approach is exemplified by situations in which those working on the invention are motivated enough (e.g., by awards, recognition, training, or discussions with others) to the need for patenting and to other IP issues that they, not their managers, initiate the invention disclosure process. The bottom-up approach, where it exists, is actually a barometer of a healthy IP culture.

In contrast, the top-down approach is the more likely approach in the early stages of establishing an IP culture. In the top-down approach, it will be up to managers, the persons responsible for the IP function, or both, to more actively seek out inventions within the company or to encourage patenting. For example, a manager who says, in effect, "this product or process is critical to our success so we need to make sure we can practice and protect it" illustrates one way to implement the top-down approach. The manager is showing IP leadership and communicating a critical organization need, driving the rest of the organization to fulfill that need. In another type of top-down approach, an intellectual property professional recommends the filing of an invention disclosure form as the result of having access to product development information, or key sales. For example, the manager may also regularly "make the rounds" within the department and identify if any impending activities (e.g., public disclosures) may require immediate patenting attention. Yet another aspect of the top-down approach, managers may seek to foster "out of the box" creativity and ingenuity.

On this last point, some of the best products, and intellectual property surrounding those products, result from a manager allowing a scientist or engineer taking a risk on an experiment or product development that is not approved in the same manner as other projects, often referred to as a "skunkworks." It may also be the result of an experiment gone bad.[68] In some situations, it is in the best interest of IP counsel to support those skunk-works activities, so that they can be properly protected. Such activities by counsel should be encouraged by senior management so that counsel will be relied upon by the organization's inventors, encouraging trust among IP personnel and inventors. Supporting inventors to pursue their ideas helps IP personnel build that trust. This does not mean that corporate budgets should be disregarded, but when IP personnel are too tightly align with management as compared to scientific endeavors, they run the risk of damaging communication lines with inventors. These communication lines are critical, and IP counsel should support even possibly unsanctioned projects or experiments (with activities such as prior art searches, expedited invention review, communication with senior management, etc.).

---

68. An example of one famous invention that resulted from what might have been characterized as a failed experiment or "bootlegging" project is the Post-It® Note. *See,* http://www.3m.com/us/office/postit/pastpresent/history.html (accessed November 22, 2007); and http://en.wikipedia.org/wiki/Post-it_note (accessed November 22, 2007).

3.5 **Skunk Works and Bootlegging**

To foster creativity and out-of-the-box free-thinking, some companies invoke "skunk-works" operations or adopt "bootlegging" policies. In the former, companies will assign a particular group of personnel to an advanced development program for a particular technology (which may even be kept secret within the company). The individuals within the group commonly will be relieved of certain of their day-to-day reporting and administrative responsibilities so that they can devote more energy toward the development. The original Skunk Works® was formed during World War II, within Lockheed, and led by Kelly Johnson. Johnson espoused fourteen rules for the Lockheed Rules of Operation, two of which illustrate the operation's flexibility:

"4. A very simple drawing and drawing release system with great flexibility for making changes must be provided.

5. There must be a minimum number of reports required, but important work must be recorded thoroughly."[1.]

"Bootlegging" is a variation on skunk works operations and frequently involves unplanned research undertaken "bottom-up" within an organization, commonly without the necessary authorization of management. Commentators trace the term back to 1967, as coined by K.E. Knight in *A Descriptive Model of the Intra-Firm Innovation Process*, *The Journal of Business*, (1967) Vol. 40, at 478-496. The bootlegging model is regarded as a valuable process for fostering innovation. *See* Augsdörfer, "Path Dependency in Unplanned R&D," Arbeitsberichte—Working Papers, ISSN 1612-6483 (2004), as posted at http://www.fh-ingolstadt.de/ABWP_04.PDF (accessed November 22, 2007). As can be appreciated, in recognition of the value that innovation can bring to a firm, the firms that encourage skunk works or bootlegging generally will also have a healthy IP culture in place.

---

1. http://www.lockheedmartin.com/aeronautics/skunkworks/14rules.html (accessed November 22, 2007).

The invention disclosure form (*See* Appendix 4) is a key document for communicating a request for legal services.[69] Two important reasons motivate

---

69. Note that Invention Disclosure documents are of a type of document that could be considered attorney-client privileged, provided they are handled properly. *In Re Spalding Sports Worldwide, Inc.*, 203 F. 3d 800 (Fed. Cir. 2000). They could, therefore, not be discoverable during litigation, unless that privilege has been waived. To avoid an opponent arguing that the privilege that has attached to Invention Disclosure has been waived, it may be prudent to restrict access to these forms, once they are completed and submitted for review. Therefore, while IP personnel may want to communicate pending matters for the Patent Committee or other sanctioned corporate functions where privilege will be maintained, posting such completed forms on a corporate intranet may prove to be an undesired use of the forms.

the submission of an invention disclosure form: first, to initiate the process of patenting by informing decision-makers of invention circumstances, and formally requesting the preparation and filing of a patent application on an invention; second, to document an idea prior to disclosure or collaborating with another organization, and, thereby, corroborate prior inventorship and ownership rights. In this context, the internal invention disclosure, if employed properly, has the potential to avoid or resolve many potential inventorship or ownership disputes without litigation or alternative dispute methods (e.g., arbitration). Inventors can use the invention disclosure form as documentation beyond notebooks or other documents. The fact that an invention record is an invention disclosure form leaves no doubt as to who considered the idea to be their own.

Considerations that apply to this form will be specific for each company, however, taking out the legalese and inserting easy-to-understand concepts should be encouraged; after all, nonlegal personnel are reading and filling in the form. The form typically breaks down into three categories of information: business, technical, and legal. Business information should convey the importance of the invention to the market, product, or company. Technical information should include the potential breadth of the invention, specific examples as well as the closest prior art. Legal information will include information necessary for determine patenting, including possible disclosure, possible sale of the invention, where the work was done (e.g., which countries), and its use in any commercial setting.

Though the information sought is for creating a legal document, replacing key IP terms can keep legalese to a minimum and avoid having nonlegal personnel provide legal opinions for which they lack qualification. For example, avoid "inventor" and use "contributors or submitters" instead; avoid "on-sale" and use "quoted" instead; avoid asking for the "first written description" or the "best mode" and instead ask for documentation showing the invention.

3.6 The Risk of Common Words or "People Say the Darnedest Things"

Patent litigation often hinges upon complex debates over the meaning of one or two particular words. This makes it difficult to believe in the possibility of "smoking guns" in a patent case. However, parties will often spend millions of dollars seeking the one or two nuggets that are likely to inflame a jury to the point that a verdict one way or the other is almost assured. As part of the establishment of any IP culture it could prove valuable to sensitize personnel to the risks they run for the organization by the words they speak and, even worse, the words they commit to writing. Below is a sampling of terms that novices to IP personnel should strive to eliminate from their vocabularies.

"infringe"

"invention"

"best mode"

"conceived"

"reduced to practice"

"equivalent"

"enable"

"obvious"

"inventor"

"offered for sale"

"copy"

One key feature of many current invention disclosure forms is information about prior art, as well as a prior art search by the submitters. In the past, particularly in the U.S., some attorneys took the attitude that it was their job to draft the applications and the job of the Patent Office to find prior art. After all, they reasoned, patent applicants pay large fees for filing an application; surely, at least a portion of the fees must go toward compensating the Office for the time examiners spend servicing each application file.

This approach has proved effective in many environments and may be suitable for a host of inventions, such as for very narrow incremental improvement inventions, for inventions where the attorney knows the prior art well, or inventions where the patentable scope of the invention is not critical. However, with patent prosecution standards tightening around the world and patenting costs sky-rocketing—particularly in the U.S. with the advent of a higher threshold for nonobviousness under the 2007 Supreme Court *KSR*[70] decision—awareness of close prior art during the drafting of a patent application can be particularly valuable to help articulate distinguishing features. The USPTO has actively sought to heighten the burden upon patent applicants to improve submissions by more rigorous prior art analysis.

Inventors can improve the efficiency of the patent application process by performing some rudimentary searching themselves and also by providing information about otherwise difficult to find prior art, such as presentations of which they are aware, products on the market, or prior products that may no longer be on the market and for which information is not readily accessible to counsel. Product brochures, catalogs, or manuals are particularly helpful in proving the state of the art for products that have been sold publicly prior to the invention.

---

70. *KSR Int'l Co. v. Teleflex, Inc.*, 127 S. Ct. 1727, 167 L. Ed. 2d 705 82 U.S.P.Q. 2d 1385 (2007).

3.7 **Foreign Filing License**
For inventions made in the U.S., a foreign filing license is required before filing the application abroad. Failure to do so, or to seek a retroactive foreign filing license, could jeopardize the validity of the patent and subject the party filing to penalties. 35 U.S.C. §§ 184 through 188. Chapter 12 addresses this in greater detail.

Ten Tips for Improving the Written Record in Invention Disclosures

1. Avoid use of unexplained internal codes, designations, abbreviations, or acronyms; an attorney or agent reading the unexplained terms will be unfamiliar with them.
2. If a disclosure refers to test standards, they should be carefully explained. It should not be assumed that a test performed within one division of a company is uniformly applied throughout the entire company. For example, some companies employ different measures on a country-by-country or region–by-region basis.
3. When a specific universal test method (e.g., ISO, ASTM, SAE, or the like exists or is used), reference to it by its proper designation will help reduce the drafting time of the attorney or agent.
4. Avoid the submission of incomplete or unexplained test data. If a patent that makes reference to experimental data is ever enforced, a great deal of energy will be spent by litigation attorneys attacking the data. By helping the attorney or agent to fully understand and explain the data, the vulnerability of the patent to such attack can be reduced.
5. Avoid poor drawing quality. The Patent Office has strict rules governing patent drawings. Seldom is the case in which drawings prepared by an inventor will suffice to meet the requirements of the Office. Drawings generally require preparation by professional patent draftspersons.
6. Avoid the use of color-coding. The Patent Office rules require black-and-white submissions except in unusual situations. In addition, it is inevitable that in the life and travels of the disclosure document, it will be photocopied or transmitted electronically—by fax machine or otherwise—and the colors will be converted to black and white format. The significance of important information that is communicated by inventors through colors, but which is received by the attorney or agent in black and white, is at risk of loss.
7. Provide at least one or more (a) generic descriptions of products; (b) technical data sheets; and (c) known patents covering the products, when identifying the products by their trade name. This greatly reduces the amount of time spent by attorneys and agents, who are unfamiliar with the products, to elicit sufficient information to appropriately describe the product in a patent application.

8. Provide the invention disclosure and any accompanying supporting materials to the attorney or agent in electronic format. A portion of the expense of drafting a patent application is due to labor-intensive word processing. Inventors can control these expenses by providing intelligible, word-processed documents or other electronic data that the attorney or agent can employ.

9. Conspicuously identify any events that may impose a deadline for filing and make sure that, when transmitted to the attorney or agent, all important facts are communicated to the attorney or agent. In addition, it is often the case that an invention disclosure will spend several months within an organization between the time it is prepared by the inventor and the time it is transmitted to an attorney or agent. It is important for the inventor or the person who transmits the disclosure to make sure that no recent events have transpired in the interim, which would impose a filing deadline.

10. Provide intelligible descriptions of the invention and the features believed to constitute an advancement over the prior art.

Planning and Strategy Communication

In addition to gathering the intellectual property of an organization, it is valuable to place it in the context of the business and plan for possible future issues. Thus, persons charged with the responsibility for administering IP should be included in product development and strategic planning, especially if the organization has an IP strategy the success of which is tied in any way to the success of any product or organizational strategy. One simple way to achieve such communication is to invite IP counsel to meetings for product development or strategic planning, and to articulate for counsel the areas in which the organization shall require legal advice from counsel.

These meetings also offer an opportunity for businesses to communicate where they are spending their resources. Such expenditures demonstrate key efforts that may need protection from competitors or freedom to operate. For example, it may be that the research and development group has spent most of its time to identify a particular additive for its formulations that dramatically reduces the costs of manufacture and avoids warranty recalls. Chances are a competitor is also focusing on solving that problem. It is helpful for counsel to understand the problem solved so that counsel can anticipate the direction a competitor may take, and seek protection to keep the competitor from doing so.

To the latter point, businesses also should communicate market information and key competitors for each protected product or process. This communication can allow the patent prosecution attorney to obtain claims that are commercially relevant. In particular, much patent prosecution takes place in a vacuum, where the attorney or agent must amend the claims to avoid the prior art and where the decisions of which claim elements can be added is simply not communicated (or, worse, unknown). Communicating market information can take place a number of ways, but including IP professionals in product shows as well as marketing plans helps them connect to the overall business.

Communicating IP Metrics and Budget

For IP professionals to perform their roles satisfactorily, it is essential for business to define and communicate what is expected of them and how much money counsel has available to meet such expectations. Expectations can be communicated with reference to some form of "metric." For present discussion purposes, metrics are regarded as performance indicators that are measurable (preferably objectively). When these metrics are properly chosen and communicated to counsel, not only will the metric help drive the business, but it will also help direct the course counsel follows.

For example, an organization might perform an IP metric of comparing the sales margin of patented products versus unpatented products. They might track the patent protection to products (helping them know which patents have value and which might not) and then can adjust factors for products that operate in different markets (so that the comparison is fairly based). In this manner, they might show the patented products command a higher incremental margin as compared to unpatented products. This metric can be used to set goals for the IP group (every business wants products with higher margins).[71] Businesses like these metrics because it gives them a goal for IP professionals to meet. In particular, internal metrics can be more valuable than external metrics[72] because internal metrics have more complete information (including confidential information such as costs, revenues, and patent mappings for individual products), and internal metrics are executed by those who understand how the technology will be used in the market. They understand how the value will be created or maintained.

No communication process would be complete without a discussion of the budget. IP expenditures are a metric of sorts, in that they can be easily measured and compared. Regrettably, whether or not the budget is met also tends to be a primary source of discontent for clients, without regard to the actual benefits derived by the organization from the intellectual property. In establishing a healthy IP culture, open communication about the IP budget is important. Elements of the budget desirably are explained and analyzed against the needs of the organization for the budgeted period.

71. *See* Dan Alderman, Remarks at Strategic IP Leadership Conference, Valuing and Promoting IP in your Organization, Hosted by Kimberly-Clark Corporation (April 12–13, 2007), "How IP Metrics Drive Business Decisions."
72. There are many external metrics today that purport to measure IP value. The Patent Scorecard, created by the Patent Board, is published in the *Wall Street Journal* on Tuesdays (*See also* www.patentboard.com). Ocean Tomo creates PatentRatings (*See* www.oceantomo.com).

3.8 Foreign Patenting: Market and Litigation Theories

Because patents are territorial, each country in the world can charge for a patent to be enforced in its country. Many countries view patents as a source of revenue (including the U.S., where millions of dollars regularly had been diverted from fees paid to the USPTO for the general fund). Patenting costs can be significant if an invention is truly to be protected around the world. Thus, businesses need to work with the IP professionals to determine a strategy to manage the costs. One commonly practiced theory is the market theory, which has two variations: (1) obtain patent protection is obtained to cover the majority of the market for the product and (2) obtain patent protection is obtained only in those countries where a competitor must manufacture or sell in order to survive in the business. Obviously, to practice either market theory, detailed market information from the businesses is critical. Another theory is the litigation theory, where patent protection is obtained only in those countries where the company is willing to actually go into court and obtain an injunction or damages. There are many countries where no enforcement will be actually undertaken because of a reputation of the country as corrupt or as having an ineffective judiciary. Thus, obtaining patent protection in those countries may simply be a waste of money.

The Rest of the Company Should Also Be Communicating

Organizational functions other than research, development, manufacturing, and legal frequently play an important role (whether direct or indirect) in the generation of IP and in extracting value from IP. It is important to engage these functions in the IP process. For example, sales and even accounting can communicate key information to assist the IP process, including providing competitive IP information, information about key lost sales (or key sales made and why they were made), analyst opinions, publicity, tax consequences of certain actions, as well as internal recognition.

In this regard, human resources (HR) can and should be involved in employee (inventor) awards, recognition at (and planning of) company IP events, and overall reinforcement of the message sent by management about the importance of intellectual property to the organization. Investor relations can and should be involved in helping investors understand why the company is taking certain IP action, as well as providing feedback regarding investors' level of agreement to those actions. Marketing can be involved, in addition to the obvious trademark issues (e.g., proper marking on promotional material, brand management) by helping the IP group understand which features of a product cause it to sell or not sell. IP counsel can possibly use this information to tailor claim elements during prosecution and provide for the greatest commercially significant claim scope.

In a culture of IP, everyone in the organization can and should provide information to the process. Communication throughout the organization is the lifeblood of this process and lines of communication must be opened and facilitated by coordinated efforts of the business and counsel.

IP Process and IP Leadership

An organization's intellectual property process will desirably have a defined workflow for handling inventions, trade secrets, outside disclosures, or other treatment of proprietary material. Ideally, an organization will have a cradle-to-grave process (or combination of "sub-processes") that establish a consistent and reproducible path the organization can follow to make its IP decisions. At the start of this chapter, six basic questions were articulated. In the sections that follow, our discussion turns to how, with the aid of the preceding communication guidance, an organization can define its IP processes based on those questions. Our discussion addresses not simply a workflow for those decisions, but also the establishment of a leadership entity (an IP Committee) or at least an individual with responsibility for administering the processes.

Decision making as it concerns the intellectual property of an organization can not be reduced to formulaic decision trees, the pursuit of which will inevitably lead to the right decision. Factors affecting satisfaction of an organization with its decisions are ever changing, and often random. Indeed, many organizations fail to recognize that the particular processes that they establish do not best serve all the needs of the organization, most of which will be influenced by dynamic considerations such as budget, commercial significance, management review, scientific "sex appeal," fit to corporate goals, speed of process, IP team buy-in, and combinations of these factors, all of which influence the exact process.[73]

One of the initial considerations in establishing IP processes is to select appropriate persons, having both correct background and authority within

---

73. For example, the process to approve a presentation before it is publicly disclosed (and hence may destroy patentability outside of, or even within, the U.S.) is a decision that many organizations do not balance well. Small companies tend to be too free with this type of decision making, meaning that IP may be lost due to lack of control (e.g., a scientist wanting to present their cool new data, but not telling IP counsel about the presentation). Large companies tend to be too restrictive or too conservative in their IP process, in many cases stifling the scientists and engineers who are excited by and want to share their work (and increasing their scientific reputations in the process).

the organization, to make the correct decisions. For example, a scientist may refrain from submitting an invention disclosure because she spoke with a scientist member of the IP team, who expressed a belief that the idea is old and unpatentable. However, the scientist did not consider all of the factors that go into a legal determination of patentability, as would have been done by IP counsel, with the assistance of the scientist. What is potentially more distressing in such situations is when a competitor or customer ultimately patents the same technology.

Another important consideration in establishing IP processes is the "need for speed." The process desirably will avoid unnecessary paperwork and approvals that will hamper prompt filing. The race to the Patent Office is particularly crucial in "first to file" systems, in which the date when an invention was made is irrelevant, even if prior to that of competitor, if the competitor filed its patent application first. Further, it cannot be overlooked that if this process is too slow, personnel within the organization will tend to avoid it.

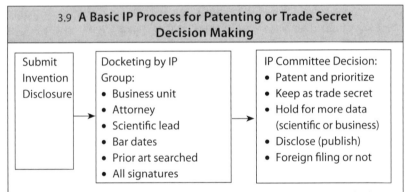

3.9 A Basic IP Process for Patenting or Trade Secret Decision Making

| Submit Invention Disclosure | Docketing by IP Group:
 • Business unit
 • Attorney
 • Scientific lead
 • Bar dates
 • Prior art searched
 • All signatures | IP Committee Decision:
 • Patent and prioritize
 • Keep as trade secret
 • Hold for more data (scientific or business)
 • Disclose (publish)
 • Foreign filing or not |

The first two sets in this process are straightforward, with an invention disclosure arriving at the IP group and the IP group making sure that all the information needed to make a decision is present or gathered. Note that sometimes the gathering of this information leads to an urgent need, at which time the process must be flexible enough to deal with the need (e.g., an immediately needed patent application filing because of a public disclosure). This example process uses an IP committee, which typically includes the business decision makers, scientific decision makers and IP decision makers.

An IP Committee

Much has been said so far about the persons charged with administering an organization's intellectual property function. In this section, an IP Committee concept is introduced as one such leadership body.[74] Typically, an IP Committee will consist of representatives from select functions of the organization, such as some or all sales, marketing, engineering, and finance personnel.

Surprisingly, organizations differ in their philosophy toward including IP counsel (whether in-house or outside counsel) as part of this committee. Some organizations believe they can manage their costs by excluding counsel. Others exclude counsel because they do not like the generally cautious approach that counsel brings to discussions. On the other hand, many of the most successful IP cultures share the common feature that IP counsel is included on the IP committee, or at least is always kept appraised of the decisions of the IP committee in a timely manner.

The precise composition of the group is organization-specific. It is useful to have the perspectives that many of these representatives will bring. However, the larger the group, the more risk that the committee will become hampered in its ability to act, inasmuch as even the simplest of tasks (such as scheduling meetings) will be bogged down by conflict.

Once selected, the IP Committee ought to be charged with some or all of the following tasks:

- Developing and overseeing an IP program and processes;
- Establishing measurable goals for the IP of the organization;
- Defining strategies for achieving the IP goals;
- Monitoring the progress toward achieving the goals and modifying strategies needed to achieve the goals;
- Meeting regularly (and frequently) as a committee for administering and assuring compliance with the company's IP program and processes;
- Helping assure the organization respects the valid and enforceable IP rights of others of which it is aware;
- Educating employees and agents about IP issues;
- Apprising employees and agents about known IP rights of others;
- Assisting to preserve records for establishing prior art, a prior user defense, inventorship contribution, independent development, or other purposes related to helping assure the continued right of the organization to conduct its business;
- Helping to assure compliance with marking and notice requirements imposed by IP laws;
- Maintaining regular and continuing communications with company management concerning IP;

---

74. Some organizations do not like the name "Committee" because it connotes a bureaucratic organizational structure. The term is used loosely in this discussion. If it makes more sense, use a substitute word, such as "Team."

- Reviewing invention disclosures and original works and approving or rejecting disclosures for patent and/or copyright registration applications;
- Preparing recommendations to management for enforcement of IP rights;
- Preparing recommendations to management for licensing or other acquisitions of IP rights;
- Identifying trade secrets and develop strategies for maintaining them;
- Maintaining regular and continuing communications with outside IP counsel; or
- Monitoring the fees incurred by Company in the process of carrying out the purposes and responsibilities of the IP Committee and exploring reasonable low-cost alternatives to manage the fees; and otherwise establishing and fostering a healthy IP culture within the organization.

As to the conduct of the IP Committee, it is expected that it will hold regular periodic meetings with a frequency appropriate to the innovation cycle of the organization. That is, the more the organization innovates, the more regularly the IP Committee ought to meet. These meetings should follow an agenda established in advance with relevant materials (e.g., invention disclosures, patents, prosecution proceedings, etc.) circulated for review in advance. Minutes, or some other written summary (ideally under the auspices of the attorney-client privilege), should be kept to record decisions.

3.10 IP Committee Meeting Minutes

Many sensitive topics are often discussed at IP Committee meetings, and the risk that harmful admissions may be recorded in the minutes is particularly acute. One benefit to including IP counsel in meetings of the committee is that minutes (or even notes taken during the meeting) that address sensitive topics may encompass communications that qualify for protection against disclosure during discovery under the attorney-client privilege. To this point, it is helpful for committee members who keep minutes or take notes at these meetings to clearly identify the communication as "Attorney-Client Privileged" and to identify the participants at the meeting. It may also prove to be good practice to have only a single person keeping record, to help reduce the risk of inconsistencies.

From a process viewpoint, there are some dangers in using an IP Committee. The committee may fail to meet. The committee may fail to make reasoned decisions. The committee may fail to make any decisions, such as by repeatedly asking for more information (thus, pushing decisions to future meetings or alternate decision-making processes). Insufficient time for the meeting may be allocated, with the effect that only some and not all important issues are addressed (which increases the risk that inventions to be considered for patenting will accumulate and fail to get properly protected). Individual members of the committee may become overwhelmed with other responsibilities, fail to show up at meetings, become bored, or simply lose interest (with the effect that certain invention disclosures can not be discussed and decisions taken). Committee members may fail to prepare for the meeting so that the agenda of the meeting becomes obsolete from the outset. These are just a sampling of the problems that can cause dysfunction of the IP Committee and which have the potential, if not monitored, to grind the IP process to a halt.

If an IP Committee proves dysfunctional or irrelevant, one possible alternative is to attempt the administration of IP by a designated "IP Advisor." An IP Advisor can effectively serve as a facilitator, who brings scientific, business, and IP together in a single person for a group or division. The role can be a fulltime or parttime job and desirably is filled by a scientist or engineer with at least a rudimentary understanding of intellectual property laws. The advisor typically will also be selected on the basis of his or her understanding of the patent portfolio and prior art, the technology being created or developed, and relevant business aspects of the organization. The advisor can help establish priorities with IP counsel and will, of course, also be charged with the important function of assuring communication within the organization.

3.11 Freedom to Operate, Prosecution, and IP Evaluation/Valuation Processes

Among the many intellectual property processes within an organization are three, in particular, that tend to get overlooked by firms that become too focused upon simply making decisions to file patent applications for their inventions.

One process is that which ought to occur when a firm becomes aware of the IP rights of another that may affect the firm's ability to commercialize its technology. This is referred to as a "freedom to operate" practice and typically involves monitoring competitive patents and determining whether the claims of the patents pose an obstacle to the firm.

The second process involves ongoing review of the portfolio of the firm to help assure that the protection sought or obtained covers the technology of the company or its competitors. It also helps to assure that patents obtained for the company are good and will be respected by competitors. For example, one such process might involve assembling a team that includes a technical person, a business person, and an attorney, who collectively can assess technical questions, assure reasonable scientific accuracy, and interrelate the IP with the business of the firm.

Finally, a process for evaluation of intellectual property that is created ought to be in place so that IP assets can be appropriately deployed, and if not used by the organization, licensed, sold, or otherwise discarded. Technology marketplaces exist for the exchange of technology (such as www.yet2.com; *See also* http://www.oceantomo.com/auctions.html).

Defining an IP Policy

Helpful to the administration of any IP function—whether through a committee, an advisor, or some other administrative authority—is a constitution document and specifically what is referred to herein as an IP policy document.[75] An IP policy can be an effective document to frame the decisions an organization needs to make and set guidelines for how individuals in the organization ought to behave. However, like any policy, it is only as good as the enforcement of that policy. Policies that are not followed are only damaging to the organization. Any IP policy that is adopted must be one that can realistically garner compliance throughout the organization.

An organization that seeks to define IP policy should consider setting forth at least two items, namely, a vision for creation and a vision for enforcement.

In defining policy for creating intellectual property, an organization is often best served by establishing a basic vision and expressing it in broad terms. One such policy statement might recite to the following effect:

> Organization regularly engages in design and development of proprietary methods, designs, compositions and other technology resulting in valuable, patents, trade secrets or in other intellectual property rights owned by Organization. Organization may seek to protect trade secrets or other intellectual property by continuing to hold the technology as trade secrets, by registration of copyrights or by patenting as the law permits. Organization expects others to respect its valid and enforceable intellectual property rights and trade secrets. It is likewise the intent of Organization to respect the valid and enforceable intellectual property rights and trade secrets of others.

---

75. Some organizations cringe at the use of the term "policy." Some view the use of "policy" as requiring senior management ratification, which the IP Committee wants to avoid. Some view the use of "policy" as requiring that the organization must follow the mandates of any such policy or face sanction. For the organizations that simply cannot accept the adoption of a "policy" concerning IP, then perhaps the organization would be better served by implementing the principles of a "policy" as "IP Guidelines" instead.

Another possible IP policy vision can be more business model specific:

> It is the policy of Organization to promote the adoption of its technology across all fields through licensing and, to that end, Organization protects it intellectual property, and seeks to license-in complementary technology.

Both policies help to frame the decisions that an organization will make with respect to its process of IP.

On the enforcement side, one sample policy statement may recite:

> Organization shall enforce its valid and enforceable Intellectual Property rights in a manner reasonably consistent with the purpose and intent of this Policy, but with the recognition that the decision to enforce must be made by management of Organization and must take into account the entirety of the circumstances surrounding a possible violation of an Organization right. Under all circumstances, Organization shall employ its Intellectual Property in a lawful manner.

Again, an alternative is an enforcement policy that reflects the organization's business model. For example:

> It is the policy of Organization to enforce its valid and enforceable intellectual property against direct competitors in the field.

In the end, corporate policy should promote ethical behavior to get strong and appropriate IP decisions. Strong corporate policies lead to a stronger IP system for all.

Making Filing and Maintenance Decisions

Technology can be evaluated along a number of different lines prior to making a filing or maintenance decision. Not all lines will apply to all organizations, but you should choose those evaluation lines that apply and weight them accordingly.

Each of these factors—business, technological and patent significance; technical and business maturity—will play out in a straightforward manner. For example, a decision not to file is easy for an immature technology that is supposed to enter a mature market with many patents already in the field. The technology obviously needs to be worked on more before it can be protected, or likely marketed, without heading into the IP of someone else. Conversely, a technology that is mature and entering a new market without many competitors preferably should be heavily protected to protect its market. Also, there may be a large incentive to patent in areas where there is

3.12 **Factors in Filing and Maintenance Decisions**	
Factor	*Description*
Business Significance	Relevance of the technology to the strategic goals of the organization
Technological Significance	Rate the significance of the technological features of the invention considering, for example, customer needs, commercial feasibility, and extensibility
Technical Maturity	Rate where in the research and development cycle the technology stands
Business Maturity	Rate the relative maturity of the business or market that the technology will enter
Patent Significance	Rate the relative closeness of the prior art and whether there is existing organization IP that already protects the technology

no significant prior art, but little incentive to patent where an organization's existing IP portfolio already protects the technology.

Once the evaluations are performed, the typical decisions of the IP committee or advisor include whether to file a patent application and set a priority or deadline for IP counsel to complete this task. If an invention disclosure is submitted for documenting ideas prior to meeting with a third party, such invention disclosures should not go to the IP committee. The IP committee may also decide to keep a particular invention as a trade secret (e.g., it is valuable and not easily discoverable from sold products or services).

One important decision is whether to publish the information of an invention disclosure. Publication creates prior art to others and should stop others from patenting the same invention as disclosed. The decision to publish involves practical questions of who will create the publication and where will it be published. Competitive concerns can also arise by promptly publishing current work; so organizations may try to find obscure publications in which to publish such information. One increasingly popular method is to publish on a Web site, such as IP.com. Such Web sites offer cheap publication costs and immediate publishing that establishes prior art. A reputable Web company should be chosen so that the prior art database will not disappear in a few years, which would defeat the purpose of publishing the information. As those in the patent field may recall, IBM published its "Technical Bulletins" for a long time in an effort to keep others from patenting the same technology. These were always hard to search and find, which could prove valuable to some or disastrous to others. An example of a framework that illustrates some considerations that go into filing decisions is provided at Appendix 9.

Making Enforcement Decisions

As discussed elsewhere in this book, there are many considerations and much work that goes into making an enforcement decision. But whatever the considerations, there are always going to be times when IP must be enforced. A cost–benefit analysis modified by the risk of winning or losing is basic to making the enforcement decision.

Identifying Goals: A Cost–Benefit Analysis

The first and most important question to ask when making an enforcement decision is: what does the organization want to accomplish? The litigation must be placed in the context of a business goal, and a value must be placed on that goal. The objectives of any enforcement can be wide and varying, even among different members of an organization. For example, does the organization want an injunction to stop a competitor? Does the organization want to obtain a cross license under the technology of the competitor? The objective must also be realistic. For example, it serves an organization little if it litigates, obtains an injunction, but is not able to itself manufacture the subject technology. That organization would probably be better served by licensing the competitor and deriving royalty income.

In terms of value, this cost–benefit analysis does not simply mean the largest damages award that an organization might win if it succeeds in the litigation. It ought to take into account the value that is realized by demonstrating to other competitors that an organization is serious about its IP and will pursue infringements.

On the cost side, there is the cost of the litigation (attorney fees, experts, etc.). In addition, there is the potential cost to reputation by enforcing and losing. There are always four major issues in patent litigation—validity, enforceability, infringement, and damages. Counsel will have to review each issue with management as well as show the financial and strategic considerations and benefits (litigation budgets, litigation counsel chosen and why, initial litigation strategy, etc.). Patent litigation requires some feel for, or understanding of, what arguments will win, and why they will win and how they will win. Answers to these questions will help management believe in the case when the going gets tough.[76]

Part of the cost consideration is whether certain "crown jewel" patents are going to be placed into dispute. After all, if such patent is lost, market entry by competitors is almost certain. Ideally, in the course of the analysis, multiple

---

76. With a motivated adversary, the going will get tough because although one party may think it has the perfect case (clearly valid, infringed patent worth millions in damages and market exclusivity), the opponent is typically not a fool simply out to spend money on litigation. They will have arguments and reasons why they should win, and ultimately a court will decide. Having someone else decide the fate of a party is always tough.

patents will be possible candidates for enforcement, each having its own risk considerations.

Other costs that organizations often overlook (and come to regret after it is too late) include the costs of distraction any organization will incur by dedicating the time of its members to supporting the enforcement effort, instead of performing their ordinary business function. Moreover, in the course of litigation in the U.S., the organization will be forced to divulge sensitive information during an intensive discovery process. Closely guarded costing and pricing information is vulnerable to disclosure to competitors and customers.

It will also do an organization well to identify what alternative means are possible in lieu of enforcement. For example, in some industries, a strategic public relations program to apprise others of information about patent grants or other industry-specific patent metrics may defer entry by competitors (this might be as simple as a chronology shared about remaining patent life that compares the patents of different competitors or a summary of key patent features). Perhaps alternative dispute resolution may suffice, or the entry of a suitable business relationship with the competitor.

Once these costs and benefits are determined, the cost–benefit analysis can go forward. Both sides in the dispute will do a cost–benefit analysis, most of the time even calculating a net present value (NPV) to the litigation. Net present values are well known in financial circles and measure the cost today of future payments and revenues. These NPVs are then used to determine if the litigation has financial value. This can be taken even further by performing an NPV on each possible outcome of the litigation, including, for example, (1) win case and get treble damages, (2) win case and settle, (3) win case and get less damages than expected, (4) win case but get minimal damages and an injunction, (5) start case and settle just before trial, etc. Each scenario has a value and an NPV, and so the possible values can be calculated. If the litigation itself does not have a positive NPV, even getting an injunction, then the litigation might still be worth the cost, if market perception or reputation for enforcement is necessary. Thus, the cost–benefit analysis can include multiple outcomes and take into account various values.

Patent Litigation Facts of Life

Most patent litigation cases settle prior to trial.[77] In 2004, there were 2,362 patent cases and 86 percent of them settled. In 2005, there were 2,231 patent

---

77. From statistics compiled by the University of Houston Law Center under Prof. Paul M. Janicke and available online at www.patstats.org.; *See,* http://www.patstats.org /HISTORICAL_ DISPOSITION_MODES__FOR_PATENT_CASES.rvz.doc(as accessed April 5, 2008): the reference further indicates for comparison, an overall civil settlement rate for 2004 of 74 percent.

cases and again 86 percent of them settled. These numbers are somewhat steady, with the settlement rate being 81 percent in 1986 and 79 percent in 1979 (but with substantially fewer cases brought in these years). There were substantial changes in patent law during 2007, and the settlement rate can be affected by these changes; for example, cases where the changes in the law can affect the case and the NPV is close to the settlement rate will more likely than not settle.

Of the cases that go to trial, the popular belief is that the patentee wins about half the time or more. In reality, the statistics are all over the place because of different people's interpretations of a win. For example, is it a win when a patent owner obtains judgment for liability on only one of six patents enforced? A true win is where the patentee prevails on all 4 major issues (validity, enforceability, infringement, and damages) in the manner they expected to prior to going to trial. Cases that go to trial are those generally where the parties disagree about the outcome of at least one of these issues, and so the risk against the patentee actually winning is substantial.

Another litigation fact of life is that the cost to litigate is significant in the U.S. a simple case will cost at least $500,000 and more complex cases will cost ten times that amount.[78] Legal talent from the largest law firms now cost upwards of $800 an hour (and the trend is higher, with some lawyers now charging over $1,000 an hour[79]). The cost to litigate is substantially less in certain foreign countries. For example, in Germany a patent litigation suit can be brought for less than $500,000 for a very complex case. Of course, the laws are substantially different in other countries; for example, in Germany there is no formal discovery process as in the U.S.

How Companies Can Keep Costs Down

Good Recordkeeping

The lifeblood of intellectual property is what can be proved in court as well as its perceived strength. Because IP is an intangible asset, it is shown by the

---

78. The American Intellectual Property Law Association reports that the average cost of litigating a patent infringement suit when more than $25 million is at stake surged from less than $3 million in 2001 to more than $5 million in 2007. American Intellectual Property Law Association, *Report of the Economic Survey 2007* at 29 (2007). The 2007 report stated that the cost of patent litigation where less than $1 million is at stake is $600,000 and the 2007 reported cost of patent litigation where between $1–$25 million is at stake is $2.5 million.

79. *See,* Nathan Koppel, *Lawyers Gear Up Grand New Fees* at B1 *Wall Street Journal* (Aug 22, 2007).

documents and things that demonstrate its existence and hence its value. Documents, samples, data, etc., must be kept to show the existence of the right. Thus, recordkeeping is critical to IP.[80] The records are important for determining dates of invention (35 U.S.C. § 102(g)), inventorship (35 U.S.C. § 102(f)), on sale or public use bars (35 U.S.C. § 102(b)), best mode (35 U.S.C. § 112), and activities outside of the U.S. (35 U.S.C. § 104). In the trademark context, the records establish a date of first use and provide samples. With trade secrets, the records define the secrets and show that they were maintained as secrets.

There are a few basics about corporate records that should be clear to everyone in the organization. First, an organization ought to clearly communicate to its employees that records are the property of the organization. They are confidential and proprietary to the organization, not to the employee. Thus, employees need to create corporate knowledge that is useful to the organization. Personnel ought to be trained to keep records that are legible, complete, and understandable. Abbreviations desirably ought to be avoided without prior definition. Terminology ought to be expressed accurately, precisely, and consistently.

It is also helpful for scientists and engineers keeping records to keep them in a scientific manner so that others can repeat their work. They should keep analytical data tied to particular experiments and in a manner that allows others to understand their work. For example, do not cross out mistakes; put a line through them so that they are still legible and can be explained at a later date. If possible, do not use Post-it® notes or other temporary records that can become dislodged or lost. It is also valuable to excise (e.g., X off) portions of pages not used (so that it will not look like you can go back and fill in a page at a later time). A sample of a format that can be adapted for use in many organizations for laboratory notebooks is provided in Appendix 7.

Indeed, records that are kept in a reliable, consistent manner according to established organizational practices are the best records for supporting IP. The reason is that with a long lapse of time common to many patent scenarios, most people will not remember the typical experiment or design or deal or whatever the record is recording. Instead, most people remember the unusual: the experiment that blows up, the spilled yield, or the business deal that was horrible or fantastic. However, most IP records document the usual, not the unusual. Thus, most people do not remember the event, but if they keep the record in the same consistent manner, they can always testify that they kept the record a certain way and the produced record looks like the way that they always kept that record. This provides authenticity and makes your records believable.[81]

---

80. Electronic recordkeeping is discussed in Chapter 2 under "Cooperation Between IT and IP."
81. *See also* Fed. R. Evid. 803(6).

Moreover, recordmakers should take into account the breadth of their potential audience. Consider the best-case scenario, in which the IP is so valuable that everyone in the market has to practice it even to stay in business. Thus, there will be a lot of infringers, lots of lawsuits, and lots of inquiries into the records surrounding the IP. The records stand the chance of being reviewed by the lawyers to the case, judges and their law clerks, and even jury members. The records have to withstand this strict scrutiny and appear reasonable under the circumstances. Abnormalities or serious deviations could place the welfare of the IP at grave risk.

In addition to defining standards and expectations within an organization for the manner and circumstances in which records are made, it is also important to assure compliance with any corporate record retention policy. These policies are generally available from counsel and provide for time periods and manner of record retention. For organizations that are newly establishing an IP culture, it is worth revisiting existing document corporate retention policies. It is likely that the organization has a relatively short retention period that may overlook the realities of patent transactions, some of which commonly will span ten years or longer.

Literature Libraries, Product Archives, and Prior Users

A literature library is a collection of publications that are relevant to the technology of an organization. It may include literature that constitutes prior art relative to a technology. It may include literature that discusses or even praises the technology of the organization. It may include literature addressing alternative or competing technologies. It is a simple fact that organizations need to compile these libraries and regularly update and organize them.

Similarly, a product archive is a repository of products that have been on the market in the past, including documentation showing the product on sale as well as samples of the products. Samples in product libraries allow for historical testing, to find possibly inherent properties of the product (e.g., properties that were not necessarily published in the past). Companies establish these libraries in order to keep a record of the prior art.

When entering a new field or selling a new product, an organization often will research the prior art, including publications and existing products, and document that status. These libraries are useful for benchmarking the organization's inventions and citing the most relevant prior art in its own patent applications. These libraries are also useful for easily finding prior art when another organization asserts an otherwise invalid patent against it.[82] In some

---

82. It is a good idea to make sure that copyright laws are complied with in connection with these libraries. *See* www.copyright.com.

cases, companies can make these libraries available to the public, such as on the internet. This public availability makes the existence of the prior art collection more widely known, such as to patent offices examining the art in your field–patent examiners search the web also.

In addition, to corporate libraries containing literature and products, companies also can document prior use of a method of doing business and in particular the sale of a product or method. Under 35 U.S.C. § 273, a prior user of a method of doing business in the U.S. can use that prior use as a defense to patent infringement. Such prior use might also help avoid liability in some foreign jurisdictions. However, it is important under this law to document the commercial sale of a product that resulted from the use of the method. Thus, some companies that want to avoid potential liability for a method of doing business patent can document what method of doing business (e.g., selling, accounting, etc.) they used for particular sales.

Patent Watches

A patent watch is a competitive intelligence tool to watch for publication of a competitor's patents or patent applications. The watch also can follow the prosecution of those patent applications to decide whether to take some action.[83] Watches can be automated periodic searches for published patents and patent applications of competitors, including automated searches for key inventors, assignees, or subject matter. For a patent application in prosecution, an organization can even format its watch to automatically monitor for office actions or other pertinent activities. Another automated search can be undertaken for citations to a company's own patents and publications, thus allowing it to see who is monitoring and citing its work.[84]

Translations

Intellectual property translations come in many shapes and forms. Some documents provide English translations of portions. For example, in searching

---

83. For clarification on the basics, a patent application typically publishes eighteen (18) months after it is filed. This is not a patent because you cannot walk into court and enforce the right to exclude anyone from the claims, but instead is a request for a patent. During prosecution, it is more likely than not that the claims will be amended. Thus people watch to see what happens. As mentioned previously, in the U.S., activities can be monitored over the internet through the Patent Application Information Retrieval (PAIR) system. See http://portal.uspto. gov/external/portal/pair.
84. There are numerous companies that will perform such automated searches, including NERAC (www.nerac.com)

the Japanese Patent Office electronic database files, English abstracts are often available, and for some recent prior art, computerized "machine" translations are available as well. In the European Patent Office, the granted claims of a European patent are translated into English, French, and German. These tools help provide a foundation for ascertaining the relevance of foreign language patent documents. However, as is often the case when prior art (patents or other published literature) exists in a language other than English, organizations invest in translations so that they can better understand what is in the prior art, avoid making incorrect arguments to the patent office, and make more informed decisions about the true patentable breadth of their inventions, or whether there is some other reason to be concerned with the foreign language documents. The investment of a few thousand dollars could avoid tens or hundreds of thousands of misspent dollars later.

On the flip side is the situation in which an organization seeks to patent in most non-English speaking jurisdictions (e.g., countries other than UK, U.S., Canada, India, Cyprus, Australia, and New Zealand), for which translations to the national language may be necessary.[85] In these instances, organizations must make intelligent decisions because the cost of translations can be very high. First, organizations ought to exercise discretion in choices of countries in which to file. To illustrate, prior to the London Agreement, to translate a patent in each country in Europe could cost upwards of one hundred thousand dollars. It may be that the only likely commercial interest is in Western Europe, in which case a number of Eastern European countries can be eliminated on that basis. Further, for many (if not most) inventions, patenting in all Western European countries may offer little added benefit, particularly if patenting in one or two jurisdictions will deter investment by a competitor in other jurisdictions. For example, it might be decided to patent in France but not Italy or Spain, because exclusion in France will have the practical effect of also excluding in Italy, or because other patents to the organization may exist in Italy that could be used effectively to exclude competitors. Thus, one way to manage translation costs is to invoke a process by which the decision to foreign file is made taking into account the cost of translations and recognizing that the cost to obtain total territorial exclusion can not be justified when effective results can be obtained by limited territorial exclusion.

Another way to manage translation costs is to include a process for the preparation and review of patent applications that helps to manage the length of the documents. Most translation services will charge per word or line. The cost is, therefore, a direct function of the length of the document. Documents that are kept shorter will be less expensive. Among the ways to

---

85. *See generally*, http://www.epo.org/topics/issues/london-agreement.html (as accessed April 1, 2008) (addressing the simplication of post-grant translation costs under the London Agreement).

keep the document shorter is to limit the number of claims. Another approach is to prepare a separate document for filing in foreign countries that is more targeted to the desired scope sought in those countries. This can help avoid the inclusion of certain redundant text portions or unnecessary written description. For example, a patent might include five pages of description of a product and five additional pages of description of the method of making it. However, it is known from the outset that the product is not likely to be manufactured in a certain country. It may be worth drafting the application to file in that country to exclude the description of the method, and thereby reduce the translation cost in that country.

Maintenance Fees and Annuities

Patents and patent applications stay in force only as long as you pay the government to maintain their status as enforceable. In the U.S., there are no fees to maintain a patent application (just the filing, search and prosecution fees), but there are maintenance fees due in the third, seventh and eleventh enforceable year of a granted patent. Outside of the U.S., it is typical that there are maintenance fees, commonly called "annuities" due each year for the patent application or patent. Generally, the annuities are due every year in every country in which the application is pending. The amount of the fee for maintenance and annuities increases as a patent or patent application ages. For example, the U.S. maintenance fee in 2007 for the third year of a patent is $930, the seventh year is $2,360 and eleventh year is $3910 (*See* www.uspto.gov), exclusive of legal service fees. Over the life of a single patent that is maintained in the U.S., Japan, and a handful of countries in Europe, it is possible that the total fees paid will exceed $100,000. Take into account that most companies committed to an IP culture will hold many patents, and it becomes immediately apparent that the cost of maintenance fees and annuities has the potential to be its largest or second-largest source of expenditures.

Therefore, in order to reduce costs, many organizations will implement a process for the periodic review of their patent portfolios to make sure that the applications and patents continue to have relevance in the marketplace. If the IP fails to continue to have such relevance, then the it can be abandoned to reduce costs in connection with maintenance fees, some organizations keep costs down by outsourcing the tasks to a fee service instead of their outside counsel.

3.13 Application of Guidelines to Process of Making Maintenance Fee Decisions

In the introduction to this chapter, six questions were posited. The following illustrates a decision-making process that applies the questions to the determination of whether to pay a maintenance fee or annuity:

1. Does the organization commercialize the technology in the country?
2. Is there a licensing opportunity that is reasonably likely in the country?
3. Is it realistic that, if an infringement is discovered, the organization will file a lawsuit in the country to protect its right of exclusion?
4. Is there dominant coverage in any other existing IP filings in that country?
5. Is there any patent coverage in any nearby country that can be employed to hamper the ability of a competitor to commercialize within the target country (e.g., would a patent obtained in France be effective to disrupt business of a competitor in Germany?
6. Has the patent filing identifiably deterred competition?
7. How much money will the payment of the fee require?

The Role of Counsel

In-House Advisor

We have already emphasized the importance of training, processes, and other practices for sharing knowledge about IP within an organization. Though senior management plays a significant role in impressing upon employees the tone or attitude of the organization toward IP, the role of executing the training and implementing processes and practices commonly is delegated to other corporate individuals or groups. We will now explore how such a role is often played by IP counsel or another IP advisor.

In its classic sense, "in-house counsel" is a designation used to denote a position held by a licensed attorney whose only client is the company. Typical large research-and-development-oriented organizations will have in-house counsel dedicated to the function of overseeing intellectual property issues. Such counsel commonly will be a registered patent attorney, but the function may be also handled by general corporate counsel. The range of functions of such counsel can be varied and diverse.

As the IP culture of an organization starts to take shape, the organization inevitably finds itself questioning whether it should have in-house counsel. For some, the association of anything "in-house" with anything "lawyer" can be a nonstarter, particularly for small and mid-sized companies in certain industries. In other industries, and particularly in high-tech, venture-capital-supported companies, in-house counsel may be one of the earliest positions filled, because of its importance, and the expectations of investors.

As will be seen, the present discussion seeks to be more encompassing by using a designation "in-house IP advisor." While defining the ideal in-house counsel as a practitioner possessing admission to a bar, this discussion seeks to redefine the paradigm qualifications for in-house IP leadership, focusing the critical qualifications away from mere legal training toward those aptly suited for fulfillment of a set of functions unique to a particular organization. By following this approach, the important outcome that is realized is not specifically the identification of someone who carries the designation of "in-house patent counsel." Rather, it is the identification of someone (even if not a licensed attorney) who can perform the most important IP functions uniquely identified for a particular organization.

In-House IP Advisor: The Role and Traits

As with many other practices described in this work, there is no "one-size-fits-all" description that characterizes the role of an in-house IP advisor or the most suitable traits for such person. Nevertheless, to help an organization identify what needs it may have for in-house IP personnel, this section enumerates a bundle of tasks and responsibilities that an organization committed to a successful IP investment will typically face. Note, though, it will likely be impossible to find the ideal candidate with all of these qualities. More likely, a person with the "correct" background (who may not necessarily be the most qualified on paper) will have to be chosen who will develop some of these qualities.

Intra-Organizational Communication

An in-house IP advisor needs to communicate well with all members of the organization—inventors, technicians, officers, program managers, etc.. The IP advisor ideally assumes the task to become familiar with the technologies developed by the organization, not only on the microscopic level, but from a broader business or "bird's-eye" perspective. A good IP advisor will attend program status meetings and identify the critical stages when a development has occurred so that appropriate IP protection can be sought and deadlines managed. As can be appreciated, therefore, important characteristics of the IP advisor include a demonstrated eagerness to seek out answers from employees, to understand and be able to navigate within the general business culture of the organization, and, perhaps most important, a willingness to challenge a practice or behavior that appears inconsistent with the objectives for IP. Simply put, successful IP advisors will not confine themselves to the safety of a cubicle but will be a highly visible presence within the organization, and will be unafraid to express a well-reasoned opinion and to seek a course of corporate behavior consistent with that opinion.

Extra-Organizational Communication

An in-house IP advisor also has to communicate reasonably well with persons outside of the organization; the three most common classes of such persons being (1) outside counsel for the organization, (2) representatives of other parties with whom the organization maintains (or with whom the organization wants to create) contractual relations, as well as (3) representatives of competitors of the organization.

The best systems for managing outside counsel issues can be in place within an organization. But if an in-house IP advisor and outside counsel do not enjoy a mutually rewarding relationship, the needs and objectives of both sides risk not being met.

Likewise, it is important that the IP advisor be capable of maintaining effective relations with joint venture or development program partners, outside consultants, licensees, licensors, vendors, and customers. Nowadays, the frequency of IP issue occurrence within these relationships is high. These third parties must be able to access and communicate openly with the in-house IP advisor to address them.

It is also important that an IP advisor communicate effectively with corporate competitors. The advisor needs to be sensitive to avoiding the creation of disputes with a competitor, to recognizing the onset of a dispute, as well as to recognizing and avoiding the type of communications with a competitor that potentially could be characterized as anti-competitive.

Addressing Technological Developments

A successful in-house IP advisor will need to take responsibility to be reasonably well versed in the state of the art to which the business of the organization pertains. For new business ventures, the advisor will understand what resources he or she needs to enlist to ascertain the state of the art (e.g., from performing his or her own literature searches, patent searches, or both, to commissioning the same to an outside searching authority). An ideal advisor will know the history of the organization intimately, including knowledge of its early developments that may not have been patented or publicly disclosed. The ideal in-house IP advisor also will have thorough knowledge of the breadth of any IP portfolio the organization may have. Such an advisor preferably will maintain an ongoing familiarity with developments in the industry that may arise outside of the organization. With such comprehensive knowledge, the advisor will be able to help the organization to realize relatively quickly whether a new corporate development may potentially qualify for one or more forms of IP protection.

Governmental Authority Communications

An in-house IP advisor who is registered to practice before a patent authority, such as the U.S. Patent and Trademark Office offers the benefit for certain filings of avoiding the need to enlist the assistance of outside counsel. Some preparation of papers (e.g., assignment documents, powers of attorney, and the like) normally performed by outside counsel may be performed by the advisor, helping to reduce the costs associated with outside counsel. In instances when the advisor is not registered to practice before a patent authority, the advisor may nonetheless become versed in one or more of the necessary administrative procedures followed by outside counsel. It may be as simple as coordinating the execution of required declarations or affidavits. It may involve the more substantive task of assuring that an invention disclosure upon which a patent application is to be prepared is complete and thorough. It may also be to help compile a thorough collection of potentially material information for consideration by the U.S. Patent and Trademark Office pursuant to 37 C.F.R. § 1.56(c)(3)(2000).[86]

---

86. Pursuant to 37 C.F.R. § 1.56(c)(3), such IP Advisor likely will be subject to the duty of candor in any event. The Rule extends to "[e]very other person who is substantively involved in the preparation or prosecution of the application and who is associated with the inventor, with the assignee or with anyone to whom there is an obligation to assign the application."

Recordkeeping

As mentioned above, an ideal in-house IP advisor will have sufficient skills and understanding of the technology at hand for helping inventors to prepare competent invention disclosure documents that can be used for drafting a patent application. The advisor, however, can also enhance record keeping practices of the organization by helping inventors to recognize the need to compile certain significant documentation to corroborate their development activities. For instance, the advisor should ideally be schooled in the significance of laboratory notebooks, test data, prototypes, early sales history documentation, and the like, so that nearly contemporaneous with the innovation activities—i.e. while they still exist and witnesses can authenticate and explain them—these records can be located and preserved for safe-keeping. Even for the advisor for whom these skills may not come easily, records of communications between the IP Advisor and innovators may provide a suitable substitute to establish evidence of the relevant activity. For example, an innovator might e-mail the advisor that she just completed testing of a new compound, and the results met the customer's specifications. While it would be nice if the innovator supplied the IP advisor with the actual test data, the e-mail itself may help to establish a record of activities in the absence of the actual data. The ability of an advisor to recognize the importance of such a record, and to preserve it properly for safekeeping, could prove invaluable in the long run.

An organization with a heavy emphasis upon defensive strategies (*See* Chapter 8) toward preserving its right to conduct its business, likely will also have established practices for preserving evidence of prior use or sale of its technologies. The IP advisor can facilitate compliance with these practices.

Strategic Planning

Yet another ideal general function that can be performed by an in-house IP advisor is in the area of strategic planning. The advisor may not necessarily be the person who designs the IP strategy of an organization. However, it can be quite valuable for the advisor to be privy to the strategy and play an active role in monitoring the implementation and effectiveness of the strategy, coordinating the IP strategy with the business strategy of the organization, and in identifying when changes need to be made to improve the chances of success for meeting identifiable goals.

4.1 Defining the Job Description of an In-House Advisor

Many functions can be assigned to an in-house advisor. Specifying which functions to require, and the particular tasks within each function, can be tailored as appropriate to meet specific needs.

1. Interfacing with management on IP issues;
2. Interfacing with outside counsel on IP issues;
3. Preparing training materials and training employees to be sensitive to important IP issues;
4. Assisting the organization to identify protectable rights and define an appropriate course of action and processes to protect the rights;
5. Drafting patent applications;
6. Prosecuting patent applications;
7. Participating in the activities of any IP Committee, carrying out decisions made by the Committee, and helping to assure the organization is practicing the principles or objectives espoused in any IP policy or strategy adopted by the organization;
8. Managing litigation and other disputes involving IP and otherwise helping to assure freedom to practice the technology of the organization;
9. Negotiating agreements with third parties (e.g., nondisclosure agreements, licenses, development agreements, government contracts, etc.);
10. Administering any employee invention compensation policies of the organization (especially important in countries having rigid inventor compensation laws such as Germany or Japan);
11. Overseeing the prioritization of patent filings;
12. Overseeing the maintenance of patent filings and abandonment or other disposition of properties of diminished value to organization;
13. Overseeing compliance with obligations under agreements of the organization;
14. Establishing an IP culture within the organization and making it contagious;
15. Remaining abreast of developments in the laws affecting the IP of the organization;
16. Competitive patent monitoring and patent searching (e.g., filing oppositions in the European Patent Office);
17. Establishing and monitoring the practices of the organization in connection with marking of proprietary designations (e.g., patent number marking, copyright notice marking, "Confidential" designations, etc.);
18. Invention record administration;
19. Archiving records of prior use or sales by the organization; and
20. Overseeing regular reviews to help assure that the goals and objectives of the organization are being met through its intellectual property.

What Type of In-House Advisor is Right for You?

An organization that is committed to establishing and maintaining a healthy and robust IP culture will invariably assign responsibilities to at least one in-house employee maintaining the health of the organization's IP. Ideally, this person is a registered patent agent or patent attorney and is, therefore, authorized to file papers and make appearances before the USPTO on behalf of the organization. However, these days, the cost of hiring a seasoned practitioner, who can hit the ground running and requires little or no skills development, is high. The 2007 Economic Survey of the American Intellectual Property Law Association reports average gross incomes for 375 corporate survey participants to be about $198,000.[87] In some areas of the country, or in some industries, this amount may be outside the budget of the organization, especially considering that the volume of filings and IP issues that the company faces will still necessitate hiring outside counsel.

In small to medium-sized organizations, the allocation of in-house IP responsibilities does not necessarily require the hiring of a fulltime, in-house patent attorney. Another option that has been pursued by some organizations is the dedication of one or more of its employees (e.g., typically engineers or scientists well-versed in the technology of the organization and that of its competitors or possibly even a paralegal) to the function of IP administration. Some organizations will select one or more such individuals and send them for training to become a registered patent agent, thereby allowing them to conduct business before the U.S. Patent and Trademark Office.[88] Still another option is for an organization to make arrangements with outside counsel to have counsel available on-site according to a predetermined schedule, or merely available to employees of the organization on an as-needed basis. The options are limited only by the imagination and the resources an organization is willing to commit to its IP investment.[89]

In some larger organizations, the role of IP administration is spread among multiple individuals as part of a team. For instance, such organizations will commonly employ one or more in-house attorneys; they also may employ an individual designated as a "patent liaison," an "intellectual asset manager," or "intellectual capital manager," or other technical personnel specifically trained to recognize and address the role and impact of patent and other IP

---

87. AIPLA *2007 Report of the Economic Survey* at I-58 (2007). The survey also indicates that for companies employing only one or two fulltime IP lawyers, the average gross income was about $174,000.
88. *See* 37 C.F.R. § 11.5-11.9.
89. Work arrangements can affect work product and effectiveness. With alternative work arrangements, appropriate IP metrics will be necessary to ensure that the IP being created, monitored and enforced meets the business needs of the organization. *See* Chapter 2 for a discussion of IP metrics.

issues on the welfare of the organization. While the assembly of such a team may be impractical for smaller companies, the role models they provide are valuable in helping them structure their respective team of professionals.

In short, the functions described here for an effective in-house advisor may be performed by a single individual or spread among multiple individuals.

Measuring Success of In-House Advisors

Measuring the performance of an advisor, like the measurement of success of an IP strategy or program generally, is not susceptible to the application of any rigid formula. While there is no specific "right way" to measure success, there are many factors that organizations can invoke to evaluate success, provided that appropriate weight is given to each such factor. Chapters 2, 3, and 8 explore various metrics.

For example, one performance indicator may be the ability of the advisor to execute a successful IP strategy. The risk of assigning considerable weight to this factor is that the successful execution of many strategies, especially those involving patent filings that are subject to considerable patent office delay, requires many years to realize. A strategy adopted in 2008 may not see identifiable results until 2013 or beyond. Similarly, an advisor may have inherited a failed strategy from a predecessor, which requires substantial time to overcome. It can be potentially unfair to the advisor to measure his or her success in the short term on this factor alone.

Another measure of the success of an advisor is in the volume of his or her workload, especially the realization of any savings as compared with the costs that otherwise would have been incurred by assigning the tasks performed by the advisor to outside counsel or a consultant. For example, suppose the advisor is paid $100,000 per year to perform 50 patent searches each year, and file and prosecute 10 patent applications. If outside counsel was engaged to perform the same services, fees are estimated at about $175,000. Assuming the quality of the advisor's work compares favorably with that of outside counsel, the ostensible cost savings may provide ample justification for maintaining the IP advisor's position.

Even for the largest companies, the common justification for eliminating dependency upon outside counsel cannot be avoided in certain circumstances. Such companies commonly keep a stable of outside law firms available to manage the occasional situation in which in-house resources are inadequate. In these instances, an IP advisor may have little choice but to depend upon outside counsel. The advisor's success in those instances will often be measured by the performance indicators of the outside counsel, such as the timeliness with which outside counsel is able to meet deadlines, interaction and communications client personnel, fees charged by outside counsel, and the overall quality of the work product delivered. An effective in-house advisor will help optimize the measurable indicators of outside counsel performance by communicating clear instructions to outside counsel, communicating the significance of the role that outside counsel plays in the process being supervised by the advisor, sharing knowledge possessed by the advisor about the particular technology under consideration, and otherwise helping outside counsel prioritize and meet deadlines. The advisor's success can also be measured in terms that the business dictates and an effective metric can satisfy the desire to measure success (e.g., higher margins for patented products as compared to unpatented products or the ability to license a technology).

4.2 **In-House Organizational Structures**

There are many possibilities for in-house IP counsel organizational reporting structures, including reporting to the General Counsel, Chief Technology Officer, President (or even its CEO or CFO), and/or Business Development. The choice of reporting structure can influence the IP culture by helping to set the tone from the top management. More specifically, whichever part of the firm controls the budget for IP will control the tone of IP for the entire firm.

Additionally, note that the client of the in-house counsel is the company, and not any individual in the company. By proper selection of the reporting structure, in-house counsel can communicate effectively with those individuals most likely representing the client company. The different reporting structures outlined below come and go inside a company as the company changes products, personnel, and markets, but someone with organizational power should own the IP process. Finally, just because there is a specified reporting structure, in-house IP counsel can have "dotted line" responsibility to all of the following for good communication.

Reporting to General Counsel: If the IP function reports to the legal side, then it may be treated like any other legal function and be considered an expense (as opposed to essentially a capital investment). As an expense, it is a function that businesses may try to minimize. On the other hand, as a legal function, IP may be given more respect for the advice provided to proceed in enforcement or licensing. Because IP is a long-term business decision, its placement in the legal side also protects these long-term decisions from short-term market pressures that businesses many feel.

Reporting to Chief Technology Officer (CTO): Reporting to the scientific side of the business clearly gives IP a more scientific feel and is appropriate where scientists or engineers are involved in it on a daily basis (e.g., as an IP advisor). It is particularly effective for invention gathering, application drafting, and prosecution to physically locate in-house IP counsel near the scientists and engineers and when the CTO may effectively set the tone for the IP. Another consideration is that in fast-moving technologies, the CTO may play a prominent role in choice of technologies that leads to intellectual property.

Reporting to Business Leaders: There are different business leaders in an organization that IP in-house counsel might report to, including the head of a business unit, president of the company, or the CEO or CFO. Generally, the higher up the organizational reporting, the clearer the tone of IP importance will be to the rest of the company. Reporting to a business leader has the benefit of clear business feedback to the IP so that corporate goals should be clear and met, including clear IP metrics from businesses. In addition, where IP has a clear business function, such as in a licensing company or where revenues from IP are desired, reporting to a separate business unit for IP may be the most efficient so that the corporate goals are met (e.g., profit and loss freedom) and IP is treated like other business units. Larger companies may have an intellectual asset management division that may be their own business unit or part of another business unit that takes responsibility for intellectual property. Further, in some organizations, IP is regarded as it own business unit or profit center. In-house counsel may, in those instances, be a business leader with his or her own profit-and-loss responsibility.

The advisor's success will also be a function of his or her credibility within the organization. An important function of many advisors is to assure compliance by employees with any policies adopted by the organization pertaining to IP. Successful performance will depend upon the personality of the advisor as well as the support he or she is provided by senior management. Senior management must vest the advisor with a certain amount of decision-making authority. When advisors make decisions within their authority, senior management must support the decisions. This tends to be a problematic area for many established organizations that hire an advisor after many years without one. It is difficult for managers historically vested with certain decision-making authority to surrender that authority to a new and unproven member of the organization.

For smaller to mid-sized organizations, the decision to hire or assign a person the responsibilities of an in-house IP advisor usually occurs after the organization is formed and has engaged in a substantial amount of research, development, or other commercial activities. Though it would be nice for most organizations to have an IP advisor from the outset of its existence, it is more common that an advisor is hired only after the organization has experienced confrontation with a competitor, an increase of patent filings of its own, or some other pattern or series of events that has caused it to rely heavily upon its outside counsel. Attendant with such reliance upon outside counsel will be an increase in attorney fees, diversion of valuable amounts of time of executives who necessarily must meet with outside counsel, and little resulting improvement in sensitivity to IP issues.[90]

As discussed in the next sections, if the decision to hire an advisor is being driven by dissatisfaction with outside counsel, it is important for the organization to perform some critical analysis to determine whether the existence of an advisor will cure the perceived ills. So often, the frustration is triggered by chronically large bills. The corporate decision for hiring an advisor often will be motivated by the desire to reduce these bills. However, in actuality, the organization's frustration is not so much the amount it is paying its outside counsel, but its perception that it is realizing little or no return on its investment. A good advisor may actually end up contributing to an overall increase in outside counsel bills, due mainly to an increased recognition of important, previously neglected value-added issues.

Some organizations hire their outside counsel as their in-house advisor, with the belief that they already know who they are getting and their abilities. This can work very well or very badly. In the latter case, it does not work out because the person chosen simply works better in the culture of outside counsel as compared to in-house advisor.

4.3 **Practical Issues to Confront When Hiring an In-House Advisor**
1. Defining job responsibilities;
2. Defining performance goals;
3. Setting compensation and incentives, which may be high for seasoned practitioners;
4. Establishing a successful working relationship between the in-house advisor and outside counsel;
5. Assimilating the advisor into the organizational structure, taking into account that if the organization previously had no such position, many employees will not understand the role of the advisor and his or her position in the organizational hierarchy;

90. For some organizations, the hiring of outside counsel becomes more palatable if counsel causes the organization to adopt a process or practice that can help avoid recurrence of a bad situation. For example, the outside counsel might establish a process for monitoring the patents of a competitor so that the organization can design its products to help assure avoidance of infringement, or otherwise to be more prepared to address the possibility of a conflicting patent in the future. Regrettably, a large number of small and mid-sized organizations, already spread thin on resources and eager to return to normal operations, are unwilling to undertake appropriate postmortem analysis of the adverse situations they just experienced. Consequently, outside counsel is not afforded the opportunity to make these suggestions. Further, if the suggestions are made, the absence of personnel within the organization to carry out the recommendations makes the likelihood of recurrence greater.

6. Skills training;
7. Organizational history and cultural training, so that the in-house advisor has the necessary foundation the make the IP culture contagious;
8. Building appropriate infrastructure may be necessary, ranging from docketing software, computing capabilities, files and other office supplies, and administrative assistant accounts for funding fee payments;
9. Establishing direction for the advisor; especially in the beginning, the advisor will seem like a drain on executive resources as the advisor will be seeking to understand the organization and its priorities; and
11. Assuring that the in-house advisor has the skills and resources to demonstrate a return on investment.

The New In-House IP Advisor and Outside Counsel

In many instances, the decision to hire an in-house IP advisor occurs on the heels of a series of complaints that an organization has with its outside counsel. One straightforward approach that many organizations take when this occurs is simply to change outside counsel. Unless the relationship with outside counsel was a poor fit from the start or, unless accompanied by some critical self-analysis and a desire to change its own attitudes toward IP and develop a stronger IP culture, the relationship with a new firm (after a brief honeymoon period) will likely lead to continued dissatisfaction, now with replacement counsel. Accordingly, one benefit of hiring an advisor is the possibility to vest the individual with the task of salvaging the relationship with existing outside counsel.

Outside counsel may misperceive the decision to hire the advisor and regard it as a threat to its relationship with the organization. There likely will be some push-back to the organization and second-guessing of the decision. Assuming that the organization indeed values its relationship with its outside counsel, it needs to prepare for how it will integrate the in-house advisor into the relationship. It is good at this juncture for the organization to candidly express its views to its outside counsel. It is possible that the decision to hire a person in-house is motivated mainly by a perception that the hiring will immediately reduce its costs. However, the reality is that cost is less the problem than the perception that the company is not realizing a satisfactory return on its IP investment. When communicated to outside counsel that the role of the advisor is to improve investment return, it tends to be more palatable to outside counsel.

4.4 **The Insider as Issue Spotter**
One common effect of hiring an in-house advisor that businesses tend to overlook is the prospect that, due to his or her ongoing presence, the advisor will identify many issues previously disregarded or ignored. This could have the practical effect of creating more responsibilities for the advisor than previously anticipated. It may also create more tasks, which will overwhelm the advisor and necessitate retention of outside counsel services.

Outside Counsel

For small to mid-sized organizations, completely avoiding any dependence upon outside counsel is unrealistic. Outside counsel is a fact of life. In accord with its poor reputation, the legal profession, and even the specific patent community within the bar at large, has its share of bad lawyers. However, by and large, the patent bar includes a respectable group of skilled practitioners with well-honed analytical and technical skills. Understanding the personality of this segment of the bar and ways that an organization can communicate with members of the patent bar can help assure a successful relationship.

Foremost, it is important to understand that in the U.S. to offer oneself out to the public as a Patent Attorney, an individual must be a licensed member of a state bar and must also be registered to practice before the U.S. Patent and Trademark Office. To qualify for the former, the individual must have received an undergraduate degree, thereafter graduated from law school and (for almost all states) have passed a rigorous bar examination. To qualify for the latter, the individual must successfully pass another exam. To even sit for this exam, the individual must have earned a college degree or otherwise have completed a prescribed amount of coursework in engineering or science, including a substantial amount of math, physics, biology, or chemistry coursework.[91] After demonstrating those qualifications, the individual must successfully pass the examination administered by the U.S. Patent and Trademark Office.[92] The passing rate for USPTO examinations historically has been relatively low, helping to assure the qualifications of licensed practitioners.[93]

---

91. *See* http://www.uspto.gov/web/offices/dcom/olia/oed/grb.pdf (accessed November 4, 2007).
92. Some individuals who have worked as an examiner at the U.S. Patent and Trademark Office are exempt from the examination.
93. By way of example, the passing rate among 4,165 individuals who sat for the examination from June 2005 to October 2006 was 58.2%. http://www.uspto. gov/web/offices/dcom/olia/oed/exam_results_mpep8ed_rev2.htm (accessed November 4, 2007). For those 1,911 individuals taking the April 18, 2001, examination, the passing rate was 47%. http://www.uspto. gov/web/offices/dcom/olia/oed/apr01ex.htm (accessed November 4, 2007). The passing rate

---

4.5 **Caution: Patent Geeks Up Ahead!**

A large segment of the patent bar includes individuals who studied engineering. Though they have been forced to adapt their personalities to the demands for verbal communication placed upon them by their legal training, these patent professionals tend to be excessively detail oriented and thorough. They often show a keen desire to understand, not simply the results realized from a particular technology, but also the manner in which the results are achieved and associated technical theory. If anything, such obsession with detail and what sometimes comes across as an inability to be able to focus on the "bigger picture" tends to be a source of frustration that clients (and many federal judges, too) have with outside counsel. Nevertheless, it is important to understand that most outside counsel bring this type of personality and training to each representation. Whether and how a firm chooses to make use of this trait is up to each firm.

How to Choose: "Choose the Attorney, Not the Firm"

One traditional maxim of counsel selection has been to choose the attorney, not the law firm. This generally has proven to be a wise practice. However, it must be borne in mind that due the unique nature of patent services, especially for representation of an organization committed to a long-term investment in its IP, successful counsel selection will necessarily involve a host of considerations.[94]

First, it can not be overemphasized that the relationship must be viewed as a long-term relationship. The transaction of obtaining a single patent alone can take several years. Factor in that a successful IP strategy could require obtaining several patents, particularly to cover improvements in evolving technologies, and it is easy to see how a relationship with outside counsel can extend for many years.

Next, it bears consideration that the technology of the organization is often multifaceted. The perceived technological background needs of an organization at time of hiring may morph into others later. For example, a company that is founded to develop and commercialize a technology for sensing

---

of 2,762 individuals who took the exam in August 1998 was 37%. http://www.uspto.gov/web/offices/dcom/olia/oed/aug98ex.htm (accessed November 4, 2007). The passing rate of 3,162 individuals who sat for the August 1997 examination was 58%. http://www.uspto.gov/web/offices/dcom/olia/oed/aug97ex.htm (accessed November 4, 2007).

94. For other perspectives on counsel selection, *see*, e.g., European Study 2006: "How mid-sized companies in Europe select and review their legal services providers," http://www.legaltechnology.com/casestudies/Study_Hodges_LexisNexis_2006.pdf (accessed November 11, 2007).

biological reactions may later find its technology having application for sensing contaminants in fluids for aircraft. The outside counsel selected for experience in the biological arts may require specialized training in the future to prepare him or her to address the aircraft application. In such an instance, a firm having diverse technological backgrounds may be an appropriate fit, as may be many an individual having proven technical versatility (e.g., individuals who have represented a variety of diverse technological clients).

Also meriting attention is the likelihood that one or more significant individuals who will service the account will depart the law firm for other career opportunities. This is a frequent occurrence in many law firms, both large and small. However, the problem tends to be particularly acute in law firms in which the billing demands placed on newer attorneys, low levels of client interaction, protracted partnership tracks, and the narrow breadth of opportunities to develop skills collectively contribute to high turnover rates.[95]

The success or failure of a relationship with outside counsel is influenced from the initial act of selection of the counsel. The choice of appropriate counsel is difficult, considering the diverse range of talents and experience levels possessed by comparatively few members of the patent bar.[96] For an organization looking to make a substantial long-term investment in IP, the selection of counsel should be treated as if entering a long-term relationship and should involve a process that may involve more than one meeting or phone interview, during which outside counsel candidates are evaluated for compatibility of the personality of the outside counsel with the culture of the organization.

Most of the time, when a company seeks to engage outside counsel to establish an IP program, it will build a pool of candidates from recommendations and referrals of others having past experience with the outside counsel candidate (e.g., its general counsel, other colleagues in the industry, and managers within the organization who previously worked with counsel while employed in another organization). Familiarity with counsel on the basis of such past experiences is valuable and often afforded considerable weight.

---

95. Turnover rates on the order of about 20% or 25% per year are common in the legal community. http://www.law.harvard.edu/news/2005/11/22_wilkins.php (accessed November 10, 2007); *see also,* http://westlegaledcenter.com/prm/prmJSF.jsf?id=5085614&sc_cid=sub_large (accessed November 10, 2007). In a speech reproduced at http://blogs.cisco.com/news/2007/01/ cisco_general_counsel_on_state.html (accessed November 10, 2007), Cisco General Counsel Mark Chandler stated, "*The Wall Street Journal Law Blog* included a note recently that associate turnover in large firms from 2001–2004 was 19%, with one major firm over 30%."

96. In the U.S., currently there are estimated to be about one million attorneys. http://www.power-of-attorneys.com/are_there_too_many_lawyers.htm (accessed November 10, 2007); and http://usinfo.state.gov/products/pubs/legalotln/lawyers.htm (accessed November 10, 2007). In contrast, the number of patent attorneys and agents in the U.S. numbers is on the order of about only 25,000. *See* http://www.averyindex.com/2007_patent_states.php (accessed November 10, 2007).

Other considerations that deserve attention in the selection process include:

1. The work sought to be performed for the organization will not pose a conflict of interest[97] with other clients of the law firm;
2. The technological training of the outside counsel provides a solid foundation to understand the technology of the hiring organization;
3. The constitution of the team that will perform the heavy lifting within the firm; and
4. The accessibility of the counsel to the organization, taking into account what commitments counsel may have to other clients that may impair the ability of counsel to serve the organization.

To amplify on the previous, selection of appropriate counsel often poses a task of balancing contradictory considerations. On the one hand, clients often select their counsel on the basis of strong reputations. The strength of the reputation, though often gained by longevity, is also a function of successes achieved from high-frequency transactions involving counsel. In other words, there is a relatively high correlation of counsel with good reputations and a heavy workload carried by such counsel. It is not realistic to expect that good counsel will confine their practices exclusively to any single client. In the selection process, therefore, the fact that counsel has a busy practice can be a positive indicator. It is important in such instances for the hiring organization to ascertain how counsel will be able to assimilate the organization into their practices and what measures will be implemented to assure that the organization feels that counsel is responding to its needs.

4.6 Conflicts of Interest

In general, when evaluating a new relationship for potential conflicts of interest, many law firms often engage in a two-fold analysis. The first part of the analysis is to evaluate whether an ethical conflict of interest exists. This analysis involves careful scrutiny of the rules of professional conduct that

---

97. A characteristic that often makes a particular candidate for outside counsel more attractive than another is the familiarity of the practitioner with the technology of the organization seeking to retain him or her. However, the organization hiring the counsel must consider how such counsel acquired its familiarity. In many instances, the familiarity is due to the past or current representation by counsel of another organization within the same field. This naturally poses the potential that the representation from the outset poses a conflict of interest or will inevitably result in a conflict of interest (e.g., a subject matter conflict). Accordingly, notwithstanding the short-term cost savings that might be enjoyed by reducing the time to ramp-up counsel on the technology, if a conflict arises and counsel must withdraw in the future, the potential cost to the hiring organization may be significantly higher.

govern the bar. For U.S. patent attorneys this involves consideration of the rules of professional conduct of the state in which the lawyer is practicing as well as the rules of the USPTO. Assuming that the proposed representation would pass muster under the ethics rules governing conflicts, law firms also will often analyze whether, notwithstanding the apparent absence of an ethical conflict, the proposed representation would pose a business conflict. That is, law firms will consider the issue of whether undertaking representation has the practical effect of angering a former or existing client and ensuing adverse consequences to that relationship. The firm will often base its decision to accept an engagement upon both of these considerations, and likely others too. The firm may even insist upon a waiver of conflicts of interest as a pre-condition for the engagement.

Looking at potential conflicts from another direction, most IP conflicts of interest come in two categories: (1) a subject-matter conflict, where the potential counsel already does work for another client on the same technology and where that existing technology might be prior art to you; and (2) a competitive conflict, where counsel represents one of your competitors.

Note that there is also one ethical conflict that many IP attorneys face and that is whether it is ethical to invest in a client (e.g., to trade in the stock of a client or to take stock as compensation for work performed). Counsel vary in their practices, but it is helpful to engage counsel in discussions about their practices in this significant area.

Choose a Compatible Reflective Personality

Much like an organization interviews candidates for positions and sometimes even administers personality assessments, it is important to interview various counsel to ascertain a compatible personality fit with the culture of the organization. Though the patent bar in general tends to be obsessed with detail, individual members of the group possess unique personality traits, leading people to wonder whether they hired a lawyer or an engineer or both. It is important to select counsel that has personality traits consistent with those of the organization.

Keep in mind, too, every attorney has his or her own individual comfort zone. It is important for the success of the relationship with outside counsel that the hiring organization understands the bounds of such comfort zone, and defines its expectations of the attorney to be consistent with the zone. For example, one of the most prevalent traits that varies from attorney to attorney is the comfort of the attorney to engage in confrontation and, more specifically, to engage in direct communication (whether hostile or not, or whether before a tribunal or not) with an adversary to squarely address a disputed issue.

An organization that has a confrontational culture may become disappointed when its counsel is unwilling to engage in confrontation. In contrast, a non-confrontational organization must expect that if it hires counsel who thrive on confrontation, counsel likely will place the organization in the position of having to face uncomfortable dialogue with its competitors.

In assessing the confrontational nature of counsel, it is important to avoid confusing it with the counsel's tolerance to risk. Though the two traits are different, it is relatively common to find both either present or absent in many attorneys. That is, it is common for confrontational counsel to also have a high tolerance to risk. Likewise, it is common for less confrontational counsel to be more risk averse. However, it is also common for risk-averse counsel to have strong confrontational traits.

Another important trait is the ability of attorneys to project themselves into the mind of the adversary, understand what motivates the adversary, and to adopt a strategy that takes such motivations into account. Along this line, another personality consideration to consider is the flexibility of perspective that counsel brings to the equation. Ideally, counsel will be both attentive to microscopic detail and also possess the capability to understand the big picture, spot patterns, and trends.

Interestingly, the personality traits mentioned above are not unique to attorneys. They are the same traits possessed to some degree by the executives and managers of the organizations who hire counsel. Some individuals have honed their traits over the years and have generated considerable goodwill and reputation for themselves and their organizations as a result of their traits. Legal representatives of the organizations have the power to jeopardize such goodwill and reputation. Alignment of personalities of counsel with that of the organization is, thus, an important consideration to protect goodwill and reputation.

4.7 Litigation Counsel Contrasted with Prosecution Counsel

Within the patent bar, two distinct groups of practitioners tend to dominate. One group fashions themselves as litigators, whose mission is to engage in battle, persuade judges and juries, and emerge victoriously. The other group generally encompasses attorneys whose main function is to procure patent rights on behalf of their clients. They tend to spend a lot of time extracting information from clients and formulating ways to present it to the Patent Office to convince the Patent Office that a patent is appropriate. Traditionally, this latter group keeps a relatively low profile, remaining behind the scenes to the extent possible. Of course, both groups understand what the other group does and how the law operates in both areas.

Define the Role and Responsibilities of Outside Counsel

Before and during any relationship with outside counsel it is important for clients to define for outside counsel its expected role on behalf of the organization. The role will differ from organization to organization. The role may include one or any combination of the job responsibilities described above for in-house counsel. The role may be broadly strategic. It may be isolated to a specific transaction. The exact role depends upon the needs of each individual organization. The fees associated with the engagement will be a function of the role played. Accordingly, to avoid creating situations in which a company is chronically dissatisfied with its outside counsel, it should define for itself outside counsel's role.

It is important also to understand that many outside counsel are quite sensitive to the costs associated with an IP investment and desire to avoid challenges to their bills. Counsel, accordingly, will not act on behalf of an organization without specific instructions from the organization. For example, outside counsel commonly will not file foreign applications on behalf of its clients in the absence of instructions from the client. The amounts are simply too high, and outside counsel will seek to avoid becoming saddled itself with such unauthorized payments because a client challenges them. Yet, an organization can decide well in advance that it wants its outside counsel to make certain filings routinely, even in the absence of instruction.

Communicate Reasonable Expectations to Counsel

One common complaint that clients have of their outside counsel stems from the failure of clients and counsel to discuss and define reasonable expectations as to the likelihood of success of a particular action, the fees that are or will be incurred on behalf of the client, and the amount of time it will take to achieve a particular result. Trying to avoid this entirely is not realistic. However, it is possible to help manage these sources of discontent by regular and open communication.

One way in which an organization can help to manage this source of potential dissatisfaction is to define a realistic budget for attaining a particular result. The organization should not be afraid to communicate the budget to outside counsel and to request of outside counsel a candid assessment of whether achievement of the result within the specified budget is likely. Moreover, if prepared sufficiently well in advance, part of the budget can be allocated toward addressing the possibility that the result sought may not be achieved. Consider, for example, an organization that seeks to patent products resulting from some preliminary research and development. The organization budgets $30,000 over a period of four years to obtain at least one patent to the product in North America and at least one European country. Sharing this expectation with outside counsel will help outside counsel draft a patent application commensurate with the budget and to invoke filing strategies that avoid unnecessary costs. Also, sharing the desired or expected patent claim coverage will help outside counsel to fashion an appropriate course of action.

4.8 **Mistakes**

Although most attorneys prefer to avoid this topic, the fact is that mistakes happen and many IP attorneys are sued for malpractice. This is not a reflection on the attorney as much as it is a reflection of today's litigious society, and the fact that the practice of intellectual property law is a date-sensitive practice. Even when following reasonable measures, deadlines get missed, and client rights get lost. As a result, it is important to recognize that with retention of outside counsel an acute level of vigilance about dates will be experienced. Often the reminders will be excruciating to receive and the effort to respond with instructions burdensome.

Engagement Issues

In the course of engaging a law firm to serve as outside counsel, it is likely that the law firm will perform an internal check for potential conflicts of interest. Thereafter, some firms will present the client with an engagement agreement. The engagement agreement effectively serves as the initial framework for defining expectations of outside counsel. As a practical matter, it should be expected that outside counsel will use the engagement agreement to establish a fee arrangement, which will serve not only to specify the expected fees, but to address how these fees will be paid. During this phase of the relationship, the client has an opportunity to seek clarification as to how certain items will be invoiced. For example, at this stage clients and counsel will often establish whether and to what extent the law firm will charge the client for photocopies, facsimiles, long-distance phone charges, scanning, file storage, and even soft drinks.[98] Clients and counsel may also establish the extent and under what circumstances the client may need to pay for secretarial overtime. The extent that counsel may charge for travel time may also be addressed, as may be the procedure that is to be followed for the advance payment of any retainer amounts.

It is not uncommon for counsel to elaborate in an engagement agreement some of the risks that the client is to face in the course of the relationship.

---

98. Fact or myth? Some law firms have vending machines into which a client code and billing matter must be entered before beverages are dispensed.

It is important for an organization to understand what is explained in the engagement agreement and recommended that it have independent counsel review the agreement.

Another issue that merits attention at an early stage in the attorney-client relationship is the manner in which fees advanced by outside counsel will be accounted for and reimbursed by the client. It is not unusual for a company filing even as few as ten to twenty patent applications a year, with some overseas filings, to incur filing fees in excess of $100,000. Faced with the prospect of this for a host of its clients, and especially in recent years with substantial government fee increases, many law firms have abandoned the practice of routinely advancing fees to its clients. Among the techniques for managing these costs that some law firms employ is the use of trust accounts that are regularly replenished by the client. Another technique has been to establish a client-maintained deposit account at the Patent Office, as to which counsel is authorized to charge fees.

Of course, it is quite helpful to address during the engagement period (and periodically thereafter) how to communicate deadlines and filing decisions.

4.9 Fee Sampler

The fees an organization can expect to pay to outside counsel will depend upon various factors, particularly the complexity of the technology and the geographic location of counsel. Also of potential influence will be the size of the law firm. The most comprehensive published guide in the U.S. for illustrating typical fees is the *Report of Economic Survey*, published every two years by the American Intellectual Property Law Association (AIPLA).[1] The following data is extracted from the 2007 AIPLA *Report of the Economic Survey* (pages I-30), reporting the average hourly billing rates of partners in private law firms.

1. 10 to 14 years of IP law experience: $371/hour
2. 25 to 34 years of IP law experience: $446/hour

For specific breakdown of fees by geographic region, it is recommended to consult the published survey results. By way of example, from the same table, it would be observed that the average fee is $512/hour for Boston counsel, $469/hour for San Francisco counsel, $367/hour for Minneapolis/St. Paul counsel.

---

1. Copies of the *Survey* are available for purchase from the American Intellectual Property Law Association, 241 18th Street South, Ste. 700, Arlington, VA 22202-3694, www.aipla.org.

Attorney-Client Privilege

The attorney client privilege is a long-standing, sacred doctrine designed "to encourage full and frank communication between attorneys and their clients by assuring clients that their disclosures will be held in confidence."[99] The bounds of the attorney-client privilege have been succinctly expressed as follows:

> [t]he privilege applies only if (1) the asserted holder of the privilege is or sought to become a client; (2) the person to whom the communication was made (a) is a member of the bar of a court, or his subordinate and (b) in connection with this communication is acting as a lawyer; (3) the communication relates to a fact of which the attorney was informed (a) by his client (b) without the presence of strangers (c) for the purpose of securing primarily either (i) an opinion on law or (ii) legal services or (iii) assistance in some legal proceeding, and not (d) for the purpose of committing a crime or tort; and (4) the privilege has been (a) claimed and (b) not waived by the client.[100]

When working with counsel, in-house or outside, it is important to exercise appropriate care to protect communications that may be protected by the attorney-client privilege. One way to do this is to include a header or footer in each written document that states conspicuously "Attorney-Client Privilege." For such documents, it is important to designate as the author (if appropriate) or recipients at least one attorney. These actions will not guarantee the privilege will be upheld as to the communication, but they will help minimize the risk they will not be.

Communications

Again, one important key to a successful relationship with outside IP counsel is regular communication. The organization must be proactive to assure that counsel understands its needs and whether those needs are being met. It must also communicate material changes of circumstances to outside counsel when they occur or very soon thereafter. Clients sometimes complain that outside counsel does not actively seek out information from the client. They might complain that counsel does not phone, write, or visit. For some outside counsel, this may be a valid complaint. Some counsel, however, take a more passive role in a sensitive effort to keep charges to the client low.

---

99. *American Standard, Inc. v. Pfizer Inc.*, 828 F. 2d 734, 745 (Fed. Cir. 1987). The attorney-client privilege is a topic of sufficient breadth that it could support its own treatise. The mention of it here merely is to raise awareness to the issue.
100. *U.S. v. United Shoe Machinery Corp.*, 89 F. Supp. 357, 358 (D. Mass. 1950).

Unfortunately, the lack of communication often leaves the client feeling (whether justified or not) as if its needs are unimportant to counsel.

A good way to avoid this type of breakdown in communications again involves defining the expectation in advance for counsel. If an organization fears it is not disciplined enough to regularly update counsel on its own initiative, an alternative approach may be to simply request that counsel take the initiative to phone periodically for updates. Another effective approach involves the establishment of a regular phone conference or even regular meetings attended in person by counsel and one or more key personnel.

4.10 **Status Reports**

One useful tool to keep abreast of developments with outside counsel is to agree to a format for a regular written status report. The content of the report will vary according to the needs of each organization. Needs change during the course of a relationship that make the periodic modification of the form and content of any status report appropriate. For example, the inclusion of a representative drawing, a written summary, or both is an effective way to jog the memory of the client and counsel. This becomes particularly important as time passes and a portfolio is grown. Among the items of information that might be included in a status report are:

1. Counsel's file number;
2. A designation, file number, or other indicator that is recognizable to members of the organization;
3. Brief summary of the commercial relevance or history of the subject of the filing;
4. Filing dates;
5. Countries in which filing made;
6. Current state of prosecution; and
7. Impending deadlines.

The status report is potentially subject to discovery in any lawsuit. So, it is worthwhile to consider adopting measures to help preserve the attorney-client privilege with proper designations and restrictions on circulation within the organization.

There are a host of published resources to assist companies managing their relations with outside counsel.[101] It is helpful to become acquainted with these. But, it is important to remember the specific and unique attributes

---

101. *See, e.g.,* American Corporate Counsel "Outside Counsel Management" (August 2003), published at http://www.legaltechnology.com/casestudies/Infopak.pdf (accessed November 11, 2007).

of intellectual property that make the universal and blanket application of the principles and practices espoused in these resources a potentially risky proposition.

Insights into Law Firm Economics

Speak candidly with any chief executive officer about his or her objectives for the organization and invariably the conversation will turn to making money. It is noble for an organization to express a desire to serve some important public function, such as feeding the hungry or leaving a "green footprint." However, it would be disconcerting, especially to any investors, if the officer subordinated its profit motive to one of these social purposes. In the for-profit world of business, the simple fact is that one of the main purposes, if not the only main purpose, of any corporate organization is to maximize profits.

Despite its efforts to self-regulate and convey an appearance that it is a profession dedicated to serving the interests of justice, it can not be ignored that the practice of law is a business and, for the most part as it relates to IP, it is a for-profit business. Like other for-profit organizations, within the bounds of their Codes of Ethics, law firms that concentrate in IP law have as one of their main purposes the maximization of profits, namely the maximization of its revenues derived from billing clients for legal services performed and the minimization of the costs to perform the services.

IP law firms do not sell mass-produced products. They sell services, which for the most part consume time. The best multitasking patent attorney can juggle a handful of open matters over a period of time. However, such attorney generally can only handle a single matter at any one point in time. For better or worse, the legal profession, including the patent bar, has adopted the billable hour as the measure of the value of services performed. That is, the fee for services is typically measured as a direct function of the time involved to perform the service. More complex matters, accordingly, will cost more than simple transactions.

As a corollary, time spent by an attorney working on a matter for one client is time that the attorney is not spending on another client. It has become accepted practice that attorneys will charge the client for consumption of their time.

Some law firms do charge certain items on a flat fee basis. Usually, this involves a predetermined fee arrangement negotiated between the client and counsel, and possibly even made part of an engagement agreement. In many instances, the fee does not reflect that actual amount of time spent by the attorney on the matter but may instead be a reasonable fee that takes into account a number of considerations, consistent with the attorney's ethical obligations.[102]

---

102. ABA Model Rules of Professional Conduct Rule 1.5 pertains to establishment of fees. It states, in pertinent part:

Exclusive of taxes, the costs incurred by a law firm for providing legal services has among its largest components:

1. attorney and staff payroll;
2. benefits and benefits administration;
3. rent or mortgage payments;
4. professional liability and other insurance;
5. telephone service;
6. computing equipment, software, and maintenance;
7. office equipment;
8. library and subscription services;
9. utilities; and
10. bar association dues.

The target profit of law firms will vary from firm to firm and will depend largely upon the size of the firm and the number of its shareholders who will share in the profit.[103] At the risk of generalizing, it is not unreasonable to expect the target profits to be on the order of about 20 to 50 percent of gross revenues or higher.[104]

To achieve these profit levels, some law firms engage in a practice known as leveraging. In its simplest terms, this involves hiring the largest possible number of associate attorneys and nonpartner/nonshareholder billing employees, and keeping them as busy as possible. The capacity of the firm to generate

---

(a) A lawyer shall not make an agreement for, charge, or collect an unreasonable fee or an unreasonable amount for expenses. The factors to be considered in determining the reasonableness of a fee include the following:

(1) the time and labor required, the novelty and difficulty of the questions involved, and the skill requisite to perform the legal service properly;

(2) the likelihood, if apparent to the client, that the acceptance of the particular employment will preclude other employment by the lawyer;

(3) the fee customarily charged in the locality for similar legal services;

(4) the amount involved and the results obtained;

(5) the time limitations imposed by the client or by the circumstances;

(6) the nature and length of the professional relationship with the client;

(7) the experience, reputation, and ability of the lawyer or lawyers performing the services; and

(8) whether the fee is fixed or contingent.

103. The analysis presented here is a simplification and does not apply for every type of law firm. Models vary from firm to firm. For additional explanations that analyze law firm profitability, *see e.g.*, T. Olson, *A Primer on Analyzing Law Firm Profitability,* http://www.gabar.org/programs/law_practice_management/law_practice_management_program_articles/a_primer_on_analyzing_law_firm_profitability/ (accessed November 11, 2007).

104. *See generally* http://www.morepartnerincome.com/blog/LawPracticeBusinessModel (accessed November 11, 2007); and http://www.juris.net/JurisPublic/Newsletters/Downloads/ADVO-CATE09.pdf (accessed November 11, 2007); *see also* AIPLA *2007 Report of the Economic Survery,* 2007 at F-19. (reporting firm overhead as a percentage of collections).

revenues is thus enhanced, while being able to cap the amount that is paid to these employees. For example, it is not uncommon that the salaries of associates in IP law firms will be kept below half of their gross income (e.g., about 25 to 40 percent). In practice, this means that firms will invoke stringent billing requirements for the associates, contributing to higher turnover rates. It also means that the likelihood that large proportions of the services performed by this firm will be performed by lesser experienced associate attorneys.

Understanding IP Counsel Invoices

Nowadays, most outside counsel bill their clients using some form of computer-generated invoice. It is a common practice for law firms to track their time and charges on a matter-by-matter basis. The typical billing cycle is monthly. However, it is not necessarily the practice of all firms to bill all services at the time rendered. Specifically, many services span a period longer than one month but are not billed until they are completed. This is a common practice employed for the invoicing of services for preparing patent applications and for the invoicing of responses to Patent Office communications.

Many law firms provide a detailed explanation of the services performed. Some will break out the actual time charged on a daily basis. Also included in the matter-by-matter reporting will be any expenses that may have been advanced by the law firm, or credits against deposits to trust accounts. Particularly when services have been rendered on a variety of different files over the course of the billing period, counsel will typically include a summary table of the fees.

Client should specify any particular requirements they have for their outside counsel invoices. For example, some clients have implemented techniques for analyzing their legal fees, which require outside counsel to assign a particular code to the task, akin to the Uniform Task-Based Management System advanced in the 1990s.[105]

A frequent source of discontent expressed by clients is their lack of understanding of the services that have been performed. This problem may be more acute when repetitive or broadly worded entries are made. Some law firms try to avoid this from the outset by providing detailed descriptions of their services, providing sufficient differentiation on a daily basis to make it clear that later services performed reasonably followed from the preceding services described. It is the practice of some attorneys to use their time entries

---

105. *See* http://www.abanet.org/litigation/utbms/home.html; and http://www.abanet.org/litigation/utbms/utbms.pdf (accessed November 11, 2007). The UTBMS was the result of collaboration by the American Bar Association Section of Litigation, American Corporate Counsel Association, and Price Waterhouse LLP, along with input from many law firms and companies.

as a way to record their meeting notes or to memorialize communications with counsel, the assumption being that if a client is going to read anything prepared by the attorney, the client is most likely to read the invoice.[106]

Ultimately, almost every client's experience with its counsel will share the common denominator of fees. Understanding IP legal bills and candid communications with counsel about them can only lead to a more positive experience.

4.11 Ten Avoidable Causes of Large Legal Bills

Assuming that a company makes reasonable efforts to follow the advice of counsel when given, the company candidly supplies all material information to counsel for counsel to properly formulate recommendations, and the company pays its bills on time, proper avoidance of the following items should help most companies feel more satisfied with their legal bills and their relationship with outside counsel.

1. Insufficient instruction to counsel about the expected deliverable from counsel;
2. Failing to vest ownership of the responsibility for IP with one or more capable individuals within the company;
3. Trying to do the job of counsel "to save a few bucks";
4. Trying to do too much by phone and e-mail instead of face-to-face;
5. Ignoring an issue and pretending it will just go away;
6. Waiting until the last minute or otherwise delaying instructions to counsel;
7. Reopening past decisions for reconsideration based upon hind-sight;
8. Not saying "no" to pursuits of low priority;
9. Not assuring adequate transfer of IP knowledge within a company; and
10. Excluding counsel from participation in strategic planning.

---

106. In the event patent infringement litigation is ever initiated, it is not uncommon for a party to seek the billing records of the opposing party. Therefore, it is important for companies to handle their invoices with sensitivity to this issue.

CHAPTER
5

Earning Respect for Your Intellectual Property

Patents Need Respect

One of the most essential ingredients for a healthy IP culture is a general sense within an organization that the intellectual efforts of its individuals are being recognized and respected by others. The recent economic climate, however, has made fulfillment of this objective very challenging.

Consider that, in recent years, the media (from classic business publications to emerging Internet blogs) has seized upon a couple of unrepresentative cases of unusual patents or unfortunate enforcement practices to cast into doubt the entire integrity of the U.S. patent system and many solid patents for deserving inventions.[107] The calls for "patent reform" have been loud and frequent, whether or not for the right reasons.[108] Not to be doubted, there have been some pretty silly patents that have granted in recent years, as there have been throughout history.[109] There also have been some unfortunate abuses of the enforcement system, again, as there has been throughout history. Regrettably, all the attention drawn to the issue and the arguments advanced in support of the reform legislation has actually weakened the U.S. patent system, making it more difficult for patent owners to earn respect for their patents.

To earn respect for their patents, nowadays, patent owners must work harder at it than ever. The simple fact of ownership is often not regarded as enough of a deterrent to secure a strong market position unless accompanied by action, which specifically means: (1) getting valid and enforceable patents and (2) enforcing those patents.

Only Get Patents That You Will Walk into Court and Enforce

What is respect for intellectual property in the business world and how is an organization to know if it has earned it? Respect can come in a variety of

---

107. The culmination of these activities occurred in early 2005 with the decision of the Court of Appeals for the Federal Circuit in the case of *In re Kretchman*, 125 F. 3d 1012 (Fed. Cir. 2005), in which the Court struck down (during a reexamination proceeding) a patent to a crustless peanut butter and jelly sandwich, commercialized (to the tune of tens of millions of dollars) by Smuckers under the name UNCRUSTABLES™. The patent in question, U.S. Patent No. 6,004,596, granted in 1999. The media ridiculed this case. *See, e.g.,* Meiser, "The Peanut Butter Jam," http://www.clevescene.com/2005-04-20/news/the-peanut-butter-jam (accessed November 23, 2007). The decision came down while the dispute brewed over the e-mail communication device patents affecting Blackberry® devices, *NTP Inc. v. Research In Motion, Ltd.,* 418 F. 3d 1282 (Fed. Cir. 2005), and also followed on the heels of the much publicized dispute between Amazon.com and Barnes & Noble over the "one-click" business method patent. *Amazon. com, Inc. v. Barnesandnoble.com, Inc.,* 239 F. 3d 1343 (Fed. Cir. 2001).

108. *See generally,* Address by Hon. Paul R. Michel to Association of Corporate Patent Counsel, (January 28, 2008; reproduced at http://ipo.informz.net/ipo/data/images/courtcases/transcript_michel (accessed April 1, 2008).

109. Web sites have been devoted in recent years to publishing various patents of unique "human interest." *See, e.g.,* http://www.patentlysilly.com/. At http://www.delphion.com/galleryarch, an archive of "obscure" patents are published, with some in the collection dating back to the 1970s and 1980s.

forms, some easy to measure and others not so easy. In its most basic sense, respect for IP (and particularly patents) is manifested in the ability of an organization to exert market exclusivity because its competitors have elected to steer clear from the patented technology. This, of course, translates into sizable profits and market share that can be readily measured. Respect may also be seen in the form payments of fees or royalties for licenses, another measurable indicator. Other forms of respect exist but are more difficult to measure. For example, some competitors abandon a technology in the face of a strong portfolio of a competitor. The existence of a strong patent portfolio often discourages any market entry by other organizations—the latter organization ceasing to be a competitor sometimes even before the patenting organization is aware that it may even have a competitor. Unfortunately, for most of these instances, there is no way for a patenting organization to learn about the decision of the potential competitor not to enter the market.[110]

One of the most basic drivers of respect for IP rights is if the right on its face is valid and enforceable. Assuring that IP rights are valid and enforceable involves no mysterious trick of the trade. Rather, to the contrary, it simply means that the right was obtained by reasonably following the rules for obtaining that intellectual property and meeting the legal requirements that confer the rights. For patents in the U.S., for instance, this typically means satisfaction of the requirements for patents as set forth in the U.S. Code Title 35 and the rules of patent practice as set forth in the Code of Federal Regulations Title 37. Cutting a corner, in even the tiniest of respects, has the potential to invite a competitor to refrain from respecting the IP rights of an organization.[111]

To illustrate, one of the most widely litigated requirements, as to which patents are attacked in the U.S. for trying to cut corners, concerns fulfillment of the duty of candor under 37 C.F.R. § 1.56, which imposes upon patent applicants (inventors, attorneys, and other involved individuals) the duty to tell the Patent Office about material information, such as prior art, that may hurt the chances to obtain a patent of broad scope. If a challenger

---

110. Respect can also be defined by what it is not. For example, when a competitor learns of a patent to an organization and disregards it, that disregard is not respect. Within the IP community, an early indication of whether a competitor will offer respect for IP of an organization is if the competitor does not respond to a letter and forces the organization to send another letter or file a lawsuit to demonstrate its seriousness.

111. As will be discussed throughout this book, there is likely no such thing as a perfect patent. In hindsight, without regard to the time and resource constraints faced at the time of procuring a patent, it is always easy to seize upon the occasional flaw in a patent and offer that as an excuse for avoiding the need to respect the patent. However valid that basis may be, it must still be recognized that a patent is a governmentally-granted right that enjoys a presumption of validity under 35 U.S.C. § 282. It is often a heavy burden to successfully attack a patent. Many organizations, accordingly, will not necessarily make a business decision to respect a patent or not on the belief that the patent is not valid or enforceable. They will take into account that they face risk, not only of losing in litigation, but in the simple fact that the organization might even face the expense, inconvenience, and uncertainty of litigation.

can prove that such "material" information was withheld and was done so with deceptive intention (e.g., it was withheld because the applicant knew it would hurt the chance to get a patent, and the applicant did not want to incur the effort to establish patentability over it), the patent could be struck down as unenforceable on the basis of inequitable conduct.[112]

5.1 How Much Prior Art is Enough to Cite?

There is no hard and fast rule about the amount of prior art to cite. Every case is different and will be fact dependent. The USPTO encourages applicants not to submit every reference of which they are aware because that adds work for the Examiners. *See* Manual of Patent Examining Procedure (MPEP) § 2004, item 13:

> It is desirable to avoid the submission of long lists of documents if it can be avoided. Eliminate clearly irrelevant and marginally pertinent cumulative information. If a long list is submitted, highlight those documents which have been specifically brought to applicant's attention and/or are known to be of most significance. *See Penn Yan Boats, Inc. v. Sea Lark Boats, Inc.,* . . . (citations omitted).

However, the whittling away of a large library of references to identify only a select few material references may open the door for an unwarranted attack on the reasonable exercise of judgment by counsel. The USPTO has demonstrated repeated difficulties in the management of this rule, especially in view of the high frequency of inequitable conduct challenges, which have caused many practitioners to exercise even greater caution and err on citing more (rather than fewer) references. Curbing inappropriate use of the inequitable conduct defense is the subject U.S. patent reform legislative efforts. The USPTO also seeks to modify the practice. *See, e.g.,* 71 Fed. Reg. 38808.

To illustrate the reason why much attention is given to citation of prior art, it is worthy to observe that in 2006 there were 53 infringement litigation cases in which the issue of obviousness of an invention (pursuant to 35 U.S.C. § 103) was decided and 49 cases where the issue of inequitable conduct was decided. Both of these defenses typically would have involved a challenge to a patent on the basis of prior art that was not in front of the examiner at the time when the patent was initially examined by the USPTO. In contrast, a comparatively slight number of cases attacked the patent on grounds that the

---

112. A determination of inequitable conduct also can provide one of the very few bases for an award of attorney fees against a patent owner in U.S. infringement litigation. *See, e.g., Bruno Indep. Living Aids, Inc. v. Acorn Mobility Servs. Ltd.,* 394 F. 3d 1348 (Fed. Cir. 2005).

written description or the wording of the claims of the patent was inadequate in violation of a requirement of 35 U.S.C. § 112. Specifically, only 2 cases decided an attack for failure to disclose the best mode, only 11 cases deciding enablement, and 13 cases decided a challenge on indefiniteness.[113] Attacks under 35 U.S.C. § 112, though recently demonstrating a surprisingly larger number of successes, historically have been regarded as carrying a relatively low likelihood of success. Accordingly, an organization should exercise considerable care in making a decision not to respect a patent to a competitor solely on such basis.

On the other side of this coin, the level of detail and care shown in the preparation of a written description may signal a reason why a patent may garner the respect of a competitor. In general, the more detailed, specific and technically sound a patent document is, the more likely it will get respect. Patents that include considerable supporting data (e.g., in the form of examples) bearing sufficient indicia of reliability may warrant respect. The depth of detail in the disclosure also assists in obtaining respect because large volumes of detail are typically indicative of a large investment by the applicant in the technology and may also sign an advanced state of efforts toward commercialization prior to writing and filing the patent application. An organization with an apparent valuable investment in its technology is more likely to take enforcement seriously, and the patent is not just a "paper patent."[114]

In the course of analyzing competitive patents, many IP professionals have come to devise practices or routines that help them recognize certain tell-tale signs that invite closer patent scrutiny. These can be gleaned from a review of the patent document itself or the public record of the USPTO file that embodies the "prosecution" communications between the applicant and the USPTO leading to the patent. It is not to say that in each of the following situations the patent is invalid or unenforceable. Rather, if any of the following signs is present, it could give reason for a competitor to scrutinize the patent more than they normally would, and could also lead the competitor to a decision that the patent need not be respected.

---

113. Based on statistics complied by the University of Houston Law Center, available at http://www.patstats.org/2006.htm.
114. The term "paper patent" can be heard in industry to refer to a patent that is based on little or no actual work, or actual reduction to practice, with the drawings or examples being used for reference to whether there is extensive work reflected in the patent. Although paper patents may be just as enforceable as any other patent, right or wrong, paper patents historically have received less respect in industry because the "paper patents" usually are not accompanied by "proof of concept." Care must be taken to avoid mischaracterizing or underestimating "paper patents." They are often filed by viable business concerns, during early stage business activities, for the purpose of establishing priority as to others, while important research and commercialization is proceeding. Helpful to evaluating the strength of a "paper patent" will often be the existence or nonexistence of other filings by the applicant, and the diligence with which the applicant prosecutes the application in the patent office.

- Prior art references were cited after prosecution is closed

In the U.S., there are time limits to the citation of prior art. Late-cited prior art is not considered by the examiner and simply placed in the file (sort of like a notice to the public). This is a ready supply by the applicant of relevant prior art that could invalidate a patent. Worse, sometimes, applicants cite relevant references during prosecution, overcome the art to get a notice of allowance, but then cite new references later (either because they did not become aware of the references until later or because they thought the additional references were cumulative), without getting the examiner to consider the references by withdrawing the case from issue or other measures. More often than not, a close review of the late references provides evidence for lack of novelty or obviousness. In the European Patent Office (EPO) and countries outside Europe, the citation of prior art is not required, so organizations need to be alert to patents granted in such countries in which the most relevant prior art applied in the USPTO or some other patent office (e.g., the Japanese Patent Office (JPO)) is not considered, even if during an opposition proceeding.

- The patent was granted in the first office action

Patents are sometimes granted without a sufficiently complete review or understanding of the claims, particularly when the patent is granted based on the examiner's first review of the claims. Patent claims are a don't-ask-don't-get situation, e.g., virtually no patent examiner in any patent office is going to write broader claims for applicant, such as by pointing out the parts of the claim that are unneeded for patentability. As a result, patent claims are almost always drafted too broadly the first time because the attorney wants to obtain as broad a scope of protection as possible for the client. Experience shows that broadly worded claims allowed without rejection upon the first review quite often tend to have a problem with the prior art.

- An Affidavit was Filed to Distinguish Prior Art

In occasional instances, a declaration or affidavit submitted during prosecution for the purpose of having the inventor or an expert distinguish a prior art reference may signal a potential weakness to the patent claims, which can not be cured by using language from the specification.

5.2 **Post-KSR Affidavit Evidence**

Not all affidavit testimony necessarily invites further scrutiny. Indeed, some testimony may warrant a more rapid determination that a patent should be respected. The rules of practice for patents, 37 C.F.R. § 1.132, authorize the presentation of objective evidence of patentability in the form of such affidavits. The courts have made clear that such evidence (e.g., evidence supporting unexpected results, prior art teaching away, commercial success, licensing by others, long-felt but unmet needs, etc.) must be afforded weight. *In re Sullivan*, 489 F.3d 1345 (Fed. Cir. 2007).

The truthfulness of statements in these filings can always be challenged and is sometimes the basis for an inequitable conduct defense.

- The Applicant Did Not Cite any Prior Art

It is often hard to believe that an inventor is unaware of even a single item of prior art that may be related to the invention. For subscribers to the philosophy that "necessity is the mother of invention," it seems improbable that an inventor is unable to point out some prior art that illustrates the problem solved by the invention, or any prior attempt by another to solve such a problem, even if from a different technical field. Accordingly, failure to cite a single reference during prosecution in the U.S. is a red flag that is sure to draw scrutiny and may likely result in payment of little respect to the patent.

Viewing the citation of prior art from another perspective, it is possible to characterize the citation (and particularly any detailed discussion) of a prior patent as a form of tacit respect to that prior patent. Bear in mind, the mere citation of a prior patent reference does not necessarily lead to a conclusion that the claims of patent have been evaluated.

- The "End of the Quarter" Patent

The "end of the quarter" refers to the time and way that patent examiners in the USPTO are evaluated for productivity. Historically, they have been judged on a periodic (e.g., bi-weekly) basis for the number of "counters" that they process (i.e., first office actions on the merits and balanced disposals), and at the end of each quarter these counters are added up to see if they are meeting their specified productivity goals. Myth has it (and experience backs it up) that near the end of each quarter, some examiners in the USPTO typically need a few counters to meet their goals, and regrettably they will seek to meet the goals by relaxing their standards and doing something involving relatively little effort, such as issuing a notice of allowance, which counts as a balanced disposal.

5.3 The "End-of-the-Quarter" Patent and You

The USPTO can not be expected to ever openly admit that it has an "end-of-the-quarter" quality problem. But, suppose you happen to receive one of these notices of allowance (or if you otherwise receive a notice of allowance for which you are skeptical), and you suspect that your broadest claim (or others) has a problem. Multiple choice, do you:

1. Take the patent, determine that the examiner was convinced by artful claim drafting, and worry about the issue if you ever enforce?

2. Take the patent, but file a response to the reasons for allowance that points out your concern and gives your reasons for why you are correct?

3. Take the patent and file a continuing application (continuation or divisional) and attempt to deal with the issue in the next patent application; or

4. Decline the patent and deal with the issue up front,filing a request for continued examination (RCE) or a continuation application?

Deciding whether to respect a patent or not will often force you to answer this question, as it can reveal certain attitudes. In a perfect world, in which time and money both were abundant, option (d) might be a prudent course. However, the right answer will differ from organization to organization and case to case. In each instance, however, one guiding consideration should be based upon the likelihood that the patent will ever be enforced, and whether the decision taken is one that you feel would withstand intense scrutiny in litigation.

Constant Evaluation of the Portfolio

If the first step toward getting respect for IP is obtaining valid, enforceable intellectual property, then the corollary to that step is that a company should not necessarily rest on the laurels of the ribbon copy of the patent grant, but should conduct an independent or otherwise reasonably objective critical assessment of the patent, attempting to see the patent as would a competitor. Situations change. What may not have been erroneous assumption at the time a patent is procured may, with the benefit of hindsight, look like an error at a later time or might be susceptible to attack by a competitor as an error. The USPTO has procedures that allow patent owners to fix innocent errors.[115]

Such a review can be performed in any number of ways. One way that has the prospect of much success (if done with the right tone and setting) is to perform periodic in-house peer reviews among IP attorneys, or possibly with outside counsel.[116] Each attorney can review the relevant documents (e.g., prosecution history, prior art, information about a competitor's product,

---

115. *See* 35 U.S.C. §§ 251–256, and 301 et seq. (respectively addressing reissue proceedings, inventorship correction, and reexamination).

116. The inclusion of management in these exercises is not forbidden. However, during early-stage reviews when warts are first exposed, there is a risk of creating undue alarm with management. It may be more productive to identify potentially problematic areas, assess risks, explore possible remedial measures before acquainting the managers with the issues.

business information, etc.) just as an adversary would do, for a granted patent of another attorney. A claim charting exercise may be performed. Opinions can, thereafter, be presented orally at a group meeting, taking care in record-making, in view of the potential for compelled disclosure of possibly privileged communications in subsequent litigation.

Another way to do this review is through the continuation or divisional process. Continuation and divisional practice almost always requires a review of the claims, prior art, arguments and the like, which were made in an ancestor patent application filing. Potential oversights made in a parent application can, in many instances, be fixed in the continuation or divisional application.

Deciding to Enforce: When to File and How to Prepare the Organization

The second part to obtaining respect is to enforce patents in a timely manner. Enforcement may assume different forms that are geared toward protecting technology from competition and preserving market exclusivity, the two most notable being infringement proceedings and licensing.

From a plaintiff's viewpoint, infringement suits are a necessary fact of life for patents to gain respect. A patent that withstands testing in court against a motivated adversary is a patent destined for widespread respect.

Enforcement is not a thing that organizations should necessarily fear. Patents should be regarded much as the land on which the organization locates its facility. Suppose a trespasser enters the land and starts drilling for oil on the land. The company will ask that person to leave. If the person refuses, police are be called or an injunction is obtained. Much as a company would protect the investment it has in its real property, it should take action to protect its investment in its technology by enforcement of its IP.

Consider the alternative: if your organization does nothing to abate an infringement—and others in your industry learn of the infringement and the lack of recourse by the organization—then soon the industry will believe that infringement is acceptable and will not be challenged.[117]

This exercise is not confined to in-house reviews, but may also be a good exercise for outside counsel to perform in reviewing files handled them, too.

117. Another consideration, but a more minor one, is laches and/or equitable estoppel. Laches is an equitable principle that denies a party's right to assert damages for infringement of the patent because they have "slept on its rights" and that, as a result of this delay, the patent holder is no longer entitled to damages. Put another way, failure to assert one's rights in a timely manner can result in damages for those claims being barred by laches. *Intirtool, Ltd. v. Texar Corp.*, 369 F. 3d 1289 (Fed. Cir. 2004). Equitable estoppel is similar, but generally looks to a pattern of behavior for a defendant to assert that the pattern of behavior has created an

No one really enjoys litigation other than some of the lawyers engaged in the fight. That said, a healthy culture of IP will not necessarily litigate for the sake of litigation. Rather, such culture will have in place processes for deciding whether and under what circumstances to initiate litigation asserting patents (or possibly challenging a pesky patent of another) and how the organization will prepare for and behave in the course of enforcement.

Turning first to the decision to enforce, there are a variety of circumstances that an organization should address and determine how they will respond in the event of occurrence. Three prominent instances are when an organization has lost sales to a competitor; when license negotiations breakdown; or when there is an appearance of a callous disregard of a patent by a competitor.

If an organization has lost sales to a competitor and has at least one claim in a granted patent having a substantial remaining life, which covers the technology of the competitor, this factor militates strongly in favor of enforcement to prevent future sales, to assure the organization is able to regain future sales, or to be reasonably compensated for the use of the IP by the competitor. That does not mean the organization must file suit immediately after it discovers the lost sales. But, most would agree that if the organization expects its patent to be respected throughout its life, at some point and in some way, the organization must enforce it, and lost sales is the strongest situation.[118]

5.4 **Having Trouble Pulling the Trigger?**

An organization that remains on the fence in an enforcement decision usually does so because its leaders, though knowing enforcement is the right thing to do, nevertheless fear confrontation, have a low tolerance for risk, or tend to regard the enforcement as an event susceptible to immediate failure or success and not as a process with many steps along the way that allow the organization a chance to stop. For these situations it is important that the organization step back and consider all the work and investment that has gone into building its patent portfolio and IP culture. It is not simply a matter of a line item for R&D on a corporate balance sheet. The goodwill and reputation of the organization is now likely affected by it, as to do nothing about the infringement

---

expectation of nonenforcement, the defendant has reasonably relied on that expectation to their detriment, and the court should not now change that reliance. *A. C. Aukerman Co. v. R.L. Chaides Constr. Co.*, 960 F. 2d 1020 (Fed. Cir. 1992) (*en banc*). Note also that under 35 U.S.C. § 286 there is a six-year limitation on damages.

118. In the pharmaceutical industry, it is an act of infringement to file an abbreviated new drug application to the Food and Drug Administration to market a generic drug. 35 U.S.C. § 271 (e)(1). For this industry, this is the same as losing sales to a competitor.

> will signal weakness to others, including competitors and prospective investors. Further, employees of the organization have come to identify themselves as fortunate members of a special organization. Infringement is not merely a loss of sales, but also harms morale of inventors, salespersons, and attorneys alike

In the course of enforcement, license negotiations may fail, which may then require litigation to resolve impasse. Litigation can break licensing impasses because it forces the parties to spend money on the litigation and incur the inconvenience and burden of preparing for litigation and meeting court-imposed deadlines, such as (in U.S. litigation) the disclosure of information (including sensitive and confidential information) during a discovery process.[119] These two events provide both motivation (reduced costs) and information to break the impasse, along with opportunities (e.g., court imposed meetings). Although it may be viewed as a licensing tactic, the tactic tends to work well and provide a different face to the licensing negotiations.

Timing may become important to the execution of litigation to break a licensing impasse. From the standpoint of an accused infringer, if litigation is started before or simultaneously with the infringer's launch of its technology, it may still be early enough that the accused infringer will modify its technology to avoid the need for the license. If royalty revenue is the true aim of the patent owner, then such aim is not served by this. In contrast, once the product has been sold for a period and gains customer acceptance, it becomes harder for the accused infringer to abandon or change its technology and makes a license more likely.

It is also important to take into account the value at risk to the parties. At some point the cost to litigate (even with its attendant risks) is regarded as considerably less expensive than the cost of royalties under a license. For such accused infringers, they will often already be on the market with the accused technology, and will be able to reserve for a potential loss from earnings on the technology.

Often, a dispute will arise because a competitor infringes a patent in callous disregard of the patent, and sometimes while openly communicating that it regards the patent as irrelevant. Such communication may be to

---

119. Litigation in countries outside the U.S., though not necessarily involving a consuming discovery process in every instance, often requires prompt action by parties to prepare their cases. For example, in many German patent infringement proceedings from the time of the initial writ to the time of the final hearing may be less than one year, and both parties typically will need to demonstrate their proofs for and against the infringement.

common customers, in which case it may also be accompanied by a dramatically lower price quote than that provided by the organization. It may also be to others, such as potential investors or analysts of the organization.

This sort of enforcement may be more difficult to justify from an organization's viewpoint because the damages might be so insignificant as not to cover the cost of the litigation. However, enforcement in this context is just as necessary as in the other situations discussed. If enforcement is not undertaken, market exclusivity will drop, and price erosion is almost a certainty. Damage to pricing of a product early in its life is especially troubling, for it may be several years before a replacement technology is developed for which higher prices can be demanded on the basis of IP rights.

Preparing for Litigation

Once the need for enforcement is clear, an enforcing organization must prepare for that enforcement, especially if the enforcement is likely to result in litigation. Differences abound in the appropriate ways to prepare for enforcement. However, in the typical enforcement scenario, it is important to do at least two things, namely, (1) define the objective of the litigation (an injunction, a license, damages (if so, how much?), customer goodwill, publicity, or combinations thereof);[120] and (2) prepare the case upfront, analyze its weaknesses objectively along with other risks and rewards, and present it to management.[121]

With management on board, particularly in U.S. enforcement, your company will need to prepare itself for discovery. Most litigation counsel will provide budget estimates, as well as progress reports toward meeting the budget. However, counsel may not always be diligent in this regard. Accordingly, it is important for a company to be proactive in seeking such information. Also, the company must seek instruction and then follow it concerning the preservation of any evidence, especially in the U.S., in view of the Federal Rules of Civil Procedure and its procedures governing discovery of electronically

---

120. This part of the analysis is critical to define strategies and establish litigation budgets.

121. Some managers like to see a risk assessment based on the statistics of winning on the issues identified in the case, overlaid with the probabilities of winning, as determined by trial counsel. Although litigation risk assessments are becoming more popular today, any statistics should be viewed with a jaundiced eye. Virtually no patent litigator will give you more than a 90 percent chance of winning on any one particular issue (and most will give you lower, much lower, percentages of winning). If you have essentially the perfect case on each of the four major issues, you will still only have a 66 percent chance of winning on all the issues by applying the statistical numbers. However, with the perfect case, most patent litigators will give you a higher chance of winning. What this means is that patent litigation requires some feel, or understanding, for what arguments will win, and why they will win, and how they will win. However, the risk assessment can help managers believe in the case when the going gets tough.

stored information (ESI) (e.g., computer- generated or computer-stored records such as emails, spread sheets, databases, presentations, etc.) as well as paper documents, samples, prototypes, patent prosecution files. At some early juncture in the contemplation of litigation, the company should place a "litigation hold"[122] on potentially relevant evidence.[123]

An organization likewise is probably well served by requesting its counsel to coordinate a preliminary document collection as part of determining the issues in the case and whether the facts, as believed by the organization, can be supported by the evidence. Ideally, the preliminary document collection is performed with the help of knowledgeable witnesses. The preliminary document collection should be very critical. It must view the evidence from the perspective of the adversary. This includes reviewing the evidence, not merely for its content, but also to assure that it will indeed be admissible. This is also a good opportunity to seek out and identify a potential "smoking gun" that could damage the case and to test the credibility of witnesses.[124]

Another important preparation step for litigation is to assure that counsel has performed a reasonable prefiling investigation, and the facts upon which the conclusions have been reached are reasonably supported. Federal Rules of Civil Procedure generally requires a patentee that initiates infringement litigation (1) to have studied the accused technology (if not acquired a sample);[125] (2) to have construed the patent claims;[126] and (3) to have applied the patent claims to the accused subject matter (the analysis typically being

---

122. *See, e.g., 3M innovative Props. Co. v. Tomar Elecs.*, No. 05-756(MJD/AJB), 2006 WL 2670038 (D. Minn. Sept. 18, 2006), and *Samsung Elecs. Co. v. Rambus, Inc.*, 439 F. Supp. 2d 524, 542–43 (E. D. Va. 2006) (addressing *Zubulake* 'litigation hold' responsibility).

123. Different organizations will accomplish a litigation hold different ways, but the organization should request its litigation counsel to advise it concerning litigation holds, along with facts about what is involved in the litigation (main issues, goals, etc.) to instruct witnesses not to discuss the case outside of the presence of counsel and to instruct witnesses to preserve documents. In the preparation for any litigation, it is especially helpful if the organization includes not only the inventors and their managers, but also representatives from the information technology group, and possibly even accounting, marketing, sales, investor relations, human resources, or any other department from which records shall be sought during the litigation.

124. There are numerous instances of such first-pass reviews being important, including Fed. R. Civ. P. 11, which requires a reasonable inquiry into the facts before signing papers filed in court. In addition, such a first pass will provide a foundation for advice to management on the strength of the case. As the plaintiff, smoking gun type documents are those that directly affect patent validity, and most importantly include prior art knowledge and its citation to the patent office.

125. *Judin v. U.S.*, 110 F. 3d 780 (Fed. Cir. 1997); *See also Q-Pharma, Inc. v. Andrew Jergens Co.*, 360 F. 3d 1295 (Fed. Cir. 2004)

126. *S. Bravo Sys., Inc. v. Containment Techs. Corp.*, 96 F. 3d 1372, 1375 (Fed. Cir. 1996).

summarized in a claim chart).[127] Patent owners often will rely upon the presumption of patent validity pursuant to 35 U.S.C. § 282 and will not necessarily exhaustively analyze all possible grounds of patent invalidity. However, if potential grounds are known to the organization, they should be communicated fully and candidly to counsel for evaluation.

Respect Through Licensing

Another significant way to enforce IP in order to gain respect for it is to meaningfully license the patents.[128] This can take many forms. It may be part of a transaction by which an organization obtains rights to patents from a competitor (e.g., cross-licensing). It may be exclusive or nonexclusive, meaning that the patent owner can decide who it wants to be able to share in the exclusive rights under the patent. It may be part of a broader business relationship (e.g., a license to practice a certain method may be granted upon the purchase from the patent owner of certain raw materials or tools to practice the method). Various basic aspects of licensing are explored in greater detail in Chapter 7.

5.5 **Unconventional Ways to Gain Respect**

In the course of investigations when making a decision about whether to enforce a patent, defects with the patent sometimes surface. For example, they may be brought to the attention of an organization by an adversary or potential licensee. How to respond in each instance is not the subject of any general rule. However, an organization committed to gaining long-term respect for its IP generally should try to do "the right thing." This may mean seeking correction of the patent. It may mean dedicating certain of the patent claims to the public. It may mean conceding value on the transaction. It becomes easier for any objective decision maker to take serious an "intellectually honest" organization that acknowledges that its patents have legally dictated boundaries than the organization that accepts no boundary.

---

127. Though not necessarily mandatory, claim charts (as in Appendix 6 are very effective tools for helping to understand how infringement is established, and to illustrate where weaknesses in an infringement case may lie. *See, Q-Pharma, Inc. v. Andrew Jergens Co.*, 360 F. 3d 1295 (Fed. Cir. 2004)

128. Licensing also is regarded as influential objective evidence of nonobviousness of a patent. *See In re Sernaker*, 702 F. 2d 989, 996 (Fed. Cir. 1983).

Licensee's Ability to Enforce

As emphasized, among the ways to gain respect for a patent portfolio is the ability to license that portfolio for royalties. Sometimes, as a result of gaining respect through a licensing relationship, an organization will need to forego some of the discretion it may have in regards to making enforcement decisions. That is, as part of many licensing relationships, it is common for a licensee to expect that the patent owner will enforce the licensed patent against third-party infringers or transfer that right to the licensee. The rationale, of course, is grounded in the understandable premise that no reasonable licensee wants to pay a royalty if a competitor using the same technology does not have to pay a royalty.[129]

The right to enforce, though ostensibly a straightforward consideration, is actually riddled with legal nuances. Organizations should make sure they understand what they are getting into when undertaking to get or give a right to enforce. By way of background, generally, an exclusive licensee can enforce a patent if the exclusive licensee "holds all substantial rights under the patent." By "all substantial," the Federal Circuit really means all.

In the case of *Morrow* v. *Microsoft Corp.*,[130] the Federal Circuit explained some of its recent pronouncements:

> Even in *Propat*, this court found that Propat had no standing to participate in an infringement suit though it enjoyed the exclusive right to sue third parties for patent infringement, the right to grant licenses to third parties, and the right to enforce license agreements. 473 F. 3d at 1191. Propat's right to license and sue third parties was subject to prior approval by the legal title holder Authentix— approval that could not be unreasonably withheld. Propat was also required to receive the consent of Authentix before it assigned rights or obligations under the agreement to another party. This court held that Authentix did not assign all substantial rights to Propat and Propat could not even sue as a co-plaintiff with Authentix. *Propat*, 473 F. 3d at 1189 (noting that even if Authentix was a party this would not ameliorate Propat's standing problem). Propat lacked sufficient exclusionary rights and therefore did not suffer statutory legal injury.

As is well known, a patent can have multiple "exclusive licensees," where each licensee has exclusive rights to a portion of the patent rights. Rights are

---

129. Along these lines, as well, is the concept of "Most Favored Nations," pursuant to which an early nonexclusive licensee might insist that if the patent is licensed to another person at a lower rate, the early nonexclusive licensee should be entitled to lower its rate and avoid unfair cost disadvantage.

130. 499 F. 3d 1332, 1342-43 (Fed. Cir. 2007) (addressing *Propat Int'l Corp. v. R Post, Inc.*, 473 F. 3d 1147 (Fed. Cir. 2007)).

often divided geographically, by field of use, and by type of use. Recently, in the case of *International Gamco v. Multimedia Games*,[131] the Court of Appeals for the Federal Circuit held that an exclusive licensee of some of the rights did not have standing to sue without the patentee joined in the suit. Gamco had received an exclusive license grant from gaming giant IGT to sell state authorized NY lottery games covered by the '035 patent.

As can be seen, the jurisprudence surrounding who must participate in enforcement litigation can create some thorny situations for patent owners. They may find themselves exposed to litigation for which they are neither prepared to undertake or lack resources to support. The litigation also has the potential to place the entire patent in jeopardy and could pose risk to a steady royalty stream from multiple existing licensees.[132]

5.6 Topics for Negotiation: The Right to Enforce

In license negotiations involving the right to enforce a patent, it is helpful for parties to squarely address the practical considerations that will arise during any enforcement litigation. The following are examples of some of the considerations they may want to explore.

  –What, if any, obligation to enforce will there be?
  –Who has the obligation to enforce?
  –What support (e.g., access to evidence, testimony, etc.) must the other party provide if enforcement and who bears the costs of support?
  –If counterclaims are asserted, or court sanctions awarded, is there an indemnification obligation for any resulting losses?
  –Who shall choose counsel?
  –Are any of the legal fees to be shared and, if so, in what proportion?

Confronting Others: Getting and Giving Notice

The decision to enforce having been made by an organization, the next step is to determine an approach to confronting the adversary. Confrontation can be accomplished in many ways. It can be aggressive and hostile. It can be cordial but firm. It can be written. It can be by telephone, face to face, or even

---

131. 504 F. 3d 1273 (Fed. Cir. 2007).
132. Another situation to consider is when there are co-owners of a patent. In that situation, all co-owners must join the suit (voluntarily or involuntarily). As expressed in *Israel Bio-Eng'g Project v. Amgen, Inc.*, 475 F. 3d 1256 (Fed. Cir. 2007), the concept is that the accused infringer should only be faced with defending against patent infringement in one lawsuit over a specific patent.

through an intermediary. Whatever the manner of the confrontation, it must occur to start the process.

Commonly, the decision to enforce is based upon some discovered competitive activity, which appears to be infringing. Accordingly, most scenarios that initiate confrontation are in the context of notification of infringement.[133] The decision whether and when to send notice of infringement will typically take into account several considerations such as (1) whether a decision to sue has been made or is still under consideration; (2) whether the notifying organization has marked its patent number on its products so that the damages period already has started; (3) whether the notifying party wants to flesh out additional information in the control of the notified party (e.g., prior art, unknown information about the structure or operation of the accused technology); or (4) the tone the notifying party wants to set for possible settlement discussions.

Why Send a Notice Letter?

There are a number of ways to give actual notice. Section 287 states that "[f]iling of an action for infringement shall constitute such notice." A primary reason to notify an infringer about an infringement is to establish the starting point for calculating damages, when the patent number has not been marked on a product. Specifically, 35 U.S.C. § 287 of the Patent Act states that "no damages shall be recovered by the patentee in any action for infringement, except on proof that the infringer was notified of the infringement and continued to infringe thereafter, in which event damages may be recovered only for infringement occurring after such notice." The courts have strictly construed this provision.

For example, consider the case of *Amsted v. Buckeye Steel*.[134] In that case, the infringer, Buckeye Steel, had been found liable for willful infringement and deliberate copying of the patent, and treble damages were awarded. Buckeye's counsel had even written a letter stating that the making of the component would infringe the patent. Nonetheless, because the patent owner Amsted failed to mark their product and failed to give actual notice until very late, Buckeye Steel avoided payment of any damages for at least the four

---

133. Infringement notification is not the only reason to initiate communication with a competitor about a patent. The communication may arise in more benign circumstances, such as in the context of inviting discussions to license a technology, even before the competitor (or potential competitor) has commenced commercialization of a technology.

134. *Amsted Indus., Inc. v. Buckeye Steel Castings Co.*, 24 F. 3d 178 (Fed. Cir. 1994).

earliest years of infringement (of the six-year pre-lawsuit "limitations" period permitted by 35 U.S.C. § 286).[135]

In most instances, organizations would like to settle their patent disputes prior to and without the need for litigation.[136] For these organizations, lying at the heart of its enforcement means is the notice letter. To be effective in resolving a potential dispute, the message delivered in a notice letter preferably is specific and firm. It does not need to employ blunt or smug accusations (e.g., "you have copied and are willfully infringing our patent") unless some other strategic purpose exists it should not necessarily be wishy washy (e.g., "we think you should take a look at our patents and how they might relate to your product line").[137] Desirably, the notice will identify any patent being asserted, along with an identification of the accused subject matter.

5.7 The Tension Between Notification and Declaratory Judgment

Until the recent changes in declaratory judgment jurisdiction jurisprudence, as exemplified in *MedImmune, Inc. v. Genentech, Inc.*, 127 S. Ct. 764 (2007) and *SanDisk Corp. v. STMicroelectronics, Inc.*, 480 F.3d 1372 (Fed. Cir. 2007), it was the practice to use "flowery" language in notice letters, to avoid creating an apprehension of litigation and triggering jurisdiction for a declaratory judgment. Nowadays, there appears little that can be said that would satisfy 35 U.S.C. § 287 to start damages accruing while still avoiding declaratory judgment jurisdiction.

If an organization is on the fence and cannot decide whether to initiate any enforcement, it is worth exploring the possible consequences of taking no action. For example, suppose an organization becomes aware of an infringement and

---

135. 35 U.S.C. § 286 states in part: "Except as otherwise provided by law, no recovery shall be had for any infringement committed more than six years prior to the filing of the complaint or counterclaim for infringement in the action."

136. As the statistics bear out, of the 2,231 patent infringement cases filed in 2005, only 314 went to trial (14 percent), with the other 86 percent settling. *See*, http://www.patstats.org/ HISTORICAL_DISPOSITION_MODES_FOR_PATENT_CASES.rev2.doc (as accessed April 5, 2008). These statistics do not reflect the number of infringement disputes settled without litigation. Though not capable of being measured, because the notifications and ensuing negotiations typically are confidential, it is a certainty that the notification alone has been sufficient in many instances to achieve respect for patents.

137. The present discussion pertains to notice sufficient for initiating a damages period under 35 U.S.C. § 287. Another context in which notice issues arise is under 35 U.S.C. § 154(d), for triggering provisional rights under a published patent application. Under that statute, the required notice is only of "the published patent application," in contrast to the required notice of the infringement.

convinces itself that it should not take action (e.g., the market is too small, the competitor's product is inferior and will fail on its own, the pricing is insufficient to justify the suit costs, etc.). The organization decides to do nothing and, consequently the alleged infringer may never receive actual notice of the infringement, let alone of the patent itself. As most such situations progress, the initial justifications for taking no action turn out to have been a short term situation, and a few years later, the infringer has successfully grown its business and has crippled the market share or pricing power of the patent owner. At that time, the patent owner wants to enforce. However, the meat of any damages claim is likely compromised as a result of taking no action when the infringement started. To add insult to injury, by then, it is not uncommon that the success enjoyed by the infringer has supported the development of its next-generation product, which either does not infringe or could readily be modified to avoid infringement.

Once notice is sent, it is important to follow the transaction through until resolution. If this becomes impossible or impractical, but an organization wants to preserve its claim, then it should communicate or otherwise demonstrate to the adversary that, though it is not going to presently pursue litigation, it is reserving and not waiving that right. Otherwise, there is a substantial risk that the notified party will take the position that the doctrine of "estoppel" precludes the claim.[138]

What to Expect When Notice Is Sent

Once in a while, upon sending notice, an infringer will contact the patent owner, confess its transgression, agree to stop its activity, and maybe even offer to pay for past damages. This is a rare occurrence, and it is not realistic to expect that it will occur with any frequency. More realistically, upon sending notice, the notifying party should prepare itself for a frustrating and time-consuming process, even if the responding party acknowledges receipt of the letter and that they are taking the matter seriously.[139]

The reality is that some delay is reasonable and is not necessarily a reason to attribute malevolence to the accused infringer. For instance, if the notified party truly was unaware of the patent, it will be necessary for it to investigate.

---

138. *See generally A. C. Aukerman Co. v. R. .L. Chaides Constr. Co.*, 960 F. 2d 1020 (Fed. Cir. 1992) (*en banc*).

139. *See e.g., Sony Elecs., Inc. v. Guardian Media Techs., Ltd.*, 493 F. 3d 1271 (Fed. Cir. 2007). In that case, the patentee sent a first notice of infringement on September 24, 1999. Sony responded by saying that it was taking the matter seriously, but needed to investigate. Sony also requested claim charts showing the infringement. The patentee sent claim charts on October 28, 1999, but did not get a response until more than six months later when Sony stated that they did not think the patents were valid.

This could involve retention of counsel, meetings to learn about the accused subject matter, ordering and studying the prosecution history of the subject patent, and formulation of a reasoned and supportable opinion. It is not unusual for this to take several weeks or longer. One way to keep the process moving forward is to have the notified party commit to a reasonable deadline for response.

Common Responses to Notice Letter

No Response at All

This is a common response from some larger organizations that are notified by a smaller organization and is often a way that the larger organization tests the seriousness of the allegation.[140] It is also common when the notified party is unsophisticated on patent matters, or the notified party knows it has a problem.

"We Are Investigating Your Letter"

While they are investigating, many, many moons may come and go. This is another way to test the seriousness of the accusation and the will of the patent owner to pursue the case. A word of caution here, an organization that says it is investigating had better truly be investigating. It will be potentially very inflammatory to a fact-finder to learn that action did not accompany the words, particularly when it comes to the issue of determining whether damages should be increased per 35 U.S.C. § 284.

"We Will Respond by a Specified Date"

The promise of a response by a specified date will seldom be met. However, sometimes it is met. In those instances, especially when the accused infringer responds with a detailed and factually supported response, it is worthy to take the response seriously, as there is likely some substance to it.

"We Need More Information"

The request for detailed, specific information typically comes after the promise to investigate and after the promise to respond by a certain date. This letter results from someone actually reviewing the patent sent and the accused

---

140. It is fair to say that large organizations have lots of products and they get lots of these sorts of notice letters. Many times the patentee goes away because they can not afford the cost of actually litigating.

products, noticing a possible problem, but not wanting to take a position; so, they ask the patentee for more information. This letter can also set the bar for how much information is in-hand at the time of alleging infringement, which can trigger Federal Rules of Civil Procedure Rule 11 issues during litigation. In particular, this letter can trigger issues surrounding whether a sufficient prefiling inquiry into the facts has been made. The request for information is either (1) so vague that you don't really know what information is needed (from which you can infer that the target has not really read the patent or really considered the issues) or (2) so detailed that they are seeking the entirety of your case without having to disclose anything so that they can just sit back, delay on disclosing any detailed information to you (e.g., sales figures for damage calculations), and take pot shots at your case to cause you more difficulty. The best response to a request for information is either (1) a meeting with business people having decision-making authority, at which both sides agree to discuss their views of the conflict or (2) filing of the complaint.

"We Have Prior Art Demonstrating Invalidity of the Patent"

Unaccompanied by any prior art, this type of response is difficult to take seriously. Therefore, this response should be met with a demand to have the prior art identified. If it is nonpatent literature or a prior use or sale that is relied upon, evidence to that effect should be requested. Many times the response of having invalidating prior art is met by continued promises of supplying that prior art, but the defendant really has no clear motivation to do so under the informal process of exchanging letters. By disclosing the prior art they have in hand to the patentee under these circumstances, they give the patentee a chance to deal with that prior art on their own terms, for example by filing a request for re-examination (which the alleged infringer does not get to participate in) or citing the prior art in a continuing application to get another patent under which that prior art was considered by the USPTO. Without identification of the prior art, the patentee runs the risk of asserting a patent that the defendant can actually defend against.

5.8 Emotions to Expect in Response to Notice

Once initial notification is made, the notifying organization must prepare itself for an unsatisfying response from the notified party. Foremost, it needs to prepare itself that the other side is not its friend and is not in the business of handing out shares of its profits to anyone who can conjure up a claim. It wants nothing to do with a patent issue and wants it to go away as fast as possible. By the time the other side responds, chances are that it will have assembled a team including its scientists, engineers, lawyers, and other business people, who will already have started to scrutinize each word of the patent (with the usual sneers and jeers: "what is that claim term supposed to mean anyhow?" or "how could the Patent Office have granted this?"). If the party has little experience with enforcement of patents, it will now be getting itself past the shock of the fees it is expected to incur, fees not forecasted in its budget. Its response is, therefore, likely to come across as annoyed, inconvenienced, or otherwise in denial that it may have a problem.

This will be unsatisfying and frustrating to the organization that initiated the confrontation, largely because the patentee has spent months preparing for the adversarial process by analyzing its patent portfolio and the accused products, assessing the merits of the possible patent infringement case, and convincing management to pursue the litigation or license. The other side is nowhere near that level of seriousness yet.

Declaratory Judgment Risks

As discussed earlier in this Chapter, the notice letter, to be effective under the damages statute and case law, typically must also be specific enough to confer declaratory judgment jurisdiction. A declaratory judgment action is a lawsuit brought to stop someone from threatening your company or organization with a patent lawsuit. This typically happens when the party being attacked with the patent wants to either become the aggressor (e.g., chose venue and/or get out of licensing) or resolve the conflict in a delayed situation that appears to suit the patentee (e.g., the patentee has market exclusivity and the other side is trying to enter the market).

The main reasons that organizations care about whether declaratory judgment cases are filed are two-fold. First, in a lot of instances, an organization wants to abate an infringement but is not ready to engage in litigation or lacks the resources. Declaratory judgment jurisdiction confers upon the accused the opportunity to force the hand of the patent owner, and thereby help situate the accused infringer in a better position for settlement. A second reason for seeking

---

5.9 First to File Rule

The courts have fashioned a body of jurisprudence around the general notion that the forum selected by the plaintiff in a first filed action ought to be the forum of the dispute, even if it appears the first filed action was merely a "race to the courthouse" to preempt the filing by the patent owner elsewhere. See generally, *Elecs. for Imaging, Inc. v. Coyle*, 394 F.3d 1341 (Fed. Cir. 2005).

When a party prepares to litigate a patent, there are many factors that influence the choice of forum, including the "home court advantage," the rules of practice within a jurisdiction for handling patent cases (e.g., N.D. California Rules, S.D. Texas Rules, W.D. Pennsylvania Rules), the experience of the court with patent cases (e.g., D. Delaware), the speed of the docket (e.g., E.D. Virginia—the brass plaque on the side of the federal courthouse in the Eastern District of Virginia states "Justice Delayed is Justice Denied."), or the like. Therefore, it is often in the interest of a party to maintain control over the choice of forum for as long as reasonably possible.

The perils of "forum shopping" is an objective of Patent Reform Legislation.

declaratory judgment is to allow the accused infringer to select the location where the lawsuit will proceed.

In the past, the Federal Circuit case law created a carefully choreographed dance of certain language in the letters that were exchanged between the parties so that the patentee could call attention to a patent, without fear of immediately inviting litigation. Recently, the law has changed dramatically in this area, and it will take a number of years for a new standard to form. In *MedImmune, Inc. v. Genentech, Inc.*,[141] the Supreme Court stated that the old test "conflicts" with the Supreme Court's precedent. Starting with the *SanDisk* case, followed closely by the Teva case, a new standard is being formed, such that declaratory judgment actions should be much easier to bring. The standard in *SanDisk v. STMicroelectronics, NV*[142] is:

We hold only that where a patentee asserts rights under a patent based on certain identified ongoing or planned activity of another party, and where that party contends that it has the right to engage in the accused activity without license, an Article III case or controversy will arise and the party need not risk a suit for infringement by engaging in the identified activity before seeking a declaration of its legal rights.

In the *SanDisk* case, there was a "friendly meeting" to discuss licensing where STM showed a claim chart mapping SanDisk's product against STM's claims. STM said at the meeting that they had no plan to sue SanDisk. About a month later, after negotiations had gone nowhere, SanDisk sued for a declaratory judgment of noninfringement and invalidity and apparently did

---

141. 127 S. Ct. 764, 774 n. 11 (2007).
142. *Sandisk Corp. v. STMicroelectronics,Inc*, 480 F. 3d 1372, 1381 (Fed. Cir. 2007); *See also Teva Pharmaceuticals v. Novartis Pharmaceuticals Corp.*, 482 F. 3d 1330 (Fed. Cir. 2007).

so properly. Under the old standard, these activities would have been insufficient to create a reasonable apprehension of suit.

In *Adenta Gmbh v. Orthoarm, Inc.,*[143] the Federal Circuit upheld a basis
for declaratory judgment when the Adenta refused to continue to pay royalties under a license agreement. Despite some evidence that the litigation was
a way to get out of the royalties agreed upon as a result of a settlement agreement, the Court found that jurisdiction was based on the fact that the patent
holder had threatened to assert its rights if Adenta failed to pay royalties
"thereby creating a substantial controversy."

Section 287: Patent Notice and Marking

As expressed earlier in this Chapter, another way to make others aware of
patents is to mark products with the patent numbers that cover the product.
This is regarded as placing the world on constructive notice of the patents. In
Nike, Inc. v. Wal-Mart Stores, Inc.,[144] the Federal Circuit summarized the
purposes of the marking statute as:

> (1) helping to avoid innocent infringement . . . ; (2) encouraging patentees to
> give notice to the public that the article is patented . . . ; and (3) aiding the public
> to identify whether an article is patented.

Thus, if a patentee fails to mark the patented product as it is released to
public view through marketing, sales, promotion, or other such endeavors,
then patentee will not be able to capture premarking damages even if they are
successful in proving infringement. However, a patentee may cure the marking defect by simply starting to mark. After the date of compliance with the
marking statute, the patentee may be able to capture damage awards.[145]

To mark a product with a patent number it is important to put the patent
number on the product itself or, if impractical, on the product packaging. All
products sold should consistently bear the marking. Marking should not be
a sporadic process. It may or may not be sufficient to mark the literature associated with a product.[146] Sometimes, the nature of the product prevents it
from being marked. In those instances, some reasonable effort at compliance
should still be attempted. For example, one approach may be to embed the

---

143. 501 F. 3d 1364 (Fed. Cir. 2007).
144. 138 F. 3d 1437, 1442 (Fed. Cir. 1998) (citations omitted).
145. Marking is not required if the patent is directed to a process or method. *See Bandag, Inc. v.
      Gerrard Tire Co., Inc.,* 704 F. 2d 1578, 1581 (Fed. Cir. 1983). However, if the process or
      method results in a tangible product, the end product should be marked.
146. *See, e.g., Calmar, Inc. v. Emson Research, Inc.,* 850 F. Supp. 861, 868 (C.D. Cal. 1994).

patent number(s) into the outside packaging of the product or displayed on the splash screen on patented software.[147] The form of the marking may be dictated by the product. For example, some products may permit the patent marking to be part of a finished product (e.g., molded or engraved into the product). Some products may permit an adhesive label or even a mechanically attached plate. Every situation will vary. The important point, however, is that some reasonable effort at compliance will create risk for the competition. No effort will impose no risk.

Some organizations encounter difficulty in marking because they own several patents, and they do not know which patents may cover a specific product. Alternatively, they have multiple versions of a product, each one being the subject of a different patent. In these instances, one approach that is followed is to simply mark all of the patents and state to the effect of: "This product may be covered by one or more of the following U.S. patents: w,www,www; d,ddd,ddd; f,fff,fff; x,xxx,xxx; m,mmm,mmm; a,aaa,aaa; or z,zzz,zzz." Though such marking cannot necessarily guarantee that damages will be awarded, it will substantially improve the likelihood of damages as compared with a situation of no marking.

In some industries, patent owners may manufacture products for assembly into a product sold by another. For example, a vendor of aircraft parts may supply to the aircraft manufacturer, which assembles the parts into a finished aircraft. It is common in these industries that the customer (e.g., the aircraft manufacturer) will insist that the product bear no markings. This makes compliance with the marking requirement difficult. In such situations, the emphasis will likely shift to reliance upon the actual infringement notice requirement under 35 U.S.C. § 287. With sparse case law on point, however, it is still in the interest of the patent owner to attempt some form of marking on associated materials, such as packaging, shipping containers, sales and shipping documentation, literature, or otherwise. Again, it will not necessarily guarantee a recovery against an infringer. But it should preserve the opportunity to raise the issue in litigation and create risk for the opponent.

Against the above, it must be borne in mind that it is illegal to falsely mark a product as covered by a patent when it is not.[148] Accordingly, it is important that any markings be properly reviewed for its propriety.

---

147. For one take on the marking statute as it applies to software, consider: James W. Soong , *Patent Damage Strategies and The Enterprise License: Constructive Notice Actual Notice, No Notice*, 2005 Duke L. & Tech. Rev. 0002 as reproduced at http://law.duke.edu/journals/dltr/ articles/pdf/2005dltr0002.pdf (as accessed April 1, 2008).

148. 35 U.S.C. § 292.

State of Mind for Infringement

In general, patent infringement is a strict liability offense; the patent laws do not care how innocent an infringer was in committing the infringement. The patent owner will be entitled to a remedy. However, where the state of mind of the infringer does matter is pursuant to 35 U.S.C. § 284, which provides that a "court may increase the damages up to three times. . . ." A court decides whether to award the enhanced damages by deciding if the infringement was undertaken with scienter.

The current state of the law is governed by the 2007 *en banc* Federal Circuit decision in the case of *In re Seagate Technology, LLC.*,[149] which overruled the duty to obtain advice of counsel as a measurement of state of mind, holding instead:

> proof of willful infringement permitting enhanced damages requires at least a showing of objective recklessness. Because we abandon the affirmative duty of due care, we also reemphasize that there is no affirmative obligation to obtain opinion of counsel.

As to what conduct will constitute "objective recklessness," that remains to be seen from the courts. In the interim, a large number of companies will continue to rely upon "advice of counsel" to support that their conduct was not objectively reckless. To the latter point, for companies that plan to rely upon "advice of counsel," it should be expected that the courts may continue to follow pre-*Seagate* case law to assess whether the reliance upon counsel was reasonable. For instance, knowing reliance upon advice from incompetent counsel could hurt a party's efforts to avoid increased damages, as may reliance upon an unreasoned opinion of counsel, or an opinion known to be grounded upon improper facts or assumptions.[150]

Duty to Investigate Third-Party Patents

The duty to obtain advice of counsel historically has been predicated upon knowledge of a patent to another. Thus, in many pre-*Seagate* circumstances, notice of a patent (even if not accompanied by an accusation of infringement) was generally considered sufficient to trigger the duty of a party to obtain advice of counsel.

---

149. 497 F. 3d 1360, 1371 (Fed. Cir. 2007) (*en banc*).
150. *See, e.g., nCube Corp. v. SeaChange Int'l, Inc.,* 436 F. 3d 1317 (Fed. Cir. 2006); *Central Soya Co. v. Geo. A. Hormel & Co.,* 723 F. 2d 1573 (Fed. Cir. 1983); but *See, DSU Medical Crop. v. Jms Co.,* 471 F. 3d 1293 (Fed. Cir. 2006) (State of mind for vicarious liability addressed).

In the absence of notice, however, there is no affirmative duty to go out and find patents that may pose a risk of infringement. Organizations that nevertheless engage in practices of locating and studying competitive patents typically do so as part of their internal risk management practices. The analysis may be in connection with competitive patent watches, in which an organization conducts a periodic search (e.g., weekly, monthly, or even quarterly) for patents that issue to a competitor, or as part of a more comprehensive state-of-the-art search.

5.10 Freedom to Operate Studies

One form of state-of-the-art searching involves a freedom to operate study. In such a study, a search for prior patents which are not expired and still in force is undertaken. Unlike other comprehensive state-of-the-art searches, the freedom to operate study is often undertaken in the context of a specific technology. More particularly, the study is undertaken to assure that the specific technology that an organization seeks to introduce to the market does not infringe any existing patents to others. Such studies will generally involve a thorough review of many patents and will consume significant resources. Not only must the searched patents be reviewed for determining the general relevance of their teachings, but their patent claims are reviewed as well, to help identify any claims that pose a potential infringement problem. In the process of clearing new technologies using this process, it is not uncommon for about a dozen or so patents to be identified as posing a potential issue. Upon identifying such patents, the organization undertaking the study has several options available to it, including one or more of: (1) abandonment of the proposed technology; (2) introduction of a design change to avoid infringement; (3) seeking a license under the patent; (4) relying upon an opinion of counsel that the patent is not infringed, invalid, unenforceable, or a combination; or (5) initiating a proceeding (e.g., reexamination, opposition, or otherwise) to seek clarification of the scope of the patent. Some organizations may choose to take no action. That conduct is risky and should rarely be done without advice of counsel.

Securing Advice of Counsel

If concerned that it might infringe a patent, and an organization wants to avoid a charge of willful infringement, then even post-*Seagate*, advice of counsel remains a viable and often-times prudent course of action.[151] It must

---

151. *Underwater Devices, Inc. v. Morrison-Knudsen Co.*, 717 F. 2d 1380, 1390-91 (Fed. Cir. 1983) (held that the duty generally required obtaining competent legal advice before engaging in any potentially infringing activity or continuing such activity).

be borne in mind, however, that reliance upon advice of counsel as a ground for avoiding increased damages in litigation shall have the likely effect of waiving the attorney-client privilege that otherwise would govern such advice. Though the organization will try to define the scope of the waiver narrowly, there is no assurance that a court will adopt such definition. For instance, prior to *Seagate* reliance upon the advice of counsel defense was a basis for seeking to waive privileged communications between an accused infringer and its trial counsel.[152] From case to case, the scope of any waiver could not be known with certainty. The scope was even sought to extend to waive immunity from disclosure as to uncommunicated work product (e.g., trial counsel's personal work that was not sent to or told to the client).[153]

Prior to 2004, accused infringers faced risk of a negative inference that an opinion of counsel was (or would have been) unfavorable if the alleged infringer failed to produce or to obtain an exculpatory opinion of counsel in response to a charge of willful infringement.[154]

As indicated, this understanding has now changed due to *Seagate*, although just how far is uncertain, and will likely remain uncertain for years. *Seagate* has the potential in the short term to help organizations save significant outside counsel costs by cutting down the need for extensive attorney opinion work. However, *Seagate* should not be considered as justification to abandon the practice of seeking advice counsel, as such advice is still valuable to help navigate the field of patents to others and likely still act to provide evidence that the behavior of an organization was not objectively reckless.

---

152. *See generally In re Seagate Tech. LLC*, 497 F. 3d 1360 (Fed. Cir. 2007) (*en banc*); *cf. In re EchoStar Communications Corp.*, 448 F. 3d 1294 (Fed. Cir. 2006) (since construed by some district courts as supporting a waiver of the privilege as to trial counsel for communicated work product).

153. *See In re EchoStar Communications Corp.*, 448 F. 3d 1294 (Fed. Cir. 2006).

154. *Knorr-Bremse Systeme Fuer Nutzfahrzeuge GmbH v. Dana Corp.*, 383 F. 3d 1337 (Fed. Cir. 2004) (*en banc*).

CHAPTER
6

Giving Respect to Valid Patent Rights

The Typical Corporation

An understanding and appreciation of the customs and principles of how, when and why to give respect to the intellectual property is important for successful development of a culture of IP. Different organizations have different tolerances for risk, with some being very risk adverse and others being very comfortable with risk abounding. The amount of risk that your company can tolerate may indicate just how well or much respect it gives to the IP of others.

Some organizations' first encounter with patents is a surprise receipt of a communication from a competitor calling its attention to a patent owned by the competitor. Other organizations will have readily anticipated the communication, and that organization may have made a conscious decision to embark on a commercial venture, aware that its competitor had a proprietary position; and in such case, by proceeding in "blind ignorance" of the competitor rights, the organization was flirting with disaster, which is certainly a risky proposition.

Another class of organizations is the obsessive–compulsive class. Such organizations are characterized as being chronically obsessed with the fear of litigation. Obsession compels them to actively seek counsel in the face of any potentially risky situation, whether it is an environmental matter, an employment matter, or otherwise. They tend to have a relatively high tolerance for legal services but seldom find themselves in disputes with others. Within those organizations, there tends to be a high level of accountability, with the managers often taken to task for errors. Fear of disputes may paralyze them.

In the middle, however, is the more typical organization, which tolerates risk when necessary and may gain its initial exposure to the patent system in an innocent manner. These organizations generally are good corporate citizens, but they may have made a mistake by not investigating patents that might affect their commercial activities, by misunderstanding the nature and scope of patent rights of the competitor, or both. Upon discovery that they have a patent issue with potential consequences, most of them become horrified that such an important issue was the subject of a mistake, but such horror is almost always simultaneously accompanied by terror, upon the discovery that, to extricate themselves from the situation, they need to incur substantial expense and divert a wealth of resources away from concentrating on their core business.

Ideally, none of the above will mark the first encounter of your organization with patents. Rather, familiarity with the topics of this chapter will enable you to enlist appropriate counsel at an early stage in commercialization.

Claim Construction: What Does That Patent Mean Anyhow?

One of the starting points for all organizations to build a healthy IP culture is to develop an understanding of the parts of patent documents and particularly how to read patent documents to decipher the scope of the right protected by the patent. Patent documents include two main parts. The first part is called the written description or the "specification."[155] This is the part of the document that describes in detail the subject matter asserted as the invention and the manner of practicing it. Though some practitioners might regard any

---

155. This is sometimes loosely called the "disclosure" of the invention, the "teachings" of a patent, or even the "specification" of a patent.

patent drawings as an independent part of the patent application, for discussion purposes herein, the written description also includes such drawings. The second part of the patent is the part that defines the scope of the invention for which the right to exclude applies. This part of the patent, called the patent "claims," consists of the numbered paragraphs at the end of the patent. The claims of a patent are to inventions what a real estate deed is to a piece of land. The claims define "the metes and bounds" of the property right. It is only the claims of a patent that can be infringed. To ascertain the bounds of real property, a surveyor would be enlisted to measure and mark the boundary parameters outlined in the deed. For patents, however, the practice of establishing the boundaries of the patent grant is done by a legal analysis of the words contained in the patent claims, in a practice universally known as "claim construction."

6.1

Perception versus Reality: In their zeal to gain or otherwise secure market share, some firms that own patents will exaggerate the scope of the protectable right that the patent provides. They may not have their own in-house patent counsel and may not necessarily look to outside counsel for explicit direction about the scope of rights. In some instances, the business people will merely state what they recall, in the most general terms, to have been their contribution to the state of the art. This could work great success in the market, for the patent owner unwittingly may create the perception in the market that the patent is much broader than it actually is.

So, you have a competitor's patent in front of you or you are trying to apply your patent to a competitor's product or process. You have to decide what the words in the patent claims mean so that you can understand the metes and bounds of the claims. Anyone who has actually done this will tell you that there is some, but little, certainty. Does that particular use of the word "a" mean one or one or more? Does the word "include" mean only the parts that follow or more parts can be added? Does the word "sandwich" (as in a material sandwiched between two ends) mean that there are no holes or leaks in the ends? Is hydrogen included in that listed group of radicals? Thus, you almost always ask, "what did (we) (they) mean by that word"? Indeed, some attorneys strive for this vagueness during prosecution so that both options may remain available to the patent owner for just this type of situation.

The claim construction depends, in many circumstances, on how someone wants to read the words. In reality, claim construction is performed in the context of comparing the claim to a potentially infringing product or process (yours or theirs). The task is approached with a desired result in mind.

As a result of this bias, words that are easily understood on one side are unclear on the other side, which is the source of many patent disputes.

Historically, the starting point of any patent analysis in the U.S. has been the determination of patent scope. In 1995, the U.S. Supreme Court solidified the role that claim construction must play in any patent infringement analysis, and assigned the responsibility of construing patent claims to judges, rather than juries. The landmark *Markman*[156] case, presented the Supreme Court with a dispute concerning the meaning of the claim term "inventory," in the context of an inventory control and reporting system for dry-cleaning stores. At issue was whether the term "inventory" included cash inventory or only articles of clothing. One reason that the court applied for its ruling that claim construction is a matter for the courts was:

> we see the importance of uniformity in the treatment of a given patent as an independent reason to allocate all issues of construction to the court. As we noted in *General Elec. Co. v. Wabash Appliance Corp.*, 304 U.S. 364, 369 (1938), "[t]he limits of a patent must be known for the protection of the patentee, the encouragement of the inventive genius of others and the assurance that the subject matter of the patent will be dedicated ultimately to the public." Otherwise, a "zone of uncertainty which enterprise and experimentation may enter only at the risk of infringement claims would discourage invention only a little less than unequivocal foreclosure of the field," *United Carbon Co. v. Binney & Smith Co.*, 317 U.S. 228, 236 (1942), and "[t]he public [would] be deprived of rights supposed to belong to it, without being clearly told what it is that limits these rights." *Merrill v. Yeomans*, 94 U.S. 568, 573 (1877).[157]

Claim construction analysis is not limited to matters of infringement. Rather, it must be performed any time the scope of patent claims is in dispute. Thus, it is also imperative to construe claims in addressing patent validity disputes.[158]

Patentee Is Own Lexicographer, or, Ascertain the Ordinary Meaning

In general, the exercise of claim construction goes like this. First, the disputed claim term is examined to see if the ordinary meaning of the claim term

---

156. *Markman v. Westview Instruments, Inc.*, 517 U.S. 370 (1996).
157. *Ibid.* at 390.
158. *See, e.g., Key Pharms., Inc. v. Hercon Labs. Corp.*, 161 F. 3d 709 (Fed. Cir. 1998) ("we observe in passing that, not unlike a determination of infringement, a determination of anticipation, as well as obviousness, involves two steps. First is construing the claim . . . followed by, in the case of anticipation . . . a comparison of the construed claim to the prior art.").

can be employed. This can be a confusing task because the patent laws allow inventors to be their own "lexicographer"; that is, inventors can take an ordinary word out of their daily vocabulary and, by a clear expression of an intent to do so, assign a unique meaning to the term, by redefining it a particularly way in the patent. By way of example, a patent may expressly state, "XXXX" as used herein means "adhashioyrwuf." But such language is not critical for establishing that a particular definition has been advanced by a patentee.[159]

Assuming that no particular meaning has been assigned, and the patentee has not been its own lexicographer, then the court will seek to ascertain the ordinary meaning of the term to a person of ordinary skill in the art.[160] This is commonly done by reference to the teachings of the specification and to the prosecution history.[161] During this part of the exercise, the patent documents are placed under a high-power microscope, and each statement and punctuation mark is scrutinized for its semantic usage made by the patent agent or attorney during the drafting and prosecution process. Attention is given to the use of "and" instead of "or." Terms of exclusion are distinguished from those of inclusion. The record is parsed for any possible hint that the patentee restricted the meaning of a patent claim term.

---

159. *See, e.g., Astrazeneca AB v. Mutual Pharmaceutical Co.*, 384 F3d 1333 (Fed. Cir. 2004) ("solubilizer" is limited to surfactants). In that case, the court stated:

> Astrazeneca seems to suggest that lexicography requires a statement in the form "I define _____ to mean _____," but such rigid formalism is not required. *See, e.g., Bell Atl. Network Servs., Inc.*, 262 F. 3d at 1268 ("[A] claim term may be clearly redefined without an explicit statement of redefinition . . . . [T]he specification may define claim terms 'by implication' such that the meaning may be 'found in or ascertained by a reading of the patent documents.'" (citation omitted)). Certainly the '081 specification's statement that "[t]he solubilizers suitable according to the invention are defined below" provides a strong signal of lexicography.

> *See also Abbott Labs. v. Novopharm Ltd.*, 323 F. 3d 1324 (Fed. Cir. 2003) (patentee was lexicographer in defining "co-micronization").

160. In some instances, an elaborate analysis is not necessary. *See Brown v. 3M*, 265 F. 3d 1349, 1352 (Fed Cir. 2001) ("The district court construed the word "or" in claim 16 as meaning that the apparatus was capable of converting 'only two-digit, only three-digit, only four-digit, or any combination of two-, three-, and four-digit date-data.' Slip op. at 9. We agree with this construction of the claim, for it is the plain reading of the claim text. These are not technical terms of art, and do not require elaborate interpretation.").

161. *See Phillips v. AWH Corp.*, 415 F. 3d, 1303, 1317 (Fed. Cir. 2005) ("The prosecution history . . . consists of the complete record of the proceedings before the PTO and includes the prior art cited during the examination of the patent.").

The "Specification" or "Written Description"

In most claim construction exercises, the first resource consulted is the "specification," or "written description" of the patent. The Court of Appeals for the Federal Circuit has elaborated on the role of the patent description in *Phillips v. AWH Corp.*:[162]

> The importance of the specification in claim construction derives from its statutory role. The close kinship between the written description and the claims is enforced by the statutory requirement that the specification describe the claimed invention in "full, clear, concise, and exact terms." 35 U.S.C. § 112, para. 1; *See Netword, LLC v. Centraal Corp* . . . . ("The claims are directed to the invention that is described in the specification; they do not have meaning removed from the context from which they arose."); *See also Markman v. Westview Instruments, Inc.,* . . . ("[A claim] term can be defined only in a way that comports with the instrument as a whole."). In light of the statutory directive that the inventor provide a "full" and "exact" description of the claimed invention, the specification necessarily informs the proper construction of the claims. *See Merck & Co. v. Teva Pharms. USA, Inc.,* . . . ("A fundamental rule of claim construction is that terms in a patent document are construed with the meaning with which they are presented in the patent document. Thus claims must be construed so as to be consistent with the specification, of which they are a part.") [citations omitted].

How the invention is described in detail is an important feature of patents. It is important to invest appropriate time and money to help assure the patent document is well drafted and consistent.

The Prosecution History

The prosecution history is also regarded as an important claim construction resource. It is the only public record that sheds light on the actual transaction that occurred at the Patent Office and by which the patent granted. As such, it serves an important public notice function:

> The public notice function of patents requires that a patentee be prevented from expressly stating during prosecution that the claims do not cover a particular device and then later suing for infringement by that same device. Allowing such a suit would be unfair to the public, particularly the manufacturer of the accused device, which was entitled to rely on the surrender of claimed subject

---

162. *Phillips*, 415 F. 3d at 1316 (citations omitted).

matter made in the prosecution history and contained in the file wrapper. *Hockerson-Halberstadt* . . . (stating that, in the context of claim construction, "the prosecution history constitutes a public record of the patentee's representations concerning the scope and the meaning of the claims, and competitors are entitled to rely on those representations when ascertaining the degree of lawful conduct. . . . Were we to accept [the accused infringer's] position, we would undercut the public's reliance on a statement that was in the public record and upon which reasonable competitors formed their business strategies"). . . ,.[163]

Illustrations

Some people will go through their careers without ever engaging in a claim construction exercise. Others may experience claim construction on a daily or weekly basis. Regardless of the experience level, there can be no denying the value of familiarity with some of the more common claim construction scenarios.

For example, a patent uses "solvent" as a claim term. The written description of the patent provides only examples in which water is used as a solvent. In fact, the specification goes further and states that "the invention is unique because the prior art always employed only organic solvents, which posed health and environment risks, and because they were organic, could not be disposed of in fresh-water bodies. The invention of the patent poses no such risks, and because it only employs water-based solvents, it can be disposed of in storm sewers." Moreover, to get the patent issued, the patent owner argued that the prior art included an organic solvent, which was "not a solvent that would be useful in the present invention." In such instance, the term "solvent" likely would be construed to exclude organic solvents.[164]

By way of further illustration, the following are instructive toward understanding how a patentee may occasion narrowing of claim scope by characterizing the claimed invention with reference to the prior art.

1. Statements that purport to distinguish a feature from the prior art by characterizing a corresponding feature in the prior art as being different from the claimed feature (e.g., a patentee in dispute over the term "textured surface" likely will be prohibited from construing the clause to cover a sand-blasted surface in a situation in which the patentee stated in the specification, the prosecution history, or both: "the prior art does

163. *Pall Corp. v. PTI Technologies Inc.*, 259 F. 3d 1383, 1393 (Fed. Cir. 2001).
164. *See SciMed Life Sys., Inc. v. Advanced Cardiovascular Sys.*, Inc., 242 F. 3d 1337 (Fed. Cir. 2001).

not teach the textured surface of the present invention, it only teaches sand-blasted surfaces";

2. Statements that purport to distinguish a feature of the claimed invention from prior art by identifying a particular disadvantage realized using the prior art, but overcome by use of the claimed invention (e.g., a patentee may be restricted from asserting a broad construction of the term "instantaneous gear shifter" to cover a gear shifter that takes 0. 7 seconds to shift between gears, when in the specification, during prosecution, or both, the patentee expressed that the invention overcomes the problems with prior art shifters, in which problematic delays of about 0. 5 seconds occur in gear change due to need for clutch engagement for shifting");

3. Express statements that the invention does not cover a certain feature (e.g., a patentee may be prevented from asserting a broad claim construction "milk processing" to cover processing whole milk when the patentee made the statement in the specification, during prosecution, or both: "the present invention finds particular application in the processing of skim milk, and in fact cannot be used for processing milk with a fat content").[165]

Notwithstanding the above scenarios, care must be undertaken at all stages of claim construction to avoid overstating the damning effect of limiting statements made by the patentee. For example, when the specification of a patent teaches only one embodiment, a court will frequently be reluctant to adopt a construction that would exclude such embodiment.[166]

Dictionaries

Claim construction also frequently involves an examination of dictionary definitions. As can be appreciated, therein lies another source of potential mischief, for dictionaries often offer several meanings for a term. More

---

165. For actual cases illustrating how the above examples have played out in litigation, *see e.g., Cultor Corp. v. A. E. Staley Mfg. Co.,* 224 F. 3d 1328 (Fed. Cir. 2000) (limiting ingredient to one prepared by use of a particular catalyst, even though claim did not specify preparation with such catalyst); *North American Container, Inc. v. Plastipak Packaging Inc.,* 415 F. 3d 1335 (Fed. Cir. 2005); *see also Ekchian v. Home Depot, Inc.,* 104 F. 3d 1299, 1304 (Fed. Cir. 1997) (analyzing the effect of statements made in an Information Disclosure Statement, the court expressed that in "distinguishing the claimed invention over prior art, an applicant is indicating what the claims do not cover, he is by implication surrendering such protection.").

166. *Vitronics Corp. v. Conceptronic, Inc.,* 90 F. 3d 1576, 1583-84 (Fed. Cir. 1996) (a claim construction that would exclude from the scope of the claim a preferred embodiment "is rarely, if ever, correct and would require highly persuasive evidentiary support").

common is the situation in which the choice of one dictionary or another may yield a different construction. This can occur among multiple different English language dictionaries. It may occur between an English language dictionary and a technical dictionary.[167] Consider, for example, the situation in which the patent claims a medication that includes a particular "suboxide." The definition of that term from *The American Heritage Dictionary* (New College ed. 1979) is "an oxide containing a relatively small amount of oxygen." In contrast, the definition from *Dorland's Illustrated Medical Dictionary* (23rd ed.) is "[t]hat oxide in any series which contains the smallest proportion of oxygen." These definitions, though overlapping, also pose the risk of excluding certain oxides from one definition, which otherwise would be included in the other.

6.2

Litigants have spent millions of dollars fighting over the scope of the following patent terms:

"a": *Elkay Mfg. Co. v. Ebco Mfg. Co.*, 192 F.3d 973 (Fed. Cir. 1999); *Crystal Semiconductor Corp. v. TriTech Microelectronics Int'l Inc.*, 246 F.3d 1336 (Fed. Cir. 2001).

"about": *Jeneric/Pentron, Inc. v. Dillon Company, Inc.*, 205 F.3d 1377 (Fed. Cir. 2000), *Ecolab, Inc. v. Envirochem, Inc.*, 264 F.3d 1358 (Fed. Cir. 2001).

"annular" and "polygonal": *Int'l. Rectifier Corp. v. IXYS Corp.*, 361 F.3d 1363 (Fed. Cir. 2004).

"composition": *PIN/NIP, Inc. v. Platte Chemical Co.*, 304 F.3d 1235 (Fed. Cir. 2002).

"golden brown": *Unitherm Food Systems Inc. v. Swift-Eckrich Inc.*, 375 F.3d 1341 (Fed. Cir. 2004).

"immediately": *MBO Labs., Inc. v. Becton, Dickinson & Co.*, 474 F.3d 1323 (Fed. Cir. 2007).

"ingredients": *Mars, Inc. v. H.J. Heinz Co.*, 377 F.3d 1369 (Fed. Cir. 2004).

"one": *Elkay Mfg. Co. v. Ebco Mfg. Co.*, 192 F.3d 973 (Fed. Cir. 1999);

"or": *Kustom signals, Inc. v. Applied Concepts, Inc.*, 264 F.3d 1326 (Fed. Cir. 2001).

"purity": *Glaxo Group Ltd. v. Apotex, Inc.*, 376 F.3d 1339 (Fed. Cir. 2004).

"substantially": *Deering Precision Instruments L.L.C. v. Vector Distribution Sys., Inc.*, 347 F.3d 1314 (Fed. Cir. 2003).

"and": *Chef America, Inc. v. Lamb-Weston*, 358 F.3d 1371, 1374 (Fed. Cir. 20040; and *Ortho-McNeil Pharmaceutical, Inc. v. Mylan Labs, Inc.*, Case No. 2007-1 (Fed. Cir. March 31, 2008).

---

167. *Phillips*, 415 F. 3d 1303 (*en banc*).

Resolution of Claim Construction Disputes

In litigated cases in which a claim term is disputed, the *Markman* Supreme Court has dictated that judges are supposed to decide the proper construction of the claim. This has been done at any of a number of stages of a lawsuit, such as during a summary judgment motion proceeding, in a pretrial order, in the course of issuing jury instructions, or even posttrial proceedings.[168] Nowadays, the most common way the issue is resolved is by a proceeding aptly named a *Markman* proceeding. In the course of such proceeding, each side will typically present its arguments, make reference to support within the intrinsic evidence (i.e., the patent and its prosecution history), and possibly introduce supporting dictionary definitions, expert witness testimony, and occasionally some other form of evidence. As to the other forms of evidence, it is common for litigants to try to introduce evidence from extra-judicial or overseas proceedings, or even inventor testimony. The courts have been resistant to admitting such evidence and especially to affording such evidence any significant weight.[169]

Probably the most disputed patent cases are the result of a dispute over claim construction. It would seem sensible that the issue be resolved at an early stage of a lawsuit, to avoid incurring unnecessary expenses of fighting over other issues that may become inconsequential. Unfortunately, the way that the traditional system of litigation has been structured in the U.S., with only slight exception, an appeal from a trial judge's claim construction must await the entry of a final judgment in the litigation.[170] This often necessarily requires further proceedings along with their attendant costs, delay, and uncertainty. The determination made by a trial judge then will be subject to a "de novo" review by the Court of Appeals, meaning that the Court of Appeals effectively will examine all of the evidence and arguments anew in its own form of *Markman* proceeding.[171] This has the potential for all sorts of unpredictable consequences. For example, in the case of *Exxon Corp. v. Lubrizol Corp.*,[172] the appeals court adopted a construction of the specified ingredients of a lubricating oil, which was different

---

168. *See* Eric Dobrusin and Katherine White, *Intellectual Property Litigation—Pretrial Practice* Chapter 15 (Aspen Law & Business 2nd ed.).

169. *Pfizer, Inc. v. Ranbaxy Labs. Ltd.*, 457 F. 3d 1284 (Fed. Cir. 2006) (The court rejected statements made during prosecution of foreign counterparts, "because they were made in response to patentability requirements unique to Danish and European law. *See TI Group Auto Sys. (N. Am.), Inc. v. VDO N. Am. LLC*, 375 F. 3d 1126 (Fed. Cir. 2004).").

170. Examples of provisions that would afford an immediate right to appeal are decisions made in the course of preliminary injunction proceedings (*see* 28 U.S.C. § 1292(a)(1)), and when the trial judge has authorized an appeal and the Court of Appeals has agreed to hear the appeal (*see* 28 U.S.C. § 1292(b)); *see also* Fed. R. Civ. Pro. P. 54(b).

171. *Cybor v. FAS Techs*, 138 F. 3d 1448 (Fed. Cir. 1998).

172. 64 F. 3d 1553 (Fed. Cir. 1995).

from the decision of the trial judge, and which was a construction that was not advanced by either party before the trial judge.[173] In denying the request for a rehearing one concurring member of the court stated:

> This is another example of the predicted mischief of *Markman v. Westview Instruments, Inc.* . . . Two judges have divined an interpretation of the claim that occurred to no one else in this extensive litigation. None of the parties or the trial court offered the interpretation that these two judges chose, and none of the extensive extrinsic evidence about how those skilled in the art would understand the claim supports it. After *Markman*, apparently the meaning of a claim has very little to do with the parties' theories of the case and the record made in support, and everything to do with what at least two judges here prefer regardless of the record.[174]

The uncertainties occasioned by this procedure has been the source of much frustration of litigants and has prompted attempts at legislation to change the process. For example, after only a few years after the *Markman* decision, the Federal Circuit commented:

> From the patent practitioner's standpoint, this court's enthusiastic assertion of its unfettered review authority has the potential to undercut the benefits of *Markman I*. *Markman I* potentially promised to supply early certainty about the meaning of a patent claim. This certainty, in turn, would prompt early settlement of many, if not most, patent suits. Once the parties know the meaning of the claims, they can predict with some reliability the likelihood of a favorable judgment, factor in the economics of the infringement, and arrive at a settlement to save the costs of litigation. *Markman I* promised to provide this benefit early in the trial court process. To provide fairness under the *Markman I* regime, trial judges would provide claim interpretations before the expense of trial. Patent practitioners would then be armed with knowledge of the probable outcome of the litigation and could facilitate settlement.
>
> The problem with this plan was in its implementation because as a question of law, a claim interpretation is subject to free review by the appellate court. The Federal Circuit, according to its own official 1997 statistics, reversed in whole or in part 53% of the cases from district courts (27% fully reversed; 26% reversed-in-part). Granted this figure deals with all issues in cases with many issues. Nonetheless, one study shows that the plenary standard of review has produced reversal, in whole or in part, of almost 40% of all claim constructions since *Markman I*. A reversal rate in this range reverses more than the work of numerous trial courts; it also reverses the benefits of *Markman I*. In fact, this reversal

---

173. *Ibid.*
174. *Exxon Chemical Patents, Inc. v. Lubrizol Corp.*, 77 F. 3d 450 (Fed. Cir. 1996).

rate, hovering near 50%, is the worst possible. Even a rate that was much higher would provide greater certainty.

Instead, the current *Markman I* regime means that the trial court's early claim interpretation provides no early certainty at all, but only opens the bidding. The meaning of a claim is not certain (and the parties are not prepared to settle) until nearly the last step in the process—decision by the Court of Appeals for the Federal Circuit. To get a certain claim interpretation, parties must go past the district court's *Markman I* proceeding, past the entirety of discovery, past the entire trial on the merits, past post trial motions, past briefing and argument to the Federal Circuit—indeed past every step in the entire course of federal litigation, except, Supreme Court review. In implementation, a *de novo* review of claim interpretations has postponed the point of certainty to the end of the litigation process, at which point, of course, every outcome is certain anyway.[175]

6.3 Public Notice Function of Patents

The emphasis placed by the courts upon the intrinsic evidence of a patent is a reflection of the recognition of the importance of the public notice function that is played by a patent document. The public notice function of patents is a term that recurs throughout the patent jurisprudence.[1] It is frequently cited as a justification for limiting the scope of a patent claim construction or of the range of equivalents that might be afforded under the doctrine of equivalents. Courts frequently ground their decisions in the rationale that a competitor should be able to reasonably rely upon the statements made by a patentee in the written public record that surrounds a patent.

Consider the following rationale expressed by the Court of Appeals for the Federal Circuit in the 2001 case of *Pall Corp. v. PTI Technologies Inc.*,:[2]

> The public notice function of patents requires that a patentee be prevented from expressly stating during prosecution that the claims do not cover a particular device and then later suing for infringement by that same device. Allowing such a suit would be unfair to the public, particularly the manufacturer of the accused device, which was entitled to rely on the surrender of claimed subject matter made in the prosecution history and contained in the file wrapper. *Hockerson-Halberstadt*. . . (stating that, in the context of claim construction, "the prosecution history constitutes a public record of the patentee's representations concerning the scope and the meaning of the claims, and competitors are entitled to rely on those representations when ascertaining the degree of lawful conduct. . . . Were we to accept [the accused infringer's] position, we would undercut the public's reliance on a statement that was in the public record and upon

---

175. *Cybor v. FAS Technologies*, 138 F. 3d 1448, 1475-76 (Fed. Cir. 1998) (*en banc*).

which reasonable competitors formed their business strategies") (internal citations omitted); *Vitronics*, . . . (in the context of claim construction, stating that "[t]he claims, specification, and file history . . . constitute the public record of the patentee's claim, a record on which the public is entitled to rely"). We accordingly must construe claims "to exclude any interpretation that was disclaimed during prosecution." *Southwall*, . . . (citations omitted).

1. *See Phillips v. AWH Corp.*, 415 F.3d, 1303, 1319 (Fed. Cir. 2005) (en banc) ("undue reliance on extrinsic evidence poses the risk that it will be used to change the meaning of claims in derogation of the 'indisputable public records consisting of the claims, the specification and the prosecution history,' thereby undermining the public notice function of patents").

2. 259 F.3d 1383, 1393 (Fed. Cir. 2001); *See also* Biogen, Inc. v. Berlex Labs., Inc., 318 F.3d 1132, 1139 (Fed. Cir. 2003) (addressing function of prosecution history "as an official record that is created in the knowledge that its audience is not only the patent examining officials and the applicant, but the interested public.").

The restricted circumstances under which an interlocutory appeal may be taken has been the subject of considerable debate and gained congressional attention, particularly in the context of the patent reform legislation sought to be enacted recently in the U.S. In a letter dated June 13, 2007, to congressional members Leahy and Specter to address the proposed amendment to 28 U.S.C. § 1292(b) for loosening the requirements for interlocutory appeals of claim construction determinations, Chief Judge Michel of the Federal Circuit offered his observations:

The current language makes automatically appealable any order "determining the construction of claims." The parties in typical patent infringement cases dispute several claim terms in many claims, often involving many different patents. Whatever the trial judge determines, one or both parties are nearly always unhappy with one or more terms as construed by the district court. Therefore, I would expect an interlocutory appeal in virtually every patent infringement case as soon as a claim construction order issues. We currently receive about 500 infringement appeals per year. A study by Professor Jay Kesan, of the University of Illinois Law School estimates that the number could double under the bill as currently drafted. Currently, the average patent infringement appeal consumes 11 months from filing to opinion. If the number of appeals per year doubles, the delay could greatly increase, possibly doubling. In my judgment, such extended delays would be intolerable from the standpoint of the corporate litigants.[176]

176. Letter from, Chief Judge Paul Michel to Congressional Members Leahy and Specter, (June 13, 2007); *see also* Kesan and Ball, *How Are Patent Cases Resolved? An Empirical Examination*,

Understanding Patent Validity

Of the organizations that maintain a patent policy, most will include some language to the effect that "it is the policy of the organization to respect the valid and enforceable patent rights of others of which it is aware." More simply stated, the policy is that if an organization is aware of someone else's patent, they will not pirate the technology unless the patent should not have been granted in the first place. As will be explored in further detail in Chapter 11, there are certain requirements for patentability. Not all innovations are entitled to patents.[177] It is the responsibility of the USPTO to examine patent applications in accordance with the statutory requirements for patentability and make the determination as to whether or not to grant a patent. Once the determination to grant a patent is made, the Patent Act confers a special status upon it for purposes of later enforcement. Specifically, the patent enjoys an evidentiary presumption in litigation that each claim of the patent is valid. In other words, the Patent Act operates on the assumption that the Patent Office, the government agency charged with knowledge of all the relevant prior art and the skill to recognize how the person of ordinary skill in the art would regard the subject innovation taking into account the state of the art, properly performed its examination function when it granted a patent for an innovation. Section 282 of the Patent Act states, in pertinent part:

> A patent shall be presumed valid. Each claim of a patent (whether in independent, dependent, or multiple dependent form) shall be presumed valid independently of the validity of other claims; dependent or multiple dependent claims shall be presumed valid even though dependent upon an invalid claim.[178]

The trust that Congress has placed in the USPTO to do a proper job of examination is so great that a party who believes the USPTO mistakenly issued the patent has a burden to prove the mistake by "clear and convincing evidence," a standard of proof not as severe as the "beyond a reasonable doubt" standard of criminal law, but still more strict than the preponderance of the evidence standard by which a patent owner need only satisfy to prove infringement.

University of Illinois College of Law, Law and Economics Working Papers, No. 52 (2006), 84 Wash. L. Rev. 2, 237–312 (2006).

177. Good IP cultures will distinguish between innovation and patentability. A great innovation might not be patentable, but that does not and should not detract from the innovation.
178. 35 U.S.C. § 282.

6.4 **Standards of Proof**

The Court of Appeals for the Federal Circuit addressed the standards of proof in the case of *Price v. Symsek,*[3] and stated:

> The issue of the quantum of proof required to establish priority in an interference with an issued patent, is one of first impression in the Federal Circuit. As articulated in *California ex rel. Cooper v. Mitchell Bros.' Santa Ana Theater*, 454 U.S. 90 (1981):
>
>> Three standards of proof are generally recognized, ranging from the "preponderance of the evidence" standard employed in most civil cases, to the "clear and convincing" standard reserved to protect particularly important interests in a limited number of civil cases, to the requirement that guilt be proved "beyond a reasonable doubt" in a criminal prosecution. See *Addington v. Texas*, 441 U.S. 418, 423-424 (1979). This Court has, on several occasions, held that the "clear and convincing" standard or one of its variants is the appropriate standard of proof in a particular civil case. See *Addington v. Texas*, supra, at 431 (civil commitment); *Rosenbloom v. Metromedia, Inc.*, 403 U.S. 29, 52 (1971) (libel); *Woodby v. INS*, 385 U.S. 276, 285 (1966) (deportation); *Chaunt v. United States*, 364 U.S. 350, 353 (1960) (denaturalization). However, the Court has never required the "beyond a reasonable doubt" standard to be applied in a civil case. "This unique standard of proof, not prescribed or defined in the Constitution, is regarded as a critical part of the 'moral force of the criminal law,' *In re Winship*, 397 U.S., at 364, and we should hesitate to apply it too broadly or casually in noncriminal cases." *Addington v. Texas*, supra, at 428.
>
> *Ibid.* at 93. A requirement of proof by clear and convincing evidence imposes a heavier burden than that imposed by requiring proof by preponderant evidence but a somewhat lighter burden than that imposed by requiring proof beyond a reasonable doubt. *Buildex, Inc. v. Kason Indus., Inc.,.* . . . "Clear and convincing" evidence has been described as evidence which produces in the mind of the trier of fact an abiding conviction that the truth of a factual contention is "highly probable." Ibid. (citing *Colorado v. New Mexico,.* . . . (citations omitted)

---

3. 988 F.2d 1187, 1191 (Fed. Cir. 1993).

Notwithstanding the heightened burden to prove invalidity, the task is not impossible. The Patent Office makes mistakes and grants patents for innovations that do not meet the statutory requirements for a patent grant.

The reasons for the mistakes are varied but generally reduce to a combination of two notable causes. First, as will be discussed in Chapter 11, the finite and compressed amount of time that a relatively small corps of patent examiners must devote to a growing body of patent application filings creates a severe strain on the ability to conduct thorough examination. Second, even if patent examiners had the luxury of an ideal amount time to comfortably examine applications, examiners simply do not have complete access to all relevant prior art. The USPTO continues to make strides toward improving examiner accessibility to prior art. The USPTO has available to it comprehensive databases that include U.S. patents, patents from the patent offices of other examination authorities, and vast archives of nonpatent literature. However, in a large number of disputes, the relevant prior art will be some source that is much less accessible. It may be a source that is not catalogued or archived in an electronically searchable database. It may be an older source that, even if stored electronically, is not stored in a text-searchable format. Examples include an obsolete product, magazine articles, advertisements, product brochures, commercial sales documentation, a trade show presentation, a lecture, or other like activities.[179] Unless this information is known by the patent applicant and cited to the examiner for consideration while the application is pending, the examiner may have no practical way to locate such information.[180]

Though the likelihood of successfully invalidating a patent is lower than avoiding liability through a determination of noninfringement, in many cases, it remains a realistic and viable consideration in the execution of any practice of affording due respect to the valid patent rights of others.

---

179. Efforts to compile nonpatent literature databases have grown. For example, the USPTO has compiled an identification of available databases for searching business method. *See, e.g.,* http://www.uspto.gov/web/menu/busmethp/figurenpl.htm (accessed July 25, 2007).

180. In the U.S., unlike most other countries, patent applicants and their attorneys and agents have an affirmative duty of candor to cite to the patent office material information. Specifically, 37 C.F.R. § 1. 56(a) provides in part:

> A patent by its very nature is affected with a public interest. The public interest is best served, and the most effective patent examination occurs when, at the time an application is being examined, the Office is aware of and evaluates the teachings of all information material to patentability. Each individual associated with the filing and prosecution of a patent application has a duty of candor and good faith in dealing with the Office, which includes a duty to disclose to the Office all information known to that individual to be material to patentability as defined in this section.

> Failure to do so, when done with intention to deceive, can render the patent unenforceable due to inequitable conduct. *See e.g., Bruno Indep. Living Aids, Inc. v. Acorn Mobility Servs., Ltd.,* 394 F. 3d 1348 (Fed. Cir. 2005). One consequence of such a determination in the U.S. is that the patent owner could be ordered to pay the attorney fees of a party defending against an infringement charge, the case qualifying as an "exceptional case" under 35 U.S.C. § 285. *Ibid.* Normally, in the U.S., each party needs to expect to bear its own costs and attorney fees. *See Mach. Corp. of Am. v. Gullfiber AB,* 774 F. 2d 467, 472 (Fed. Cir. 1985) (explaining deviation from "American Rule" concerning fee shifting in patent cases).

Getting Rid of the Occasional Bad Patent

Notwithstanding the frequency that patents are mistakenly granted, the procedures available for attacking patents without a costly legal proceeding are scarce. In fact, in the U.S., challenges to patents may be done through litigation in the courts or in a private arbitration,[181] through a reexamination proceeding in the USPTO,[182] or both. Regrettably, both approaches are costly, involve uncertainty, and take a significant amount of time to resolve.

In the U.S., historically, the most preferred approach to revoke an invalid patent is to pursue an invalidity proceeding in a federal court. Such a proceeding affords the challenging party complete resort to discovery proceedings available under the Federal Rules of Civil Procedure, as well as the ability to raise every possible reason for invalidity. This is a potential benefit to a challenger because, at the outset of such proceeding, the challenger may lack evidence to support, or even an awareness of, certain potential defenses. Many grounds for challenging a patent are based upon facts exclusively within the control of the patent owner, or other third persons, to which the challenger ordinarily lacks access. For example, evidence of the state of mind of a patent owner may be relevant to a challenge under the 35 U.S.C. § 112 best mode requirement, which imposes an obligation on the part of inventors to describe the "best mode contemplated by the inventor of carrying out his invention." Evidence pertaining to commercial activities or public uses of the patent owner also is the type of evidence that discovery would afford access.

In addition, invalidity proceedings offer a significant benefit in that they afford challengers complete rights to participate in the attack of a patent and to respond to positions taken by the patentee. This is a right that commences at the start of a proceeding and does not conclude until the final appeal has been exhausted.

One of the biggest drawbacks to patent invalidity proceedings is the cost, both actual and opportunity cost, and the threshold requirements for invoking the jurisdiction of the courts. In the U.S., invalidity proceedings normally occur as part of a patent infringement litigation, in which the issue of infringement also is in play. Not only is there the expense of hiring attorneys, incurring expert witness fees, costs of court filings, transcripts, photocopying, and other associated expenses, there is also the cost of allocating valuable employees to many hours of record collection, interviews, preparation, and testimony. In addition, challengers are vulnerable to divulging confidential of other sensitive commercial and technical information.

Gaining access to the U.S. courts is another drawback. Article III, Section 2, clause 1, of the Constitution grants access to the courts only upon a "case or

---

181. *See generally* 35 U.S.C. §§ 294 and 135(d).
182. 35 U.S.C. § 301 et seq.

controversy." Mere awareness of a patent, and grounds for its invalidity, is not sufficient to grant jurisdiction. There must be some engagement of the patent owner with the challenger concerning the patent. Specifically, as discussed in the previous chapter, the Court of Appeals for the Federal Circuit has specified that the Constitutional threshold for invoking declaratory jurisdiction may be met upon assertion of the patent rights. Specifically, the court held:

> Article III jurisdiction may be met where the patentee takes a position that puts the declaratory judgment plaintiff in the position of either pursuing arguably illegal behavior or abandoning that which he claims a right to do. We need not define the outer boundaries of declaratory judgment jurisdiction, which will depend on the application of the principles of declaratory judgment jurisdiction to the facts and circumstances of each case. We hold only that where a patentee asserts rights under a patent based on certain identified ongoing or planned activity of another party, and where that party contends that it has the right to engage in the accused activity without license, an Article III case or controversy will arise and the party need not risk a suit for infringement by engaging in the identified activity before seeking a declaration of its legal rights.[183]

As seen from the table below, a reexamination proceeding offers many attractive features, most notably its relatively low cost and the ability, if successful, to achieve a complete revocation of a patent.

Notwithstanding the above benefits, since their commencement in 1982, reexamination proceedings have never been fully embraced by the patent community. Most patent challengers value the right to fully participate in litigation proceedings, with the attendant burdens and intrusions of discovery, then to face the prospect of a patent owner surviving reexamination unscathed, or possibly blemished by only a mere change to some or all of the claims.

As discussed above, the intrinsic evidence that is considered for claim construction could include the prosecution history of a patent. The prosecution history for claim construction, or for establishing prosecution history estoppel, can also include the record created during a reexamination proceeding.[184] It is often the case that a patent emerges from prosecution with insubstantial basis for narrowing the construction of a term on the basis of the prosecution history. Initiating a reexamination proceeding is one way in which a

---

183. *SanDisk Corp. v. STMicroelectronics Inc.*, 480 F. 3d 1372, 1381 (Fed. Cir. 2007); *See also Teva Pharmaceuticals USA Inc. v. Novartis Pharmaceuticals Corp.*, 482 F. 3d 1330 (Fed. Cir. 2007), *But see Benitec Australia, Ltd. v. Nucleonics*, 495 F. 3d 1340 (Fed. Cir. 2007) (addressing justiciability of declaratory judgment action upon dismissal of infringement claim).

184. *See, e.g., Intermatic, Inc. v. Lamson & Sessions Co.*, 273 F. 3d 1355 (Fed. Cir. 2001); *Cole v. Kimberly-Clark Corp.*, 102 F. 3d 524, 532 (Fed. Cir. 1997); *Cf. Arlington Indus., Inc. v. Bridgeport Fittings Inc.*, 345 F. 3d 1318 (Fed. Cir. 2003); *Abbott Labs. v. Novopharm Ltd.*, 323 F. 3d 1324 (Fed. Cir. 2003).

competitor might force a patent owner to take a position in the written record that could be used by a competitor to support a business decision.

Consider the situation in which a patent covers a "mechanically driven garage door opener with an optical motion sensor." The only embodiment of the patent shows a belt-driven opener. During the original prosecution of the application, claims to a garage door opener with a sensor were rejected based on a prior art patent that disclosed a thermal motion sensor with a chain-driven opener. The "optical" feature was added to the claim by the applicant and deemed enough to distinguish over the prior art. The prosecution history, thus, did not address how the opener having driven. A competitor would like to enter the market with a piston-driven garage door opener with an optical motion sensor. The competitor searches some foreign language patents in the European Patent Office and discovers a reference that teaches the piston feature in combination with a motion sensor. The reference appears more relevant to the claims than any of the prior art of record and would satisfy the requirement of 35 U.S.C. § 303 for creating a "substantial new question of patentability." *Ex Parte* reexamination is sought by the competitor and ordered by the USPTO. In the course of prosecution, the patent owner amends the claims to cover a "belt-driven garage door opener with an optical motion sensor," and argues that such "belt-driven" feature is not shown in the prior art and is different from the piston-driven opener of the prior art. Effectively, the patentee has disclaimed from the scope of its patent the feature sought to be employed by the competitor. By pursuing this strategy, the competitor has cleared a potential obstacle. Of course, this strategy should not be tried in every instance. It is considerably more effective when the patentee is unaware, during the reexamination, of the products sought to be offered by the competitor seeking the reexamination.

6.5		
	Litigation	*Ex Parte Reexamination*
Jurisdictional threshold	A contention of a "right to engage" in an accused activity	Substantial new question of patentability
Any reason for invalidity may be asserted	Yes	No
Reasons for invalidity other than patents or printed publications can be asserted	Yes	No

Discovery may be conducted to support assertions	Yes	No
Challenging party can fully participate in the proceeding	Yes	No (but consider inter partes reexamination)
Decisions are appealable	Yes	Yes (by Patentee)
Cost range	More than $1,000,000 est.	Less than $100,000 est.
Challenging party can fully participate in the appeal	Yes	No (but consider inter partes reexamination)
Patent claims can be revoked during proceeding	Yes	Yes
Patent claims can be amended by narrowing their scope during the proceeding	No	Yes
Length of proceeding	Several years	1–2 years

As will be explored further in Chapter 8, elsewhere such as in Europe, there is another way to get rid of the occasional bad patent, and it is called an opposition. In the European Patent Office (EPO), an opposition to a granted patent can be filed within nine months of the grant date and can raise pretty much any issue (usually other than clarity), as well as the citation of new prior art. The proceeding is first on the papers but culminates in an oral hearing at which a panel of three examiners hear the arguments on each issue, and immediately decide whether the patent should be revoked or not. Statistically, only about 5 percent of the granted EPO patents are opposed.[185] However, oppositions may be used as a viable business strategy to cast doubt on the worldwide patent family of a competitor while the opposition is pending, and after, if the EPO revokes the patent.

---

185. *See generally*, http://www.aplf.org/2005-statistics-for-epo-oppositions-and-appeals-2/ (as accessed April 5, 2008).

Infringement

In general, the right granted by a patent is the right to exclude others from making, using, selling, offering to sell, or importing the patented invention, as set forth in 35 U.S.C. § 271(a). The patent claims (the numbered paragraphs at the end of the patent) define the metes and bounds of the invention.[186] The claims are the only part of a patent that a person can infringe.[187] Thus, it does not necessarily matter if a competing machine has the identical structure as a machine shown in the drawings of a patent. If the claims do not cover the competing machine (and thus also the machine of the drawings), there is no infringement. Along these lines, another confusing scenario involves the situation when a competing product is identical to a commercial product, purported to be commercialized by the patent owner under a patent. If at least one claim of the patent does not cover the competing product (and thus also the patent owner's product, even if it is marked with the patent number), then there can be no infringement.[188] Again, infringement is only

---

186. *Hoechst-Roussel Pharms., Inc., v. Lehman*, 109 F. 3d 756 (Fed. Cir. 1997) (citing *Corning Glass Works v. Sumitomo Elec. U.S.A, Inc.*, 868 F. 2d 1251, 1257 (Fed. Cir. 1989)).

187. *SRI Int'l v. Matsushita Elec. Corp. of Am.*, 775 F. 2d 1107, 1121 (Fed. Cir. 1985) (*en banc*). In *Phillips v. AWH Corp.*, 415 F. 3d 1303, 1312 (Fed. Cir. 2005) (en banc), the *en banc* court reiterated:

> It is a "bedrock principle" of patent law that "the claims of a patent define the invention to which the patentee is entitled the right to exclude." *Innova*, 381 F. 3d at 1115; *See also Vitronics*, 90 F. 3d at 1582 ("we look to the words of the claims themselves … to define the scope of the patented invention"); *Markman*, 52 F. 3d at 980 ("The written description part of the specification itself does not delimit the right to exclude. That is the function and purpose of claims. "). That principle has been recognized since at least 1836, when Congress first required that the specification include a portion in which the inventor "shall particularly specify and point out the part, improvement, or combination, which he claims as his own invention or discovery." Act of July 4, 1836, ch. 357, § 6, 5 Stat. 117, 119. In the following years, the Supreme Court made clear that the claims are "of primary importance, in the effort to ascertain precisely what it is that is patented." *Merrill v. Yeomans*, 94 U.S.568, 570 (1876). Because the patentee is required to "define precisely what his invention is," the Court explained, it is "unjust to the public, as well as an evasion of the law, to construe it in a manner different from the plain import of its terms." *White v. Dunbar*, 119 U.S.47, 52 (1886); *See also Cont'l Paper Bag Co. v. E. Paper Bag Co.*, 210 U.S.405, 419 (1908) ("the claims measure the invention"); *McCarty v. Lehigh Valley R. R. Co.*, 160 U.S.110, 116 (1895) ("if we once begin to include elements not mentioned in the claim, in order to limit such claim . . . , we should never know where to stop"); *Aro Mfg. Co. v. Convertible Top Replacement Co.*, 365 U.S.336, 339 (1961) ("the claims made in the patent are the sole measure of the grant").

188. The courts are prohibited from making infringement determinations on the basis of a comparison of an accused product and a commercial product offered by the patent owner under the patent. In *AquaTex Indus., Inc. v. Techniche Solutions*, 479 F. 3d 1320, 1327-28 (Fed. Cir. 2007), the Federal Circuit reiterated:

possible on the basis of a comparison of the competing product with the subject matter described in the patent claims.

Most patents have more than one claim. However, there need not be infringement of every claim to establish infringement. A patent owner need only prove infringement of a single patent claim, and the patent is deemed to be infringed.[189] In litigation, the burden of proving the infringement is placed on the patent owner and need only be satisfied by a preponderance of evidence.[190] The difference between independent claims and dependent claims can be determined from looking at the claims; if a claim refers to an earlier claim (e.g., A method of claim 1. . . .), then it is a dependent claim.[191] If the competitor can establish that the underlying independent claim is not infringed, then the dependent claim cannot be infringed either, because the feature missing from the independent claim is also missing from the dependent claim, which incorporates such feature by reference.[192]

6.6
It is a common misconception, particularly by persons with limited exposure to patents, to conclude they are foreclosed from practicing the feature of the dependent claim, even when such persons do not employ each feature of the independent claim. This tends to work wonderful advantages for patent owners, who themselves often lack knowledge of the difference between independent and dependent claims, and will make inaccurate statements in the marketplace about the coverage of their patents.

"Infringement, either literally or under the doctrine of equivalents, does not arise by comparing the accused product . . . with a commercialized embodiment of the patentee." *Johnson & Johnston Assocs. Inc. v. R. E. Serv. Co.*, 285 F. 3d 1046, 1052 (Fed. Cir. 2002) (en banc) (internal quotation marks omitted); *See also* Donald S. Chisum, 5A *Chisum on Patents* §18. 04[1][b] (2005). Similarly, we noted in *Amstar Corp. v. Envirotech Corp.*, 730 F. 2d 1476 (Fed. Cir. 1984), "[i]nfringement is not determined . . . by comparison between commercial products sold by the parties." *Ibid.* at 1481–82.

189. *Pall Corp. v. Micron Separations, Inc.*, 66 F. 3d 1211, 1220 (Fed. Cir. 1995) (citing *Intervet Am., Inc. v. Kee-Vet Labs., Inc.*, 887 F. 2d 1050, 1055 (Fed. Cir. 1989)).

190. *Mannesmann Demag Corp. v. Engineered Metal Prods. Co.*, 793 F. 2d 1279, 1282 (Fed. Cir. 1986); *see also Mariquip, Inc. v. Fosber Am., Inc.*, 198 F. 3d 1363 (Fed. Cir. 1999)

191. By way of refresher, the independent claims are the complete paragraph claims that do not refer to another claim. The dependent claims, by definition (*See* 35 U.S.C. § 112), will directly or indirectly refer to an independent claim and will incorporate by reference all of the features of the independent claim.

192. *Wahpeton Canvas Co. v. Frontier, Inc.*, 870 F. 2d 1546, 1553 (Fed. Cir. 1989) ("dependent claims cannot be found infringed unless the claims from which they depend have been found to have been infringed").

The above addresses where to look to conduct an infringement analysis. But as to what constitutes an appropriate analysis, there are two types of infringement. The first type, literal infringement, requires that every feature recited in the claim is found in the competing subject matter.[193] The second type, infringement under the doctrine of equivalents, addresses the situation when the competing subject matter omits one or more features of the claim, employing in its place an insubstantially different feature. In the analysis of both types of infringement, the starting point is claim construction.[194] As discussed above, this involves an examination of the intrinsic evidence for the patent and may also explore extrinsic evidence.[195]

After construing the claims, the resulting construed claims are compared with the competing subject matter (e.g., by claim charts, as discussed in Chapter 2). If a single feature is absent, there is no literal infringement. The claim could have 300 individual features and the competing device can copy 299 of them, even including the feature that distinguished the claim from the prior art. But if just a single feature is omitted, there is no literal infringement.

6.7 "Single" Axioms

1. Infringement of a single patent claim constitutes infringement of the entire patent.
2. Omission in a competing product of a single feature of a single claim can avoid infringement of that claim.
3. Noninfringement of a single patent claim does not avoid infringement of the entire patent.

---

193. *Maxwell v. J. Baker, Inc.*, 86 F. 3d 1098, 1105 (Fed. Cir. 1996) ("[t]o literally infringe, the accused device must contain every limitation of the asserted claim"); *See also Bayer Ag v. Elan Pharm. Research Corp.*, 212 F. 3d 1241 (Fed. Cir. 2000).

194. The Court of Appeals for the Federal Circuit stated, in *Lifescan, Inc. v. Home Diagnostics, Inc.*, 76 F. 3d 358, 359 (Fed. Cir. 1996):

> [I]nfringement is determined by a two-step analysis. In the first step the claims are interpreted by the court, as a matter of law. In the second step, the claims are applied to the accused device by the trier of fact. This procedure applies whether the issue is of literal infringement or infringement by equivalency.

195. Pursuant to *Markman v. Westview Instruments, Inc.*, 577 U.S. 370, 134 L. Ed. 2d 577 (1996), claims are interpreted as a matter of law by a court. The matter of claim construction must be determined based upon a review of intrinsic evidence, namely the claims, the specification and the file history (if in evidence); *See Pitney Bowes, Inc. v. Hewlett-Packard Co.*, 182 F. 3d. 1298 (Fed. Cir. 1999), *Vitronics Corp. v. Conceptronic, Inc.*, 90 F. 3d 1576 (Fed. Cir. 1996) (regarding the use of extrinsic evidence only if an ambiguity exists after consideration of the intrinsic evidence); *See also, Phillips v. AWH Corp.*, 415 F. 3d 1303 (Fed. Cir. 2005) (*en banc*) (addressing the use of dictionaries or treatises to establish the ordinary meaning of a claim term).

> 4. Noninfringement of a single independent claim avoids infringement of all claims dependent from the independent claim.
> 5. Invalidity of a single patent claim does not render the entire patent invalid.

Even if a product does not infringe a claim literally, the inquiry does not end, because the product may still infringe the claim under the doctrine of equivalents. The doctrine of equivalents has its historical basis in case law in which the U.S. Supreme Court recognized that certain circumstances will make it unfair for a competitor to avoid a finding of infringement as a result of the mere omission of a claimed feature. Arising out of the desire to prevent patent piracy the court has formulated certain standards for analyzing infringement under the doctrine of equivalents, which focus upon the "substantiality of differences" between the claimed subject matter and the competitive subject matter.[196]

Perhaps the most well known landmark Supreme Court case in the U.S. addressing the doctrine of equivalents is the case of *Graver Tank & Mfg. Co. v. Linde Air Prods. Co.*[197] In that case, the court determined that there was infringement of a patent claiming a welding flux that employed an alkaline earth metal silicate when the accused substituted manganese (not an alkaline earth metal) for magnesium. In the *Graver Tank* case, the Supreme Court introduced the "function, way, result" test for analyzing infringement. That test remains in use presently and remains the most common analysis applied by the courts. The court reasoned:

> It is difficult to conceive of a case more appropriate for application of the doctrine of equivalents. The disclosures of the prior art made clear that manganese silicate was a useful ingredient in welding compositions. Specialists familiar with the problems of welding compositions understood that manganese was equivalent to and could be substituted for magnesium in the composition of the patented flux and their observations were confirmed by the literature of chemistry. Without some explanation or indication that Lincolnweld was developed by independent research, the trial court could properly infer that the accused flux is the result of imitation rather than experimentation or invention. Though infringement was not literal, the changes which avoid literal infringement are colorable only. We conclude that the trial court's judgment of infringement respecting the four flux claims was proper, and we adhere to our prior decision on this aspect of the case.[198]

---

196. *See Warner-Jenkinson Co. v. Hilton Davis Chem. Co.*, 520 U.S. 17 (1997).
197. 339 U.S. 605 (1950) ("The essence of the doctrine is that one may not practice a fraud on a patent.").
198. *Ibid.* at 611–12.

As can be appreciated, the existence of the doctrine of equivalents, while serving an important function of preventing appropriation of inventions by skirting imprecise verbiage in the patent claims, presents considerable opportunity for mischief by patent owners. Consequently, in the context of upholding the public notice function of patents, the courts have imposed restrictions on the application of the doctrine of equivalents. For example, among the restrictions now imposed on the doctrine of equivalents is "prosecution history estoppel." This doctrine focuses on the public notice function performed by the patent application file that is published by the Patent Office for each patent. Premised upon the consideration that competitors[199] should be entitled to rely upon the record surrounding a patent, the doctrine effectively dictates that amendments or material representations made during the prosecution of a patent, in order to obtain allowance of an applicant's claims, may estop or prevent a subsequent different or broader interpretation of the claims asserted by way of the doctrine of equivalents.

The Supreme Court addressed this doctrine in *Festo Corp. v. Shoketsu Kinzoku Kogyo Kabushiki Co.,*[200] and ruled:

> A patentee's decision to narrow his claims through amendment may be presumed to be a general disclaimer of the territory between the original claim and the amended claim. . . . There are some cases, however, where the amendment cannot reasonably be viewed as surrendering a particular equivalent. The equivalent may have been unforeseeable at the time of the application; the rationale underlying the amendment may bear no more than a tangential relation to the equivalent in question; or there may be some other reason suggesting that the patentee could not reasonably be expected to have described the insubstantial substitute in question. In those cases the patentee can overcome the presumption that prosecution history estoppel bars a finding of equivalence.

> This presumption is not, then, just the complete bar by another name. Rather, it reflects the fact that the interpretation of the patent must begin with its literal claims, and the prosecution history is relevant to construing those claims. When the patentee has chosen to narrow a claim, courts may presume the amended text was composed with awareness of this rule and that the territory surrendered is not an equivalent of the territory claimed. In those instances, however, the patentee still might rebut the presumption that estoppel bars a claim of equivalence. The patentee must show that at the time of the amendment one skilled in the art could not reasonably be expected to have drafted a claim that would have literally encompassed the alleged equivalent.

---

199. *Haynes Int'l., Inc. v. Jessop Steel Co.,* 8 F. 3d 1573, 1578 n. 4 (Fed. Cir. 1993).
200. 535 U.S. 722, 740–41 (2002).

Prosecution history estoppel is not the only basis for restricting the doctrine of equivalents. Other doctrines have emerged, including the "all-limitations" or "all-elements" rule, and the "disclosure-dedication" rule.[201]

By way of illustration of the "disclosure-dedication" rule, suppose a patent expressly discloses that the subject device can be made of metal or plastic, but the claims specifically require that the device be made of plastic. Under the "disclosure-dedication" rule, the disclosure of alternative metal and plastic materials, with the claiming of only plastic, dedicates to the public the use of metal. A competitive device made of metal, thus, should be deemed to avoid infringement, even though it may have been considered an equivalent when the application was drafted.

In contrast with the relatively straightforward analysis invited by the "disclosure-dedication" rule, the body of cases that has emerged under the "all-limitations" or "all-elements" rule makes the application of that rule and its outcome less predictable. Essentially, the rule calls for an analysis under the doctrine of equivalents such that each feature of the claim finds correspondence somewhere in the accused device. Along these lines, if the claims recite a certain feature in a way that would specifically exclude certain subject matter from its scope, the rule may be invoked. One particular case from the Federal Circuit that illustrates application of the "all-limitations or all-elements" rule is that of *Moore, U.S.A., Inc. v. Standard Register Co.,*[202] in which the court explained:

> If our case law on the doctrine of equivalents makes anything clear, it is that all claim limitations are not entitled to an equal scope of equivalents. Whether the result of the All Limitations Rule, *See Pennwalt Corp. v. Durand-Wayland, Inc.,* 833 F. 2d 931, 934-35, (Fed. Cir. 1987) (*en banc*), prosecution history estoppel, *See Warner-Jenkinson*, 520 U.S. at 33–34, or the inherent narrowness of the claim language, *see Sage* . . . , many limitations warrant little, if any, range of equivalents . . . .
>
> In this case, we hold that the applicant's use of the term "majority" is not entitled to a scope of equivalents covering a minority for at least two reasons. First, to allow what is undisputedly a minority (i.e., 47.8%) to be equivalent to a majority would vitiate the requirement that the "first and second longitudinal strips of adhesive . . . extend the majority of the lengths of said longitudinal marginal portions." '464 patent, col. 10, ll. 56-60. If a minority could be equivalent to a majority, this limitation would hardly be necessary, since the immediately preceding requirement of a "first and second longitudinal strips of adhesive disposed in

---

201. *Johnson & Johnston Assocs., Inc. v. R. E. Serv. Co.*, 285 F. 3d 1046 (Fed. Cir. 2002) (*en banc* Court addressing effect of disclosed but not claimed subject matter); *See also, Wilson Sporting Goods Co. v. David Geoffrey & Assocs.*, 904 F. 2d 677, 684 (Fed. Cir. 1990), *cert. denied*, 112 L. Ed. 2d 547 (1990) (addressing more complicated "hypothetical claim" analysis).
202. 229 F. 3d 1091, 1106 (Fed. Cir. 2000) (citation omitted).

said first and second longitudinal marginal portions, respectively, of said first face" would suffice. Second, it would defy logic to conclude that a minority—the very antithesis of a majority—could be insubstantially different from a claim limitation requiring a majority, and no reasonable juror could find otherwise.

In some instances, it is also possible to avoid infringement by equivalents merely by virtue of the fact that the competitive technology realizes the same disadvantages sought to have been overcome by the patented subject matter.[203] Thus, for example, a patent claiming a method for operating a motor using wood as a fuel source might characterize operation of a prior art gasoline burning motor as disadvantageous because its fuel source emitted particulates of a certain size that could not be filtered using off-the-shelf filters. The claimed subject matter overcame that disadvantage by the selection of wood. The accused subject matter burns ethanol, in contrast, and emits particulates of such a size that off-the-shelf filters can not be employed. Under these facts, the competitor in this scenario likely would have a sound basis for avoiding infringement by equivalents. In short, the law of the doctrine of equivalents has the potential to make murky the analysis of infringement.

"But We Sell Only One Part; Someone Else Assembles It Elsewhere"

Another common misconception in the patent world is that infringement can be avoided by virtue of commercializing less than the entirety of a claimed combination. For example, a competitor may seek to avoid infringement of a patent claiming a jet engine by selling a turbine blade, but not the turbine rotor or the engine housing. Likewise, a competitor might seek to avoid infringement of a patent for a sweetened beverage by merely supplying the artificial flavoring, which is incorporated by the beverage manufacturer into the ultimate beverage.

The Patent Act recognizes the potential for these kinds of situations, in which a patent might not be infringed by any of a number of components but

---

203. *Dawn Equip. Co. v. Ky. Farms, Inc.*, 140 F. 3d 1009 (Fed. Cir. 1998), the court held:

> The '282 patent, in its Background of the Invention section, describes the problems with prior art "multi-hole pinned height adjustment" mechanisms. The patent teaches that such mechanisms are time-consuming to adjust and are prone to misadjustment by inserting the pin in the wrong holes, and furthermore the loose pins in such mechanisms are easily lost. '282 patent, col. 2, ll. 12-29. Kentucky Farms' multiple-hole, pinned height-adjustment mechanism is such a mechanism and shares these same problems. In contrast, the '282 patent teaches that the mechanism provided by the patented invention is directed at solving these problems. *Ibid.* at col. 2, ll. 31-34. These statements in the patent alone strongly suggest, if not mandate, judgment in Kentucky Farms' favor.

would be infringed when those components are assembled or used in combination.[204] Specifically, 35 U.S.C. § 271 effectively creates vicarious liability (contributory infringement or inducing infringement) provisions for situations in which substantial contributors—or persons who aid and abet or otherwise participate indirectly in a patent infringement—may become liable for infringement though their individual acts do not amount to a direct infringement. The prohibitions apply not only to acts contributing to the supply of less than all of a claimed combination, but could apply to acts performed abroad.

Paying respect to the patent rights of others, thus, requires not merely an examination of an organization's own conduct. It generally will also require due consideration of activities all along the supply chain, as well as an examination of how the subject matter will be used by any of its customers.

---

204. 35 U.S.C. § 271; *See Aro Mfg. Co. v. Convertible Top Replacement Co.*, 365 U.S. 336, 339 (1961), and *Microsoft Corp. v. AT&T Corp.*, 127 S. Ct. 1746 (U.S. 2007).

Instructive of the policy underlying the doctrine of contributory infringement is the case of *Dawson Chemical Company et al. v. Rohm and Haas Company,* 448 U.S. 176, 187-88 (U.S. 1980), where the Supreme Court stated:

As we have noted, the doctrine of contributory infringement had its genesis in an era of simpler and less subtle technology. Its basic elements are perhaps best explained with a classic example drawn from that era. In *Wallace v. Holmes,* supra, the patentee had invented a new burner for an oil lamp. In compliance with the technical rules of patent claiming, this invention was patented in a combination that also included the standard fuel reservoir, wick tube, and chimney necessary for a properly functioning lamp. After the patent issued, a competitor began to market a rival product including the novel burner but not the chimney. 29 F.Cas., at 79. Under the sometimes scholastic law of patents, this conduct did not amount to direct infringement, because the competitor had not replicated every single element of the patentee's claimed combination. Cf., e.g., *Prouty v. Ruggles,* 16 Pet. 336, 341 (1842). Yet the court held that there had been "palpable interference" with the patentee's legal rights, because purchasers would be certain to complete the combination, and hence the infringement, by adding the glass chimney. 29 F.Cas., at 80. The court permitted the patentee to enforce his rights against the competitor who brought about the infringement, rather than requiring the patentee to undertake the almost insuperable task of finding and suing all the innocent purchasers who technically were responsible for completing the infringement. Ibid. *See also Bowker v. Dows,* 3 F.Cas. 1070 (No. 1734) (CC Mass. 1878).

The *Wallace* case demonstrates, in a readily comprehensible setting, the reason for the contributory infringement doctrine. It exists to protect patent rights from subversion by those who, without directly infringing the patent themselves, engage in acts designed to facilitate infringement by others. This protection is of particular importance in situations, like the oil lamp case itself, where enforcement against direct infringers would be difficult, and where the technicalities of patent law make it relatively easy to profit from another's invention without risking a charge of direct infringement.

6.8 Consequences of Patent Infringement

—**Money Damages:** minimum of reasonable royalty[4]; lost profits possible[5]
—**Injunction:** not automatic[6]
—**Prejudgment Interest:** authorized[7]
—**Increased Damages:** possible under Section 284 up to three times

It is tempting for many competitors to gauge their downside if faced with litigation as merely their unit sales totals multiplied by a percentage royalty. As a matter of likelihoods, most litigated cases will result in resolution on the basis of such a license. However, the occasional case sometimes goes astray and, in addition to a claim for triple damages for willful infringement, will include a claim for damages under the "Entire Market Value" rule, which can take a royalty foreseen as cents per unit sales and quickly escalate it to dollars per unit.[8]

---

4. 35 U.S.C. § 284; *See also Georgia-Pacific Corp. v. U.S. Plywood Corp.*, 318 F. Supp. 1116, 1120 (S.D.N.Y. 1970).
5. *See generally Rite-Hite Corp. v. Kelley Co., Inc.*, 56 F.3d 1538, 1545 (Fed. Cir. 1995) (*en banc*) ("The *Panduit* test requires that a patentee establish: (1) demand for the patented product; (2) abs ence of acceptable non-infringing substitutes; (3) manufacturing and marketing capability to exploit the demand; and (4) the amount of profit it would have made."); and *Panduit Corp. v. Stahlin Bros. Fibre Works, Inc.*, 575 F.2d 1152 (6th Cir. 1978).
6. *eBay, Inc. v. MercExchange*, LLC, 126 S. Ct. 1837 (2006).
7. *See* 35 U.S.C. § 284; *Gen. Motors Corp. v. Devex Corp.*, 461 U.S. 648 (1983).
8. Referring to *Rite-Hite Corp. v. Kelley Co.*, 56 F.3d 1538 (Fed. Cir. 1995) (*en banc*). The Federal Circuit concisely explained the "entire market value" rule as applying where the customer demand for an entire apparatus is based upon the patented feature in the case of *Imonex Servs., Inc. v. W. H. Munzprufer Dietmar Trenner GmbH*, 408 F.3d 1374 (Fed. Cir. 2005).

License When You Can

As will be discussed in greater detail in Chapter 7, another way of paying respect to the valid patent rights of others is to license patent rights. A license is effectively a grant of permission by a patent owner to infringe a patent. Normally, the quid pro quo for a license is a royalty payment, which may be a lump sum, an on-going obligation, or some other arrangement. In some instances, it is a cross license, by which the challenger grants to the patent owner a license, such as under a patent right owned by the challenger.

A very important point that an organization must consider is that the grant of a patent license is not an automatic right in the U.S. Though some countries have provisions for compulsory licenses, the U.S. does not.[205] Indeed, the law does not regard the unilateral refusal of a patent owner to license its technology as anticompetitive.[206]

Of course, it should also be borne in mind that recent Supreme Court case law makes clear that a patentee is not automatically entitled to an injunction upon prevailing in an infringement action.[207] The inevitable outcome of an infringement dispute may very well be a compulsory license.

Designing Around a Competitor's Patent: What's the Problem?

Of all the ways to pay respect to the valid patent rights of others, perhaps the one most misperceived, but most consistent with the policies underlying the patent system, is the practice of designing around a patent. Designing around a patent involves first performing a claim construction, comparing the claim to the product or process at issue, and then finding at least one claim element that can be eliminated from the product or changed in the product such that it is not included either literally or under the doctrine of equivalents. Typically, a team of people, including patent attorneys, engineers, sales and marketing, and business people will be involved in any product changes. Regrettably, to most novices in the patent world, the phrase "designing around" connotes some sinister or cheating state of mind, but that is not the case.

The practice of "designing around" a patent is favored by the courts. The Court of Appeals historically has expressed its positive attitude toward design-around programs. For example, in the case of *WMS Gaming Inc. v. International Game Technology,*[208] the Federal Circuit stated that:

> the patent law encourages competitors to design or invent around existing patents. See *Westvaco Corp. v. International Paper Co.,* . . . ; See also *State Indus., Inc.*

---

205. See also Chapter 7; one illustrative comparative analysis of compulsory licensing is provided in http://www.ipo.org/AM/CM/ContentDisplay.cfm?ContentFileID=6484&FusePreview=Yes (accessed July 26, 2007).

206. See 35 U.S.C. § 271(d)(4):
  d) No patent owner otherwise entitled to relief for infringement or contributory infringement of a patent shall be denied relief or deemed guilty of misuse or illegal extension of the patent right by reason of his having done one or more of the following:
  (4) refused to license or use any rights to the patent. . . .
  See also *Intergraph Corp. v. Intel Corp.,* 195 F. 3d 1346 (Fed. Cir. 1999).

207. *eBay, Inc. v. MercExchange, LLC,* 126 S. Ct. 1837 (2006).

208. 184 F. 3d 1339, 1355 (Fed. Cir. 1999); see also *Slimfold Mfg. Co. v. Kinkead Indus., Inc.,* 932 F. 2d 1453 (Fed. Cir. 1991) (citations omitted).

v. A. O. Smith Corp., . . . (explaining that designing around existing patents promotes competition to the benefit of consumers)."

Likewise, in the case of *Westvaco Corp. v. Int'l Paper Co.*,[209] the Federal Circuit expressed:

"[D]esigning or inventing around patents to make new inventions is encouraged." *London v. Carson Pirie Scott & Co.*, ... [K]eeping track of a competitor's products and designing new and possibly better or cheaper functional equivalents is the stuff of which competition is made and is supposed to benefit the consumer. One of the benefits of a patent system is its so-called "negative incentive" to "design around" a competitor's products, even when they are patented, thus bringing a steady flow of innovations to the marketplace. It should not be discouraged by punitive damage awards except in cases where conduct is so obnoxious as clearly to call for them. The world of competition is full of "fair fights". . . . *State Indus., Inc. v. A. O. Smith Corp.*, . . .

It is true that, in some instances, a design around will involve only slight changes from the patented subject matter. In those instances, a successful design around is in reality a testimonial to the weakness of the particular patent. A patent that is written so that only a slight change avoids infringement (even under the doctrine of equivalents) is typically a patent that grants in a crowded technological field for an incremental improvement to the state of the art. It is for that reason that the patent did not grant with broad claim scope in the first place.

A more typical design around will have the effect contemplated by the courts. In the course of designing around a patent, the examination of the teachings of the patent will cause the competitor to identify newer and better ways to accomplish the result sought, to accomplish better results, or both. The solutions developed by the competitor, in turn, could form the basis of a patent for the competitor. The resulting disclosure of the competitor's solution contributes to progressing the state of the art, and invites further progression by other competitors.

Unless done by a person well versed in the principles of patent laws, design-around activities should almost always be conducted under the supervision or with the assistance of experienced patent counsel. As will be gleaned throughout this book, the patent laws are loaded with subtleties and nuances. Even though most analyses are undertaken from the viewpoint of the person skilled in the art, it is difficult to expect the skilled artisan to be able to know and comprehend the vast body of patent jurisprudence that exists.

---

209. 991 F. 2d 735, 745 (Fed. Cir. 1993) (citations omitted).

Designing around patent claims should be contrasted with reverse engineering a product. In the first, you are examining your own product versus another's patent, while in the latter, you are taking apart another's product. With certain exceptions (e.g., when an agreement precluding reverse engineering exists, or when copyrights or other IP rights must be violated to deconstruct the product) reverse engineering is generally lawful. As the Supreme Court stated, "the competitive reality of reverse engineering may act as a spur to the inventor, creating an incentive to develop inventions which meet the rigorous requirements of patentability."[210]

---

210. *Bonito Boats, Inc. v. Thunder Craft Boats, Inc.*, 489 U.S. 141, 161 (1989).

CHAPTER
7

Constructively Sharing and Transferring Intellectual Property

Different Scenarios

Just as some social cultures have become refined because of the diversity of experience and customs that its respective members bring, the potential for some intellectual achievements to best serve a group is by some form of technological integration or sharing by members of the group. Sharing IP can take many forms, from the disclosure of confidential information, to licensing, and even to complete transfers of rights. Sharing IP within an organization, as well as outside of an organization allows other organizations to invest in the IP, often with a synergistic result that improves the technology for the benefit of both the originating entity and the investor.

Intellectual property sharing occurs in a number of different scenarios, which may be prompted by any number of different stimuli. It may be voluntary or involuntary. For instance, an infringement lawsuit may result in the patent owner being unable to get an injunction against the infringer. Alternatively, a common customer may insist that certain IP be licensed to a competitor to ensure that supply will be uninterrupted. The patent owner, in both of these instances, will need to share the patent involuntarily with an infringer, hopefully at least being subject to some royalty payment.[211] More commonly, intellectual property sharing is a voluntary process. For example, it may arise from a plan of an organization to derive royalties by licensing its IP. This is a common model with university-invented technologies. In industry, for example, Texas Instruments and IBM have been lauded for their licensing programs.

The good and bad about sharing IP is that it usually comes down to an issue of money. In some industries, this works well. For example, in the pharmaceutical industry, rights to exploit a drug in a particular territory are commonly licensed for substantial payments. In the computer or integrated circuit industry, royalties per unit sold are also common.[212] In these industries, the strength of the intellectual property is tested, but respected, with full value coming from the product it protects.

IP sharing may be mutual. For example, cross-licensing is a mutual process commonly employed when two or more organizations require the use of the other's IP to commercialize a technology. It is especially common when the technology of each party does or will infringe a patent of the other. In that scenario, the parties have the option to sue each other (spending years in

---

211. The touchstone of almost every transaction that involves sharing of IP is the consideration paid for the right to share. The most widely practiced measurement of consideration is the royalty payment. Determination of a royalty is never easy, and the theories for setting a royalty are numerous. A royalty may be paid as a percentage of sales. It may be paid on a per use basis. It may be a lump-sum payment or series of payments. In some instances, a technology has yet to be proven or the IP has yet to be validated. In those situations, it is not uncommon for royalties to be structured as milestone payments (e.g., the payment of a certain amount upon the occurrence of a certain event, such as first sales, regulatory approval, grant of a patent, or otherwise).

212. Indeed, some companies have a business model that relies upon sharing IP. For example, Tessera Technologies (www.tessera.com) invented packaging technologies for the electronics industry and licenses those technologies to manufacturers, without fabricating a product themselves. Fallbrook Technologies, Inc., ARM Ltd., and Rambus, Inc., are other examples of companies that operate on a licensing business model.

court and millions of dollars) or cross-license to eliminate the obstacles to each. Both parties are equally motivated.

Related to cross-licensing is another form of sharing known as "patent pools," pursuant to which core enabling patents are made available by a group of pool members. Patent pools used to have a strong antitrust taint, but more recent successful models have gone a long way toward fostering this as a preferred practice in many industries.[213] For example, patent pools are widely used in the electronics industry.[214]

Another common way in which IP sharing is manifested is in the area of standards setting.[215] In particular, it has been observed that in various industries interoperability of proprietary components is essential. To ensure interoperability, it is often beneficial for an industry to adopt a common technology platform. This could work out very well for an organization if its technology is adopted as the industry standard. However, standards setting may raise difficult conflict of interest issues, which are often addressed by requiring that members who participate on a standards setting board agree to license their IP "on fair and reasonable terms." Yet, each organization has its own perception about the value contributed by its technology, so the determination of "fair and reasonable" royalties is not easy. Standards setting boards may also require a daunting disclosure of what IP each member has that would impact each possible standard.[216]

---

213. One definition of patent pool has been proffered in a White Paper commissioned by the USPTO;

> A "patent pool" is an agreement between two or more patent owners to license one or more of their patents to one another or third parties. 5 Alternatively, a patent pool may also be defined as "the aggregation of intellectual property rights which are the subject of cross-licensing, whether they are transferred directly by patentee to licensee or through some medium, such as a joint venture, set up specifically to administer the patent pool."(footnotes omitted)

J. Clark et al, *Patent Pools: A Solution To The Problem of Access in Biotechnology Patents?* (December 5, 2000) available at http://www.uspto.gov/web/offices/pac/dapp/opla/patent-pool.pdf (accessed December 7, 2007).

214. The most successful patent pools protect protocols or parts that allow interoperability of products manufactured by diverse competitors. For example, there is an open source patent pool (*see* http://www.patent-commons.org/ last accessed December 1, 2007). There are patent pools for the MP3 compression standard, for the IEEE 1394 ports (commonly called fire-wire ports), and a pool is forming for RFID tags. Patent pools typically collect patents from a variety of owners and pay out royalties based on a formula tied to the contribution of each pool member's IP.

215. *See generally, Justin Hurwitz, "The Value of Patents in Industry, Standards, Avoiding License Arbitrage with Voluntary Rules,"* 36 AIPLA Q.J. 1 (2008) at 1.

216. Perhaps the most infamous case on standards setting is the Rambus case where Rambus was accused of deceiving a standards setting board into believing that Rambus did not have any IP covering a standard that the board decided to adopt on memory chips used in computers. *See Rambus, Inc. v. Infineon Techs. AG,* 318 F.3d 1081 (Fed. Cir. 2003) for a discussion of the

7.1 Drafting Licenses, Generally

Sharing and transferring IP is substantially about written licenses and agreements, and counsel should spend much time and care in crafting the language of these documents as in crafting the language of the claims of a patent. There are two ways to transfer IP: explicitly and implicitly. Companies strive to only transfer explicit licenses because the intellectual property is transferred in a controlled manner, with the maximum value. And, while there are many circumstances that can create implied licenses, most agreements include explicit elimination of implied licenses.

There are many different types of agreements for sharing IP, as well as aspects of transactions pertaining to such sharing. "Licensing" is a common term used to address typical sharing arrangements that do not involve a complete transfer of IP rights between or among parties, the complete transfer being known as an "assignment."[217]

But, there are other arrangements as well, such as development agreements, disclosure agreements, sales and distribution agreements, enforcement agreements, joint defense agreements, and many others. Familiarity with available types of agreements will provide an active IP culture with the ability to select the correct agreement for the correct situation. In the area of technology sharing, the possibilities of arrangements are infinite, limited only by the imagination. Thus, the following will cover a few common types of agreements that are used surrounding the creation of IP and some of the more basic sharing transactions.[218]

Confidentiality Agreements

As discussed in Chapter 2, and as will be discussed further in Chapter 10, confidentiality agreements are also called nondisclosure agreements, and they cover the disclosure and use of confidential information. Outside of the typical employment scenario, these agreements are used so that different organizations can share confidential information with each other. It may be

---

fact. Since then, the Federal Trade Commission (FTC) sued Rambus for attempting to monopolize the DRAM chip market. The high visibility and high profits has raised the awareness of IP issues among many standards setting boards.

217. *See generally Waterman v. Mackenzie,* 138 U.S.252, 255 (1891).
218. There are treatises on licensing IP and every possible consideration cannot be covered in this overview. *See* Brian G. Brunsvold and Dennis P. O'Reilly, Drafting Patent License Agreements (5th ed. BNA Books 2004) for a concise how-to book on patent licensing.

for the purpose of initially ascertaining if there is a mutual interest in a business relationship. It may be for governing the conduct between the contracting parties, during the course of performing under another arrangement. For example, it may govern how parties share information during a development program or even pursuant to a licensing relationship, such as when know-how or other sensitive information is transferred. The discussions can lead to further agreements where a license to use the IP is actually transferred, such as testing products or processes, a joint development agreement, a contract research agreement, a license agreement, or another sort of agreement that shares or transfers IP (e.g., mergers, acquisitions, assignments, trademark concurrent use agreements, etc.).[219]

Confidential information is disclosed under these agreements. To maintain the value of confidential information it is important that the information remain confidential. So, nondisclosure agreements typically restrict how information shared can be used. Often, the agreements expressly acknowledge that the agreement does not confer any license rights under the information. Such agreements may also express restrictions against reverse engineering or even against chemically analyzing formulations.

Materials Testing or Service Agreements

Materials testing or service agreements are the next step up the ladder of IP sharing after a confidentiality agreement. In the relationships that these agreements govern, typically, others are granted a limited right to the use of IP (though perhaps under confidentiality obligations). Specifically, one party might be granted a right to test or experiment with your product or ideas.[220] The use is typically limited to the purpose of the agreement. However, this type of use (beyond the disclosure use of simply determining whether to enter into a business relationship) creates a number of IP issues. Perhaps the most prevalent issue pertains to addressing the possibility that in the course of testing or performing services, a new invention or original work may be made. To contemplate this possibility, parties will often seek to determine, up front, who is

---

219. Nondisclosure agreements are also commonly used for job candidates, vendors, consultants, and contractors. In one sense, as was discussed in previous passages herein, these sorts of agreements form the foundation of IP because they ensure that information is not considered disclosed for legal purposes, such as for protecting trade secrets, protecting against disclosure for absolute novelty purposes, and for stopping any improper use of those secrets. In the abstract, however, the security that the agreements afford also fosters candid information sharing by which technology can be improved upon through a relationship with the parties.

220. The permitted use that is granted by these agreements is essentially a license to the IP, albeit one that is quite limited in the scope of use and duration.

entitled to ownership of the discovered rights. Take for example the situation in which an organization develops a new jet engine component, but the organization does not have access to an entire engine, or a test machine to see how the component works. It finds another organization that does have such capabilities. In some instances, the latter will simply charge a flat price for access to the facilities. In others, the latter may choose instead to actively assist in the testing (for perhaps a lower fee) but insist upon a share in ownership of (or possibly a right of first refusal or option to license) any IP rights for discoveries made during the testing. Another example is a service agreement with companies that are commonly called contract research organizations (CROs) that may perform complicated research or testing on materials or ideas or concepts.

Because of the possible generation of intellectual property in these agreements, most often the company that initially owns the samples or ideas will also want to own exclusively any newly created IP. Generally, there are four IP-generation scenarios that will result from a testing or services agreement:

1. Rights in the data itself,
2. Rights in any IP that can be derived from the data (e.g., conclusions about inventions over the prior art),
3. Any IP that relates to the materials or ideas, and
4. IP that enables the testing.

At the outset of negotiations for these rights, parties often understand that the first three types of IP will belong to the party commissioning or paying for the testing or services. There are a number of ways to write such ownership clauses, but most CROs prefer a positive statement of the IP that is being generated. Another way to handle CROs or service agreements is to define all the IP that the CRO or service partner will keep and designate ownership of everything else to the client.

The fourth type of intellectual property that may be created in connection with the testing or services is often regarded as being reserved to the CRO. Accordingly, if in the prior hypothetical case, the owner of the engine testing machine devises a method for testing or unique equipment necessary for the testing, that organization will want to own rights to that development, so it can use it to offer like services to other customers. As such, they typically need to own the IP that enables the testing. If the commissioning party needs access to the newly developed testing technology in order to demonstrate the efficacy of its technology to others, it is not unusual or unreasonable for the commissioning party to seek permission back (e.g., in the form of a license) from the CRO, so that the commissioning party can most fully enjoy its technology and demonstrate its capabilities to others. Thus, with reference again to the aircraft testing illustration, if the CRO had developed a unique test fixture for allowing the test to be performed and had negotiated to own the IP rights to it, the commissioning party may reasonably insist upon a limited right to be able to use such test fixture IP rights for future testing.

> ## 7.2 Example Clause That Assigns All Rights to Company
>
> Company shall own all right, title, and interest in and to all results, including all data, protocols, analysis, conclusions, and reports forming, including, or being derived from such research results, in each case as created by Recipient, alone or jointly with the Company, during the term of and in connection with the Services under this Agreement ("Service Results"). Company shall own all right title and interest in and to all Intellectual Property made or conceived or reduced to practice, in whole or in part, by one or both of the Parties, solely or jointly, during the term of this Agreement, and arising out of the Service activities under this Agreement, or where such Intellectual Property is in any way based on or derived from the Service Results ("Agreement Inventions"). Recipient will record and document all Service Results and all Agreement Inventions in a scientifically and legally acceptable manner, and Recipient will disclose and provide all Service Results and Agreement Inventions to Company. Recipient hereby assigns and agrees to make all assignments necessary to accomplish and perfect Company's ownership in all Service Results and Agreement Inventions. Recipient shall assist Company, at Company's expense, to further evidence, record and perfect such assignments, and to perfect, obtain, maintain, enforce, and defend any interests and rights assigned.

Another popular testing scenario involves the situation in which an organization owns IP that it is trying to commercialize or license to another organization. The latter organization, however, must satisfy itself prior to entering an agreement that the IP has value. In this situation, a "license" is granted to test the subject of the IP effectively. In the course of the testing, the testing organization may identify alternative applications for the technology or ways to improve the technology. In such instances, it is not unreasonable to expect that the organization that owned the IP in the first place would want to exclude the testing party from acquiring IP ownership rights.

Joint Development Agreements

A joint development agreement is an agreement in which two or more organizations agree to work together to research or develop a technology.[221]

---

221. Each joint development scenario will provide a unique set of facts, and it is difficult to apply universal provisions for these agreements. It is a common situation that business people will negotiate a memorandum of understanding or letter of intent without evaluating all of the possible scenarios. It would do well in many instances, therefore, to confer with business persons prior to negotiations to help define topics to negotiate, especially provisions

One form of joint development involves an agreement between two or more distinct organizations, which remain legally distinct. Another form, a joint venture, involves two or more organizations forming another distinct organization. The expected result from any joint development agreement is that the technology will be developed, along with IP rights. Joint development agreements are somewhat unique because usually the parties to them each will bring certain IP to the table at the outset, and each will be expecting certain IP ownership rights upon conclusion. In a crude sense, a joint development program contemplates a marriage of sorts between or among the parties, with the joint development agreement serving as the prenuptial agreement if, and more likely when, the marriage fails. Accordingly, the most heavily negotiated subject in joint development agreements is the ownership of IP rights upon termination of the relationship. Another heavily negotiated subject is the access that the parties are willing to grant to their underlying technologies upon termination.

For example, consider the situation in which two organizations are jointly working to develop a new reinforced composite material. One organization owns proprietary technology in a reinforcement material. The other owns proprietary technology in the matrix material into which the reinforcement is to be introduced. If the technology is a success, both parties stand to win because a demand will be created for each of their respective materials. The issue that is faced, however, is the possibility that the development will succeed, but the relationship between the parties will fail. With such an occurrence, use by one party of the new technology may be prevented because the other party has an IP right that prevents the use of the material owned by that party.

To address this issue, parties to a joint development agreement normally will identify categories of IP and will negotiate the use of each such category upon termination. Two popular temporal-based categories are Background IP and Agreement IP.[222]

Background IP is the IP that each party brings to the joint development activity. Licenses to the Background IP are typically necessary for carrying out the research and development activities of the parties, which are anticipated to occur as part of performance of the joint development agreement.[223]

---

concerning the eventuality of termination and the effect that will have on ownership and license rights.

222. Other synonymous terms are sometimes employed, such as "Existing IP" and "Resulting IP" to distinguish between categories of IP.

223. Research and development activities are an act of infringement in the U.S. because there is no general research use exception other than for pharmaceuticals. Instead, the experimental use exception is very narrowly applied to research that is performed for noncommercial reasons. *See Merck KGaA v. Integra Lifesciences I, Ltd.,* 545 U.S.193 (2005) for a discussion of the safe harbor for pharmaceuticals in 35 U.S.C. § 271(e)(1). There is no general research

This is seldom a problem, as the parties entering the agreement typically seek a mutual benefit, and it makes little sense to hamstring the relationship at the outset by denying access to the technology. The bigger issue lies in addressing the continued use of the Background IP upon a successful development and, thereafter, upon termination of such relationship. This contingency is handled most frequently by some sort of licensing relationship. For example, a license to the Background IP of one party may be granted to the other so the other can exploit the technology being jointly researched and developed. With a joint venture, the Background IP of each party is typically licensed to the joint venture.

Agreement IP can include patents, know-how, and data which arise during and as a result of joint development activities. It is possible that rights in Agreement IP can be divided upon termination of a joint development. However, joint developments sometimes end with hard feelings between the parties, e.g., one party feels the relationship was either a success or failure because of its own action (success) or the other party's actions (failure). Negotiation for resolution of ownership will be difficult in such circumstances, and, thus, it is much better to address the issue up front when negotiating the agreement.

There is no single approach that works best in the negotiation of these provisions. However, patience and sensitivity to the commercial needs of the other party will go a long way to avoiding breakdown of a joint development relationship before it begins.[224] If one party to the agreement is the likely commercialization party, then that party will typically want to own as much of the rights as possible, while granting a license back to the other party.

Each of the different types of Agreement IP can be handled separately for allocating respective post-termination uses. For example, if the IP that results is in the form of patents, they may be licensed to one or both parties, with or without a right to sublicense to others, absent the permission of the other party. It might be possible that only the resulting patents can be licensed for further use but that know-how or other IP created during development is not

---

use exemption to patent infringement in the U.S. *See Madey v. Duke Univ.,* 307 F.3d 1351 (Fed. Cir. 2002). In many countries, however, there is a general exemption to patent infringement for research. For example in Germany, there is no patent infringement for research into a patented invention, but the exemption does not extend to research with a patented invention. *See* Art. 11. 2, German Patent Act of 1981, *In re Clinical Trials I,* German Federal Supreme Court (BGH) published July 1995, and *In re Clinical Trials II,* German Federal Supreme Court (BGH) published 1997.

224. The unfortunate part of negotiating termination rights before a relationship begins is that it necessarily involves projecting into the future the possibility that the other side has failed to live up to the bargain. This is done at a time when the parties have just identified each other as partners; when they are in the "honeymoon" period and otherwise ought to be experiencing an inspirational and creative surge.

to be shared with others. Alternatively, the resulting patents and know-how might be shared.

Joint development agreements can also provide for specific technologies that may belong to one party or another, which are sometimes referred to as "carve-outs" because the IP directed to this specific technology is carved out of the joint development agreement and specifically allocated to a party from the outset. Carve-outs are common when one party has an established business in a related area where the agreement may be used or further developed during the joint activities. For example, suppose that the manufacturer of the reinforcement material in the above hypothetical instance has an existing business in which it is investigating new uses for its reinforcement materials. It may carve out improvements to its reinforcement materials from the consequences of the joint development agreement, to protect the right of that business to continue to develop and not be blocked by joint development activities.

The parties can also define fields of use to which they each will be confined with their respective commercial activities, e.g., one party may choose to commercialize the hypothetical composite as catalysts for olefin polymerization while the other seeks a field for using the composites in integrated circuits. A field can be defined as broadly or narrowly as the parties desire. The IP that is generated in joint development can be allocated to one or another party, both inside the field and outside of the field. The agreement can also define certain fields that the parties plan to later address.

With regard to IP, joint development agreements will typically include many other provisions, such as provisions defining who has responsibility for getting and paying for patents, how the parties will report new inventions to each other and make patent filing decisions, how the parties will cooperate in the process of prosecuting the applications for patents, who will pay the costs for patenting, who is responsible for infringements of third-party rights and possible indemnity for such potential infringements, how the parties will enforce resulting IP rights, how the parties will share in the proceeds from any enforcement, as well as other responsibilities the parties may each have upon termination of the agreement.

Each of these topics is part of a bundle of rights that result from IP and can be addressed as part of an overall negotiation process targeted at allocating business risk and costs between the parties. A full discussion of the pros and cons of each topic is well beyond the scope of this book. The appropriate negotiated resolution will differ from situation to situation. An open mind and creativity will lead to the most successful outcome.

Of course, as with many of the more complex agreements addressed in this chapter, joint development agreements may have many other clauses and provisions unrelated to IP, including scope of work, division of work, payments, resource allocations, indemnity clauses, representations, warranties, notices, choices of law, and alternate dispute resolution.

License Agreements

Licensing intellectual property can convey a full right to the IP and, as such, is generally near the top of the ladder when it comes to sharing IP.[225] With licensing of IP, conceptually an owner examines the bundle of rights that is conferred by the IP and then decides if, how, and for how much to share each right. As a result, there are many different types of license agreements. At one extreme, in the case of various exclusive licenses, the licenses may look more like assignments in the vast amounts of rights conferred. Some may be much more restrictive, or nonexclusive, resembling nothing more than an agreement that the IP owner will not sue ("covenant not to sue") the other party for infringement of the IP right.

There are many considerations in licensing intellectual property and a complete discussion of each possibility is beyond the scope of this book. However, to understand whether and when to consider licensing in the context of an active and healthy IP culture, the following topics will give some necessary background and will be touched upon, including, exclusivity, cross-licensing, grant-backs, reservations (or exceptions), limitations, improvements, sublicensing, most-favored terms, royalty basis, and term and termination provisions.

Exclusivity

The first, and typically most important, issue is the type of license, exclusive or nonexclusive. This defines the extent that a licensor (i.e., the party owning the IP right) is willing to share its right to exclude others under the IP. "Exclusivity" means that the licensee (i.e., the party to whom the license to use the IP is granted) is the only party that can use the IP. There is also co-exclusivity, where the licensee and licensor are the only parties that can use the IP.[226] With nonexclusive licenses, there may be a number of licensees, who may compete directly with each other.

Granting complete exclusivity under a license has the potential to invoke a number of issues, including possible antitrust implications, how to protect the licensor (given that the licensor is effectively turning over its right to

---

225. Many organizations use the term "in-licensing" to refer to licensing to obtain rights under the IP of someone else and "out-licensing" to refer to licensing of the IP of the organization to others outside the organization.

226. In lieu of granting an exclusive license, some parties grant what they call "sole licenses," meaning that the party receiving the license need not fear that some other party will also get a license. However, in those situations, the party granting the license often reserves IP rights to itself. Therefore, a sole licensee is not immune from competition from the licensor.

exclude others and must retain some assurance it will get compensated), and enforcement.

Antitrust issues may arise when the license creates market exclusivity. The Department of Justice has taken a number of different positions on the topic of the interplay between patent licensing and anticompetitive activities.[227]

Protection of the licensor is also important with exclusivity because typically no licensor wants to see its technology licensed exclusively and then put onto the shelf and not commercialized. To help avoid this situation, licensors may include provisions to assure commercialization (and hence a royalty payment) by the licensee or to otherwise return the rights to the licensor so the licensor can exploit the IP some other way. For example, if the exclusive licensee does not exploit the licensed technology sufficiently, a number of remedies may be agreed to in the license such as (1) termination of the license, (2) conversion of the exclusive license to a nonexclusive license, or (3) minimum guaranteed royalty payments. Many exclusive licenses will have a finite (but extendable) term, and will also require due diligence by the licensor toward commercialization (e.g., dates for achieving milestones toward commercialization are defined), which is sometimes called a "best-efforts" provision.

Enforcement of infringement of the licensed intellectual property is also a potentially key consideration for the exclusive licensee because the licensee is paying for and wants to maintain exclusivity. Attendant with the right of exclusivity is the right to sue others for infringement of the IP right. Thus, the parties will have to consider and agree upon a method for policing infringement of the licensed IP. This has the potential to cause headaches for some IP owners because many have no interest in becoming a party to a lawsuit, especially a party against which the owner does not compete. However, for judicial reasons, sometimes owners are required to participate in the lawsuit.[228] Therefore, the parties will often need to determine the mechanism for identifying infringements by others, who will be named as a plaintiff in any lawsuit, who will pay for the lawsuit, and how any proceeds from the lawsuit will be divided.

Cross-Licensing

In "cross-licensing," parties own IP that they agree to share with each other. Cross-licensing is extensive in some industries (e.g., the computer and software industries) where a single product can be covered by hundreds of patents

---

227. *See, e.g.,* U.S. Dept. of Justice and Fed. Trade Commn., *Antitrust Enforcement and Intellectual Property Rights: Promoting Innovation and Competition* (2007) available at http://www.usdoj.gov/atr/public/hearings/ip/222655.pdf (accessed December 8, 2007). Especially in the U.S., and in Europe, it is wise to consult antitrust counsel when licensing exclusively.
228. *Israel Bio-Engineering Project v. Amgen Inc.,* 475 F.3d 1256 1558 (Fed. Cir. 2007).

and every party that makes a product needs a license.[229] In some circumstances, one party's IP is dominant over the other party's IP (meaning the first party's IP is necessary for using the technology generally because it is first in time, and it broadly covers a whole new technology, but the second party's IP may cover only certain improved features or aspects of the technology; e.g., a party patents wheel generally while another party later invents an alloy for specific use to make the wheel). The grant from the dominant owner of a license will typically be met by a return grant to the dominant owner of a license under the other's IP. The grant of a cross-license may form part of the consideration, with a monetary royalty typically making up the remainder of the consideration.

Grant-Backs

"Grant-backs" are licenses from the original licensee back to the original licensor and may be a form of cross-license or a license to improvements made by the licensee. An improvement is where the licensee starts with the licensed technology and makes a further invention or creates new IP that is based on the licensed technology. Licensors may demand a license back to any improvements made by the licensee, in the form of a grant-back, so that the licensor can then provide the improvement to all of its licensees. But grant-backs that over-reach may also raise an antitrust concern, in the context of requiring the licensee to provide the licensor with market power through exclusivity to the granted-back IP (e.g., related IP or improvement).

Reservations and Exceptions

"Reservations" or "exceptions" are clauses that take back a portion of what was licensed as part of the license grant. Such reservations or exceptions become important as the complexity of the licensing of the technology grows. For example, if one party licenses exclusively in a field of use and then tries to license another party to a specific piece of technology that is not specific to the field, then the second license may need an exception to the earlier exclusive license. Consider, for an example, a new technology for a detergent. The licensor may grant an exclusive license to a licensee for use in laundry detergents, while reserving the field of hard surfaces. A second licensee may come along and want a license to use the detergent for dishes. The licensor then improves the detergent using a new ingredient. The license to the second party under

---

229. It has been heavily documented that there are hundreds of patented components in a computer, which has been used as a reason for patent reform. Stephen A. Merrill et al. eds *A Patent System for the 21st Century* (National Academies, National Research Council, 2004).

the improvement will need to be limited to its use for dish detergent. Otherwise, the first licensee may become undermined. As another example, suppose one or more nonexclusive licenses are granted to different licensees, and then a party arrives that wants an exclusive license. The licensor must either terminate the nonexclusive licensees, or make the exclusive license grant subject to the existing nonexclusive licenses. Similarly, a licensor may seek to grant an exclusive license to another party, but reserve for itself an exception under the agreement.

Field of Use Limitations

License "field of use" limitations are also common, and are used to divide up the licensed rights. Common field of use limitations are (1) geographical (e.g., licensing a party to an exclusive territory); (2) application fields of use (e.g., to a specific product or process); and (3) nature of use (e.g., a right to sell only, but no right to make or use). Limitations on the license give greater flexibility to the licensor to obtain maximum value for the licensed technology. There is generally no restriction on the types of limitations that can be incorporated, as long as they do not create an antitrust issue.

Sublicensing

In "sublicensing," a licensee further shares the licensed IP with another party. This most often occurs with exclusive licenses but may also occur with non-exclusive licenses. The sublicensing may be required to be for a specific purpose (e.g., commercialization of a product) and may be required in some industries to allow for an important license to be part of a merger or acquisition. In other contexts, sublicensing terms may be required to be of less scope that the original license grant. This reduced sublicensing scope stops the licensee from substituting a third party into the licensee role. For example, if the license has important commercialization requirements that the original licensee later wants to avoid, the licensee might try sub-licensing all of its rights to a third party. However, the licensor might never have agreed to the original license with the third party (e.g., it is a direct competitor or has bad credit or no market history).

Grant Provisions

As can be appreciated from the above, a key provision in any license agreement is the "grant" provision, which defines the license grant. Not only is it important to specify the nature of the grant (e.g., exclusive, nonexclusive, any exceptions, carve-outs, fields of use, etc.), it is also very important to specify the precise intellectual property that is being licensed. When specific IP is being licensed, attention ought to be paid to its identification, either through specific numbers (e.g., patent numbers) or specific criteria.

The bundle of rights in license agreements includes the following pieces that may or may not be included in the grant clause: the right to make, have made, sell, offer to sell, use, practice methods, lease, barter, import, export, sublicense, or otherwise exploit the IP. When detailed negotiation of the grant clause happens, a licensee may become concerned that the grant clause does not include all the rights needed to practice the technology being licensed. In this situation, a representation or warranty or covenant not to sue can be used to clarify that the licensee is getting all the rights needed from the licensor. By way of example, sometimes a license is granted under a certain patent. However, another related patent application is pending in a patent office that may have equal significance to the licensee. The licensee, accordingly, may seek, not just a license to the specific patent, but to "any other patent properties owned by the licensor which may be necessary for the license to practice the licensed technology." No licensee wants to learn shortly after starting to pay royalties that it now needs to pay additional royalties to the same licensor under another patent.

Royalty Payments

"Royalty" or other payment terms are also important and should be tied to the intellectual property being licensed. The royalty rate in license agreements is typically the measure of the value of the IP to both the licensee and the licensor. Customary royalty rates vary from industry to industry. There is no hard and fast rule for calculating royalties. Though some "rules of thumb" can be found, their application in practice has not been consistent.[230]

---

230. *See, e.g.,* Gordon Smith and Russell Parr, *Intellectual Property: Valuation, Exploitation, and Infringement Damages* (Wiley 2005); Choi, et al., *An Analytical Solution to Reasonable Royalty Rate Calculations,* 41 J. L. & Tech.. 49 (2001); Cromley, "Twenty Steps for Pricing a Patent" (Nov. 2004) available at http://www.aicpa.org/pubs/jofa/nov2004/cromley.htm (accessed December 9, 2007). Various online databases offer services to help ascertain reasonable royalty rates in industries, *see, e.g.,* www.royaltysource.com; www.royaltystat.com; *see also* www.ipresearch.com/books.html. It should be borne in mind that many of the existing licenses are confidential and may not be reflected in the databases.

Among the most widely referenced criteria employed in a royalty determination are those from the case of *Georgia-Pacific Corp. v. U.S. Plywood-Champion Papers, Inc.*:[231]

1. The royalties received by the patentee for the licensing of the patent in suit, proving or tending to prove an established royalty.
2. The rates paid by the licensee for the use of other patents comparable to the patent in suit.
3. The nature and scope of the license, as exclusive or nonexclusive; or as restricted or nonrestricted in terms of territory or with respect to whom the manufactured product may be sold.
4. The licensor's established policy and marketing program to maintain its patent monopoly by not licensing others to use the invention or by granting licenses under special conditions designed to preserve that monopoly.
5. The commercial relationship between the licensor and licensee, such as whether they are competitors in the same territory in the same line of business, or whether they are inventor and promotor.
6. The effect of selling the patented specialty in promoting sales of other products of the licensee, the existing value of the invention to the licensor as a generator of sales of his nonpatented items, and the extent of such derivative or convoyed sales.
7. The duration of the patent and the term of the license.
8. The established profitability of the product made under the patent, its commercial success, and its current popularity.
9. The utility and advantages of the patent property over the old modes or devices, if any, that had been used for working out similar results.
10. The nature of the patented invention, the character of the commercial embodiment of it as owned and produced by the licensor, and the benefits to those who have used the invention.
11. The extent to which the infringer has made use of the invention, and any evidence probative of the value of that use.
12. The portion of the profit or of the selling price that may be customary in the particular business or in comparable businesses to allow for the use of the invention or analogous inventions.
13. The portion of the realizable profit that should be credited to the invention as distinguished from nonpatented elements, the manufacturing process, business risks, or significant features or improvements added by the infringer.
14. The opinion testimony of qualified experts.

---

231. *Georgia-Pacific Corp. v. U.S. Plywood-Champion Papers, Inc.*, 318 F. Supp. 1116 (S.D.N.Y.1970), *modified*, 446 F.2d 295 (2d Cir. 1971).

15. The amount that a licensor (such as the patentee) and a licensee (such as the infringer) would have agreed upon (at the time the infringement began) if both had been reasonably and voluntarily trying to reach an agreement; that is, the amount which a prudent licensee—who desired, as a business proposition, to obtain a license to manufacture and sell a particular article embodying the patented invention—would have been willing to pay as a royalty and yet be able to make a reasonable profit and which amount would have been acceptable by a prudent patentee who was willing to grant a license.

As can be appreciated from the above, because established royalty rates may be a factor that would influence the determination of a royalty, in the event of litigation, a licensor should expect to have to make available all licenses during an infringement suit.[232] This could pose some practical issues, particularly with protecting sensitive information that a licensee does not wish to be divulged.

On this point, it is also difficult to gauge what constitutes an established royalty. Because payment terms vary from license to license, each license presents a unique situation making it difficult for that particular license to set a precedent for the reasonable royalty. For example, a putative royalty rate may appear to be 5 percent. Upon scrutiny, it is learned that a lump sum payment was made in addition, making the total "royalty" amount actually higher. In other situations, licensors may get nonmonetary compensation such as a cross-licenses, a valuable right to license improvements, or a grant-back rights. Each license agreement is different from the others, and these additional forms of consideration need to be considered, especially when efforts are made to rely upon published data about royalty rates.

Another common issue with royalty rates is the basis of the royalty calculation. Some licenses call for the ongoing payment of a royalty based upon units sold. However, it may be possible to structure the royalty on the amount of product produced, on a per use basis, on a flat fee per period basis or otherwise. In some instances, difficulty in setting a royalty is encountered because the parties cannot agree on how much of a technology the royalty rate should be based. For example, a licensed invention may pertain to a piston for an engine. The parties will argue whether the royalty should be a percentage of the piston price or a percentage of the engine price. That is, should the basis of the royalty be a single component or the entire machine that includes

---

232. 35 U.S.C. § 284 states that "Upon finding for the claimant the court shall award the claimant damages adequate to compensate for the infringement, but in no event less than a reasonable royalty. . . ." This language brings into issue what a licensor believes is a reasonable royalty to infringe the IP, and the royalty rate in a license agreement can set the ceiling for damages.

the component. This hotly contested issue is the subject of extensive research in different industries to identify customary practice.

Still another common issue is just how closely the IP must be tied to the use of the technology. For example, if a licensor has tens or hundreds of patents directed toward a particular technology, neither the licensee nor licensor may want to go through the task of identifying each possible use that would fall under a valid claim of the patents (or within the scope of the licensed know-how). And if the royalty basis is very specific and the exact use of the technology changes (e.g., slightly different products or different processes), the task may have to be repeated multiple times in order to determine what royalty to pay. In these circumstances, a royalty basis can be agreed upon that applies to an entire defined technology. However, it may raise antitrust concerns to demand a royalty for technology that is not covered by the licensed intellectual property. This situation can be structured to occur, but typically it will require the parties to agree and it should arise under circumstances such that the license offer is not presented as a take-it-or leave-it licensing offer.[233]

License Term and Termination

Finally, term and termination of the license are important features of a license. The most common term of the license is the life of the IP, but shorter terms can be used. The good and bad thing about shorter terms is that they expire before the IP, leading to new negotiations under different market, IP, and technology conditions. The changed circumstances are usually good for one side, but not the other, and you should carefully consider which side of that coin you may be on when the initial term ends. Termination rights are also hotly contested because the licensor might want the ability to terminate the license in certain circumstances, such as transfer of the commercialization of the licensed product to a third party that the licensor might not have licensed in the first place. On the other side of this issue, the licensee may need the ability to transfer the license upon the sale of all or substantially all the assets of the business, without risking termination because the business may be depending on the license to be in business.

Compulsory Licensing

Compulsory licensing addresses the situation where an IP owner must license another under an IP right. Compulsory licensing is a repugnant term in the

---

233. *See* the litany of cases leading to and subsequently citing *Hazeltine Research, Inc. v. Zenith Radio Corp.,* 395 U.S. 100 (1969).

U. S. because the case law and tradition is that an IP owner gets a right to exclude.[234] If the owner is unable to exclude someone from using its IP because of a mandatory license, then the intellectual property is essentially being taken from him (albeit at a price determined to be fair by the courts) and is not the meaningful right to exclude that it is purported to be. For example, a case involving Xerox held that a patent owner does not have to sell a patented product to anyone who asks, the so-called "refusal to sell" situation.[235] In contrast, the Supreme Court held that injunctions for patent infringement are not automatic and will grant only when the traditional four-factors test applied to other legal situations is met.[236] The four-part test may be difficult to meet for IP owners in some business models, e.g., a licensing company may have a difficult time showing irreparable harm if there is always a licensing option. This inevitably puts forth a compulsory license scenario, because the IP owner cannot keep the infringer from the market.[237] Indeed, since *eBay* the district courts have been working through various fact scenarios in an attempt to clarify the state of the law.[238]

Joint Ownership

In many situations—such as joint development scenarios or license situations in which the licensee plans to invest significantly to develop a technology—the issue of joint ownership must be addressed. One approach to resolving the issue is to simply say that any technology that is created during a certain time period, and under certain circumstances, will be jointly owned. Sometimes, however, this is not acceptable to a party. In the latter situation, parties often resolve the issue by agreeing that ownership of the IP will be based on inventorship. That is, only the party that invents gets to own the intellectual property.

234. Compulsory licensing outside of the U. S. may be common in some technologies. However, many countries are changing or not enforcing these older laws in an effort to comply with the Agreement on Trade-Related Aspects of Intellectual Property Rights, including Trade in Counterfeit Goods, of the Uruguay Round of the General Agreement on Tariffs and Trade (GATT TRIPS Agreement). art. 31 of the GATT TRIPS Agreement allows for compulsory licensing on a case-by-case basis under certain circumstances.
235. *In re Indep. Serv. Orgs. Antitrust Litig.*, 203 F.3d 1322 (Fed. Cir. 2000).
236. *eBay, Inc. v. MercExchange LLC,* 126 S. Ct. 1837, 78 U.S.P.Q.2d (BNA) 1577 (2006).
237. The law concerning compulsory licenses varies around the world and often is technology-specific. A big issue in recent years has been the efforts in some countries to impose compulsory licensing upon drug companies because the social justification is asserted to far exceed the economic justification for not doing so.
238. *See, e.g., Finisar Corp. v. The DirectTV Group, Inc.,* No. 1:05-CV-264, 2006 WL 2709206 (E. D. Tex. Sept. 1, 2006); There is also a blog that keeps track of the permanent injunction cases that have come out since the Supreme Court's eBay decision.. *See* http://www.fr.com/news/articledetail.cfm?articleid=561, last accessed December 3, 2007.

In the U.S., inventorship may be determined based on conception, reduction to practice, or combinations of both activities, and almost always will require proof by corroborated documentary evidence. In this manner, the IP is assigned to whichever company's personnel came up with the idea. While this may be an easy out of a sticky issue in negotiation, there are several problems with this approach, not the least is how to prove who came up with the idea and how to resolve disputes over who came up with the idea. These problems should be understood prior to agreeing to this arrangement, Therefore, it is wise when negotiating ownership based upon inventorship to specify a procedure for resolving any claims.

When joint ownership is agreed upon, it is important to recognize the possibility of issues that parties will later face. One of the most sensitive issues, of course, is enforcement. Often, one joint owner does not want to get involved in disputes that the other joint owner may have. However, the courts may require participation. Accordingly, it is common to negotiate provisions that contemplate this situation and address the consent needed to bring suit, who bears costs, who controls the litigation, and how proceeds are split.[239]

Joint ownership creates limitations in prosecution of patent applications. This occurs when the patent applications are drafted and look too similar to one of the party's Background IP (i.e., prior art), and terminal disclaimers cannot be filed because the ownership is different. This level of similarity can also raise inventorship issues. Joint ownership can also create conflicts of interest among the attorney prosecuting the joint application if that attorney also has one of the parties as a client.

To solve the joint ownership issue, the parties can agree that one party will own the IP but that the other party has a license for all purposes. In some industries, the parties will have a difficult time with this solution because they are otherwise competitors and the ownership by one party gives them some measure of control over the other party. Moreover, they simply cannot accept another owning the IP that they may be relying upon for a particular product or process. Thus, business considerations may limit the possible solutions to joint ownership, but joint ownership, from a strictly legal viewpoint may prove limiting to full IP exploitation.

Implied Licenses

Licenses may be implied out of the terms of agreements, circumstances alone, or a combination of explicit terms and circumstances. Similar to implied contracts, implied licenses may arise out of the law or out of the facts. As discussed in Chapter 2, one example of an implied license created by operation of law is a "shop right." Most licensing agreements try to be specific enough

---

239. Absent agreement, joint patent owners are not required to account to each other. 35 U.S.C. § 262.

to avoid an implied right, and in most agreements, implied licenses are explicitly denied. However, they may still exist.

Many implied licenses arise out of the first sale or exhaustion doctrine, which applies to many forms of IP (e.g., patents and copyrights). Under the first sale doctrine, the first authorized sale of a protected product transfers with it all the intellectual property covering the transferred product. The IP has been exhausted. This eliminates the owner's ability to control the use or further sale of the product (so long as it is a true sale and not just a lease). For example, if you have both patents and copyrights covering software that you make and sell. Upon your sale of the software, you cannot stop the purchaser from using the software by agreeing to only a license to the copyrights in the sale documents. The purchaser will get an implied license to use what was purchased, even under the patents that you tried to keep from being licensed. See generally *Medeco Security Locks, Inc. v. Lock Technology Corp.*,[240] in wherein the Court expressed: "[l]ike any other implied contract, an implied license arises out of the objective conduct of the parties, which a reasonable man would regard as indicating that an agreement has been reached".

In the area of copyright law, the IP holder needs to be particularly careful. As technology advances, making copying easier and a variety of new types of publication available, an implied license can result from activities that previously would not have resulted in a license. For example, in *Boosey & Hawkes Music Publishers, Inc. v. Walt Disney Company*,[241] the court addressed whether new media publication was included in the copyright grant given in boiler plate language. But there are cases on both sides of this issue. Note though that implied licensing can go no further than any other license. As expressed in *Monsanto Co. v. Scruggs*,[242] "a seller cannot confer broader rights via an implied license than it has been granted by the patent holder".

There are many factual and legal circumstances that can give right to an implied license. Paying damages in a lawsuit, sales of non-staple components, most favored licensee clauses, patents acquired after an earlier license, and use of a purchased item in a patented process are all circumstances that should be carefully considered for implied licenses.

Transferring IP

Intellectual property is transferred in a written agreement that is typically called an assignment.[243] Assignments transfer all right, title, and interest in

240. 199 U.S.P.Q. (BNA) 519, 524 (S.D.N.Y. 1976); *See also Quanta Computer, Inc. v LG Electronics Inc,* 453 F.3d. 1364 (Fed.Cir.2006), cert.granted.

241. 145 F.3d 481 (2d Cir. 1998).

242. 459 F.3d 1328, 1336 (Fed. Cir. 2006).

243. The U.S. Copyright Act requires transfers to be in writing. 17 U.S.C. § 204. Recordation of the document with the Copyright Office may be necessary to prevail against a conflicting

the IP to the new owner. The assignment agreement is fairly straightforward. However, the business transaction leading to the assignment is often complicated. For example, the transaction can call for an assignment of the IP, but then grant back licenses from the assignee to the original owner. If those licenses include substantial rights (e.g., an exclusive license), the court may interpret the assignment more as license than as assignment. The point is that the agreement will be interpreted by the substance of the rights in the IP that the parties have after the agreement is executed.

The standard assignment agreement has a few key parts. First, the assignment typically defines the invention or IP as being assigned, and is not typically limited to a single patent application or patent. Next, the assignment identifies a patent or patent application specifically (typically by number and filing date) and then includes all continuations, divisionals, extensions, etc., as well as all foreign counterparts to the specifically identified IP. Assignments can be for a whole series of patents and patent applications that are identified specifically in an appendix. Finally, the assignment typically conveys all right, title, and interest, as well as a right to act. Sometimes, the assignment goes further by identifying specific rights that the assignment includes (e.g., the right to enforce and collect damages), but these may be redundant.

7.3
In many contract scenarios, parties may want to agree at the outset to a form of dispute resolution. The most common forms of alternative dispute resolution (ADR) are mediation, which is a nonbinding settlement facilitation process, and arbitration, which can be a binding proceeding that results in a decision on the merits. When negotiating an ADR provision, the following are examples of topics to negotiate: mediation; arbitration; -selection of neutral party; whether to have discovery; sharing of costs; and when proceeding must be completed.

Due Diligence

As with real property, or any asset previously owned by another, a prospective purchaser of IP rights typically wants to investigate the rights it is buying. Purchasers do not want to be surprised by invalid patents, patent applications that fail to properly claim the commercially significant part of the invention,

---

transfer. 17 U.S.C. § 105. *See also* 35 U.S.C. § 261 (governing recordation of patent assignments).

or lack of complete ownership by the seller (e.g., inventors are properly named and have all assigned their rights to the seller). To be sure that there are no surprises, purchasers use a process called "due diligence" to investigate the IP. Due diligence is considered a necessary precursor prior to business transactions that rely at least in part on intellectual property, including funding a venture, mergers, acquisitions, initial public offerings, and licensing.

Due diligence typically starts with clearly defined questions to be answered, with the purchaser obtaining advice throughout the process, based upon answers to those questions. Questions asked in due diligence are geared toward learning *inter alia*:

- What is the value of the IP in terms of the likelihood it will be respected, including but not limited to where there are any apparent defects in the IP?[244]
- Is there clear title to the IP including whether there is any third party who might claim an ownership right?[245]
- Is there a risk of infringing someone else's IP (a potential liability) if the IP being purchased is used or practiced?[246]
- Is there any other apparent obstacle to the ability of the acquiring party to fully enjoy the rights it will obtain.[247]

Looking at the first question, its value is tied to two broad questions. The first question is: what does the IP actually cover; that is, will it cover the technology, products, or processes that the purchaser seeks to commercialize and will it also provide a reasonable sphere of protection to exclude competitors from offering similar technology? The second question tends to focus on whether the IP is valid and enforceable, so that if enforcement through litigation ever becomes necessary, will the IP withstand challenge? These questions can be phrased many different ways, but they are going to be at the heart of a standard due diligence investigation. If the acquiring company has an expectation that patents will protect a specific commercial product, then that expectation must be investigated and confirmed. The remaining duration of the IP right, as well as its territorial limitations, will also be addressed.

---

244. Claim construction, analysis of prior art, and investigations of prior art activities not previously considered are among the activities undertaken.
245. A review of any funding agreements, developmental agreements, licenses, or other relationships of an organization pursuant to which someone else might claim an IP right is a common focus of this analysis.
246. It is possible with this part of the analysis to conduct searching, perform freedom-to-practice studies.
247. The results of the due diligence on all these considerations will often dictate the nature and extent of any warranties that may be sought, or the purchase price to be paid.

Different types of intellectual property may provide different scopes of coverage, and this will also have to be investigated. For example, copyright protection will have different coverage for a key software purchase as compared to the coverage that patents may have for the same software purchase. If the work is highly creative, the copyright protection may be considered to be of broader scope than if the work is less creative. Also, for example, trademark value may depend on the strength of the mark and market recognition (e.g., secondary meaning).

Any question pertaining to validity and enforceability of the IP will also vary according to the type of IP (e.g., an analysis of patent validity could involve a much different level of rigor than analysis of the validity of a copyright). Validity and enforceability investigations may not be conclusive, in part, because they depend on searching for prior art or failure to disclose a reference or other evidence that may be hard to find. Also, for example, even if material prior art is already in the hands of the target company and that prior art is given to the due diligence investigators for the purchasers, it may be hidden in a huge collection of prior art and difficult to find. Outside prior art searches are many times conducted but may lead to only marginally relevant prior art or no previously marketed products (a prior use). Thus, validity and enforceability should be carefully considered in great detail. However, the acquiring company should realize that validity and enforceability will remain an issue even after the transaction is completed. This may help avoid satellite litigation regarding transfer of potentially worthless assets.

Clear title is usually a straightforward question. The seller should be able to present clear title to the IP, and the purchaser should ask the seller to provide such documentation. This includes, for example, proper assignments from all inventors or contributors and possibly employment agreements that key contributors agree to assign IP to the seller. One area that should form the basis for due diligence inquiry is whether the selling party is under any obligations to another organization, such as a prior development agreement, or a licensing agreement. The purchaser can also investigate assignments of some IP online (e.g., the U.S. Patent and Trademark Office and the U.S. Copyright Office maintain Web sites for searching assignments).

Questions of potentially infringing a third party's intellectual property focus on two main areas, (1) whether the target company has any pre-existing IP infringement problems and (2) whether any identifiable third party's IP will be infringed by doing the things that the transaction is anticipating (e.g., marketing a product). The first inquiry looks to pending litigation, any notices or other claims of infringement sent by other, or even any licenses that might be expiring or are nontransferable. The second inquiry is more difficult, but typically starts with a search for the patent position of the target company's direct competitors. These searches are usually called "freedom to operate" searches.

The due diligence process itself involves asking questions, interviewing key personnel (e.g., patent attorneys, scientists), obtaining documents from the seller (target company), and obtaining information from independent sources.

There are so many potential areas of inquiry that many people rely on a due diligence checklist to remind them of the possible areas for investigation. However, checklists may be insufficient because every transaction is different, and it is the substance of the IP that must be evaluated. Thus, comprehensive checklists might shift the focus to an issue that actually requires little attention, which not only wastes time and money, but worse, may be at the expense of overlooking a more important issue that requires detailed attention.

In most transactions, the IP attorneys who created the IP will often know its potential faults and weaknesses. Budget and time permitting, it may be worthwhile to conduct a personal interview with them. In many situations, there is not much time to assess the IP; thus, in a major transaction, a due diligence team may need to be assembled comprising attorneys (corporate and IP), accountants, scientists, and appraisers. In such instances, it is helpful to have a clear line of communication and well-defined objectives and parameters to govern the contribution each team member is expected to make.

While there is no set way to conduct due diligence, due diligence typically has two phases, an initial review and a detailed analysis. In the initial phase, the general nature of the purchase is considered, including what types of IP the seller should have for the subject matter of the transaction. A software company may have more valuable trademarks and copyrights than patents. In contrast, an automobile parts manufacturer may have trade secrets and patents that protect the value of the company's products. Companies that market consumer products may have valuable trademarks, trade secrets, and know-how. Pharmaceutical companies may have only patents. Also in the initial phase, the seller should be asked for a preliminary indication of the IP that they have, if any, and for copies of documents showing the IP. The initial phase is intended to scope out the detailed review (e.g., determine how long the detailed review will take and what resources will be needed, including people and money). A suitable nondisclosure agreement may need to be executed.

After the scoping of the detailed due diligence, the next step is a request for detailed information, including access to certain people. It might be appropriate to start interviewing corporate officers, in-house attorneys, key inventors, and IP prosecution attorneys. These interviews (by phone or in person) may need to be sensitive to attorney-client privilege issues, and thus a common interest agreement may be needed to protect the privilege.[248] Tours, personal

---

248. A common interest agreement allows the parties to a transaction to disclose attorney-client privileged information with each other without waiving the privilege. These agreements are common, and may not be necessary depending on the circumstances, but are added protection for those situations where there is a waiver concern. *Compare Katz v. AT & T Corp.,* 191 F.R.D. 433, 438 (E.D. Pa. 2000) ("plaintiffs failed to prove that the parties to the [license] negotiations shared an identity of interests such to invoke the common interest doctrine") *with Hewlett-Packard Co. v. Bausch & Lomb,* Inc., 115 F.R.D. 308 (N.D. Cal. 1987) (no waiver where defendant and potential purchaser "anticipated litigation in which they would have a common interest").

inspections, and product testing also may be considered, depending on the time, cost, and reasonableness of such activities.

7.4

The following is an example of how a company might seek to structure requests for information about IP covering the XYZ product line that the company seeks to acquire from a seller. The list provides a starting point for a due diligence inquiry, but is far from exhaustive:

1. all IP (including but not limited to patents, patent applications (published and unpublished), invention disclosures, trade secrets, copyrighted works or otherwise) owned by Seller that Seller relies upon to protect rights to the XYZ product line;
2. all information possessed by Seller that affect the strength, validity or both, of any of the identified IP;
3. all ownership documentation evidence title to the IP;
4. all contracts (including but not limited to assignments, licenses, development agreements, research agreements, testing agreements, security agreements, or otherwise) with employees, contractors or third parties that may affect the ownership of rights in the IP;
5. all documentation concerning payment of maintenance fees or annuities for the IP;
6. all information about possible infringements by the XYZ product line of third party IP rights (including but not limited to accusations, opinions of counsel, lawsuits or otherwise);
7. all information about possible infringement of Seller's IP by any third party (including but not limited to accusations, opinions of counsel, lawsuits or otherwise);
8. any investigations undertaken by Seller to determine the value of its IP;
9. the patent marking practices made by Seller with respect to the XYZ product line;
10. any challenges made to the validity of the IP (e.g., by reexamination, reissue, opposition, protest, or otherwise);
11. any governmental or regulatory submissions made by Seller pertaining to the XYZ product line; and
12. any other information about the XYZ product line or its associated IP that may affect the ability for company to fully enjoy the benefits it seeks from the transaction.

CHAPTER

8

Toward a Successful Intellectual Property Strategy

Introductory Strategy Considerations

The benefits to be realized from a healthy IP culture, and even the recognition that an IP Culture exists within an organization, sometimes occur by happenstance. More often, however, they occur as a result of planning and coordination.

With surprising frequency, however, you will encounter new small and mid-sized organizations, and even large organizations, that own some trade secrets and may even have patented some of their technologies. When asked what they want to accomplish with their IP, they pause, reflect, and shrug their shoulders. Some will attempt to proffer an answer they have read in some business journal, such as, "we want to hold our patents defensively to protect our right to do business." But, when pressed with one or two further questions, such as how they intend to accomplish their IP objectives and whether they would sue a competitor who copied one of their patented inventions, invariably they will confess they do not know. Many times the IP obtained is not tied to any particular business strategy.[249]

Ask the same persons about how they have structured their personal retirement plans, and they will likely identify a process by which they regularly study their investment statements and fund prospectus information, and select and switch funds in response to current market conditions and identifiable short- and long-term goals commensurate with their age, their income, and their future specific family needs. In short, through the exposure to retirement plans at their places of employment, to television, magazines, and other readily accessible media, these persons have come to learn and appreciate the value of personal investing. They treat personal retirement savings with the care and purpose of nurturing a valuable investment. But as to their IP, they have no similar experiences, and they have not been exposed to a healthy IP culture that would foster an awareness of IP strategy.

In a healthy IP culture, owners foster attitudes that treat intellectual property as an investment, which requires care, measured prudence, and responsiveness

---

249. The need for correlating IP strategies with business strategies has become so acute that an entire consulting industry has emerged to help companies with IP portfolios obtain value for them. For example, ipvalue.com has partnered with British Telecom (BT), Xerox's Palo Alto Research Center (PARC), and others aiming to "maximize return on invention through commercialization of their patent portfolios." *See* http://www.ipvalue.com/partners/index.html last accessed December 7, 2007.

to an ever-changing landscape. Maximization of return on a typical IP investment typically warrants the development and implementation of a strategy
with measurable goals, realistic and flexible means to achieve them, a reasonable budget to support the necessary actions, and the willingness to confront
an adversary.

In the following, the reader is introduced to a handful of IP strategies.
On the overall spectrum of IP strategies, the strategic aspects addressed
are among those often employed by some of the most IP-savvy and sophisticated organizations. Yet, they are readily within the conceptual grasp of
novices.

Offensive or Defensive

IP strategies can be characterized in one of two ways: defensive (to protect the
right to do business) or offensive (to exclude competition). While both of
these purposes are legitimate, they are not mutually exclusive. Therefore, to
treat them as "either/or" propositions could be the first mistake of any organization seeking to establish an IP strategy. The more notable mistake, however, is to overlook a more fundamental and overarching purpose of having
an IP strategy, and that purpose is to make money.

IP strategies generally have several themes, which deserve a proper introduction. First, as alluded to, strategies may be viewed from its defensive
elements, its offensive or exclusionary elements, and more preferably as a
combination of each. A defensive strategy does not necessarily mean that the
strategy is invoked in response to an attack by an adversary. Commonly,
organizations invoke defensive strategies as a routine manner of conducting
business, regardless of the presence of a competitive threat.

Typically, a defensive strategy is invoked for the purpose of clearing intellectual property obstacles that may affect the ability of an organization to
practice its technology, and thus to assure its "freedom to practice," also commonly referred to as "freedom to operate" or "right to practice." Defensive
strategies usually focus on avoidance of infringement of competitive IP,
whether by invoking design changes to avoid infringement of the IP, by
attacking the validity of the IP, or by obtaining a license.

Defensive strategies also focus on preventing competitors from obtaining
patents in the first place, such as by precluding a competitor from
patenting by publishing and, therefore, creating prior art. By avoiding
infringement disputes, and by precluding competitor patenting in the first
place, an organization helps to preserve its right to do business, allowing
it or its licensees to sell product unencumbered by patent infringement
baggage.

8.1 Survey of Popular Defensive Strategies

In general, a successful defensive strategy will often involve a combination of some or all of the following practices:[1]

1. Ongoing publishing of literature about technology developments; Filing patent applications for purpose of publication (with subsequent prosecution to issuance or abandonment);
2. Maintaining an archive of information about prior technological developments (whether sold or merely used) of a company—including preservation of sales records, photographs, samples, and the like—to establish the existence of the technology as of a certain date;
3. Marking patent numbers on products covered by a patent;
4. Drafting extremely detailed descriptions of technology for creating a sufficient disclosure to prevent a competitor from later obtaining an improvement of its own patent;
5. Disseminating or citing obscure prior art information so that patent authorities and others are able to access the information;
6. Engaging in freedom to practice patent searches to identify existing potentially problematic patents;
7. Challenging the validity of patent grants, such as through invalidity, opposition, or reexamination proceedings; and
8. Licensing dominant patents.

---

1 As with many of the topics of this book, the description of certain of the practices and strategies in this chapter is for purposes of raising awareness and is not necessarily an endorsement of the practice. Though applicable over a range of circumstances, the success of the practices will often depend upon consideration of facts unique to a particular situation. The practices are not to be construed as mutually exclusive. It will be seen that combinations of practices (even the combinations not discussed here) could lead to substantial success.

Offensive or exclusionary strategies, in contrast, usually are invoked with an eye toward preserving or gaining market share, or command higher pricing by keeping competitors from competing in a market. The potency of these strategies is derived mostly from infringement lawsuits (actual or threatened) and their attendant costs, inconveniences, and the serious consequences that can follow from a judicial determination of infringement. The possibility of a large money damage award, an injunction, and even an award of attorney fees causes considerable angst to competitors of a patentee.[250] It is the elucidation of this fear that drives an offensive strategy.

---

250. In reality, these worst-case scenarios seldom occur. The actual number of patent disputes that arise is not known nor readily ascertainable. However, it can be assured that only a

8.2 **Survey of Popular Offensive Strategies**

In general, a successful offensive strategy will often involve a combination of some or all of the following practices:

1. Seeking broad patent coverage;
2. Building a collection of many patents in a field of technology, including filings for covering variations of the basic underlying technology of an invention and filings in different territorial regions (or a related strategy called patent flooding, which involves creating a large collection of patents and patent applications in a field of technology, where each patent has only minor or commercially insignificant features);
3. Setting an example by attacking weak infringers (especially those from which a quick and favorable acknowledgement of patents and cessation of activities is likely);
4. Educating the customer base of the existence and scope of patents and the potential risk of infringement with competitive technologies;
5. Notifying competitors of the existence;
6. Marking the patent number on a product covered by a patent;
7. Engaging in litigation in foreign jurisdictions; and
8. Conspicuously maintaining the pendency of at least one patent application that pertains to a technology.

---

fraction of all disputes will progress to the point of an infringement lawsuit. For example, it is reported that in 2006, of the approximately 260,000 federal lawsuits filed in the U.S. Courts, only about 2,800 (roughly 1 percent), were patent infringement suits. http://www.patstats. org/Historical_Filings_PatentSuits_OtherSuits.rev2.doc (accessed October 29, 2007). Consider also that in the years 2004 and 2005, about 86 percent of patent infringement lawsuits (disputes that are actually filed in the courts) in the U.S. will settle (frequently with some form of a license).
http://www.patstats.org/HISTORICAL_DISPOSITION_MODES_FOR_PATENT_CASES. rev2.doc (accessed October 29, 2007). In turn, of the cases that ultimately proceed through a trial, only a portion will result in a determination of infringement; for example, in 2006 only about 29 percent of surveyed cases resulted in a determination of literal infringement, while only about 15 percent of surveyed cases resulted in a determination of infringement by equivalents. http://www.patstats.org/2000-04.htm; and http://www.patstats.org/ 2006.htm (all accessed October 29, 2007). The same source of data reports that during that period only 56 cases resulted in an increase in damages due to willful infringement. Therefore, though the prospect of a severe consequence is modest, if a lawsuit ever proceeds to judgment, it is apparent that the frequency of such worst-case occurrence in the U.S. is generally relatively small.

Strategies

Looking deeper into the above defensive strategies, it is clear the primary objective of many of them is to prevent competitors from obtaining patents. However, a strategy premised upon assuring freedom to practice by creating or making prior art known has its limitations. There is no certainty that, even if prior art exists, it will be located and considered by a Patent Office. Lots of patents withstand rigorous examination that fails to locate the most relevant prior art. Even the most vigilant practices cannot assure that occasionally troublesome patents will not grant.

8.3 Publication Pitfalls

Among the major pitfalls that make it difficult to rely upon publication as a successful defensive strategy are: (1) assuring that the published information can and will be searched and retrieved by patent authorities and others *See generally, SRI Int'l, Inc. v. Internet Security Systems, Inc.*, 511 F.3d 1186 (Fed. Cir. 2008); and (2) the incentive to publish often does not coincide with the patenting activities that are sought to be obviated by the defensive publication.

Even assuming that all relevant prior art is available for electronic database searching, the wide range of synonymous terms available to a patent applicant to describe an invention and the ability of a patent applicant to "be his or her own lexicographer" and define his or her own terms make it impossible to assure that a complete search can be performed. Suppose an applicant seeks to distinguish a material by a property called its "squishy Q factor." The patent describes a specific test made up by the applicant for measuring the squishy factor. A literature search likely will not turn up any reported "squishy Q factor." Unless the defensive publication prophesized such a "squishy Q factor," defensive publication would not likely help a competitor. Likewise, a competitor might have disclosed the possibility of the employment of an oxide of iron, but the patent claim simply states "rust." To a patent examiner not well versed in materials, a search might overlook the defensive publication.

Another frequent occurrence is that by the time a competitor seeks to enter a market or adopt a new and developing technology, it is too late to publish defensively. Patents already may have granted or applications are already pending. As to the latter, an effort to publish defensively actually could have the unintended consequence of alerting the patent owner to the possibility of competition.

Invalidity Challenges: Defensive Strategies

Once a patent has granted to a competitor, the most popular ways to assure freedom to practice, independent of obtaining a license, are to establish that the practice of a technology would not infringe a patent, that the patent is invalid, or both. As discussed previously, the practice of seeking advice of counsel, though not necessarily required for avoiding a claim for triple damages,[251] is a substantial step toward mitigation of patent risks. In the best-case scenario, the advice of counsel will be embodied in a reasoned written opinion. However, attorney opinions have no binding legal force. The legal force that assures freedom to practice is obtained through a governmental mandate, such as a court order, judgment, or other determination by an administrative authority.

As discussed previously, though there are ways that a competitor may invoke the jurisdiction of a U.S. court, before being sued for infringement, the circumstances allowing such declaratory judgment proceedings at a minimum require that there be "identified ongoing or planned activity of another party . . . where that party contends that it has the right to engage in the accused activity without license. . . ."[252] This frequently is not the case. Nor is a declaratory judgment and the attendant costs and risks of patent infringement litigation a particularly attractive option to organizations looking to compete in a particular market.

At present, short of a declaratory judgment proceeding, there is no proceeding in the U.S. by which an organization could seek a governmental mandate that would declare that the organization does or will not infringe a patent with a particular technology. However, there do exist ways in which an organization, in the absence of an infringement dispute, can gain greater certainty about the meaning or validity of a particular patent.

In the U.S., for example, an organization is free to request that the Patent Office reexamine a patent in view of patents or printed publications. Another mechanism available in some countries is a proceeding called an "Opposition Proceeding." Moreover, in some countries, even in the absence of an actual dispute between an organization and a patent owner, the organization may file proceedings to revoke a patent, sometimes referred to as "Nullity Proceedings." The following is a brief overview of these proceedings. It should be borne in mind that the proceedings are sometimes protracted, expensive, and typically subject to appeal. They are not recommended in every instance. However, as will be seen, for situations in which an organization seeks greater certainty in making its business decisions, these proceedings offer an attractive risk management vehicle.

251. *In re Seagate Tech. LLC*, 497 F.3d 1360 (Fed. Cir. 2007) (*en banc*).
252. *SanDisk Corp. v. STMicroelectronics Inc.*, 480 F.3d 1372, 1381 (Fed. Cir. 2007).

8.4 **WARNING**

The following discussion addresses unique procedures that are only available in certain territories. The outcome of a successful European Patent Office opposition, though helping to establish greater certainty concerning the scope or validity of a U.S. patent, may be excluded from evidence in a U.S. proceeding. Likewise, a successful attack in a U.S. reexamination will not assure consideration of the outcome by a foreign patent authority. Accordingly, for organizations that want the greatest assurance of success for litigating a case to conclusion, these procedures will not necessarily sway an outcome. However, for the vast majority of other situations, in which a resolution of a dispute is negotiated privately between or among parties, the authoritative imprimatur associated with a decision in these proceedings frequently has tremendous psychological impact.

Reexamination

As was discussed in Chapter 6, reexamination proceedings in the U.S. are available both to patent owners who seek greater certainty over the scope and validity of their own patents and to any other third party seeking the same. All that the requesting party must show to invoke the jurisdiction of the USPTO to reexamine a patent is the presence of a "substantial new question of patentability" in view of prior art that is either a patent or a printed publication.[253] Reexamination proceedings follow one of two courses, ex parte and inter partes.

The ex parte approach can be filed by anyone. It can even be filed anonymously. Once filed, the requesting party will have a limited further opportunity to participate. Once proceedings reach a certain stage, however, they proceed in the absence of the requesting party, as if the patent owner were prosecuting the application for the patent anew with the Patent Office. Among the possible results of a reexamination proceeding are that some or all of the patent claims will be revoked or amended. In some instances, the claims will be upheld in entirety. However, in the process of being upheld, the patent owner will almost always be compelled to make statements in the prosecution history that can be used to limit the claims in a later dispute.

Due to the limited opportunity for a requesting party to participate, reexamination requests are relatively inexpensive. For example, costs will typically be well below $50,000 (USD). However, though relatively inexpensive, many

---

253. *See* 35 U.S.C. § 301 et seq. Section 303, 35 U.S.C. § 303, specifically states in part: "Within three months following the filing of a request for reexamination under the provisions of Section 302 of this title, the Director will determine whether a substantial new question of patentability affecting any claim of the patent concerned is raised by the request, with or without consideration of other patents or printed publications."

organizations opt against ex parte reexamination, precisely because of the limited opportunity to participate. Accordingly, ex parte reexamination has not gained overwhelming popularity.

8.5 Reexamination to Clarify Claim Scope

Suppose that MUDCO owns a U.S. patent for a method of dredging a swamp comprising the steps of positioning a dredging apparatus above a swamp, removing swamp muck from the swamp, and separating the muck into its solid and liquid constituents.

DIRTCORP has been dredging swamps since 2004, well after the 2001 issue date of the MUDCO patent. DIRTCORP based a portion of its technology on a system it remembers seeing in a prior 1993 article published by a now-defunct company named MUCK. The MUCK and DIRTCORP systems each operate by boiling the muck so that water is removed. The steam from the water is released to the atmosphere. DIRTCORP fears that MUDCO will sue it and say that such a step constitutes "separating the muck into its solid and liquid constituents." DIRTCORP files an anonymous reexamination request and cites the MUCK article, telling the patent office that under a broad construction of "separating the muck into its solid and liquid constituents," it might be argued that MUCK teaches that step.

Upon determination that a substantial new question of patentability is raised, the USPTO rejects the claims in view of the MUCK article. MUDCO responds by arguing that MUCK is different because the steam is a vapor phase that is released to the atmosphere, and there is no resulting water constituent. The USPTO agrees and withdraws the rejection. Under principles applied by the U.S. Court of Appeals for the Federal Circuit, any attempt by MUDCO to thereafter apply the claim to the DIRTCORP process has been weakened by the distinction made during prosecution. Accordingly, though not revoking the patent, DIRTCORP has used the reexamination proceeding as a vehicle to gain greater certainty about the meaning of the MUDCO claims.

Inter partes reexamination affords additional participation (including during appeals) to the requesting party. However, it also limits how the requesting party can use the results of the proceeding. An adverse decision could result in an estoppel, and the process is costly. Though seeing increased frequency of usage, inter partes reexamination still has not seen its desired intended usage level.[254]

---

254 *See* http://www.uspto.gov/web/offices/dcom/olia/reports/reexam_report.htm (as accessed May 4, 2008).

Opposition

An Opposition Proceeding is another vehicle useful for competitors to establish business certainty. Though most common in Europe, the practice is followed in other countries as well. In the U.S., efforts have been made to legislate an Opposition Proceeding, and it is widely expected that some form of Opposition proceeding will eventually exist. An Opposition Proceeding is a post-grant proceeding in which members of the public, without the need for any dispute with the patentee, may challenge the grant of a patent for prior art and other reasons. For example, in the European Patent Office, opponents may challenge a patent grant for prior art reasons as well as "added subject matter" and even "sufficiency of the teachings" reasons.[255] Provided that the opposition is filed with the European Patent Office within nine months from the grant date of the European patent, a decision on the opposition will have sweeping territorial effect. If the opposition tribunal determines the patent to be invalid, in whole or in part, the decision will apply to the patent in each country in which the European patentee had ratified the grant.

For example, suppose that a patentee obtained a European patent on January 1, 2006, and immediately validates the patent in Germany, France, The Netherlands, Greece, the United Kingdom, and Italy, incurring the cost of translations into the national language of each such country. Though the patents of each such country are then in force, an opponent can successfully revoke the European patent in an opposition proceeding filed nine months later. The effect of such revocation impacts, not only the European patent, but each patent in the ratified countries. All such patents are susceptible to revocation on the basis of the opposition outcome.[256]

In the case of typical oppositions, a patentee facing a revocation challenge is provided opportunity to salvage patentable subject matter. The patentee, of course, is given a fair chance to respond to the grounds of the opposition, with argument, evidence or both. The patentee is also usually given the opportunity to present amendments to the patent grant, particularly the patent claims, in order to more specifically claim the subject matter of the patent. In a European patent opposition, this practice is referred to as the presentation of "Auxiliary Requests." Provided that the subject of the auxiliary requests does not present added subject matter, and is sufficiently taught in the written description of the patent, the European Patent Office opposition tribunal will ordinarily consider the auxiliary requests, and in many instances, will uphold the patent on the basis of one of the auxiliary requests.

The result of a complete patent revocation, though desirable, is not always a realistic ambition. Accordingly, in many instances, it can be a success for an

---

255. These are similar to challenges in the U.S. (in invalidity court litigation) for violations of 35 U.S.C. § 112, which governs the sufficiency of patent descriptions.
256. *See* European Patent Convention Article 68.

opponent to have only some of the original claims revoked or even substituted with more narrow claims. Consider a situation in which a patentee obtains a patent on a unique chocolate chip cookie. What makes the cookie unique is that (in the preferred embodiment of the patent) the chocolate chips have a unique "core/shell" configuration, by which the shell has a pure cocoa content of 85%, while the core is sweeter, with a pure cocoa content of only 35 percent. The effect is to yield a burst of sweet flavor, while allowing the patentee to feature that its chips have a high flavenoid content. The patent claims "a cookie having a dough matrix and a plurality of core/shell chocolate morsel bits distributed throughout the matrix." The opponent has been in plans to launch a new line of cookies that have a dough matrix and "core/shell" chocolate morsels that feature a hard butterscotch candy shell and a milk chocolate core. Though clearly different from the patented cookie, the opponent's cookie would fall within the claims of the patent. Accordingly, it is valuable for the opponent to be able to limit the scope of the patent—if not revoke it in its entirety—even if the opponent is unable to find prior art that taught the precise combination of preferred high cocoa content shell and sweeter low content core. For instance, reliance upon prior art cookies that use M&M® candies as the morsel could greatly benefit the opponent.

It will be appreciated that, even though a common practice, the response of patentees to an opposition request will vary and will largely be a function of the regional culture of the patentee. For example, in Europe, and other countries where oppositions are common proceedings, patent owners that patent frequently within those jurisdictions are sensitive to the likelihood of oppositions and will not necessarily react as if under attack. In contrast, opposition proceedings are not familiar for many smaller and mid-sized American companies. If one of their patents comes under scrutiny in a European opposition, a more confrontational and suspicious reaction may ensue. As a result of years of sensitization brought on by the American legal system, the patentee will likely immediately perceive that some nefarious activity is afoot that requires vigilant enforcement. Simply on the basis of such fundamental cultural differences, it is wise for prospective opponents to thoroughly consider whether the desired results sought by an opposition reasonably can be achieved, without provoking a larger dispute.

For some companies, oppositions are a business strategy to gain a license to the patent being attacked in opposition. In particular, it is a common request in Europe for the opponent to request a free license to withdraw from an opposition, which will leave the patent available to the patentee to assert against others. One study of oppositions filed in the cosmetics industry showed that one company had filed almost as many oppositions as the number of patents granted and another company had filed three times more oppositions than patents.[257] The ostensible strategy is to disrupt efforts at

257. Dietmar Harhoff and Bronwyn Hall, *Intellectual Property Strategy in the Global Cosmetics Industry*, A Soap Opera presented at the CEPR/IFS Conference in November 2002, available

8.6 **The Opposition Backup**

In some instances, an organization may believe that its chances of success in an opposition proceeding are good, but there are other compelling reasons why it does not make sense to pursue an opposition. If challenge is not made within the allotted period for opposition, the only other way to challenge patent validity will be through the courts. In Europe, for example, this would mean that a challenger would need to attack validity in each individual country in which the patent was ratified. While this is a viable option, it is expensive, and it will necessarily require a substantial likelihood of success to justify pursuit. It is important in every instance in which an opposition has been considered and rejected, nonetheless, to archive and document the bases upon which the opposition would have been pursued. Information upon which a party would rely to attack validity, and which may become necessary later, in the event of a future dispute, should be carefully preserved. This becomes especially critical if any of the bases is grounded upon some prior commercial or other activity that will require proof by witnesses and documents (e.g., prior use, prior sale, prior invention, etc.). Records of these activities desirably should be gathered and preserved for safekeeping.

broad patenting of competitors, thereby reserving a larger field in which to practice a company's own technology or to concentrate its research efforts.

Also meriting careful consideration is the limited territorial effect that opposition proceedings have, particularly in multi-jurisdictional patent disputes involving patents from various countries. For example, evidence regarding the outcome of a European Opposition Proceeding will likely face challenge if sought to be introduced before a U.S. court.[258] The sovereignty of the patent system of each regional territory will receive much deference. In some instances, simple arrogance of patent authorities of one region may even bias them to reject or seek to contradict a decision of which they are aware by a patent authority of another region. Therefore, it is not necessarily prudent to place extensive weight on a decision from one jurisdiction on its perceived potential influence on a tribunal in another jurisdiction.

---

at http://elsa.berkeley.edu/~bhhall/papers/HarhoffHall02%20IP%20Cosmetics%20slides.pdf (last accessed December 7, 2007).

258. *See, e.g., TI Group Automotive Sys. (North America) Inc. v. VDO North America LLC*, 375 F.3d 1126 (Fed. Cir. 2004); and *Caterpillar Tractor Co. v. Berco, S. p. A.*, 714 F.2d 1110, 1116 (Fed. Cir. 1983) ("Though no authority is cited for the proposition that instructions to foreign counsel and a representation to foreign patent offices should be considered, and the varying legal and procedural requirements for obtaining patent protection in foreign countries might render consideration of certain types of representations inappropriate, there is ample such authority in decisions of other courts and when such matters comprise relevant evidence they must be considered").

However, where such a decision tends to garner much influence is in the Boardrooms of the parties to a dispute. For the vast majority of smaller and mid-sized organizations (and even the large multinationals), their primary business arena is the marketplace and not a courtroom. To justify difficult decisions, these organizations nevertheless often feel compelled to have their day in court. However, it is the fact of having such day in court that tends to carry the greater influence. Of lesser concern to these organizations is the particular court chosen. That is, what is sought for the business decision is the weight of authority derived from a decision by an impartial tribunal. Of secondary concern for a large number of these companies is the location of the tribunal. Thus, an adverse outcome to an organization from the European Patent Office in an opposition will typically have a sobering effect on its business leaders, in weighing its options for confrontation in the U.S. Local oppositions, thus, can provide a relatively low cost means to influencing the future direction of a global dispute.

Judicial Invalidity or Nullity Proceedings

Judicial invalidity or nullity proceedings are another vehicle for gaining certainty regarding the scope or validity of patents. Unlike oppositions, these proceedings are generally pursued on a country-by-country basis. They will be subject to the patent laws of the respective country of the dispute. The determination of invalidity in one country will not assure an invalidity determination in another country. Thus, a successful attack that revokes a patent in Germany will not assure that the corresponding patent in France will be revoked, even if it has identical claims derived from a European patent application.

Country by country the governing procedures may vary as well. For example, some countries will require the challenging party to establish some dispute or threshold business interest to warrant assertion of jurisdiction. Some

8.7 **Comparison of Validity Court Proceedings in U.S., U.K., and Germany**			
	United Kingdom	*Germany*	*United States*
Can be filed by anyone without jurisdictional threshold	Yes	Yes, for unexpired patents or utility models	No
Amendments to patent allowed during case	Yes	Yes	No
Assessment of fees to prevailing party is automatic	Yes, actual fees are assessed	Yes, amount established according to value of case	No

countries will allow claim amendments during the proceedings. Also, some countries will assess fees against a losing party.

Offensive Strategies

Turning now to more thorough consideration of certain of the offensive strategies, the present discussion addresses three popular approaches for creating risk (or at least the perception of risk) for competitors. Successful execution of each of these, usually contemplates the filing of more than one patent application that claims priority to or the benefit of the filing date of a previously-filed application. This might be done through the use of one or more filing applications under the Patent Cooperation Treaty (PCT), the continuation and divisional statutes (e.g., 35 U.S.C. §§ 120 or 121) of the U.S. or other countries having such laws, or through the use of Paris Convention. As will be illustrated through the example of the German Utility Model, depending upon where protection is sought, such filings may not even require examination for requirements of patentability.

One alternate strategy (that does not rely on claims of benefit) is sometimes referred to as patent flooding. In this offensive patent strategy, multiple patent applications are filed into the same space as a competitor's new technology. Each individual application may or may not be very long nor very broad, and many times not thoroughly considered. Instead, many, many applications are filed, each containing a seemingly minor or commercially irrelevant technical difference between each application as well as between the filed applications and the competitor's original technology. The object is to flood the new technology with many patents and patent applications as compared to a competitor's patents and to effectively block out various pockets of the field into which the competitor may seek to commercialize. This strategy may work well, particularly where the competitor has limited resources to deal with the many patent filings or where the competitor may not see the commercial advantage of the technology sufficiently to justify the patent expense.

Continuation/Divisional Practice

Before starting in depth on the practice of divisional or continuation filings, a word of caution is in order. In recent years, this topic has polarized the U.S. legal community and the USPTO. The practice has been widely favored among U.S. practitioners for many years and has statutory authority.[259] In general, the practice allows a patent applicant to file multiple patent applications that claim the benefit of the filing date of an originally filed application so long as the

---

259. *See* 35 U.S.C. §§ 120 and 121.

inventors are common, the new application is filed while a prior application in the chain remains pending, and the invention claimed in the continuation or divisional application is described as required by 35 U.S.C. § 112 in the earlier application. Accordingly, for example, suppose a patent applicant files Application 1 on January 4, 2005, describing a paper or laminated plastic film shipping label that has a radiofrequency identification device (RFID) embedded in it. Due to a prior art reference from Korea discovered by the examiner, which disclosed a metallic foil label, the Application 1 claims are amended to require that the label be a plastic film. The claims are immediately allowed on January 31, 2007. While the Application 1 is still pending, the applicant decides to seek claims to the paper embodiment, and files Application 2 on March 23, 2007, as a continuation of Application 1. Though it has a March 23, 2007, filing date, Application 2 is entitled to the benefit of the January 4, 2005, filing date of Application 1, for purposes of avoiding application of prior art.

The above example illustrates one common use of continuation applications, namely to secure additional patent coverage beyond that which is obtained in the normal course of prosecution. A decision on whether to invoke this approach often involves the consideration of several factors, such as (1) whether commercial circumstances necessitate that a patent be granted in short order and (2) the costs and delays that are associated with appealing a rejection to the Patent Office Board of Appeals, or even to the Court of Appeals for the Federal Circuit. In other words, it has often been the case that the cost of filing a continuation or divisional application (e.g., commonly from $1500 to $3,000) is considerably cheaper than an appeal (e.g., commonly from $7,000 to $15,000). Further, the patent life is measured from its original filing date, not from the date of patent grant. For some applications, even with the patent term being adjusted for Patent Office delay, the time of an appeal can significantly eat away useful portions of the patent life. This is even more acute when the technology being patented has a short life cycle.

Securing a patent at a relatively early stage in the process also has the potential to open the door for commercial opportunities to an organization. This benefit can be as simple as the value to be derived from being able to mark (pursuant to 35 U.S.C. § 287) a patented technology with a patent number or publish in product literature or advertisements that the technology is patented[260] with prospective investors, development partners, or other commercial venture candidates. The mere fact that a patent is obtained demonstrates a commitment by an applicant to the patent process. It sends a message that the patentee will see the process through, despite the appearances of adversity in the face of patent office rejection. It is an acknowledged fact among

---

260. The ordinary consumer is often less concerned with the scope of any patent than it is with the fact that the product is sufficiently new and unique that it has been awarded patent protection.

some companies that they will not even entertain consideration of technology for "licensing in" to the company, unless and until a patent grants. The fact of a patent, notwithstanding the potentially limited scope, also generally has proven to be a valuable consideration given significant weight by investors. The grant of a patent, albeit of relatively limited scope, particularly if coupled with the pendency of a continuing application that could lead to additional claim scope has proven to be a successful practice.[261]

The availability of continuation/divisional practice also provides other strategic benefits, such as the ability to direct claims to cover specific improvements that are made to the technology underlying the original filing. Using the above example, suppose that on April 5, 2007, the applicant discovers a new combination of paper materials that allows it to embed its RFID sensors at half the cost it envisioned at the time of its original filing. A potential licensee approaches the applicant on April 17, 2007, and wants to license the technology but fears there will be insufficient coverage. The applicant can file a continuation for the broad concept of the paper embodiment and get the benefit of the January 4, 2005, filing date (while possibly also filing a new application with a 2007 filing date to cover the new combination of materials).[262] Thus, as seen, another important use of continuation and divisional applications is to cover later improvements to an applicant's own technology.

Yet another strategic use of continuation and divisional applications, and one that has caused the most controversy in recent years, is the filing of such applications to cover later-introduced technologies of competitors. The Court of Appeals for the Federal Circuit has expressed that such practice is not improper, provided that the amended claim is encompassed within the written description of the application as originally filed. In one instance, the Court has stated:

> While it is legitimate to amend claims or add claims to a patent application purposefully to encompass devices or processes of others, there must be

---

261. Comments offered by the USPTO in defense of its adoption in 2007 of rules limiting the right of an applicant to file continuation applications have come down harshly on the practice of filing continuation applications. While no one can dispute that the USPTO faces a backlog of its applications, its efforts to address this problem appear to be misdirected and likely will result in the unintended consequence of creating considerable additional burden upon the limited resources of the Office. The published case law that the USPTO relies upon to justify its actions illustrates situations on the extreme end of the continuation practice continuum, in which the applicant maintained pendency for many years, with clear evidence that diligent prosecution was lacking. At the time of this writing, district court litigation had invalidated the proposed rules, rejecting the asserted rule making authority of the USPTO. See *Tafas. v. Dudas*, 511 F. Supp. 2d (E. D. Va. 2007); and Memorandum Opinion dated April 1, 2008.

262. In this scenario, the continuation application would cover the broad concept of a paper label. A new application, with no claim to the January 2005 filing date will be needed to cover the specific new combination of paper materials, assuming such combination was not described in the January 4, 2005, filing.

support for such amendments or additions in the originally filed application. *See Kingsdown Med. Consultants, Ltd. v. Hollister Inc.*, 863 F.2d 867, 874, 9 U.S.P.Q.2d 1384, 1390 (Fed. Cir. 1988) ("[N]or is it in any manner improper to amend or insert claims intended to cover a competitor's product the applicant's attorney has learned about during the prosecution of a patent application. Any such amendment or insertion must comply with all statutes and regulations, of course, but, if it does, its genesis in the marketplace is simply irrelevant.")[263]

The U.S. Patent and Trademark Office has criticized this practice. However, such criticism appears to be founded upon its experiences in extraordinary situations.[264] Nonetheless, efforts to amend rules now governing continuation practice in the U.S. are certain to play a significant role in shaping the future of practice in the U.S. for monitoring competitive activities and seeking patent protection in response to the activities.

Foreign Filings and Litigation

Responsible foreign filing practice is another aspect deserving attention when designing and implementing a patent strategy. The economy is now an established global economy. This means that vast amounts of successful technology that originate in one geographic region will find application in a remote region. The identification of the remote regions and the determination of whether to patent in the region frequently turns on many considerations. These include the location where products are made, the location where the products are to find end use, or even the existence of prospective licensees for capturing market share in which an organization is not able to invest in infrastructure to commercialize the technology but nevertheless would like at least to derive some revenue from the market.

The practice of widespread foreign filings is quite expensive. To file in every country, let alone even the most industrial countries, is simply cost-prohibitive for all but a handful of organizations, and even then, generally

---

263. *Pin/NIP, Inc. v. Platee Chemical Co., 304 F.3d 1235, 1247 (Fed. Cir. 2002); See also, State Industries, Inc. v. A. O. Smith Corp.*, 751 F.2d 1226, 1235-36 (Fed. Cir. 1985) (addressing permissibility to "maintain[] pendency of an application . . . while competitors' products appear on the market in an effort to later draft and obtain the allowance of claims that read on the competitors' products").

264. The Patent Office cites two specific cases: *In re Bogese*, 303 F.3d 1362 (Fed. Cir. 2002), a series of 12 applications pending for 8 years; and *Symbol Technologies Inc. v. Lemelson Medical, Education & Research Foundation LP*, 422 F.3d 1378 (Fed. Cir. 2005), where applications were delayed in the USPTO for 18 to 39 years. A study of those cases indicates extraordinary circumstances that simply do not exist in most patent filings. Moreover, the *Bogese* court expressly acknowledged, 303 F.3d at 1370 that "[a]n applicant's attempt to obtain new claims directed to inventions that he or she believes are fully disclosed and supported in an earlier application, however, is easily distinguishable from appellant's failure to further the prosecution of his application toward the issuance of any claims."

only for their most important inventions. Consequently, most smaller and mid-sized organizations must make thoughtful strategic decisions. As a result, a few factors (apart from the short-term costs of pursuing the investment) tend to rise to the top as the most influential considerations for the location of foreign filings, among them being:

1. The strength of the court system and procedural advantages that may exist for patentees seeking relief for infringement;[265]
2. The ability of a patent in a specific region to impact commercialization by a competitor in other regions in which no patents are filed;[266]
3. The size of the market in the respective region;[267] and
4. The likelihood of adoption of a technology in the region of interest.[268]

The Utility Model

Once again, the cost of an investment in foreign patent protection tends to drive the decision making of many organizations. It is not simply the cost of the government filing fees and translation costs. The investment costs also tend to involve a significant amount of legal fees to prosecute the applications in the foreign patent offices.[269] One possible way to avoid the latter costs, and also to avoid the delays occasioned by the prosecution activities, is to employ

---

265. As will be discussed momentarily, some countries (such as Germany) traditionally have structured their patent systems in a way that offers considerable procedural advantage to patent owners. Other countries have been criticized for the apparent reluctance to facilitate enforcement against infringers.

266. Consider how a patent in France and Germany could stifle the introduction of a consumer product designed and built in Switzerland for the entire European market, even if a patent is not pursued in Switzerland. A manufacturer might be able to make modifications to its products for the respective market in each different country. However, this imposes burden to manage distribution of the products to assure noninfringement and will also require various redundancies in the sales and marketing functions of the organizations. Accordingly, it can be seen that even though it would be nice to have protection in as many European countries as possible, a strategy for protecting market share has the prospect of succeeding even absent such protection.

267. The shear magnitude of the size of the market in China, even taking into account the perceived inability to reliably enforce patent rights, has caused large numbers of organizations to pursue patent protection in China.

268. Consider the market for large sport utility vehicles. The cost of fuel and simple considerations of lifestyle preferences and space (even if just for parking) have limited the adoption of these vehicles in Europe. In the U.S., in contrast, fuel has been considerably less expensive and real estate is more abundant. Patents for technologies that are specific to large sport utility vehicles may have less value in Europe than in North America.

269. Remember, each country has its own laws and will examine applications pursuant to their own respective patentability standards. A grant of a patent in the U.S. offers no assurance of a grant in a foreign country.

a procedure, offered in a select few countries, of registering the invention as a "utility model."[270]

For this process, effectively, the patent application of the priority country is filed in the patent office of the intended country, with the desired claims. In relatively short order, possibly months, the invention will be registered. It will then confer rights upon the owner to sue for violations, typically subject to the ability of the accused to challenge the validity of the patent.

Why a Utility Model?

The main reasons for pursuing a utility model are that it is a relatively quick way to secure some form of a protection right, and overall costs may be lower than patenting because of the absence of a significant prosecution phase.[271] Further, in some countries, the standards for obtaining a utility model may be less stringent than those required for obtaining a patent.[272] Despite its advantages, pursuit of a utility model has certain disadvantages as compared with an ordinary patent. Among them is that the term of protection of a utility model is going to be shorter than the term of a patent. In Germany the maximum term of the utility model or *Gebrauchmuster* is ten years from filing.[273] In contrast, German patents typically enjoy a maximum life of twenty years from filing. In addition, utility models are not an option available for protecting certain technologies. For example, in Germany, though many mechanical, chemical, and electrical innovations can be protected by a utility model, processes generally will not receive protection by a utility model.

---

270. Among the examples of countries that afford invention registrations are Japan, various European countries, Mexico, and China. http://www.wipo.int/sme/en/ip_business/utility_models/where.htm (accessed October 29, 2007). Since 2001, Australia has offered the possibility of an *Innovation Patent*, which protects innovations that may lack "inventive step," but which nonetheless exhibit an "innovative step." *See* http://www.ipaustralia.gov. au/patents/what_innovation.shtml#1 (accessed October 29, 2007).

271. The pursuit of utility model registration is not a guarantee of lower costs in every instance. There are various strategies that can be invoked in the drafting of claims for the utility model, which can cost a lot. However, it is common in many instances of utility model filings that a dispute with a competitor is imminent. Accordingly, the costs are incurred for the purpose of avoiding potentially greater costs in the course of any litigation of the dispute.

272. *See generally* http://www.wipo.int/sme/en/ip_business/utility_models/utility_models.htm (accessed October 29, 2007).

273. There are many technologies for which a term of ten years may be more than adequate. For example, certain consumer-oriented technologies, such as that found in cars or personal electronics, become obsolete merely a few years after their introduction. The value in the right to exclude competitors is heavily weighted in the phase immediately following market introduction, and much less in the ten-to-twenty-year period following the introduction.

Why Germany?

The pursuit of a utility model in Germany can offer many benefits.[274] Though it is not intended as a substitute for seeking ordinary patent protection, it can provide an interim measure of potentially enforceable rights, particularly during the period when an application for a European patent or a German national patent is pending. Germany offers many benefits commercially, given its role as one of the most dominant global economies. As discussed above, a risk to a competitor of enforcement of utility model rights in Germany likely can significantly impact competition elsewhere within Europe.

A substantial portion of costs will reside in translation fees. Due to the highly competitive nature of the legal services community within Germany, applicants should expect to incur relatively modest legal fees, particularly as compared with certain other European countries, in which legal fees historically are reputed to be high.

It should be borne in mind that a party charged with violation of utility model rights has the right to challenge the validity of the utility model claims. If successful, this could result in an assessment of legal fees against the proprietor of the rights.[275] However, during any such proceedings in which the validity of the claims is challenged, the proprietor may amend the claims (provided the amendment does not constitute added matter).

Measuring Success of a Strategy

How to know whether a strategy has been effective escapes definition by any straightforward objective formula. Success will be measured differently in every instance. In the case of for-profit corporate organizations, even though the underpinnings of every strategy will be maximization of profits, it is unrealistic to expect success to be defined by readily identifiable data. Earlier discussions in Chapters 2 and 3 identified some possible metrics that businesses can use to measure if their IP is doing what they want.[276] However, there are various

---

274. It is reported that about 400 German utility models are published every week, with about 70 percent pertaining to mechanical inventions. http://scientific.thomson.com/support/patents/patinf/patentfaqs/utility (accessed October 29, 2007).

275. In German litigation, though assessment of fees to a losing party is automatic, the amount of fees is predetermined by German law and is based upon the value of the case. Consequently, seldom will an adverse outcome to a proprietor result in assessment of the total actual fees incurred by the other party. In contrast, other countries frequently award the entire amount of fees actually incurred by the prevailing party. The losing party, nonetheless, will also be assessed the court costs (again, the amount being based upon the value of the case) in German proceedings.

276. *See also* Williamson, How Metrics Can Put IP at the Heart of Your Company's Agenda, Intellectual Asset Management (August/September 2004) at 35-39, reproduced at http://64.233.167.104/search?q=cache:NYvsj9T8vhwJ:www.ipperform.com/Metrics-IAM-Mag-ARTICLE-ISSUE-7.pdf±williamson±metric±heart±agenda&hl=en&ct=clnk&cd=1&gl=us (as accessed April 7, 2008).

questions that an organization can ask itself to help assess success. The questions generally are directed at ascertaining from available data the response of an organization, its investors, its competitors, and its customers to patenting by the organization.

1. *Is there a direct and identifiable revenue stream attributable to the patents of the strategy?* The easiest and most understandable way to determine the success of a strategy is to identify a sum of money directly linked to the patents. This may be from such varied sources as a damages award or other remedy in litigation, from a settlement of a lawsuit, from royalties under a license, or even the purchase price realized from the sale of patents. Patents also have become a popular asset for use as collateral for loans or other financing.

2. *Is there data by which the relative profits of subject matter sold under the patent can be compared with the profits of a technology offered by the organization that is not covered by the patents?* Some organizations are able to point to an identifiable discrepancy in the profitability of subject matter sold under its patents, as compared with technology that is not. For example, suppose an organization sells patented coatings and realizes a profit of one dollar per kilogram of material. However, the same organization sells various commodity coatings that are not patented, and only realizes ten cents per kilogram profit. For a variety of circumstances, it may be reasonable to attribute a substantial portion of the one dollar profit to the existence of an exclusive market position secured to the organization by a patent.

3. *Are competitors filing oppositions to the patents overseas or reexamination requests in the U.S.?* In some instances, the filing of a challenge to the scope of a granted patent by a competitor is merely for malicious purposes. However, for many respectable challengers, it is also a sign that the challenger takes the patent grant seriously. The challenge to its scope is, therefore, a sign of respect for the value conferred by the patent right. On the flip side, relative to the challenger, a successful challenge to the patent could clear the way for the challenger to access a market with its own technology.

4. *If the organization is a publicly traded company, is there any correspondence with patenting activities and share price of the company?* The announcement of an award of a patent (and the implicit benefits to be derived and enjoyed from such grant) for a key technology is a common basis upon which stock prices tend to rise. Likewise, news of a license granted under a patent of a company also frequently is employed to bolster investor confidence.

5. *Is there a liability or expense that has been avoided due to the existence of the IP?* Examples of such liability or expense include the avoidance of litigation with a competitor. It may also involve forgiveness of a past infringement by the organization, which a competitor elects not to

pursue out of fear of a counter-strike by the organization under one of its patents. The mere avoidance of defending an infringement lawsuit could save an organization millions of dollars, even if they won the lawsuit.

6. ***Can any award of business be attributed to the existence of a patent?*** It is common that some vendors will assert valuable patent rights as a means to help enhance the likelihood of an award of competitively bid business. The possible risk of supply disruption to a customer that an injunction might bring, or even the potential that the cost of a license royalty will be passed through to a customer, often provides the incentive for a customer to award a business opportunity in favor of a patent owner. Thus, it may be possible through the simple act of notifying a customer about a patent that an organization may be able to secure an award of business to itself.

7. ***Are there any identifiable instances where the goodwill of the organization has been or could be enhanced by publicity from patenting activities?*** In recent years, the *Wall Street Journal*® has taken to publishing a list called the PATENT SCORECARD.[277] Every Tuesday, a different industry sector is featured. The basis for inclusion in the featured listing is a demonstrable commitment to patenting. Apart from the potential value to be derived from the recognition of the company as innovative, data such as this is coming to be relied upon as a metric for evaluating companies with a heavy emphasis upon research and development.

8. ***Are there any identifiable changes in market share that coincide with the implementation of the strategy?*** Sometimes it is not immediately possible to isolate a specific allocation of revenue. It may be necessary to view the change macroscopically, in terms of a change of market share. For some technologies, this may require a period of time, during which multiple patents granted. This is often the case with the introduction of a next generation, "improved" product for which a family of patents has been sought to cover different aspects of the technology. For some technologies, even a gain in market share of one percent attributable to an exclusively protected technology can translate into millions of dollars.

9. ***Has a competitor changed its product in apparent response to patent filings?*** The manifestation of a successful strategy may be simply in the expense or inconvenience caused to a competitor by causing the competitor to change a design. While these are often not immediately felt by a patent owner, over the long term substantial benefits can be realized. A company faced with implementing a design change to its product often will need to validate the redesigned product, which costs money and takes substantial time (especially when the product is required to

---

277. *See generally* http://www.patentboard.com/our_services/wsj_overview.asp (accessed October 29, 2007).

be subject to rigorous testing under conditions simulating actual use), often delaying market entry by the competitor.

10. ***Has the organization otherwise been able to accomplish the objective originally set forth to justify pursuit of the patenting strategy?*** So many organizations tend to lose sight of the justifications they offered at the outset of any patenting strategy. Sometimes it is because they simply do not memorialize the initial objectives of the strategy. Other times, it is because the organization starts to enjoy some success (well beyond that initially contemplated) that when they suffer some set-back, an element of greed prompts them to want more than what they have. A simple reminder of the initial objectives of the strategy, and whether those objectives have been met, may be the most straightforward approach to measuring success.

Case Studies

As mentioned earlier, IP strategies tend to be divided into two categories, defensive strategies and offensive strategies, with the terms defensive and offensive being used generally to describe the primary objective of the strategy.[278] Within the above categories there are a number of subcategories. Albeit not necessarily mutually exclusive, the subcategories each tend to invoke unique courses of action.

With the offensive strategies herein, the primary objective is the maximization of revenues by the exercise of the right of the IP owner to exclude others from commercializing the protected subject matter within a particular market. Such exclusion may be in the form of a complete and total exclusion, such as may be possible by invoking a patentee's right to seek an injunction for preventing future patent infringement.[279] The exclusion may be more subtle, and may involve something short of preventing competition. For example, the exercise of a patent owner's right to exclude may involve the grant of a license to a competitor within a particular market, subject to the payment of a royalty. This has the potential to benefit the IP owner, as it is

---

278. The latter offensive strategies typically are founded upon the exercise by an intellectual property owner of its right to exclude others under its IP. In the present discussion it will, therefore, interchangeably be called an exclusionary strategy.

279. There is no automatic right to an injunction when patent infringement has been established. The courts will apply an equitable analysis *eBay, Inc. v. MercExchange, LLC*, 126 S. Ct. 1837 (2006).

expected that the competitor having the royalty obligation will need to charge a higher price to its customers to achieve a desired profit level, which places the competitor at a competitive disadvantage relative to the IP owner.

The strategy may involve the grant of a license to an entity that does not necessarily compete with the patent owner in the same market (e.g., a naval architecture firm might license certain of its IP developed for ocean-going vessels to a manufacturer of automobiles for passenger vehicle applications). Still other companies have a business model that relies almost totally upon a strategy of offense, with such licensing companies creating new technology of their own (e.g., Tessera[280]) or only licensing the technology created by others (e.g., ipvalue.com).

Another subcategory of strategies arises when two competitors actively compete within a common market, and both competitors actively patent their respective inventions. In these instances, a collision course between competitors is virtually inevitable. Strategies are, therefore, devised, and measures taken, with an eye toward establishing a peaceful coexistence.

Defensively, the strategies devised and the measures invoked typically will involve the existence of one or more patents held by a competitor or other third party, which may cause, or have caused, a dispute over infringement. In these situations, strategies aim to eliminate the patent as a threat, prevent other patents from issuing and posing further obstacles, or exercise damage control by reducing the severity of any consequence that may flow from an adverse outcome in any dispute.

Yet another subcategory of strategies invokes a hybrid of defensive and offensive elements. Characteristic of this subcategory is the situation in which an organization has embarked upon market analysis and has identified potential marketing opportunities in which to expand its business. In the course of its due diligence, the organization identifies a scattering of patents to third parties that pose potential obstacles to market entry. Accordingly, to enter the market and have any chance at enjoying any exclusionary position, it must also engage in defensive measures to mitigate the potential consequences of the existing third-party patents.

Selecting the appropriate strategy must be done on a case-by-case basis, taking into account the company's particular needs and market conditions. It must not be performed in a legal vacuum, devoid of meaningful business influence. Indeed, a strong patent strategy can in no way substitute for a strong business model. A patent strategy must, therefore, be regarded as merely one tool in a larger tool kit necessary for building a successful business.

---

280 *See generally*, http://www.tessera.com/company/licensees (accessed December 13, 2007).

Case Study 1: Licensing with Ensuing Pricing Disadvantage

Suppose A Company owns a patent for a solar-powered personal entertainment system for a passenger railcar. A Company sells each of its units for $10,000. For each system, A Company is able to demonstrate a net profit of $1,200. B Company has introduced an infringing competitive system that it offers to the same customers as A Company but at a price of $9,600. B Company boasts to its shareholders, in public filings, that its expected net profits for sales of these new systems are $1,000. For a variety of reasons, including the main reason of avoiding shutdown of supply to a common customer of A and B Companies, A Company decides to grant B Company a license under its patent at a royalty of $600 per system. In order to meet the profits projected for shareholders, B Company must pass the royalty through to the customer, in the form of a price increase to $10,200. Alternatively, B Company can show a lower price increase or no price increase, and accept a lower profitability. As seen, the exercise of total exclusion from the market need not be sought by the patentee for the patentee to still benefit from an offensive strategy.

Case Study 2: Cross-Licensing

YCO owns a number of patents in the field of power generation. YCO has derived a significant competitive advantage from the use of solar cells on the tips of the windmills. The technology is such that YCO windmills are able to generate power from the conversion of both solar and wind energy. YCO has a portfolio of patents that address the solar/wind energy combination solution. ZINC has engaged in the field of solar cell manufacture for twenty years and holds several patents in that field. ZINC has developed and patented a unique solar cell for use in windmills to achieve a 50 percent efficiency increase as compared with prior solar cells used for the purpose. ZINC desires to enter the solar/wind energy market, potentially in competition with YCO, but fears that the YCO patents impose an insurmountable barrier to entry.

ZINC and YCO each recognizes the value to their respective organizations of having access to the other's technology. Taking care to avoid an anticompetitive relationship, ZINC and YCO enter a cross-licensing relationship. As a result, ZINC is able to make and sell windmills under YCO's patents, which employ ZINC's unique solar cells, subject to the payment of a royalty to YCO. In turn, and likewise subject to payment of royalties, YCO gains access to the improved solar cell technology under the ZINC patents.

Case Study 3: Total Exclusion

K9 has a policy of excluding competitors from competing in any field in which K9 possesses market share. K9 sells a line of patented textiles used for aircraft interiors and recently raised the prices for textiles it is selling to an aircraft manufacturing customer. The customer has sought to obtain a similar textile from BW, a competitor of K9. Though employing some technological differences, the BW material nonetheless arguably falls within the claims of the K9 patents. K9 charges BW with infringement. Consistent with its right to unilaterally refuse to license its patents, in seeking to maintain an exclusive market position, K9 refuses to license BW.[281] As a result, the customer is faced with continuing to purchase from K9 at the higher price, purchase from BW subject to the threat of unavailable supply due to an injunction, or encourage BW to engage in a program to design around the K9 patents, the costs of which likely would be borne (at least in part) by the customer.

Case Study 4: Entering a Market Populated with Patents[282]

BC makes insecticides, and wants to apply one of its insecticides to a new use in the field of surgical instrument sterilization. BC performs a patent search and learns that a company named PS previously attempted to enter such a market using an insecticide as an active ingredient. PS holds several patents to the technology, some of which could pose a barrier to the ability of BC to successfully launch a product. BC studies the patents to PS and determines that several are potentially invalid as anticipated by the prior art. One patent, though likely valid, would not pose an infringement issue for BC, provided that BC stays within design guidelines prepared by its counsel. The sole remaining patent is clearly a likely infringement issue. The cost and effort to design around the patent are prohibitive. BC remains steadfast in its commitment to enter the market. Accordingly, BC secures counsel to determine if the patent can be established as invalid. If not susceptible to invalidation, then BC determines it will seek a license from PS. Simultaneously, BC

---

281. *See generally Intergraph Corp. v. Intel Corp.*, 195 F.3d 1346, (Fed. Cir. 1999), and *Data Gen. Corp. v. Grumman Sys. Support Corp.*, 36 F.3d 1147, 1182 (1st Cir. 1994) ("the desire of an author to be the exclusive user of its original work is a presumptively legitimate business justification for the author's refusal to license to competitors."

282. A similar, albeit defensive, strategy is to enter a market populated with patents by making and selling enough products to get the attention of the patent holders, but not so much that it will break your company if you have to shut down and pay damages. Sort of like getting your toe wet to test the water. You can collectively test the patent validity, willingness of the patent holders to license, and market reception of a technology.

engages in a campaign to patent various ideas it has pertaining to solving particular technical problems unique to the intended application. When granted, BC's patents could provide them with something to potentially cross-license to PS. BC also contemplates the possibility of forming a joint venture with PS, by which each would contribute its respective proprietary technologies.

Case Study 5: Reexamination to Reduce Damages Exposure

XCorp holds a U.S. patent that is five years old and has two patent claims. ZCo discovers the patent and forms an opinion that it infringes both claims from its activities with its AAA machine introduced four years ago (which is relevant only to claim 1 of the patent) and from its BBB machine introduced one year ago (which is relevant only to claim 2 of the patent). But there is a reasonable likelihood that the claims are invalid due to a prior art patent located by ZCo. ZCo files a request for reexamination and succeeds in invalidating claim 1. Claim 2 survives reexamination. By pursuing the reexamination, without costly litigation, ZCo has reduced its potential exposure for damages significantly; any XCorp claim for damages for four years of infringement by the AAA machine is extinguished.

Case Study 6: Acquisition of Rights to Resolve Dispute

H obtains a dominant patent that broadly covers a new technology. H does not practice the technology. However, two entities, K and L, each practices the technology and both are sued by H for infringement. As a means for quick resolution of the infringement dispute, K purchases the H patent from H, along with the right to sue for past infringements. Thereafter, K persists in the suit against L for infringement of the H patent.

Case Study 7: Avoidance of Litigation

ONE owns several dominant, but aging, patents that cover unique modular office furnishings. TWO decides to enter the market in competition with ONE. The technology of TWO is unique unto itself and is visibly different from the ONE furniture. However, giving a broad construction to the ONE patents, it is possible that ONE could state a claim for infringement against TWO and cause inconvenience through litigation. The TWO technology, meanwhile, gains immediate market acceptance and includes many features (for which TWO obtains patents) that consumers now demand of ONE's products as well. Though ONE owns the earlier dominant patents, the risk created by the existence of the TWO patents causes ONE to refrain from suing TWO for infringement.

Case Study 8: Licensing to Foster Adoption of Technology

BX holds broad patent coverage to a unique method for preparing an alternative fuel from corn. The technique has proven to have yields and efficiencies in excess of ten percent of any prior technology. BX also sells unique patented equipment for use in the process. In recognition of the vast market size, BX embarks on a widespread licensing program, offering its processing technology for license at a nominal royalty rate in order to foster widespread industry acceptance of the technology.

Case Study 9: Same as 8, with Collateral Sales of Goods

The same facts are present from Case Study 8, however, with the acceptance of the technology, BX also realizes a demand for its unique equipment and generates substantial revenues from the sales of the equipment.

Case Study 10: Licensing to Maintain Innovation Advantage

DKX holds a family of patents covering a process for making a water-repellant textile for low-cost upholstery applications. DKX is about to launch an alternative process that will enable it to use its textiles for many of the more profitable high-end upholstery applications, where DKX has decided to concentrate its business efforts. MV competes with DKX and has been attempting to capture some of DKX's market share with its own textile for low-cost applications. MV has received only lukewarm acceptance of its technology. Industry rumors have it that, unless an immediate business upswing occurs, MV is contemplating a venture with an off-shore competitor, with inexpensive labor and a growing research and development function, which will afford MV access to a broader range of technology (and the potential to hurt DKX). DKX enters into a license with MV, by which DKX grants rights to MV to manufacture its low-cost upholstery process technology.

Trade Secrets and Other Intellectual Property

Intellectual Property Types

To help define the appropriate IP culture for an organization, it is important to have an appreciation for the diverse disciplines within the IP field. The most common types of intellectual property are patents, trade secrets, copyrights, and trademarks.[283] The latter two provide a significant basis for supporting various industries. For example, the software industry, along with the entertainment and recording industries, heavily depends upon copyright for protection of its assets. The merchandising and consumer products industries, from sports teams to car companies, likewise, depend upon trademarks for capturing revenues. However, the needs of each of these industries are not necessarily unique. Any business that sells unique products or services expects to invest in more than one type of intellectual property protection to safeguard valuable assets. The key to securing the greatest return on such investment is an understanding of the differences among the subject matter that can be protected and with various forms of available protection.

The Trade Secret and Patent Dichotomy

Historically, technology oriented companies have protected their processes, formulations, and future product designs by either or both trade secrets and patents. In generations past, the balance of protection tipped in favor of trade secrets. However, in the late 1980s and the 1990s the pendulum started to shift toward patent protection as an emphasized, if not preferred, form of protection for proprietary technology developments.

Though not entirely mutually exclusive, protection through a patent grant is contradictory to protection afforded by trade secrets. On the one hand, a patent provides its owner with a limited monopoly to exclude others from exploiting the patented technology. The *quid pro quo*, however, is that the monopoly is granted only as part of an information exchange–the patent owner must disclose the innovation so that others can reproduce it when the monopoly period ends. In a pronouncement on these policy considerations, in 1974 the U.S. Supreme Court reiterated the public disclosure requirement that necessarily must occur in exchange for a patent grant:

> The patent laws promote this progress by offering a right of exclusion for a limited period as an incentive for inventors to risk the often enormous costs in

---

283. The term "trademarks" covers the general category of intellectual property that concerns itself with identifiers of source or origin. As will be discussed, such identifiers may be a trademark if they serve to identify a good, a service mark if it serves to identify a service, or even trade dress, for product configurations.

terms of time, research, and development. The productive effort thereby fostered will have a positive effect on society through the introduction of new products and processes of manufacture into the economy, and the emanations by way of increased employment and better lives for our citizens. In return for the right of exclusion—this "reward for inventions," . . . the patent laws impose upon the inventor a requirement of disclosure. To insure adequate and full disclosure so that upon the expiration of the 17-year period "the knowledge of the invention enures to the people, who are thus enabled without restriction to practice it and profit by its use, "*U.S. v. Dubilier Condenser Corp.*, 289 U.S. 178, 187, 157 (1933), the patent laws require that the patent application shall include a full and clear description of the invention and "of the manner and process of making and using it" so that any person skilled in the art may make and use the invention. 35 U.S.C. § 112. When a patent is granted and the information contained in it is circulated to the general public and those especially skilled in the trade, such additions to the general store of knowledge are of such importance to the public weal that the Federal Government is willing to pay the high price of 17 years of exclusive use for its disclosure, which disclosure, it is assumed, will stimulate ideas and the eventual development of further significant advances on the art.[284]

By the public record nature of a patent grant, anything that is disclosed in a patent is not a secret. Thus, although the social policy advanced by compulsory disclosure in patents necessarily seems incompatible with the basic premise underlying trade secret law, the following sections show that despite the ostensible incompatibility between patents and trade secrets, a successful technology portfolio derives much value from a combination of both protections.

---

284. *Kewanee Oil Co. v. Bicron Corp.*, 416 U.S. 470, 480-81 (1974). Similarly, Justice O'Connor expressed the view of the court in *Bonito Boats, Inc. v. Thunder Craft Boats, Inc.*, 489 U.S. 141, 146-47 (1989) (citation omitted):

> From their inception, the federal patent laws have embodied a careful balance between the need to promote innovation and the recognition that imitation and refinement through imitation are both necessary to invention itself and the very lifeblood of a competitive economy. Soon after the adoption of the Constitution, the First Congress enacted the Patent Act of 1790, which allowed the grant of a limited monopoly of 14 years to any applicant that "hath . . . invented or discovered any useful art, manufacture, . . . or device, or any improvement therein not before known or used." In addition to novelty, the 1790 Act required that the invention be "sufficiently useful and important" to merit the 14-year right of exclusion. Section 2 of the Act required that the patentee deposit with the Secretary of State, a specification and if possible a model of the new invention, "which specification shall be so particular, and said models so exact, as not only to distinguish the invention or discovery from other things before known and used, but also to enable a workman or other person skilled in the art or manufacture . . . to make, construct, or use the same, to the end that the public may have the full benefit thereof, after the expiration of the patent term."

Trade Secret Protection

Trade secret law always has occupied a significant place in the body of intellectual property law available for protecting proprietary information. At least one survey of 138 survey respondents reported that the respondents suffered proprietary information losses in excess of $50 billion.[285] Even though patent filing have grown exponentially over the past couple decades, a considerable portion of proprietary information in the form of trade secrets still remains, and a basic understanding of the trade secret law is, therefore, essential.

The Civil Law

The body of law giving rise to protection of trade secrets derives from state law, which for the most part developed from the common law. In the past several decades many states have codified their trade secret laws, based upon the initiative of a subcommittee of the Patent Committee of the American Bar Association commenced in the late 1960s. An on-again/off-again/ on-again progression of activities then transpired through the 1970s by advocates for a uniform system of trade secret protection, with renewed momentum by the early 1980s. By 1985, a committee acting for the National Conference of Commissioners on Uniform State Laws had adopted the Uniform Trade Secrets Act (UTSA), which has since formed the basis of the trade secret statutes of most states.[286]

Coincidentally, at the time when the committee adopted the UTSA, confidence in the U.S. patent system was at a low point.[287] The Court of Appeals for the Federal Circuit, whose formation was based at least in part on unifying patent law across the circuits, had only been operating for a couple years. Many technology companies still suffered from the effects of many years of inconsistent treatment of patents among the various judicial circuits. The situation was so poor, that not only was uniformity lacking among the Circuits, consistent application of the law could not be relied upon even within an individual Circuit.[288]

---

285. PriceWaterhouseCoopers, *Trends in Proprietary Information Loss, Survey Report*, ASIS Foundation and the U.S. Chamber of Commerce (September, 2000).
286. Uniform Trade Secrets Act with 1985 Amendments (Prefatory Note).
287. In a Prefatory Note, the committee expressed that "[i]n view of the substantial number of patents that are invalidated by the courts, many businesses now elect to protect commercially valuable information through reliance upon the state law of trade secret protection." Uniform Trade Secrets Act with 1985 Amendments (Prefatory Note).
288. *See also* http://www.terry.uga.edu/~jlturner/HenryTurnerJLSJune2005Two.pdf. In a 1975 case, *Campbell v. Spectrum Automation Co.*, 513 F.2d 932, 937 (6th Cir. 1975). the Court of Appeals for the Sixth Circuit considered whether to adopt a preponderance of the evidence

9.1 Life Prior to the Federal Circuit

The Prefatory Note to the Uniform Trade Secrets Act makes passing reference to the large volume of patents being invalidated by the courts in the period leading up to the 1985 adoption. Just how bad was it? Prior to the Federal Courts Improvement Act of 1982, which created the Court of Appeals for the Federal Circuit, it was widely known among practitioners that certain circuits looked upon patent validity favorably, while many others regarded the issue of validity with hostility. For example, it was widely known that an accused infringer stood a much greater chance of success when attacking a patent in the Eighth Circuit than in the Seventh Circuit. Forum shopping was rampant. A survey of the law under the "first to file" rule, and declaratory judgment jurisdiction would show a vast body of jurisprudence that emerged in the 1970s for determining where venue was appropriate when a declaratory judgment plaintiff seeking to invalidate a patent with a claim of invalidity would race to the courthouse before the filing of an infringement action by the patent owner. Though forum shopping remains an issue still today, the creation of the Court of Appeals for the Federal Circuit has mitigated it. For an interesting review of the impact of the Federal Circuit on the practice of forum shopping in patent cases, see Atkinson, Scott, and Marco, Alan C., and Turner, John L., *The Economics of a Centralized Judiciary: Uniformity, Forum Shopping and the Federal Circuit*, Vassar College Department of Economics, Working Paper Series 86. (January 2007); http://irving.vassar.edu /VCEWP/VCEWP86.pdf (accessed August 5, 2007). The authors conducted an extensive survey of certain reported case decisions, starting in 1953, and reported (in Table 1) the following pre-Federal Circuit rates in which the patents were upheld as not invalid (classified according to whether the patent owner was the plaintiff or was the defendant in a declaratory judgment action).

Circuit	Patentee-Plaintiff	Patentee-Defendant
Third	.250	.273
Fourth	.519	.571
Eighth	.424	.357

standard (which would have the effect of easing the burden upon a challenger to prove invalidity) or a clear and convincing evidentiary standard (which would favor patent owners). In the context of a dispute over inventorship, the court presented a survey of the prevalent standards among the circuits:

In view of the recognition by the Supreme Court that state trade secret law is not pre-empted by patent laws, the Act has since been adopted as is, or with modifications, by a majority of states.[289]

The UTSA provides for monetary relief, injunctive relief or both, for the unauthorized taking or misappropriation of trade secrets. The UTSA defines a trade secret as:

1. Information, including a formula, pattern, compilation, program, device, method, technique, or process, that:
2. derives independent economic value, actual or potential, from not being generally known to, and not being readily ascertainable by proper means by, other persons who can obtain economic value from its disclosure or use, and
3. is the subject of efforts that are reasonable under the circumstances to maintain its secrecy.[290]

The UTSA is a codification of civil law, affording aggrieved trade secret owners the right to seek relief from violators. In the U.S., however, misappropriation of trade secrets may also be prosecuted criminally.

We find no recent decisions of the Supreme Court delineating the burden of proof in patent validity actions. The application of the "clear and convincing" standard varies among the Circuits. Two Circuits seem to apply the "clear and convincing" standards regardless of the asserted ground of invalidity. *See Hobbs v. United States*, 451 F.2d 849, 856, (5th Cir. 1971); *Universal Marion Corp. v. Warner & Swasey Co.*, 354 F.2d 541, 544, (10th Cir. 1965), cert. denied, 384 U.S. 927 (1966). Four Circuits have applied the standard in cases where patented prior art has been urged as a ground for invalidity, without explication. *See Trio Process Corp. v. L. Goldstein's Sons, Inc.*, 461 F.2d 66, 70 (3d Cir.), cert. denied, 409 U.S. 997 (1972); *Ever-Wear, Inc. v. Wieboldt Stores, Inc.*, 427 F.2d 373, 375, (7th Cir. 1970); *L & A Products, Inc. v. Britt Tech Corp.*, 365 F.2d 83, 86 (8th Cir. 1966); *Moon v. Cabot Shops, Inc.*, 270 F.2d 539, 541 (9th Cir. 1959), cert. denied, 361 U.S. 965 (1960). We find two Circuits that have applied a lesser standard to the usual patent case. *Rains v. Niaqua, Inc.*, 406 F.2d 275 (2nd Cir.), cert. denied 395 U.S. 909 (1969) (preponderance of the evidence); *Universal Inc. v. Kay Mfg. Corp.*, 301 F.2d 140, 148 (4th Cir. 1962) . . . .

We conclude that the clear and convincing standard should be applied in the present case. In doing so, we do not commit this Circuit to any general rule requiring the application of this standard in all patent cases.

In contrast, only about four months later, when addressing the issue of proving invalidity by obviousness, the same Court adopted a preponderance of the evidence standard. *Dickstein v. Seventy Corp.*, 522 F.2d 1294 (6th Cir. 1975), *cert. denied*, 423 U.S. 1055 (1976)

289. *Kewanee Oil Co. v. Bicron Corp.*, 416 U.S. 470 (1974); *See also Aronson v. Quick Point Pencil Co.*, 440 U.S. 257 (1979).

290. Uniform Trade Secrets Act Section 1(4).

Economic Espionage Act: Federal Trade Secret Criminal Laws

In 1996, federal legislation called the "Economic Espionage Act" was passed in the U.S. criminalizing the theft of trade secrets.[291] Although this may look like a protectionist law, Congress enacted the Economic Espionage Act in response to a growing threat of overseas theft of trade secrets, whether for a foreign national company or government. It was also enacted the same year as the enactment by Congress of an Act criminalizing certain acts of trademark counterfeiting and in recognition of the concern that U.S. companies shared that:

> Inventing new and better technologies, production methods, and the like, can be expensive. American companies and the U.S. Government spend billions on research and development. The benefits reaped from these expenditures can easily come to nothing, however, if a competitor can simply steal the trade secret without expending the development costs. While prices may be reduced, ultimately the incentives for new invention disappear, along with jobs, capital investment, and everything else that keeps our economy strong.[292]

The gist of the Economic Espionage Act is reflected in 18 U.S.C. § 1832, which states in pertinent part:

> (a) Whoever, with intent to convert a trade secret, that is related to or included in a product that is produced for or placed in interstate or foreign commerce, to the economic benefit of anyone other than the owner thereof, and intending or knowing that the offense will, injure any owner of that trade secret, knowingly—
>
> (1) steals, or without authorization appropriates, takes, carries away, or conceals, or by fraud, artifice, or deception obtains such information;
>
> (2) without authorization copies, duplicates, sketches, draws, photographs, downloads, uploads, alters, destroys, photocopies, replicates, transmits, delivers, sends, mails, communicates, or conveys such information;
>
> (3) receives, buys, or possesses such information, knowing the same to have been stolen or appropriated, obtained, or converted without authorization;
>
> (4) attempts to commit any offense described in paragraphs (1) through (3); or
>
> (5) conspires with one or more other persons to commit any offense described in paragraphs (1) through (3), and one or more of such persons do any act to effect the object of the conspiracy,
>
> shall, except as provided in subsection (b), be fined under this title or imprisoned not more than 10 years, or both.

---

291. 18 U.S.C. §§ 1831 et seq.
292. 142 Cong. Rec. S12201-03 (daily ed. Oct. 2, 1996) (statement of Sen. Specter), 142 Cong Rec. S12208 *S12207-S12208 (WL).

The legislative history of the Economic Espionage Act includes a number of qualifications (expressed in Manager's Statements), which effectively underscore various differences between the patent laws and trade secret laws. Though expressed in the context of the criminal conduct proscribed by the Economic Espionage Act, the statements also find application in the civil law governing trade secrets. Among them:

1. "a person who develops a trade secret is not given an absolute monopoly on the information or data that comprises a trade secret";[293]
2. "[i]f someone has lawfully gained access to a trade secret and can replicate it without violating copyright, patent or this law, then that form of "reverse engineering" should be fine";[294]
3. "unlike patented material, something does not have to be novel or inventive, in the patent law sense, in order to be a trade secret";[295]
4. an individual's "general knowledge and skills or experience that he or she obtains or comes by during his tenure with a company" are normally going to be safeguarded by trade secret law;[296]

---

293. 142 Cong. Rec. S12201-03 (daily ed. Oct. 2, 1996) (statement of Manager), 142 Cong Rec S12208 *S12212 (WL). The Manager's Statement further states:
Other companies can and must have the ability to determine the elements of a trade secret through their own inventiveness, creativity, and hard work. As the Supreme Court noted in *Kewanee Oil Co. v. Bicron Corp.*, 416 U.S. 470 (1974): "If something is to be discovered at all very likely it will be discovered by more than one person. . . . Even were an inventor to keep his discovery completely to himself, something that neither the patent nor trade secret laws forbid, there is a high probability that it will be soon independently developed. If the invention, though still a trade secret, is put into public use, the competition is alerted to the existence of the inventor's solution to the problem and may be encouraged to make an extra effort to independently find the solution this known to be possible." *Ibid.* at 490-91.

294. *Ibid.* at S12213. By way of illustration, the Statement further expresses:
For example, if a person can drink Coca-Cola and, because he happens to have highly refined taste buds, can figure out what the formula is, then this legislation cannot be used against him. Likewise, if a person can look at a product and, by using their own general skills and expertise, dissect the necessary attributes of the product, then that person should be free from any threat of prosecution.

295. *Ibid.* Nonetheless, in recognition of the concern that a secret that lacks novelty is prone to a characterization as being "general knowledge", the Manager's Statement further expresses:
While we do not strictly impose a novelty or inventiveness requirement in order for material to be considered a trade secret, looking at the novelty or uniqueness of a piece of information or knowledge should inform courts in determining whether something is a matter of general knowledge, skill or experience.

296. *Ibid.* The Manager's Statement further expresses:
As the Pennsylvania Supreme Court noted in *Spring Steels v. Molloy*, 400 Pa. 354, 363 (1960):
It is not a phenomenal thing in American business life to see an employee, after a long period of service, leave his employment and start a business of his own or in association with others. And it is inevitable in such a situation, where the former employee has dealt with customers on a personal basis that some of those customers will want to continue

The Economic Espionage Act has been invoked to convict a number of offenders, for various violations. For instance, the first jury trial under the Economic Espionage Act[297] involved charges that an adhesives researcher at Avery Dennison provided trade secret information about acrylic adhesives to a Taiwanese competitor of Avery Dennison. In another early case, in Silicon Valley, a former Intel Corporation employee pleaded guilty to having copied computer files having trade secret information pertaining to the Itanium microprocessor, intending to use it at his new job at Sun Microsystems.[298] In another Silicon Valley case, a research and development project team leader for Cisco Systems, Inc., pled guilty to having accessed the Cisco computer system to burn CDs that had trade secret information about a voice-over and optical networking project at Cisco.[299] The defendant left Cisco to work for a potential competitor, at which he copied the trade secret files onto a laptop and the company network.[300]

Reasonable Security and the Other Crux of the Challenge to Keep Trade Secrets: Reverse Engineering

A vulnerability of trade secrets, under the law of trade secrets, is the policy reflected in the law to allow free use of information in the public domain. For instance, the definition of trade secrets under the UTSA and the Economic Espionage Act both specifically exclude from the scope of protectable trade secrets subject matter that is "readily ascertainable through proper means." Speaking to the right of a patent owner to prevent reverse engineering,

---

to deal with him in < that> new association. This is . . . natural, logical and part of human fellowship . . .

This legislation does not criminalize or in any way hamper these natural incidents of employment. The free and unfettered flow of individuals from one job to another, the ability of a person to start a new business based upon his or her experience and expertise, should not be injured or chilled in any way by this legislation. Individuals must have the opportunity to take advantage of their talents and seek and accept other employments that enables them to profit from their abilities and experience. And companies must have the opportunity to employ these people. This measure attempts to safeguard an individual's career mobility and at the same time to preserve the trade secrets that underpin the economic viability of the very company that would offer a person a new job.

297. *See U.S. v. Yang*, 281 F.3d 534 (6th Cir. 2002).
298. *See* http://www.usdoj.gov/criminal/cybercrime/OwSent.htm (accessed July 30, 2007).
299. *See* http://www.usdoj.gov/criminal/cybercrime/MorchPlea.htm (accessed July 30, 2007).
300. *See also* http://www.usdoj.gov/opa/pr/2007/August/07_nsd_572.html (accessed August 5, 2007), at which a Department of Justice August 2, 2007, press release describes a guilty plea by a defendant under the Economic Espionage Act for possessing a trade secret military training simulator belonging to his former employer, a California company, which he altered to make it look as if it came from his current employer. The unit was installed for the People's Republic of China ("PRC") Navy Research Center.

in *Bonito Boats, Inc. v. Thunder Craft Boats, Inc.,*[301] the Supreme Court expressed:

> This is clearly one of the rights vested in the federal patent holder, but has never been a part of state protection under the law of unfair competition or trade secrets. *See Kewanee*, 416 U.S., at 476 ("A trade secret law, however, does not offer protection against discovery by . . . so-called reverse engineering, that is by starting with the known product and working backward to divine the process which aided in its development or manufacture") . . . .

Although reverse engineering is allowed by the law, there is no general statutory or common law guarantee of a "right" to reverse engineer. Thus, you can contractually give up your ability to reverse engineer (or force the other side to do so), particularly in licensing. This issue has been examined extensively in the context of shrink-wrap or click-wrap licensing of software,[302] and the result can depend on how the prohibition against reverse engineering is presented in the license agreement. The issue can be handled differently in different states because it depends on the exact state trade secret law as well as state contract law as it applies to copying restrictions. In one example, a shrink-wrap license was breached where the license prohibited all reverse engineering. *Bowers v. Baystate Technologies, Inc.,*[303] applied Massachusetts contract law and upheld breach of contract even though the contracted restriction was far broader than copyright protection would have allowed.

When reverse engineering leads to copying the competitor's product or product features, that activity may not be "stealing" a trade secret, but the activity can result in liability for contract breach (e.g., if there is an agreement not to reverse engineer), copyright infringement or patent infringement. To try to avoid some of the liability that comes with copying, some have argued that federal copyright law preempts contractual restrictions on copying. This is one way to argue for a federal "right" to reverse engineer. The argument goes that the "fair use" provisions of copyright law give a right to copy up to the point that the use is no longer "fair." The majority in *Bowers* did not accept that a federal right to copy existed in the fair use provisions, however a dissent by Judge Dyk agreed with the concept. The Ninth Circuit has held that reverse engineering is a "fair use" (discussed later in this chapter) under

---

301. 489 U.S. 141, 160 (1989).
302. Shrink-wrap refers to the licenses that come attached to a box containing software, which are generally licenses written to say that you agree to those licenses by opening the package. Click-wrap refers to the licenses that are presented to you to download software over the Internet. Both licenses are generally unread by the users and both typically contain restrictions on reverse engineering the software.
303. 320 F.3d 1316 (Fed. Cir. 2003).

copyright law. *Sega Enterprises, Ltd. v. Accolade, Inc.*,[304] and *Sony Computer Equipment v. Connectix Corp.*,[305] held that reverse engineering of computer code may be a fair use of a copyrighted work if it is the only way to gain access to the ideas and elements of the software, and there is a legitimate reason for such access. Thus, when undertaking reverse engineering activities, it is important to keep in mind that contractual provisions may prohibit reverse engineering, and that trade secret law is not the only legal consideration. There might be other IP rights that govern.

As technology continues to march forward, particularly in the areas of information management and high throughput research and analytical tools, the ability of a competitor to reverse engineer a trade secret grows, too. With only limited exceptions, it is a naïve for an organization to believe that its competitors are incapable of reverse engineering. Though for the foreseeable future, the trade secret owner likely will be able to extract a brief lead time relative to the competitor; in the years to come, it is imperative to recognize that the lead times will shrink and may even disappear. For organizations that need to preserve their lead times, and which do not currently engage in patenting, it is imperative to consider that option. With typical patents, even if reverse engineering of a patented devise is successful, the patent grant should be able to exclude the competitor from exploiting the patented technology.

9.2 Reverse Engineering Tools

Anyone who remains skeptical that their technology is safe from deconstruction by a competitor would benefit from a review of some of the powerful tools that have become readily available over the past couple decades and which find considerable use to support reverse engineering activities.

Glow Discharge Mass Spectrometry: trace elemental detection precise to parts per billion

Fourier Transform Infrared Spectroscopy: inorganic and organic analysis; particularly useful for polymer analysis

Nuclear Magnetic Resonance: compound identification

X-Ray Diffraction: Crystalline solid analysis

Electron Microscopy: Material structure characterization to magnifications beyond 100 million times magnification

Laser Profilometry: Surface topography and roughness analysis; film thickness and depth profiling capable of measurements to hundredths of a micron

---

304. 977 F.2d 1510 (9th Cir. 1993).
305. 203 F.2d 596 (9th Cir. 2000).

> Three-Dimensional Scanning: generation of computer-aided design data for replicating solid structures
> In addition to the above, it is becoming increasingly common to obtain university coursework and training in reverse engineering. *See, e.g.*, http://fie.engrng.pitt.edu/fie95/3a5/3a53/3a53.htm (accessed August 12, 2007)

It is, therefore, important to take appropriate care in creating situations that may provide another party with an opportunity to reverse engineer. It would be unfortunate to lose the value of trade secrets, not through a nefarious security breach, but rather through the diligent, and legally accepted, efforts of a competitor to identify the result obtained by a trade secret technology, and to ascertain the way in which the result has been accomplished.

Security and confidentiality precautions that trade secret owners can exercise to prolong the life of their trade secrets are discussed in Chapter 10. From the elaboration of the law, as set forth above, under state laws and the Federal Economic Espionage Act, confidentiality preservation is paramount. There is simply no avoiding the burden upon trade secret owners to protect themselves by reasonable physical and electronic security measures, as well as prophylactic contract provisions with their employees, contractors, business partners, and other risk groups (possibly including a contractual obligation prohibiting reverse engineering). A 2002 survey undertaken by PriceWaterhouseCoopers, ASIS Foundation, and the U.S. Chamber of Commerce revealed that the top four risk groups for intellectual property and proprietary technology loss were:[306]

1. former employees;[307]
2. foreign competitors;[308]
3. onsite contractors; and
4. domestic competitors.[309]

---

306. PriceWaterhouseCoopers, *Trends in Proprietary Information Loss, Survey Report*, ASIS Foundation and the U.S. Chamber of Commerce (September, 2000).
307. *See also* David Hannah, *Keeping Trade Secrets Secret* 47 No. 3 MIT Sloan Mgmt. Rev. 17-20 (Spring 2006) (emphasizing the importance not simply of nondisclosure agreements, non-compete agreements, and IP assignment provisions, "access restrictions", and "handling procedures", but also the importance of new-employee orientation, on-going training, and the proper handling of departing employees).
308. According to the 2006 Science and Engineering Indicators (*See* Figure 3-23), the percentage of foreignborn college graduates in science and engineering positions grew from 11.2 percent in 1980 to 19.3 percent in 2000.
309. PriceWaterhouseCoopers, *Trends in Proprietary Information Loss, Survey Report*, ASIS Foundation and the U.S. Chamber of Commerce (September 2000) at Table 3.1.

Notably, the highest risk area was research and development, accounting for 43 percent of the dollar value loss.[310] Good organizational practices and employee sensitivity training are essential to build an IP culture that is aware of the *daily* risks and vulnerabilities to which the organization's trade secrets are exposed, whether they arise from internal personnel, physical plant layout and practices (e.g., monitored entrances, visitor sign-in, visitor escorts), or the conduct of the organization's personnel when they are off the corporate premises (e.g., at meetings, at trade shows, in a restaurant or coffee shop, while traveling).

The Shift Away from Trade Secrets

What caused the shift toward a more aggressive stance toward patenting in the past couple decades cannot be attributed to any one factor. In one respect, confidence in the 1982 creation of the Court of Appeals for the Federal Circuit and the uniformity in patent law it sought to create finally started to gain traction.[311]

Additionally, in the U.S., significant court decisions confirmed the patentability of life science technologies, software-oriented inventions, and even business methods. All of these, in turn, bolstered innovator confidence that their innovations could support protection. During the same time period, technology saw rapid progression in electronics, enabling faster and more efficient data processing and storage. Revolutionary software products dramatically enhanced the ability to gather and generate data. Historic obstacles that impeded innovation started to give way to tools designed and built simply for the purpose of facilitating innovation.

---

310. PriceWaterhouseCoopers, *Trends in Proprietary Information Loss, Survey Report,* ASIS Foundation and the U.S. Chamber of Commerce (September 2000) at Table 3.1 (According to Table 3.5 of the survey 49 percent of the participating surveyed companies report research and development losses.).

311. Sitting *en banc* in its first case, the Court of Appeals for the Federal Circuit stated in *South Corp. v. **United States,*** 690 F.2d 1368, 1371 (Fed. Cir. 1982) (*en banc*):

    As a court of nationwide geographic jurisdiction, created and chartered with the hope and intent that stability and uniformity would be achieved in all fields of law within its substantive jurisdiction, we begin by adopting as a basic foundation the jurisprudence of the two national courts which served not only as our predecessors, but as outstanding contributors to the administration of justice for a combined total of 199 years, the Court of Claims and the Court of Customs and Patent Appeals.

    See also, Christianson v. Colt Indus. Operating Corp., 486 U.S. 800, 813 (1988) ("one of Congress' objectives in creating a Federal Circuit with exclusive jurisdiction over certain patent cases was 'to reduce the widespread lack of uniformity and uncertainty of legal doctrine that exist[ed] in the administration of patent law.' H. R. Rep. No. 97-312, at 23 (1981)").

The global emergence of economies bent toward capitalism, in the late 1980s and early '90s also opened the door for global business.

Of course, these developments were all superimposed on a landscape that included cellular phones, the Internet, and even wireless e-mail. The world rapidly started becoming much "smaller" than ever before, by unprecedented ability to spread and share information and new ideas. New ideas surfaced and spread at a rate and in an amount never before seen. With them also grew the opportunity for misappropriation of the ideas and the technological means for achieving such misappropriations. Security concerns expanded beyond the concern for a breach of the perimeter of a physical plant. It extended into computer networks.

The human dimension also can not be overlooked. Since the late 1980s, companies around the world have seen a frenzy of mergers, acquisitions, and divestitures. With each one of those transactions, people have lost jobs.[312] Some have gone to work in an unrelated field, but many others have stayed within their field, merely relocating their experiences and wisdom to a competitor. Combined with the public policy considerations that allow employees to apply general knowledge gained from past employment, an already congested court system simply could not keep pace with the transient and fluid workforce that the business world had brought upon itself. Enforcement of confidentiality obligations in every instance simply is not a practical option.

In short, many of the basic premises upon which the law of trade secrets developed, and the tools for assuring preservation of confidentiality, no longer exist in some companies. Changing times have rendered obsolete the sole reliance upon trade secrets to protect crown jewel technology. What has occurred in recent years is the slow awakening of business to this fact and a resulting shift toward patenting.

In a number of industries, the awakening has occurred simultaneously between or among competitors. In others, it has occurred according to a specific sequence. For instance, one competitor recognized that trade secret protection alone would not adequately protect its technology, and patents could help. That competitor obtains patents, which it then uses in the marketplace to exclude another competitor. Seeing the effect of being excluded by the patenting, the excluded competitor soon follows the lead of the first competitor and starts its own patenting.

---

312. During the period from 1990-1994, through mergers and acquisitions in the U.S., it has been estimated that 5.25 million employees who worked for one company in 1990, found themselves working for another company by 1994. *See* http://www.sba.gov/ADVO/stats/ m_a.html (accessed August 7, 2007). The same study also indicated that "business locations acquired from large firms by other large firms lost 9.3 percent of their jobs, on average."

Trade Secret and Patent Coexistence

Though the preceding discussion underscores the differences between patent and trade secret law, the selection of one form of protection over another does not preclude protection by the latter as well. For example, two significant sets of circumstances may compel paying close consideration to both patents and trade secrets. In one, an organization seeks to protect, not merely an isolated innovation, but the technology portfolio that surrounds it. In another, an organization seeks to protect merely the innovation.

Building a Trade Secret Moat around a Patent Fort

It is quite common that an innovation subject to patent protection is also part of a larger pool of valuable intellectual property (a "moat of intellectual property"), for which protection under the trade secret laws is important.[313]

In the course of developing a technology, vast amounts of valuable data and know-how are generated, which could qualify for trade secret protection. The data and know-how may reflect efforts to optimize a technology for a particular application. It may reflect avenues pursued by the innovator that were successful or even avenues that the innovator pursued which were unsuccessful. There may be inventions made that are determined to be unpatentable due to a publication by a third party. The best mode, enablement, and description requirements under 35 U.S.C. § 112 may not necessarily require disclosure of all data and know-how in the patent application. However, possession of the data and know-how would be of great value to a competitor in developing its own competing technology. Before the competitor can even scale the walls of the patent fort that lies before it, the competitor must cross the moat surrounding the fort.

It is also possible that much of the data generated is generated after the date when a patent application is filed. Recall, the relevant date for the obligations to disclose details about an invention is the date of filing the application. Provided that the requirements for patentability otherwise have been met, the duty does not compel supplementing the written description when post-filing developments are made, and no new application is filed.[314]

---

313. In "The Role and Value of Trade Secrets in IP Management Strategies," presented at 35th PIPA Congress, Toyama, Japan (October 20, 2004), Professor Jorda emphasized the compatibility of patents and trade secrets, and the important role that trade secrets play in building value for an organization in its innovations. Advancing the harmonious relationship between trade secrets and patents, and the "shortsightedness" of choosing one form over the other, he expressed that "the bulk of R&D data and results or associated, collateral know-how for any commercially important innovation cannot and need not be included in a patent application but deserves, and requires, protection which trade secrets can provide."

314. The existence of subsequent contradictory date may raise other issues associated with the duty of candor. Therefore, it is helpful for clients to communicate about such information

Trade Secret Protection When Opting to Patent an Innovation

In some instances, the major value an innovation may bring is in the right to exclude others from using a technology, and data and know-how will be relatively small in volume or otherwise not significant enough to warrant the expenditure of resources to protect associated trade secrets. Nevertheless, a value still remains in the ability to defer a competitive market entry for as long as possible. Those organizations stand to benefit from adherence to reasonable security precautions before filing a patent application and during its initial period of pendency in the Patent Office, which could help to assure that competitors do not access information that might help provide a head start with their own technology.

Nowadays, unless a patent applicant abandons its application at a relatively early stage, it should be assumed that after some period of time (roughly eighteen months in most instances) the patent application will publish and any trade secrets contained in it will be revealed. However, prior to such time, the application files are kept secret by the Patent Office.[315]

In addition, it may be critical to preserve confidentiality in the time leading up to the filing of a patent application. Public activities trigger the deadlines to file patent applications to avoid forfeiting rights. As a general rule, in the U.S., the public activity will trigger a one-year deadline to file.[316] Elsewhere, outside the U.S., where absolute novelty standards apply, there is generally no grace period.[317] Accordingly, in efforts to build a patent-oriented culture, benefit can also be realized by the establishment of a culture sensitive to practices for safeguarding trade secrets.

---

with counsel to best address how to treat it and to assure compliance with patenting requirements.

315. 35 U.S.C. § 122 imposes an affirmative obligation upon the U.S. Patent and Trademark Office to keep patent applications confidential for at least eighteen months; *See also* Article 93 of the European Patent Convention and Article 64 of the Patent Act of Japan (Act No. 121 of 1959).

316. 35 U.S.C. § 102(b) states in part:

A person shall be entitled to a patent unless—

(a) the invention was known or used by others in this country, or patented or described in a printed publication in this or a foreign country, before the invention thereof by the applicant for patent, or

(b) the invention was patented or described in a printed publication in this or a foreign country or in public use or on sale in this country, more than one year prior to the date of the application for patent in the United States. . . .

317. *See, e.g.,* Article 54 of the European Patent Convention, which states in part:

(1) An invention shall be considered to be new if it does not form part of the state of the art.

(2) The state of the art shall be held to comprise everything made available to the public by means of a written or oral description, by use, or in any other way, before the date of filing of the European patent application.

See also Articles 29 and 30 of the Patent Act of Japan (Act No. 121 of 1959).

Trade Secrets, Patents, or Both

Every organization is unique and faces its own individual challenges in protecting its proprietary technology. It is not uncommon to still encounter an organization that believes its interests can best be served by careful trade secret protection. For some of these organizations, this probably makes good sense. However, in a majority of cases, the resistance to patents is less founded upon confidence in trade secrets but rather on lack of a decision-making framework and the overwhelming amount of education often needed to embark upon a successful patent strategy.

The following illustrative survey questions can help in deciding whether to patent an innovation or keep it as trade secret.

1. Who within the organization has access to the information?
2. Of those persons with access, which ones are bound by confidentiality obligations under their employment agreement?
3. Of those persons with access, what is the likelihood they will remain employed by the organization?
4. Of those persons with access, have any been formerly employed by a competitor?
5. Will personnel from the organization travel in its efforts to commercialize the technology?
6. Is the information inaccessible to temporary or contract employees?
7. Is the information recorded in a single location and stored there in a fireproof safe inaccessible to all but the most key employees of the organization?
8. What effort is needed by a competitor to reverse engineer?
9. Can the idea be kept secret for 20 years?
10. Is the likelihood negligible that within the next 20 years someone else independently will come up with the same information?[318]
11. Is the information a process performed within a restricted access, secure facility?

---

318. Consider the prophetic musings of the Supreme Court in *Kewanee Oil Co. v. Bicron Corp.*, 416 U.S. 470, 490-91 (1974):

Even were an inventor to keep his discovery completely to himself, something that neither the patent nor trade secret laws forbid, there is a high probability that it will be soon independently developed. If the invention, though still a trade secret, is put into public use, the competition is alerted to the existence of the inventor's solution to the problem and may be encouraged to make an extra effort to independently find the solution thus known to be possible. The inventor faces pressures not only from private industry, but from the skilled scientists who work in our universities and our other great publicly supported centers of learning and research.

12. Upon grant of a patent to cover the information, will it be practical or convenient to police competitive activities?

9.3 **Policing Secret Processes**

One familiar ground for reluctance to patent processes is the belief that it is nearly impossible to monitor a competitor's activity without access to the competitor's facilities. This is a valid concern and deserves consideration in fashioning an appropriate strategy. However, with the Process Patent Act in 1988, Congress sought to alleviate the burden upon a patentee in those circumstances by adding 35 U.S.C. §295:

> In actions alleging infringement of a process patent based on the importation, sale, offered for sale, or use of a product which is made from a process patented in the U.S., if the court finds-
>
> (1) that a substantial likelihood exists that the product was made by the patented process, and
>
> (2) that the plaintiff has made a reasonable effort to determine the process actually used in the production of the product and was unable so to determine,
>
> the product shall be presumed to have been so made, and the burden of establishing that the product was not made by the process shall be on the party asserting that it was not so made.

Copyrights

The same clause that creates the authority for the Patent Act in the U.S. also authorizes the Copyright Act. Article 1, Section 8, Clause 8 of the U.S. Constitution vests Congress with the power: "[t]o promote the Progress of Science and useful Arts, by securing for limited Times to Authors and Inventors the exclusive Right to their respective Writings and Discoveries." Copyright law protects original works of authorship that are fixed in a tangible medium.[319]

---

319. *See* 17 U.S.C. § 102(a), which authorizes copyright protection for the following categories of works:
  (**1**) literary works;
  (**2**) musical works, including any accompanying words;
  (**3**) dramatic works, including any accompanying music;
  (**4**) pantomimes and choreographic works;
  (**5**) pictorial, graphic, and sculptural works;
  (**6**) motion pictures and other audiovisual works;
  (**7**) sound recordings; and
  (**8**) architectural works.

Novelty is not necessarily a prerequisite, only originality.[320] Moreover, it is not the idea nor the facts that are protected from an author's work, but rather the "expression" of the idea or the fact.[321]

In general, the courts have come to recognize two classes of copying that give rise to an action for copyright infringement. The first is regarded as "reproductive" copying, and generally occurs when there has been an exact reproduction made of a copyrighted work. For example, a photocopy of a copyrighted work is a reproductive copy. Proving copying is relatively straightforward in an instance of reproductive copying. The resulting copy pretty much speaks for itself.

In contrast, when exact duplication is not made, but some transformative measures are taken in the creation of a work, such an act may still be actionable copyright infringement. Proof of this type of copyright infringement tends to be more difficult, requiring proof of access by the accused party to the copied work, and substantial similarity between the copied work and the accused work.

Not all copying, whether transformative or reproductive, gives rise to liability for copyright infringement. The copyright laws embody a doctrine called "fair use," which allows certain limited copying.[322] Thus, it may be OK

---

320. *Feist Publ'ns, Inc. v. Rural Tel Service Co.*, 499 U.S. 340, 346 (1991)(" In two decisions from the late 19th Century—*The Trade-Mark Cases*, 100 U.S. 82 (1879); and *Burrow-Giles Lithographic Co. v. Sarony*, 111 U.S. 53 (1884)—this Court defined the crucial terms 'authors' and 'writings.' In so doing, the Court made it unmistakably clear that these terms presuppose a degree of originality.").

321. *Ibid.* at 349-50 ("copyright assures authors the right to their original expression, but encourages others to build freely upon the ideas and information conveyed by a work. *Harper & Row, supra,* at 556-557. This principle, known as the idea/expression or fact/expression dichotomy, applies to all works of authorship."). *See also* 17 U.S.C. §102(b), which states:
   In no case does copyright protection for an original work of authorship extend to any idea, procedure, process, system, method of operation, concept, principle, or discovery, regardless of the form in which it is described, explained, illustrated, or embodied in such work.

322. The doctrine of fair use is found in the Copyright Act of 1976. 17 U.S.C. § 107 provides:
   Notwithstanding the provisions of sections 106 and 106A, the fair use of a copyrighted work, including such use by reproduction in copies or phonorecords or by any other means specified by that section, for purposes such as criticism, comment, news reporting, teaching (including multiple copies for classroom use), scholarship, or research, is not an infringement of copyright. In determining whether the use made of a work in any particular case is a fair use the factors to be considered shall include—
   (1) the purpose and character of the use , including whether such use is of a commercial nature or is for nonprofit educational purposes;
   (2) the nature of the copyrighted work;
   (3) the amount and substantiality of the portion used in relation to the copyrighted work as a whole; and
   (4) the effect of the use upon the potential market for or value of the copyrighted work.
   The fact that a work is unpublished shall not itself bar a finding of fair use if such finding is made upon consideration of all the above factors.

to copy a work if, for example, the copy is only a small portion of the overall work. Another familiar situation in which the fair use doctrine is often employed is for educational or classroom purposes. The U.S. Supreme Court has authorized videotaping of television shows, a reproductive copying, for "time-shifting" purposes.[323] The U.S. Supreme Court also has upheld parody as a legitimate fair use for transformative works.[324]

Among the common misconceptions with copyright law is that, regardless of whether fair use exists, a work that employs only a small amount of a copyrighted work, employs a copyrighted work in a different tangible medium than the original copyrighted version of the work, or is based only in limited part on the copyrighted work, will avoid infringement liability. The exclusive rights afforded to copyright owners are enumerated in 17 U.S.C. § 106, and include the exclusive rights "(2) to prepare derivative works based upon the copyrighted work. . . ."[325], where:

> A "derivative work" is a work based upon one or more preexisting works, such as a translation, musical arrangement, dramatization, fictionalization, motion picture version, sound recording, art reproduction, abridgment, condensation, or any other form in which a work may be recast, transformed, or adapted. A work consisting of editorial revisions, annotations, elaborations, or other modifications which, as a whole, represent an original work of authorship, is a "derivative work."[326]

Accordingly, suppose that an organization receives a trade publication on a periodic basis. Instead of ordering copies for all personnel, it excerpts portions of each article into an abbreviated summary document, which is copied and distributed to personnel. Alternatively, the organization may prepare an audio recording of each article and make it available for download to employees. It is possible that either of these acts could give rise to an assertion of copyright infringement for violation of the exclusive right of the owner to prepare derivative works.

Another misconception is that the absence of a copyright notice (e.g., "©") means that it is okay to copy a work. The absence of the notice does not excuse copying from being an actionable infringement. The copyright comes into existence at the time when the work is created. In 1988, acting to conform the U.S. Copyright Act with the Berne Convention international agreement for the protection of copyrighted works, Congress eliminated the requirement of

---

323. *Sony Corp. of America v. Universal City Studios, Inc.*, 464 U.S. 417,451 (1984) (introducing presumption of unfair use when the purpose of the copying is a commercial purpose).
324. *Campbell v. Acuff-Rose Music, Inc.*, 510 U.S. 569 (1994) (upholding as permitted fair use the use by the band 2Live Crew of portions from the Roy Orbison song, "Pretty Woman").
325. 17 U.S.C. § 106.
326. 17 U.S.C. § 101.

copyright notice.[327] A work need not bear a notice to be protected. Further, a work need not even be registered with the copyright office prior to the infringement for the copyright owner to be entitled to a remedy.[328]

In extreme situations, copyright violations are subject to criminal prosecution under 17 U.S.C. § 506.

9.4 **Managing Copyright Risks**

In addition to policing its use of licensed software, an organization should monitor control over unauthorized copying of trade literature and journal articles to avoid unexpected copyright infringement accusations. Securing appropriate permission to reproduce a copyrighted work is the most straightforward way to avoid liability for copyright infringement. A popular collective rights organization that offers a licensing service for this purpose is that offered by the Copyright Clearance Center. *See* www.copyright.com. Licenses are available on a pay-per-use basis or even on an annual basis. Similarly, for organizations that broadcast music or other audio content, licenses are available through the American Society of Composers, Authors and Publishers (ASCAP) and may be a worthy precaution. *See* www.ascap. com. A variety of other entities offer similar collective rights services, in the U.S. and abroad.

Trademarks

Distinguishing Trademarks, Service Marks, and Trade Dress

Virtually anything that can function as a source designation is capable of protection as a trademark, a service mark, or trade dress. This form of intellectual property protection is normally associated with names or logos, but can extend to other source indicators, such as colors or even sounds. The body of law pertaining to this form of intellectual property is referred to generally as trademark law, and it is actually a form of the broader laws of unfair competition,

---

327. 17 U.S.C. § 401 (discussing the notice requirements as optional, using the discretionary clause "may be placed," instead of "shall be placed").

328. The right to sue for infringement necessarily will require a copyright registration (even if "ex post facto."). 17 U.S.C. § 411. Copyright remedies, including (but not limited to) money damages, injunctive relief or both, are authorized by statute. *See* 17 U.S.C. §§ 412, and 501 et seq. The appropriate remedy will depend upon the timing of any registration relative to the infringement and any publication of the work. *See* 17 U.S.C. § 412.

misrepresentation or passing off.[329] As explained by the U.S. Supreme Court:[330]

> Traditional trademark infringement law is a part of the broader law of unfair competition, *See Hanover Star Milling Co. v. Metcalf,* 240 U.S. 403, 413 (1916), that has its sources in English common law, and was largely codified in the Trademark Act of 1946 (Lanham Act). *See* B. Pattishall, D. Hilliard, & J. Welch, Trademarks and Unfair Competition 2 (4th ed. 2000) ("The United States took the [trademark and unfair competition] law of England as its own"). That law broadly prohibits uses of trademarks, trade names, and trade dress that are likely to cause confusion about the source of a product or service. *See* 15 U.S.C. §§ 1114, 1125(a)(1)(A). Infringement law protects consumers from being misled by the use of infringing marks and also protects producers from unfair practices by an "imitating competitor." *Qualitex Co. v. Jacobson Products Co.,* 514 U.S. 159, 163–164 (1995).

Though a registration is necessary to obtain certain remedies for infringement, these rights can come into being simply upon first use of the designation. The latter is referred to as "common law rights" and, even in the absence of a federal trademark registration, might provide a basis to invoke federal court jurisdiction for enforcement. State law protection is also possible.

Trade dress is a unique subcategory of source designators. Simply put, the unique shape of an item might cause the courts to afford exclusive protection to the owner. Among the examples of the many litigated items that have been subject to trade dress protection are:[331]

1. an automotive vehicle body;[332]
2. packaging;[333]

---

329. In the case of *Gibson Guitar Corp. v. Paul Reed Smith Guitars LP,* 423 F.3d 539 (6th Cir. 2005), the Court of Appeals for the Sixth Circuit recognized that:
    trademark and trade dress are two distinct concepts under the Lanham Act. *See Wal-Mart Stores, Inc. v. Samara Bros., Inc.,* 529 U.S. 205, 209-210 (2000). The Lanham Act defines a trademark as "any word, name, symbol, or device, or any combination thereof" which is used or intended to be used by a person "in commerce . . . to identify and distinguish his or her goods, including a unique product, from those manufactured or sold by others and to indicate the source of the goods, even if that source is unknown." 15 U.S.C. § 1127. By contrast, trade dress is not explicitly defined in the Lanham Act, but has been described by the Supreme Court as the "design or packaging of a product" which has acquired a "secondary meaning" sufficient "to identify the product with its manufacturer or source." *Traffix Devices, Inc. v. Mktg. Displays, Inc.,* 532 U.S. 23, 28 (2001). (footnote omitted)
330. *Moseley v. V Secret Catalogue, Inc.,* 537 U.S. 418, 428 (U.S. 2003).
331. *TrafFix Devices Inc. v. Marketing Displays Inc.,* 532 U.S. 23, 29-30 (2001) (addressing functionality limitation upon trade dress protection).
332. *Chrysler Corp. v. Silva,* 118 F.3d 56 (1st Cir. 1997) (Dodge VIPER® vehicle).
333. *Rose Art Indus., Inc. v. Swanson,* 235 F.3d 165 (3d Cir. 2000).

3. a dictionary cover;[334]
4. furniture;[335] and
5. a restaurant.[336]

One of the main policies underlying trademark law is the protection of the consuming public from being confused in its purchasing decisions by similar designations. Being a prophylactic measure, the law does not require that there be actual consumer confusion. Instead, the mere risk of confusion may warrant relief. Accordingly, the courts widely apply an analysis for determining infringement on the mere basis of a "likelihood of confusion." This normally entails a contextual analysis that looks at commercial marketplace considerations surrounding a use of a mark. By way of illustration, the Sixth Circuit Court of Appeals reiterated the eight-factor test of that circuit, which examines:(1) strength of plaintiff's mark; (2) relatedness of the goods; (3) similarity of the marks; (4) evidence of actual confusion; (5) marketing channels used; (6) degree of purchaser care; (7) defendant's intent in selecting the mark; and (8) likelihood of expansion in selecting the mark.[337]

It is not always easy to know if someone claims a proprietary interest in a mark or trade dress.[338] Certain markings should help to alert the need for possible further investigation. For example, the use of °, TM, or SM is an indication that someone asserts a proprietary interest in a mark or trade dress.

---

334. *Merriam-Webster, Inc. v. Random House, Inc.*, 35 F.3d 65 (2d Cir. 1994).

335. *Herman Miller, Inc. v. Palazzetti Imports and Exports, Inc.*, 270 F.3d 298 (6th Cir. 2001).

336. *Two Pesos, Inc. v. Taco Cabana, Inc.*, 505 U.S. 763 (1992).

337. *Audi AG v. D'Amato*, 469 F.3d 534, 542-43 (6th Cir. 2006). The Ninth Circuit expressed the following in *Au-Tomotive Gold Inc. v. Volkswagen of America Inc.*, 457 F.3d 1062, 1075-76 (9th Cir. 2006):

   A "[l]ikelihood of confusion 'exists when customers viewing [a] mark would probably assume that the product or service it represents is associated with the source of a different product or service identified by a similar mark." *Fuddruckers, Inc. v. Doc's B. R. Others, Inc.*, 826 F.2d 837, 845 (9th Cir. 1987) (quoting *Lindy Pen Co. v. Bic Pen Corp.*, 725 F.2d 1240, 1243 (9th Cir. 1984)). The Ninth Circuit employs an eight-factor test (the "*Sleekcraft*" factors) to determine the likelihood of confusion: (1) strength of the mark(s); (2) relatedness of the goods; (3) similarity of the marks; (4) evidence of actual confusion; (5) marketing channels; (6) degree of consumer care; (7) defendant's intent; (8) likelihood of expansion. *Surfvivor Media, Inc. v. Survivor Productions*, 406 F.3d 625, 631 (9th Cir. 2005); *See also AMF Inc. v. Sleekcraft Boats*, 599 F.2d 341, 348-49 (9th Cir. 1979). These elements are not applied mechanically; courts may examine some or all of the factors, depending on their relevance and importance. *See Surfvivor*, 406 F.3d at 631; *Thane Int'l*, 305 F.3d at 901 ("The list of factors is not a score-card-whether a party wins a majority of the factors is not the point. Nor should the factors be rigidly weighed; we do not count beans.") (internal punctuation and citations omitted).

338. As with the preceding treatment of copyright protection, this discussion merely scratches the surface of the law surrounding protection of designations of origins, and only for the purpose of trying to highlight the differences among the various forms of intellectual property.

Except in limited circumstances, the absence of such a marking will not excuse an infringement of a protected right.

One caution for an internal IP program is the proper marking of the trademarks or services marks of the organization. It can be an act of unfair competition to incorrectly mark your products with the wrong type of notice (e.g., ®, TM, or SM). Thus, care should be taken in proper marking.

It must be borne in mind that one of the basic policies behind the likelihood of confusion analysis is to protect consumers from confusion in the marketplace, even though trademark owners are often the party to invoke the rights. Another doctrine also protects the rights of mark owners from a diminution of mark value by users of the mark, even for uses that do not directly compete with the goods or services of the mark owner. This doctrine is addressed by a body of law prohibiting dilution of the marks, such as may result from "blurring" or "tarnishing" of the value of a mark.[339]

Trademark Counterfeiting

Another illustration of how the interests of the consuming public are sought to be protected by the law, when it comes to trademarks, is embodied in the Trademark Counterfeiting Act of 1984 and the Anticounterfeiting Consumer Protection Act of 1996. Specifically, 18 U.S.C. § 2320 makes it a crime to intentionally traffic or attempt "to traffic in goods or services and knowingly uses a counterfeit mark on or in connection with such goods or services. . . ."[340]

IP Overlap: Selecting the Best Intellectual Property Protection

The overlap of trade secrets and patents has been discussed, with the conclusion that the two are not necessarily mutually exclusive when seeking to protect an innovation and the technology that surrounds it. Likewise, the laws of trade secrets and patents do not necessarily preclude protection of intellectual property under trademark law, copyright law, or both.[341] As with copyright

---

339. *See* 15 U.S.C. § 1125 (Federal Trademark Dilution Act – "FTDA"); *Moseley v. V Secret Catalogue, Inc.*, 537 U.S. 418 (U.S. 2003). As enacted, 15 U.S.C. § 1127 defined "dilution" to mean: "the lessening of the capacity of a famous mark to identify and distinguish goods or services, regardless of the presence or absence of—(1) competition between the owner of the famous mark and other parties, or (2) likelihood of confusion, mistake, or deception."

340. *See e.g., United States v. Foote*, 413 F.3d 1240 (10th Cir. 2005) (prosecution for trafficking in counterfeit Mont Blanc pens).

341. In considering the generalities embodied in the present discussion, it must be borne in mind that, historically, the law has been quick to respect the freedom of competitors to

protection, merely because an item is the subject of trademark, service mark, or trade dress protection does not prevent the item for qualifying for another form of intellectual property protection. For example, the design of a distinctive logo for a trademark or service mark might qualify for copyright protection as an original work. Likewise, a product shape might form the basis for trade dress protection and for design patent protection. One long-standing example from the case law that has supported such dual protection is the case of *In re Mogen David Wine Corp.*[342] In that case the court authorized trade dress protection for a distinctive wine bottle configuration. Moreover, it is possible that functional features in a product having associated protectable trade dress may be patented under an ordinary utility patent. As to the latter, it must be borne in mind that design patent and trade dress protection is not supposed to extend to primarily functional features of an article.

9.5 **IP Comparison**			
	Patent	*Trade Secret*	*Copyright*	*Marks/Trade Dress*
Primary Legal Basis	The Patent Act 35 U.S.C	State law; Economic Espionage Act	The Copyright Act, 17 U.S.C.	U.S. Constit. Art. 1, Sect.1, cl.1; The Lanham Act15 U. S.C. § 1125; state law
Governing Agency Granting	USPTO	None	U.S. Copyright Office	USPTO
Duration	Finite	Indefinite	Finite	Indefinite if used (with renewals for registrations)
Marking	"U.S. Patent No.___"	"Confidential" or "Proprietary"	©	®, SM or TM

practice subject matter that has entered the public domain. *See Sears, Roebuck & Co. v. Stiffel Co.*, 376 U.S. 225 (1964), and *Compco Corp. v. Day-Brite Lighting*, Inc., 376 U.S. 234 (1964); *Bonito Boats, Inc. v. Thunder Craft Boats, Inc.*, 489 U.S. 141 (1989); *TrafFix Devices, Inc. v. Marketing Displays, Inc.*, 532 U.S. 23, 29 (2001)("Trade dress protection must subsist with the recognition that in many instances there is no prohibition against copying goods and products. In general, unless an intellectual property right such as a patent or copyright protects an item, it will be subject to copying").

342. 328 F.2d 925 (C.C.P.A. 1964).

Protectable Subject Matter	Ornamental designs, articles of manufacture, compositions, processes, software, business methods	Secrets that provide competitive advantage	Artwork, literature, software, music, recordings, compilations,	Names, logos, colors, shapes, slogans, etc.
Act Giving Rise to Protection	Patent Office registration proceeding	Confidential measures	Creation of the work; Copyright Office registration proceeding needed for enforcement	Use of designation (in interstate commerce for federal rights); registration proceeding affords benefits
Ability to Exclude Independent Creation or Reverse Engineering	Excludes independent creation and reverse engineering	Independent creation or reverse engineering are defenses	Independent creation is a defense	Not Applicable (first use governs)
Where Suit Brought	U.S. Federal Courts	U.S. Federal Courts or State Courts	U.S. Federal Courts	U.S. Federal Courts or State Courts

Talk the Talk

By their very nature, IP attorneys are precise and obsessed with proper word choice. The following are examples of the most common mistaken statements lay persons make when first engaging with an IP attorney, along with how the IP attorney translates the statement.

9.6		
Statement	*What patent attorney hears*	*Better way to say it*
I want to patent my company's name	Does she want to trademark her company name?	I want to trademark my company name

I want to patent my engineering drawings	Does she want to copyright the drawings or does she want to patent the device that is depicted in the drawings?	I want to copyright my drawings; or I want to get a patent on the invention shown in my drawings (as case may be)
I want to copyright my invention	Does he want to protect his invention or some literature he wrote to describe it?	I want to patent my invention; or I want to copyright an article I wrote to describe my invention (as case may be)
I want to copyright my company's name	Does he want to protect the artwork of his company logo or merely protect the word used as the company name?	I want to copyright the artwork used for my company logo; or I want to register a trademark for my company name, my company logo, or both (as case may be)
I want to trademark my invention	Does she want me to help her pick a name for her invention, or does she want me to patent her invention?	I want to trademark a name for my invention; or I want to patent my invention
I want to trademark my song	Does he want to protect the title of his song, or does he want to protect the music or lyrics of his song?	I want to protect the name of my song; or I want to protect the music or lyrics of my song with a copyright

CHAPTER
10

Confidential Information and
Effective Corporate Trade Secret Programs

An Underpinning

Confidential information is a foundation to intellectual property. It is a basic underpinning to trade secrets and patents and a seed from which intellectual achievements of an organization can grow. Though the concept of confidentiality is fairly well known, a full appreciation of its role and value in fostering healthy IP attitudes often tends to be misunderstood. In general, information disclosed without restriction on its dissemination loses its status as a trade secret. Once lost, it is gone forever (and with it, potentially valuable IP is also lost). Similarly, patenting (especially in absolute novelty countries outside of the U.S.) depends on the first disclosure of information outside of an organization being made first to a patent office and not to a party under no restriction of confidentiality.

In Chapters 2 and 7, the importance of agreements to the protection of confidential information was underscored, both as to the need for agreements with employees and contractors, as well as with outside organizations with whom an IP-sharing relationship is sought (*See also* Appendices 1–3). The discussions were generic to situations in which a patent program is sought or whether a trade secret program is sought. In this chapter, concepts underlying confidentiality are explored more particularly as they pertain to organizations biased toward trade secrets. Beyond the use of agreements, the chapter addresses other important considerations for such organizations, such as security measures, employment practices, and other business practices consistent with a healthy IP culture.

Preliminary Definitional Matters

"Confidential" means secret. In its most basic sense, "confidential information" is not necessarily defined by what it is but, rather, what it is not. Consider the following, which is relatively common illustrative definitional language found in agreements concerning confidentiality.

> "Confidential Information" means any Company information, technical information, business information, trade secrets or know-how, including, but not limited to, research, product plans, products, services, customers, customer lists, markets, equipment, software, developments, inventions, processes, formulas, electronic data, technology, samples, designs, drawings, engineering information, calculations, algorithms, hardware configuration information, marketing, finances or other business information disclosed by the Company either directly or indirectly, in writing, visually, orally or by drawings or inspection of parts, samples or equipment.

Most such agreements would then start to carve away, from the broad scope of information in the above, certain classes of information that disqualify the information from being confidential (e.g., information that goes outside of the organization without an obligation of confidentiality—even if disclosed to only one person). For example, typical exceptions to the definition of confidential information might include:

> (i) information that is generally known at the time of disclosure, (ii) information that is publicly known and made generally available through no wrongful act of the recipient, or (iii) information that a recipient rightfully has received from a third party who is authorized to make such disclosure.[343]

---

343. Sometimes an obviousness-type combination is eliminated from these defined exceptions to avoid going back to records with hindsight of what the confidential information is to try

The word "proprietary" confuses many people, especially when it is used along with the word confidential or, worse, in a circumstance in which the term "confidential" should otherwise have been used. However, proprietary more accurately means having an ownership interest in something.[344] It is not necessarily synonymous with "confidential." An ownership interest is much different from a secret. For example, a patent application that is published (as is commonly done eighteen months after filing) becomes a public disclosure. The information in the application remains proprietary but (by virtue of the public disclosure) is no longer confidential. Similarly, information can be confidential but not necessarily proprietary to a single owner. For example, the fact or content of business discussions between companies might be confidential, but there is not necessarily an ownership interest in the discussions.[345]

10.1 Proprietary: The Adaptive Designation

The term "proprietary," if used appropriately, could be a "stem cell" sort of term—adaptable to any number of different purposes. For example, it might be possible to create a triable issue of fact on whether the designation "Proprietary" means confidential or merely an assertion of ownership. If a party is a plaintiff in a trade secret case, it could argue that the designation meant the information was confidential. In contrast, in defending a patent infringement lawsuit on grounds of a public use, the same party (assuming it had not taken an inconsistent position elsewhere), might assert that the purpose of the designation was merely to put others on notice that a party owned rights.

---

and show that the confidential information falls into one of the exceptions (typically the "known at the time" exception). Thus, you can exclude from the definition of confidential information combinations of records that might collectively show the confidential information unless those records tie the confidential information together in the records themselves. For example, in *Mike's Train House, Inc. v. Lionel LLC.*, 472 F.3d 398, 411 (6th Cir. 2006), the court stated, in dicta, that trade secrets can be based on a "unique combination of both protected and unprotected material."

344. *Black's Law Dictionary* defines the adjective "proprietary" as "belonging to ownership; belonging or pertaining to a proprietor." Black's Law Dictionary at 637 (5th ed. West Publishing 1983).

345. This has to be compared to the stealing of a corporate opportunity and intentional interference with a business relationship. Both are state court causes of action that could provide common law and/or statutory remedies for business discussions that were supposed to benefit one party but ends up not doing so. These are based on fiduciary duties or common law torts and assessed on a state-by-state basis.

The term "classified information" refers to a species of confidential information. Normally, "classified information" refers to information that is restricted from dissemination by statute or regulation. Access to classified information typically requires certain governmental security clearances.

"Secrecy" is often used synonymously with "confidentiality." However, some parties prefer to avoid usage of the term because it may tend to insinuate the involvement of governmental information.[346]

10.2 Confidential Information v. Classified Information

The lowest level of classified information in the U.S. is called "confidential information" and is defined as information that "would cause 'damage' or be 'prejudicial' to national security if publicly available." Executive Order 13292, the latest in a long series of Executive Orders, restricts access or the handling of classified information that rises to the level of confidential information. As a result of the use of the word "confidential" in the classified information system, most government contracts or laws use the word "proprietary" to mean confidential or they simply avoid use of the term "confidential information." For example, the Economic Espionage Act of 1996 (18 U.S.C. §§ 1831-39) relies on the terms "trade secrets," which is defined as requiring the owner to have "taken reasonable measures to keep such information secret." Additionally, many laws refer to or use "proprietary" to mean "confidential business information." *See* for example, 18 U.S.C. § 1905, which restricts disclosure of confidential information by government employees; 5 U.S.C. § 552(b), which provides an exemption from the Freedom of Information Act (FOIA); and 41 U.S.C. § 423, which provides for procurement integrity. Technology that could be considered important to national security may also fall subject to certain compliance with the Patent Act or the Rules of Practice. *See generally* 35 U.S.C. § 184 and 37 C.F.R. § 5.2.

Measures to Preserve Confidentiality

There is no hard and fast rule that will dictate whether adequate measures have been taken to qualify information as "confidential." To help assure that information will be regarded as confidential, many organizations hold themselves to a standard that is consistent with that needed to establish information as a trade secret under applicable state trade secret laws. In general, this means that the

---

346. In view of the above, it is a relatively widespread practice for organizations to identify agreements for protecting confidential information as "nondisclosure agreements" or "NDA's."

protective measures taken for the information must be reasonable under the circumstances. What is reasonable under the circumstances will vary from industry to industry, or even business to business within the same industry.

Attention to answering two basic questions should help most organizations to establish reasonable confidentiality measures.

1. How is information designated as confidential?
2. What physical measures are taken to limit access to the confidential information?

One basic step to protecting confidential information is to conspicuously mark it to denote its sensitivity. What is appropriate marking will vary from case to case. In some instances, a designation of "CONFIDENTIAL" on the cover page of a multipage document may suffice. In others it may not, or it may unnecessarily subject the document (or isolated parts of it) to risk of treatment as not confidential. For example, it is sometimes the case that a party will mark only a cover page of the document as confidential, but an unmarked page gets separated from the document.

Another common issue encountered in marking of confidential information is when the marking has been abused to the point that it becomes impossible to take a claim of confidentiality seriously. Consider, for example, the situation in which a party shares one hundred pages of documents, all marked as "Confidential" with another party under a confidentiality obligation. Among the one hundred pages are ninety-five pages from a catalog that the disclosing party makes publicly available, three pages are from a Material Safety Data Sheet that the disclosing party submitted to its local Occupational Health and Safety Administration and posted on its website, and the remaining two pages are formula sheets word-processed on corporate letterhead. It is difficult to know in this instance whether, in fact, all of the information is indeed confidential. If litigation ever ensued, the credibility of the disclosing party may also be called into question from the excessive marking.

Overall, the marking used on disclosure of information documents (e.g., presentations, e-mails, etc.) is an industry-by-industry judgment call. For example, in some industries, the tendency is to treat anything without a proprietary marking as public domain and free to copy.

There are different schools of thought on best practices, and the best practice selected must take into account the particular circumstances of each disclosure. That said, however, one common practice is to employ, in addition to a "CONFIDENTIAL" designation, a copyright notice to the effect of "© COPYRIGHT OWNER, DATE. All rights reserved."[347] Use of such a notice should help to deter blatant copying of a disclosure.

---

347. *See* 17 U.S.C. § 401.

If the intention is to make a public disclosure, then care should be taken to avoid using the "CONFIDENTIAL" designation. In fact, the use of such a designation, even if erroneous, could sabotage the value the document might otherwise have for establishing a prior public use. For example, suppose that an organization is accused of infringing a patent. The organization defends on the basis that it publicly used the accused subject matter years before the application for the patent was filed. However, to support its assertions, the organization must rely for its proofs upon documents that are marked as "CONFIDENTIAL." On its face, the marking contradicts the premise for which the document is offered. In such instance, it would have been better not to have employed any confidentiality designation or to have only employed a copyright notice. In the latter example, depending upon the facts of the particular case, the mere use of the designation "PROPRIETARY" might have been sufficient to create an issue of material fact that would warrant a trial on public use.

10.3 **The Trade Secret Identification Conundrum**

There is a temptation in many organizations to maintain a comprehensive detailed list of trade secrets, (e.g., (i) the temperature at which the formula is baked is 400°C, (ii) the amount of stabilizer is 2.72 percent, (iii) the flame retardant is purchased from XCO under code name "Falcon," etc.) to help personnel recognize what information requires sensitive treatment. Some organizations keep a list of trade secrets, but opt for general categories instead, e.g., (i) formulations for welding compound, (ii) process conditions for welding compound, (iii) vendors of welding compound ingredients. As can be seen, there is some value to having a catalog of the company trade secrets. However, there is a danger that if too specific and, upon misappropriation of merely the list, competitive advantages will be lost). Trade secret laws vary widely, from state to state, in how clearly the trade secrets must be identified.

See "Identification of Trade Secret Claims in Litigation: Solutions for a Ubiquitous Dispute" by Graves and Range, for a comprehensive discussion of when and how trade secrets are identified during litigation at http://www.law.northwestern.edu/journals/njtip/v5/n1/3.

The reasonableness of physical measures to preserve confidentiality will vary from case to case. Examples of measures companies can take are:

1. Storing the information in a locked or password protected storage site;
2. Placing sign-in sheets at reception;
3. Requiring escorts for visitors to facilities;
4. Requiring visitors to undertake an obligation of confidentiality as condition for access to premises;
5. Restricting trade secret information to locations having limited access;

6. Requiring employees or other personnel to sign a nondisclosure agreement, and otherwise taking precautions with both new and departing employees;
7. Dividing access to formulation ingredients among multiple persons, with each having access only to some of ingredients;
8. Using code names for parts or ingredients;
9. Screening items (e.g., containers, documents, cameras, etc.) that leave the premises and which may include confidential information; and
10. Restricting access to the information to a limited number of individuals within the organization.[348]

10.4 Reasonable Measures May Differ

To illustrate how "reasonableness" may differ depending upon the circumstances, consider the following scenarios. In each scenario, the company possesses secret formulations recorded on 3 x 5 index cards. The index cards are kept in a tray on the desk of the company's president. No one is entitled access to the president's office without supervision. However, in one instance, a cleaning crew accesses the office in the evening when the business is closed. In the other instance, the cleaning crew cleans during normal business hours and only cleans the president's office while the president or an administrative assistant are present. It might be argued that in the former situation, reasonable measures have not been taken, but in the latter they have.

Situations Posing Disclosure Risks

To maintain the value of confidential information, the confidential information should be kept confidential. Disclosure destroys confidentiality, and with it any potentially valuable trade secrets,[349] possibly some patent rights, and may even violate some government regulation or statute restricting disclosure. Disclosure can take place through verbal, visual, or documentary communication, including e-mail.

---

348. Additional guidance can be gleaned from http://my.execpc.com/~mhallign/protect.html (accessed November 26, 2007). *See also* D. Hannah, *Keeping Trade Secrets Secret*, 47 MIT Sloan Management Review, 17-20 (Spring 2006).
349. The Uniform Trade Secret Act (UTSA) defines trade secrets as information,
    including a formula, pattern, compilation, program device, method, technique, or process that: (i) derives independent economic value, actual or potential, from not being generally known to, and not being readily ascertainable by proper means by other persons who can obtain economic value from its disclosure, and (ii) is the subject of efforts that are reasonable under the circumstances to maintain its secrecy.
    Uniform Trade Secret Act § 1.

Disclosure may occur purposefully or by accident. The state of mind of the party making the disclosure is immaterial because, once disclosed outside a confidentiality obligation, the confidential information typically has thus lost its status as confidential.

While many organizations spend a great deal of time seeking to protect against intentional taking of confidential information by third parties, often the greater risk lies in the accidental disclosure of confidential information by its own personnel. The following is a listing of scenarios in which organizations often unwittingly disclose aspects of confidential information.

1. Patent application publishing eighteen months after filing, or publications in journals, trade magazines;
2. Presentations at conferences;
3. Displays at trade shows;
4. Conversations with professional collegues;
5. Advertising, brochures, or other marketing activities;
6. Cell-phone conversations in public locations (e.g., restaurants, airplanes, etc.;
7. Sales activities, including presentations without a confidentiality agreement or product demonstrations or bid proposal (including to the government);
8. Social gathering or entertaining customers;
9. Web site postings, including by bloggers or message boards;
10. Unescorted vendors or contractors on premises, (e.g., to fix equipment, make a delivery, conduct a meeting, or otherwise);
11. Investor or analyst presentations by senior management; and
12. Customer sales calls.

10.5 The Perils of Having Customers

Customer disclosure of confidential information is a common source of improper disclosure, even when a confidentiality agreement is in place (the other common source of improper disclosure is employees). In a frequent scenario, the customer is an original equipment manufacturer that relies upon vendors for the supply of unique components. On the one hand, the customer wants to benefit from the most advanced state of technology the vendor possesses. On the other hand, the customer does not necessarily want to pay the price the vendor seeks to command. As a result, the customer will employ a competitive bidding process, during which confidentiality obligations are sometimes overlooked. Unfortunately, the vendor is left with little recourse, unless it wants to sue its customer. Nevertheless, this should not discourage organizations from following prudent practices, including reminders to their customers verbally and in writing that the information being provided is confidential.

Potential Consequences of Disclosure

Section 102 of the Patent Act in the U.S. affords a one-year "grace" period within which to file a patent application following a nonconfidential external disclosure. This means that a patent application has to be filed in the U.S. Patent and Trademark Office within one year of the public disclosure or rights will be lost.[350] By one account, the grace period is used by 20 percent of all patent applications filed in the U.S.[351]

In contrast, patentability outside of the U.S. generally requires "absolute novelty," which means that the first public disclosure of the invention must be in the filing to a patent office.[352] It is typical that, due to the frequency of use of the U.S. grace period, if an American entity asks a European Patent Attorney to file a patent application for an invention in the European Patent Office, the first question the Patent Attorney will ask is "was it disclosed before the filing date?" If the answer is "yes," the attorney will either decline the case or immediately start to issue caveats to start preparing the applicant for an unsuccessful result.

10.6 Ameliorating a Novelty Bar

Though the law seems to impose a "bright-line" rule, it is possible that the adverse consequences of the disclosure might be avoided.

Some organization try to fix this situation with a retroactive confidentiality agreement, but these may not be effective unless confirming a verbal understanding of confidentiality made at the time of the disclosure.

Simply because a public disclosure was made, the facts may not necessarily give rise to an actual bar on patentability. For instance, in European practice, if the subject of the claim could not reasonably be ascertained from the subject matter disclosed (e.g., the patent claims an intermediate compound that does not appear in the finished compound), the disclosure might not necessarily give rise to a bar to patentability. The analysis will invariably boil down to the scope of the patent claims under consideration, as compared with the subject of the disclosure.

It is important in any close case to provide the material facts to counsel for guidance on the patenting.

---

350. 35 U.S.C. § 102(b) bars patentability if the invention was described in a printed publication more than one year prior to the effective filing date of a patent application.

351. *See Grace Period and Invention Law in Europe and Selected States*, published by the European Commission and can be found at www.ipr-helpdesk.org.

352. Art. 54 European Patent Convention (EPC). Generally, there is an exception to this rule if the disclosure of the confidential information was in breach of an agreement (e.g., a confidentiality agreement or an employment agreement). art. 55(1) EPC.

Important Confidentiality Lessons for Employees

Almost every organization pays some lip service to confidentiality. However, for employees to adhere rigidly to corporate confidentiality policies, corporate leaders must lead by example, and they must establish infrastructure and teach practices that foster confidentiality. Training should start by defining for employees that confidential information is an asset owned by the company. In a healthy IP culture, this will be reinforced by corporate employment policies and desirably by express language in an employment agreement as well. However, notwithstanding these express obligations, it is remarkable how much employees need reminding.

10.7 **Confidentiality Restrictions**

Example Clause in Employment Agreement Giving Ownership, and Limiting Disclosure and Use of Confidential: Employee agrees that all Confidential Information is the property of and owned by the Company. Employee agrees not to disclose Confidential Information without the consent of the Company and not to use Confidential Information for any purpose other than in furtherance of his duties at the Company.

Employees desirably are also trained to protect the confidential information of the company, just like other corporate assets. For example, employees understand readily that if someone is office supplies from the company for use at their home, that is probably wrong. However, in the time leading up to the establishment of a healthy IP culture, the same employees may not think twice about discussing the results of a secret pilot study while in a public restaurant. Employees need to be given concrete examples for how to recognize confidential or sensitive information and how to conduct themselves with such information.

The following are examples of practices that organizations can school their employees to follow in efforts to foster a strong IP culture.

- Clear conference rooms after use, including erasing white boards;
- Close and put away lab notebooks;
- Log-off computers, especially on conference room computers;
- Ask visitors who are unescorted if they need some help (don't let an unknown, unbadged person pass in the hall);
- Do not talk on airplanes or in public spaces where you can be overheard;
- Do not tailgate through or hold open security doors, which are intended to restrict access;

- Follow company policy on taking company data or information off-site, including in laptop form;
- Do not prop open doors;
- Check with your legal group to see if a confidentiality agreement is in place if you have a visitor or are visiting another company (do not guess or take someone else's word for it unless they have checked);
- Make sure job candidates that are being interviewed have signed confidentiality agreements;
- Do not assume that once a confidentiality agreement is in place it lasts forever; make sure it is currently enforceable;
- Follow-up verbal or visual disclosures of confidential information with a letter or e-mail listing what was disclosed;
- Only disclose what needs to be disclosed; a confidentiality agreement permits disclosure in confidence, it does not require disclosure;
- Mark presentations, e-mails, or other documents with the appropriate label;
- Check with legal counsel to make sure vendors, fabrication shops, or outside consultants have the correct agreement in place before you send them your designs or data; and
- Have visitors sign in at the lobby, making clear that it is not a formality for which apologies are needed, it is a requirement for all visitors.

In a successful IP culture, these activities will become second nature and infectious. Employees will take responsibility for knowing what is confidential and protecting it.

10.8 **Third Party Information**

Another aspect of confidentiality for which training of employees is important is in the protection of confidential information received that belongs to third parties (such as other companies that they work with or to whom they will disclose confidential information under an agreement). This can be achieved in an employment agreement, in employee policies, or both, with language consistent with the following.

Example Clause on Third Party Confidential Information: Employee recognizes that the Organization has received and in the future will receive from third parties their confidential or proprietary information subject to a duty on the Organization's part to maintain the confidentiality of such information and to use it only for certain limited purposes. Employee (or consultant) agrees that Employee (or consultant) owes the Organization and such third parties, during the term of this Agreement and thereafter, a duty to hold all such confidential or proprietary information in the strictest confidence and not to disclose it to any person, firm, or corporation or to use it except as necessary in carrying out the services for the Organization consistent with the Organization's agreement with such third party.

It is important to protect the confidential information of a third party in the same manner that an organization would protect its own information. Most organizations do not want to be the source of leaks of confidential information, or to gain a reputation for leaking confidential information.

Unsolicited Proposals or Disclosures

Sometimes companies get information that they do not want, for example, information that is disclosed in violation of an agreement, information that contaminates an organization with trade secrets, or other confidential information of another organization, or even information from a customer on how to improve a product. The most effective way to handle information that is improperly disclosed, or otherwise potentially contaminates it (particularly when the organization has reasonable basis to know that the information was improperly disclosed or is contaminating), is to return the information to its source, and to advise the source that the information received was not circulated within the organization or used for any purpose. Simply put, one of the best courses of action is to put the information in an envelope and mail it back to the source or (if received by e-mail) a return e-mail notifying the source of the destruction of the information, making no copies.

Many companies protect themselves from an accusation of misappropriation, in the context of unsolicited disclosures, by placing limitations on unsolicited information from third parties.[353] The limitations are also an attempt to protect their own research and development and claims against disclosing trade secret information.

---

353. Misappropriation of proprietary information is a common law tort that is not the same as misappropriation of trade secrets. Common law misappropriation is sometime referred to as unfair competition and should be applied to those cases where other forms of intellectual property do not apply. For example *U.S. Sporting Prods. v. Johnny Stewart Game Calls*, 865 S. W. 2d 214 (Tex. App. 1993) cites three elements to this tort:

    (1) creation of the information through time, skill, labor or money, (2) defendant's use of that information in competition with the plaintiff and thereby gaining an advantage and (3) commercial damage to the plaintiff.

    Recently, some states have cut back common law misappropriation based on preemption by Section 7 of the Uniform Trade Secret Act. For example, in *AirDefense, Inc. v. Airtight Networks, Inc.*, No. C05-04615JF, 2006 WL 2092053 (N.D. Cal. July 26, 2006) claims to conversion of trade secrets, common law unfair competition through the theft and attempted use of trade secrets and statutory unfair competition through the theft and attempted use of trade secrets were all dismissed as pre-empted by the statutory trade secrets act.

As an example, many web sites of venture capitalists have the warning statement (under the legal or submission section) that no confidential or proprietary information should be submitted. For example, CMEA Ventures (www.cmeaventures.com) states, "Due to the large number of business plans and related materials that we review, and the similarity of such plans and materials, we cannot accept responsibility for protecting against misuse or disclosure of confidential or proprietary information or other materials in the absence of our express written agreement."[354] Also, for example, Xerox has an entire "submissions booklet" that explains what the rights of the organization are when you submit an idea.[355]

Once an unsolicited idea is presented and received within an organization, however, what it does next will vary depending upon the circumstances. For instance, some companies take the submissions into the legal department, file them, and make sure that the research and development teams never see the idea. This procedure ensures that no claim of misappropriation is possible. However, this might also stifle innovation, particularly if the submission is a good idea.

10.9 **Clean Rooms**

Some organizations may receive a submission, and identify a potential conflict with ongoing work of the organization. Upon recognizing the potential conflict, the organization might attempt to establish a "clean room," to isolate the disclosed information from the ongoing information. Clean room development also can be used by starting with a specification of the results of a desired technology of a competitor, assembling an isolated research group to achieve the results without using information about a competitive technology. It is a popular technique used in software development.

Some organizations will accept outside submissions, but will impose a waiver requirement. In particular, the organization will accept an outside submission, but only after the disclosing party agrees to waive any claim of confidentiality. Assuming the waiver is clear and unambiguous, the waiver can work, but needs careful drafting. For example, in *Burten v. Milton Bradley Co.*,[356] the plaintiff independent inventors created a game that they hoped to

---

354. *See*, www.cmeaventures.com/contact-us.php.
355. http://www.xeroxtechnology.com/ip1.
    nsf/0/6D277FFB3B110E7885256A69004F5FFA/$FILE/OutsideSubmissions.pdf   (accessed November 27, 2007).
356. 763 F.2d 461 (1st Cir. 1985).

sell to Milton Bradley. Milton Bradley expressed that it would accept the idea only if the plaintiffs first signed a disclosure agreement that stated that there was no relationship between the parties, that Milton Bradley assumed no obligation to accept the product idea and that the disclosing party (the plaintiffs) were to retain all rights under U.S. patent laws, but that otherwise Milton Bradley would accept their idea for consideration. Milton Bradley declined the plaintiff's idea, but a year later came out with a game that the plaintiffs considered pretty much the same thing. A jury verdict awarded substantial damages for misappropriation, but it was overturned on a motion for judgment notwithstanding the verdict. The court specifically stated that the waiver issue was a close call under Massachusetts law, illustrating how these cases do not always pose bright-line scenarios.

The following are examples of possible waiver clauses that have been found sufficient by courts:

- No confidential relationship is to be established by such submission or implied from consideration of the submitted material, and the material is not to be considered submitted in confidence.[357]
- No obligation of any kind is assumed by, nor may be implied against the company unless or until a formal written contract between the parties is signed.[358]
- All of inventor's rights arising out of the submission shall be limited to any rights accorded under U.S. patent and copyright laws.[359]
- I do not hereby give Chrysler Corporation any rights under any patents, trademarks, or copyrights I now have or may later obtain covering my suggestion, but I do hereby in consideration of the examination of my suggestion release it from any liability in connection with my suggestion or liability because of use of any portion thereof except such liability as may arise under valid patents, trademarks, or copyrights now or hereafter issued or obtained.[360]

One key to these clauses is the explicit denial of a confidential relationship, which destroys any implied contract obligations.

If an organization decides to accept a confidentiality obligation, safeguards might be installed. A foremost consideration is the protection of ideas already in its possession. This can be proven by written documents, provided that reliable records have been made and kept. Another consideration is to limit dissemination of the idea within the organization and possibly even require

---

357. *See MH Segan Ltd. P'ship. v. Hasbro, Inc.*, 924 F. Supp. 512, 517 (S.D.N.Y. 1996)
358. *See Id.*
359. *See Id.*
360. *Hassel v. Chrysler Corp.*, 982 F. Supp. 515 (S.D. Ohio 1997).

the execution of individual confidentiality by those who review the proposals. Good training to sensitize employees throughout an organization can help to reduce the possible risk of contamination from unsolicited disclosures.

Securing Premises

As this chapter and Chapter 9 make clear, reasonable measures to preserve confidentiality are key, especially to meet the often-rigorous requirements for trade secret protection. It is important not only to take the measures, but to document the measures taken. This could be achieved with a procedures manual, checklists, or both. It might also be achieved with log books, which could mean keeping a contemporaneous written proof showing that the steps designated were indeed followed.

What is reasonable under the circumstances obviously changes from industry to industry, but consider the following aspects of security for a typical premises of an organization:

1. Physical security at organization premises, both inside and outside;
2. Electronic security for servers, individual computers and network and/ or e-mail access;
3. Handling and training of employees; and
4. Policies or practices for disclosure of information.

Physical Security

Strict physical security at premises is not necessarily a requirement for asserting trade secret protection, but it sends a strong message about how much an organization cares about its secrets and confidential information.[361] Apple, Inc., is reputed for its physical security measures, including internal doors that only electronically keyed employees may enter, and with a posted sign to "not tailgate" (meaning don't follow someone with access into a place that you do not otherwise have permission to enter).[362] For a more typical organization, it is often sufficient to install physical security measures to the degree that

---

361. *See, e.g., Electro-Craft Corp. v. Controlled Motion, Inc.,* 332 N. W. 2d 890, 220 U.S.P.Q. (BNA) 811 (Minn. 1983), stating that "ECC's physical security measures did not demonstrate any effort to maintain secrecy." There, ECC had a plant that had some secure entrances, but 7 unlocked entrances without warning signs. This was among a list of things that were not done at ECC to maintain security.
362. *Wall Street Journal* (WSJ) article reprinted at http://www.appleinsider.com/articles/06/06/28/wsj_on_apple_and_its_obsession_with_secrecy.html.

visitors and employees alike recognize, when on the premises, that security is valued by the organization. Limiting access might ruffle some feathers, but it will send a clear message that the organization has a security ethic.

Other possible approaches to securing the premises include, where reasonable and appropriate, the use of guarded entrances (including at night), locked doors, and fences to enclose the premises or portions of it. Unfettered access to company facilities can not be allowed. Small organizations that share space with others must take special precautions to assure that confidential information is not accessible. A reception area should feature a visitor log and should limit or restrict access to the facilities beyond the reception area. For some portions of the facility, an organization might restrict all visitors. A vigilant receptionist, who is not easily intimidated, also can assure that visitors sign-in and receive appropriate escorting.

Within R&D or laboratory facilities, it is prudent to employ abundant locks (doors, filing cabinets, etc.). Individual employee access to specified labs helps to limit access. A company might wish to avoid windows for the most sensitive parts of the premises and even to invoke procedures on whether or not blinds can be kept open. Procedures may also be invoked to monitor chain of custody and control of lab notebooks.[363] If guests are escorted through a facility, protection of sensitive information might be as simple as covering the sensitive information with a sheet or tarp.

In manufacturing and production facilities, it is helpful to conceal the identity and model numbers of equipment, as well as packaging for raw materials. A procedure for monitoring inventory is helpful to assure part samples or prototypes are not stolen and used to reverse engineer the technology. If there are key processing steps, they should be kept in secure locations. Gauges that would reveal critical operating parameters (e.g., pressure or temperature settings) might also be concealed or kept out of plain view. Questions by visitors to persons on the shop floor should be monitored and shop floor workers instructed not to answer.

Executive offices are another source of valuable information, and reasonable precautions to secure them are suggested. It may simply mean placing a lock on a door, invoking practices to avoid leaving sensitive information in plain view, or locking away certain sensitive business information (e.g., in locking desks, safes, or file cabinets).

Each organization will adopt its own security system and may issue badges or key fobs to employees (some may still issue regular keys). Electronic or

---

363. One company trying to attract customers, but keep certain trade secrets confidential, used a black tarp covering. Whatever was confidential in their laboratories was covered with a black tarp, and, of course, the first question asked by visitors was, "what's under the tarp?" So it worked.

radiofrequency access badges are common, which require employees to use the badge to gain access to facilities. A number of such systems are tied to a computer system that records or logs which employees entered which doors and when. These badges also allow management to decide which rooms or facilities should have restricted access (e.g., a server room might be limited to Information Technology employees or a laboratory might be limited to employees working on the projects located in the laboratory). It is important when issuing such badges to track who the recipients are and to ensure badges are reported promptly if lost or returned if an employee departs. In this regard, it is also common to install alarms, security lighting, or closed circuit television cameras to deter or record those breaking or entering premises.[364] Of course, posted signs warning of the security measures that are in place, and that unrestricted access is forbidden, should help.

To protect its information, a company needs to attend to its methods of waste management. "Dumpster-diving" has been widely encountered in the trade secret and confidential information arena. It is worthwhile to contract with a reputable paper-shredding service and also to invoke measures to destroy superfluous samples or prototypes.

Finally, an increasing problem facing many companies is the loss of information by using computers that travel outside of company premises, personal digital devices, cameras, e-mail messaging devices, or other electronic devices. The portability and size of many of these devices, as well as storage devices (such as USB drives, memory cards, etc.), could make them relatively easy targets.

One important, last point with physical security measures: it is important to regularly maintain physical security measures, not only to keep them in good working order, but to demonstrate a consistent long-term commitment to the measures. As with all company policies or practices, those that cannot be shown in court to have been practiced regularly will have a difficult time withstanding challenge. Documenting the approaches taken and how they have been maintained is helpful.[365]

---

364. It may seem amazing, but it pays to be paranoid. Many Silicon Valley start-ups have had their trade secrets stolen by thieves working for foreign competitors. Edward Iwata, *USA Today*, quoted Supervisory Special Agent Donald Przybyla, of the FBI's Palo Alto, California, Office as stating, "In Silicon Valley, at least 20 foreign nations have tried repeatedly to steal U.S. trade secrets over the past 5 years." *See* Jan. 15, 2003 *WSJ Online*, "Two Silicon Valley Cases Raise Fears of Chinese Espionage," where computer chip designs and software were allegedly stolen and people were stopped at the airport with the information in their bags; *See also* www.economicespionage.com for a list of cases of outright theft.

365. *See, e.g., Nw. Airlines v. Am. Airlines*, 853 F. Supp. 1110 (D. Minn. 1994) (where on a motion for summary judgment questions of fact existed regarding whether reasonable precautions were taken by American Airlines because employees that were leaving were allowed access to files with trade secrets).

Electronic Security and Document Control

Today, electronic security is just as important as physical security. Electronically stored information (ESI) now comprises the vast majority of information created in an organization. Computers, servers, and networks must be protected from unauthorized access. Thus, beyond the physical security of the boxes that contain the electronic information, the following policies and practices should be considered and implemented as needed to demonstrate an effort to keep information secret.[366]

Among the various electronic security measures that may be invoked are:

- Main drives on computers can not be accessed without proper log-in
- Networks that can only be accessed through proper log-in
- Passwords for log-in should change on a periodic basis (e.g., every six months)
- Passwords should meet a certain level of complexity to avoid deciphering (e.g., must use at least one number and nonalpha numeric character and/or no common names).
- Virtual private networks (VPN) may be used to make sure that anyone who accesses the organization network from a location outside the premises has an organization computer that was registered with the organization and special software that identifies the computer to the network prior to access to the network.
- Restrict access to files or software so not everyone can access the entire network.
- Change restrictions imposed on certain files to provide an additional level of security by allowing only identified users to change or print documents on a system.
- Automated warnings and lock-outs may be used in certain circumstances, such as when passwords are typed in incorrectly too many times; a user's account might become frozen and a warning sent to an IT administrator.
- E-mail restrictions on sending confidential information.

The Sarbanes-Oxley Act of 2002 (SOX)[367] dramatically changed corporate IT departments and has helped gain acceptance and understanding of policies

---

366. In addition, organizations today should have a document retention and security policy (as emphasized by the Federal Rules of Civil Procedure). An extra measure of document security might be achieved by numbering sensitive documents and maintaining an inventory and distribution list, to identify who obtains which documents and the ensuing chain of custody.
367. Pub. L. No. 107-204, 116 Stat. 745.

that aid an effective trade secret program. Technically, the specific portion of SOX relates to internal controls over financial data, which are mostly driven by IT systems (*see* 15 U.S.C. § 7262). Chief information officers are now responsible for security, accuracy, and the reliability of the systems that manage and report the financial data, which benefits the trade secret program. Thus, public companies will have many of the IT policies and practices in place that will help an effective trade secret program.

These precautions show that the organization is serious about its secrets. However, as these precautions become common, they can create an impression among employees that there are exceptions or that the security is not really intended for them. For example, in *Northwest Airlines v. American Airlines*,[368] sophisticated employees of American Airlines thought it was acceptable to take documents with valuable trade secrets to their new jobs at Northwest Airlines, despite numerous precautions by American, including special nondisclosure agreements, disclosure of information on a need-to-know basis, and strict computer access. The employees changing jobs still believed that e-mailing a document containing American's secrets was acceptable. It can only be assumed that training and constant reminders would reduce the likelihood of a future similar recurrence.

10.10 **What If?**

What if, after a few days on the job, it becomes apparent that a new employee took trade secret information from a former employer and is using it at the new job? In such instances, legal advice should be sought immediately. The employee and his or her equipment and belongings should be quarantined, with such materials being locked in a secure area, inaccessible to others in the organization. In many instances, damage control will include some contact with the former employer to explain the problem and to help assure precautions are taken to avoid proliferation of the problem. Such occurrences are rare, but when they do occur, they constitute some of the most egregious and damaging forms of IP theft.

A level of annoyance or irritation may be created by computer security, electronic security, or any of the other security measures illustrated herein. Many employees will find ways around the policies or procedures that company security imposes. In fact, on July 30, 2007, the *Wall Street Journal* published "Ten Things Your IT Department Won't Tell You," which was a list of the top ten ways to avoid your company's policies, such as how to send giant files, how to use software your employer does not want you to use, and how

---

368. 853 F.Supp.1110 (D.Minn.1994).

to store work files online.[369] Each entry on the list contained the "problem", which in fact is the annoyance that employees found with electronic security, the "trick" to avoid the problem, and the "risk" of using the trick. Many in the IT community have denounced the *WSJ*'s downplaying of the issues at stake (e.g., SOX compliance), but it shows that if you impose computer policies that make the lives of your employees more difficult, they will find ways around the policies, and this will impact the effectiveness of any program to safeguard trade secrets and other confidential information.

Practical solutions exist to most computer security issues that employees can raise, and an organization that fosters a healthy IP culture will not simply avoid those issues but will seek to solve them in a way that helps employees do their jobs and protects the trade secrets. While these may become dated with time, here are three of the "problems" on the *WSJ*'s list and solutions that companies can employ to make computers easier to use yet still show concern for confidential information and the trade secrets therein.

1. Sending "giant files": Organizations often limit the size of files sent by e-mail. One justification is to avoid cluttering storage, and servers. It also has a side benefit to help avoid the transmission of valuable database files. But, for the typical organization that engages in activities that lead to IP, the occasional need to send a large file is inevitable. The *WSJ* suggests using a reputable Web service and taking appropriate measures tominimize the risk of interception.

2. Accessing work files from home: Some organizations forbid taking work files home to avoid loss or disclosure. However, in today's virtual workplace such an expectationmay be unrealistic.[370] The *WSJ* suggests using a service like Google Desktop to make a document accessible to both computers. However, loading to the server of a third party risks disclosure of sensitive information. One possible solution for an effective trade secret program is for an organization to establish its own secure FTP site that allows employees to access and save documents among the computers. Even under this scenario it is important to train employees to not only upload or download critical documents through the secure site, but to avoid thereafter transmitting the document over an unsecured connection.

---

369. V. Vara, *Ten Things Your IT Department Won't Tell You*, Wall St. J. at R1 (July 30, 2007), available at http://online. wsj.com/article/SB118539543272477927.html?mod=fpa_mostpop (accessed November 28, 2007).

370. The U.S. Patent and Trademark Office is one of the U.S. Government's largest "telework" employers, with over 3000 employees participating, available at http://www.uspto.gov/web/offices/com/speeches/07-45.htm (accessed November 28, 2007). This is accomplished notwithstanding the statutory burden on the Office to maintain applications in confidence. *See* 35 U.S.C. § 122(a).

3. Storing work files online: Recognizing that many people want their work files available on demand from any remote location, the *WSJ* suggests using an online storage service. However, this might not be considered reasonable under the circumstances, especially if it violates company policy.

One possible alternative solution is training employees to be sensitized to the practice and its risks. Trained employees will find that using a USB memory stick or an assistant or colleague (who is left behind at the home base) to e-mail, via a secure connection, the desired files (or using a file transfer service) is just as simple and more in-line with company policy.

Computer security is here to stay and should not be circumvented for employee convenience. IP and IT need to work together because if IT policies are being circumvented then IP policies also will suffer.

Handling Employees

Employees may be one of the biggest leaks of improperly disclosed trade secrets. Employee training and employment agreements are covered elsewhere in this book and are important here as well. An effective trade secret program uses additional employee handling techniques, including selective disclosure of trade secrets, noncompetition agreements, and employee exit procedures.

Selective disclosure of trade secrets refers to specifically choosing what to disclose to whom and when. Although impractical for small companies, larger companies can effectively keep important trade secrets hidden from most employees by segregating information and only disclosing information on an as-needed basis.

The following examples illustrate opportunities in which organizations can sensitize their employees to the importance of confidential information and the value of trade secrets.

- Job Interviews: Candidates should be informed that their job responsibilities will necessarily expose them to trade secrets and confidential information and that there is an enforced policy or established practices in place to maintain confidentiality. A simple question about whether the candidate is up to the task sometimes leads to surprising answers.
- Newly hired: Upon joining the company, employees should be given orientation, with particular guidance on trade secrets and confidentiality. This can be administered by a knowledgeable HR employee even prior to any formal training scheduled with an IP professional. For example, an orientation process can explain the employment agreement the new employee will be asked to sign, as well as part of a review of any company employee handbook or policy manual.

- After work begins: Employees should be monitored for compliance at least on a random basis. IT now has the capability to monitor all activity through the company's network, and these capabilities can be used for random checking for compliance on issues other than whether improper Web sites are being visited.
- Job promotions usually mean exposure to additional corporate trade secrets (e.g., financial information), and employees may need to be reminded or have new information subject to new rules.
- Termination requires re-emphasis of the company's expectations, especially with disgruntled employees or nonvoluntary termination. Exit interviews are common as are termination agreements, which re-emphasize the confidentiality of the trade secrets the employee has learned, the return of company documents and information, and additional restrictions as needed.

Categorizing employees by job function and crafting confidentiality agreements and training to certain job functions can also handle disclosure of trade secrets. For example, hourly workers and contractors will see fewer trade secrets and often may need only a general confidentiality agreement. Officers, directors, and executives will generally be exposed to more trade secret and confidential information, and, thus, may require a more detailed confidentiality agreement, possibly including some sort of noncompete agreement. Research and development employees may be exposed to the most sensitive trade secrets, and consideration should be given to imposing even greater restrictions on the use of trade secrets and confidential information learned during employment.

Noncompetition agreements are also widely used to protect trade secrets. The general idea is that former employees cannot use or disclose trade secrets for some period of time after employment ends in order to give the company time to cause the secrets to become obsolete. Another basis is that some trade secrets are so vital to the company's business that employees should be restricted from using or disclosing those secrets. While the specifics of such agreements are beyond the scope of this book (they are more appropriate to human resources and require extensive analysis for reasonableness), they merit some attention as they are an effective tool for trade secret programs.

In general, noncompetition clauses are reviewed with strict scrutiny to ensure that they are crafted to protect only that which deserves protection. The contracts are disfavored on the basis that they restrain individuals from making a living by practicing their skills. However, this is a state-by-state issue, with some states striking down most if not all such clauses (e.g., California[371]), while

---

371. California Business and Professions Code § 16600 states, "Except as provided in this chapter, every contract by which anyone is restrained from engaging in a lawful procession, trade or business of any kind is to that extent void."

other states allow such clauses as long as they are reasonable (e.g., Texas[372]). Even those states that allow for noncompete clauses or agreements require that the restrictions be reasonable, typically looking to the time length of the restriction, geographic restrictions, and functional areas or fields of restriction for balancing reasonableness versus the employees' ability to earn a living. If your state allows noncompetition agreements or clauses, they should be employed, especially for highly valued employees.

A closely related issue is the doctrine of inevitable disclosure, in which an individual can be restrained from using an organization's trade secrets at a new job if the trade secrets of the old organization will inevitably be disclosed in the practice of the new job. Again, this is a state-by-state issue, with some states adopting the doctrine and others not.

Practices for Information Disclosure

Suppose an organization wants to implement an effective program but not chill its employees from working creatively or making the best use of trade secrets or other confidential information as possible, which may necessarily include disclosure of such information outside of the organization. One approach is to establish a fundamental process by which a group of select individuals within the organization reviews information that is to be disclosed publicly for the first time. This review shows a commitment to protect trade secrets, as well as providing a basis for demonstrating prior art publications and fostering the application of valuable information to solve problems faced by customers and others.

An example of this practice in a healthy IP culture might call for all employees desiring to disclose information outside of the organization to send their disclosures (e.g., papers, presentations, or other disclosures) to the IP Committee, or another designated group, for review and authorization prior to disclosure. Decisions on the review can be made and records kept so that, over time, what has already been disclosed will become known within the organization. An additional benefit is that a record is created of what has been disclosed, which can serve as a prior art repository against competitors trying to patent what you have already disclosed. Appendix 8 illustrates a form that an organization might employ as part of such a process.

---

372. Texas Business and Commercial Code, Title 2, Chapter 15, Subchapter E, § 15. 50(a) states "a covenant not to compete is enforceable if it is ancillary to or part of an otherwise enforceable agreement at the time the agreement is made to the extent that it contains limitation as to time, geographical area, and scope of activity to be restrained that are reasonable and do not impose a greater restraint than is necessary to protect the goodwill or other business interest of the promisee."

CHAPTER
11

Patenting Inventions

A Defining Moment

The decision to adopt a practice of patenting innovations is often a defining moment for the organization, and reflects a refined appreciation for the value that its intellectual achievements can bring to the organization. It will often be the first time the organization spends large amounts of money to enlist outside assistance to help assure its intellectual property is protected. With that investment comes expectation of a return. To ensure the greatest return on investment, it is important for organizations to have a solid understanding of the nature of the patent asset and the processes that go into obtaining it. This chapter seeks to lay a foundation for such understanding.

Requirements for Patentability

In its most basic sense, the predicate act required for a patent is the occurrence of an invention. But, what is an invention? When does a "discovery" or an "innovation" become an invention? Do all inventions qualify for a grant of a patent? As will soon be seen, though grounded in certain common principles, the substantive requirements for an innovation to qualify for a patent vary from country to country and among different technical disciplines.

Though conceptually the grant of a limited monopoly for a contribution to science or the arts dates earlier, the modern patent system traces its roots back more than six centuries to medieval Venice, coinciding with the emergence of Europe from the Dark Ages, during which matters of politics, philosophy, and religion dominated.[373] The earliest reported patent from this era was granted to an architect named Filippo Brunelleschi for a ship to transport marble used to build the Duomo of Florence.[374] The Venetian Patent Act of 1474 granted a limited monopoly for a term of ten years, for "new and ingenius devices."[375] A century and a half later, England enacted its first patent act, the "Statute of Monopolies," which outlawed monopolies, except for affording a fourteen-year monopoly to "the true and first inventor" covering "any manner of new manufactures."[376] England had not awaited the Statute of Monopolies before granting patents. Indeed, it is reported that at least as early as 1449, England had awarded its first patent to John of Utynam for stained glass for Eton College.[377] From 1561 through 1590, the Crown had granted monopolies for the manufacture and sale of various staple commodities.[378] The practice came to be abused, prompting King James I to revoke all patents in 1610.[379]

The U.S. patent system has its basis in Article 1, Section 8, Clause 8 of the U.S. Constitution, which grants Congress the power "[t]o promote the Progress of Science and useful Arts, by securing for limited Times to Authors and Inventors the exclusive Right to their respective Writings and Discoveries."

---

373. It is reported that as early as 1443, Venice granted its first patent for inventions. However, Venice did not adopt a patent statute until March 19, 1474. Craig Nard and Andrew Morriss, *Constitutionalizing Patents: From Venice to Philadelphia, Case Research Paper Series in Legal Studies*, Working Paper 04-12 (August 2004).
374. *Ibid.*
375. *Ibid.* citing Donald Chisum, Craig Allen Nard, Herbert F. Schwartz, Pauline Newman, and F. Scott Kief, Principles of Patent Law at 11-12 (West 2004).
376. www.ipo.gov.uk/about -history-patent.htm (accessed June 25, 2007).
377. http://www.uh. edu/engines/epi2002.htm (accessed July 4, 2007).
378. *Ibid. See also* Nard and Morriss, *supra* note 1, at 39-40. Citing extensive resources, Nard and Morriss outline the history of the earliest efforts to enforce patent rights, in the case of *Darcy v. Allen*, 74 Eng. Rep. 1131 (K. B. 1603).
379. www.ipo.gov.uk/about -history-patent.htm (accessed June 25, 2007).

Though adopted in 1787, the first codification of patent laws in the U.S. did not occur until 1790. The 1790 Act established a three-person panel consisting of "the Secretary of State, the Secretary for the department of war, and the Attorney General of the United States" tasked with examining patent applications to determine if an invention or discovery "not before known or used" was "sufficiently useful and important to warrant a fourteen year patent grant.[380]

Inventorship Generally

In the U.S. inventions are secured to "Inventors." In some countries (e.g., Germany and Japan) compensation obligations may also flow from inventing. Therefore, it will be important to correctly identify the inventors of any particular invention, both for patent validity and inventor compensation issues.

By definition, an invention is subject matter that is conceived and reduced to practice. *Pfaff v. Wells Electronics, Inc.*[381] emphasized that the main act of inventing is the conception part: "The primary meaning of the word 'invention' in the Patent Act unquestionably refers to the inventor's conception rather than to a physical embodiment of that idea." Reduction to practice, however, shows that the invention and testing it is completed (e.g., that the thinking part is done). Reduction to practice can be accomplished by actually making the claimed invention and testing it to assure it works or by writing it down in a patent application and filing it (called a "constructive reduction to practice").

Thus, an inventor is generally regarded as a person who contributes to the conception of the invention where the invention is that which is claimed in a patent and is the definition of what you are excluding others from doing. For co-inventors or joint inventors, there does not need to be work performed in the same place, at the same time or even the same level of contribution.[382] Activities of joint inventors do, however, have to be linked together in some fashion.

Sometimes inventorship is determined by what it is not. For example, merely carrying out another's instructions or assisting the true inventor (i.e., being a "pair of hands") is typically regarded as not contributing to

---

380. Patent Act of 1790, Ch. VII, Sec. 1. At the time, Jefferson was Secretary of State, Henry Knox was Secretary of War, and Edmund Randolph was the Attorney General. Knox and Randolph are remembered by the naming of two buildings that comprise the campus of the present day U.S. Patent and Trademark Office. .

381. 119 S. Ct. 304 (1998).

382. See 35 U.S.C. § 116 and *Eli Lilly and Co. v. Aradigm Corp.*, 376 F.3d 1352 (Fed. Cir. 2004).

the conception.[383] Contributing what is already known in the prior art is also not generally regarded as invention.[384] Suggesting a result instead of how to accomplish the result also is not necessarily an invention.[385]

Determinations of Inventorship

In the context of an IP culture, there will likely be discussions and determinations of inventorship. If monetary awards are used as incentives, for example, sometimes a long list of contributors will appear on the invention disclosure form. Also, corporate recognition of inventorship will give an incentive to be named an inventor. Moreover, if companies are working together in a joint development program, then each company may have an incentive to have their employees named inventors while excluding those from the other company. Thus, having a good idea of what the requirements are and how to apply those concepts will prove useful.

A helpful approach for determining inventorship is to show each person claiming to be an inventor the actual claim, and then ask them to point to some part of the claim that they contributed. This can be a good simulation of what to expect as a test because it is what would likely happen if the patent is ever enforced, and the result can then be documented in the file of the patent application (e.g., for amending inventorship if the claims are restricted or amended). In some organizations, there tend to be two types of employees who get excluded from inventorship–managers and assistants. Managers may approve a project or review progress but may not contribute to the conception of the claimed invention, and approval or review is not enough. Assistants may be involved in the detailed experiments but may not be involved in thinking up the experiments or direction to take in the research.

Thus, clearly, naming inventors is not the same as naming co-authors in a journal publication or giving recognition in a presentation. Inventorship comes with rights (e.g., ownership right to the invention) and responsibilities. One responsibility is to read and understand the patent application, including the claims (as listed in the oath required of each patent application in the U.S.), and to make sure the application sufficiently enables the invention and teaches the "best mode."[386] Another responsibility in the U.S. is to cite prior art to the U.S. Patent and Trademark Office, which most inventors accomplish by citing that prior art to their patent attorney.[387]

---

383. *Ethicon, Inc. v. U.S. Surgical Corp.*, 135 F.3d 1456 (Fed. Cir. 1998).
384. *Hess v. Advanced Cardiovascular Sys., Inc.*, 106 F.3d 976 (Fed. Cir. 1997).
385. *Garret Corp. v. U.S.*, 422 F.2d 874 (Ct. Cl. 1970).
386. 35 U.S.C. 112.
387. 37 C.F.R. 1. 56.

Finally, stealing someone else's invention does not confer IP rights upon the thief. "Derivation" is the term used when the accusation is that one party takes another's idea (invention) as its own.[388] Inventorship disputes can lead to these accusations, and they are hard to resolve because of the fact-specific nature of the inquiry.

Utility Requirement

In general, the utility requirement goes to the nature of the innovation and is the product of value judgments as to whether the type of innovation is that which is deserving of a monopoly. In its most basic sense, underlying the analysis of "utility" is a determination of whether an innovation produces a "useful, concrete, and tangible result."[389] Historically, the patent system has been unwilling to grant patents for discoveries of laws of nature, physical phenomena, or abstract ideas.[390] For example, recognition that an apple falling from the sky is a result of gravity is a law of nature, and the patent system is unwilling to award a monopoly to the person who discovers it.[391] A mathematical algorithm (e.g., a sequence of steps used to process a given input value) similarly is not regarded as the subject of an exclusive right. However, when the law of nature, the algorithm, or a combination of both is put to some new and extraordinary use, particularly to deliver a "useful, concrete and tangible result," society has deemed such innovations as appropriate subject matter for patenting.[392]

The issue of utility has surfaced several times over the past several decades. In 1981, in the *Diehr* case, the Supreme Court held that an algorithm applied in a practical way to produce a tangible result, in that case for curing a material, qualified as patentable subject matter.[393] Live microorganisms for breaking down oil, such as from oil spills, were upheld as being patentable "manufactures" or "compositions of matter," even though argued to be

---

388. See 35 U.S.C. § 102(f).
389. *State Street Bank & Trust Co. v. Signature Fin., Inc.*, 149 F.3d 1368, 1373-74 (Fed. Cir. 1998) (deeming as patentable subject matter a business method in patent entitled: "Data Processing System for Hub and Spoke Financial Services Configuration.").
390. *See Diamond v. Diehr*, 450 U.S. 175, 185 (1981).
391. *Diamond v. Chakrabarty*, 447 U.S. 303, 309 (1980)(" Thus, a new mineral discovered in the earth or a new plant found in the wild is not patentable subject matter. Likewise, Einstein could not patent his celebrated law that E=mc 2; nor could Newton have patented the law of gravity").
392. *Diamond v. Diehr*, 450 U.S. at 188.
393. *See also In re Alappat*, 33 F.3d 1526 (en banc) (data transformed by a machine through math calculations to provide smooth waveform display on a rasterizer monitor).

merely products of nature.[394] Patents for business methods were officially recognized by the Court of Appeals for the Federal Circuit in the *State Street* case of 1998.[395]

On the particular issue of business method patents, though recognized as patentable subject matter in the U.S., the European Patent Convention specifically excludes business method patents from patentable subject matter.[396] Notwithstanding, it has been reported that the European Patent Office received numerous such application filings.[397]

Similar value judgments have arisen in the context of medical procedures. For example, in the U.S., the patent laws allow medical procedures to be patented. However, a patent owner is restricted in the parties from whom relief for infringement may be sought.[398] In contrast, the European Patent Convention specifically excludes medical procedures from the scope of patentable subject matter.[399] Efforts to patent such innovations have required special treatment in Europe.[400]

---

394. *Diamond v. Chakrabarty*, 447 U.S. at 303.

395. According to the USPTO, "Financial apparatus and method patents date back to this period. These early financial patents were largely paper-related products and methods. The first financial patent was granted on March 19, 1799, to Jacob Perkins of Massachusetts for an invention for "Detecting Counterfeit Notes." http://www.uspto.gov/web/menu/busmethp/index.html#origins (accessed June 30, 2007).

396. E.P.C. 52(2) states: (2) The following in particular shall not be regarded as inventions within the meaning of paragraph 1:. . . (c) schemes, rules and methods for performing mental acts, playing games or doing business, and programs for computers. . . .

397. http://www.iusmentis.com/patents/businessmethods/epc/ (accessed July 4, 2007) ("The European Patent Office (EPO) reported in late 2000 that it has about 2,000 pending "business method" applications. . . . In contrast, the U.S. Patents and Trademark Office (USPTO) had over 8,000 pending business method applications in 2000 alone.").

398. 35 U.S.C. § 287(c) excludes medical practitioners from various remedial provisions for patent infringement: "(1) With respect to a medical practitioner's performance of a medical activity that constitutes an infringement under section 271(a) or (b) of this title, the provisions of sections 281, 283, 284, and 285 of this title shall not apply against the medical practitioner or against a related health care entity with respect to such medical activity."

399. *See* E.P.C. Article 52(4): Methods for treatment of the human or animal body by surgery or therapy and diagnostic methods practiced on the human or animal body shall not be regarded as inventions which are susceptible of industrial application within the meaning of paragraph 1. This provision shall not apply to products, in particular substances or compositions, for use in any of these methods.

400. One approach for circumventing the effect of the exclusion, for new uses of medications, has been what is regarded as "Swiss claims" or "second medical use" claims, a manner of claiming having its roots in a directive of the Swiss Patent Office. *See* E.P.C. Article 54(5) and Swiss Federal Intellectual Property Office Official Journal E.P.O. 581 (1984).

11.1 **Business Method Filings**

Following the *State Street* decision, the USPTO faced a surge of business method patent application filings. Based upon data obtained from the USPTO, the popular and informative blog of *patentlyo.com* reported on May 5, 2005, that the USPTO had encountered a backlog of more than 19,000 business method patent application filings, with a mere 11 percent allowance rate for fiscal year 2004.[1]

---

1. http://www.patentlyo.com/patent/2005/05/updated_busines.html (accessed July 4, 2007).

A Basic Novelty Discussion

The novelty requirement, which addresses the basic issue of whether the subject matter is new, is a globally accepted threshold standard for patentability. In general, the requirement demands that the subject matter sought to be patented (as recited in the patent claims) include at least one feature that is not present in a single piece of prior art (e.g., a reference or product). This requirement is one of the most straightforward principles of the patent law. However, it is also one of the most easily confused. To illustrate, consider the following example: a machine with a new element.

For this example, suppose a machine has been created that recycles plastic milk bottles. The machine has a single opening into which plastic milk bottles are inserted, while the bottles still have their caps on them and are filled with spoiled milk. The machine has a first station that removes the bottle caps. At a second station, a pump connected to a hose sucks the spoiled milk from the bottle and sends it to an incinerator. At a third station, the remaining empty bottle is shredded. At a fourth station the resulting shreds are melted and compacted with a circular die to form a small disc shaped like a hockey puck.

The closest prior art is a patent from several years earlier in which an apparatus is described that includes the identical structure as the above apparatus. In fact, the development that lead to the innovation used a commercially available machine made under the prior art patent. However, the prior patent describes a rectangular die, which forms a brick rather than a disc. The prior art only discloses embodiments and examples in which whole milk is removed.

How the patent claims are drafted would, therefore, determine whether the structure of the machine was novel.

Example 1: Claimed Subject Matter Lacks Novelty
A milk bottle recycling apparatus, comprising:
a) a bottle cap removal station;

b) a milk removal station;

c) a shredding station; and

d) a melting and compacting station.

Example 2: Claimed Subject Matter Possesses Novelty

A milk bottle recycling apparatus, comprising:

a) a bottle cap removal station;

b) a milk removal station;

c) a shredding station; and

d) a melting and compacting station that includes a circular die for forming a compacted disc from molten shreds of the milk bottle.

As seen, the elements of Example 1 "read on" the prior art. That is, each of the elements recited can be found in the prior art. In contrast, the elements of Example 2 include the recitation (or what is regarded as a "limitation") that the melting and compacting station includes "a circular die for forming a compacted disc." This feature is not described in the prior art patent. Therefore, its presence is deemed under the patent laws to make the claimed combination "new" or "novel." Remember, the discussion right now is to illustrate *only* novelty. Whether the difference of employing a circular die as opposed to a rectangular die deserves a patent still requires an assessment of obviousness/inventive step.

Among the many issues that arise under a novelty determination, there are two particular issues that tend to generate confusion. A first issue is when a feature or result of an apparatus, device, composition, or process is present in an innovation but is not explicitly described in a prior art reference. In this instance, the issue will generally come down to an analysis of proofs of inherency of the teachings of the prior art. For example, a prior art patent talks about "steam." The question arises does that inherently mean that water is present at a temperature above 100°C?

A second issue is when an apparatus, device, or composition performs a function or is used for a purpose not disclosed in the prior art. In this instance, the typical practice is to set forth a claim as a process claim, instead of an apparatus or composition of matter claim. Consider the following examples.

Suppose that the innovative apparatus of the previous Example 1 is specifically used for the limited purpose of recycling bottles of chocolate milk at least 30 days after the expiration date of the milk as marked on the bottle.

Example 3: Claimed Subject Matter Lacks Novelty

A milk bottle recycling apparatus, comprising:

a) a bottle cap removal station;

b) a milk removal station for removing chocolate milk from the milk bottle;

c) a shredding station; and

d) a melting and compacting station.

As can be seen, the structure claimed for the apparatus could be urged as reciting no features that distinguish over the prior art. The law has typically treated new uses of existing structures as lacking novelty. To pursue a patent, the practice has evolved of claiming not the old structure, but a process of using the old structure for a new purpose.

Thus, one approach for introducing novelty could involve claiming a method of using the apparatus for the purpose of recycling chocolate milk bottles such as:

Example 4: Claimed Subject Matter Possesses Novelty as Process Claim

A process for recycling a chocolate milk bottle, comprising the steps of:

a) removing a bottle cap from the chocolate milk bottle at least 30 days after its expiration date;

b) removing chocolate milk from the chocolate milk bottle;

c) shredding the chocolate milk bottle; and

d) melting and compacting the resulting shreds of the chocolate milk bottle.

From the above, an argument can be advanced that novelty is now present because the prior art patent does not describe the specific application of recycling chocolate milk bottles. Prevailing case law would support that position with considerable likelihood of success.

Innovations Must Not Be Obvious

Without more facts, you are probably struck that the innovations of the above examples are not the type that ought to be patentable. Should the mere change of a rectangular die to a circular die merit a valuable property right with its attendant monopoly? Has there been a significant enough contribution to the state of the art from the recognition of a new use (recycling chocolate milk bottles 30 days after expiration date) of a prior art recycling machine to justify affording the right to prevent others from doing the same for the next 20 years? As it is, mere novelty is insufficient to entitle an innovator to a patent. Something more has been required, and specifically some determination that the innovation is sufficiently extraordinary that it would not have been obvious to a person of ordinary skill in the art at the time of the invention.

Obviousness

Though modern patent acts typically frame the requirements in terms of lacking obviousness or as possessing "inventive step," the essence is the same, requiring that some act of innovation must occur before a government will grant a patent monopoly. That said, however, obviousness or nonobviousness or inventive steps are typically difficult determinations. The requirement has its foundation in the historic and ongoing balancing of a reward of exclusivity to pioneers who explore the frontiers of science and technology against the stifling effects that a legal monopoly might have upon investors who drive the economy. The concept of obviousness in the U.S. patent law dates back to the 1850 case of *Hotchkiss v. Greenwood*,[401] in which the Supreme Court upheld the invalidation of a patent for making knobs from potter's clay, stating:

> unless more ingenuity and skill in applying the old method of fastening the shank and the knob were required in the application of it to the clay or porcelain knob than were possessed by an ordinary mechanic acquainted with the business, there was an absence of that degree of skill and ingenuity which constitute essential elements of every invention. In other words, the improvement is the work of the skilful mechanic, not that of the inventor.

The *Hotchkiss* principles are regarded as the foundation for the codification (a century later) of the obviousness requirement in 35 U.S.C. § 103, of the Patent Act of 1952. The Supreme Court added to the jurisprudence with the landmark case of *Graham v. John Deere Co.*,[402] exploring the Constitutional underpinnings of the Patent Act. Speaking of Article 1, Section 8, Clause 8, the Court explained:

> The clause is both a grant of power and a limitation. This qualified authority, unlike the power often exercised in the sixteenth and seventeenth centuries by the English Crown, is limited to the promotion of advances in the "useful arts." It was written against the backdrop of the practices—eventually curtailed by the Statute of Monopolies—of the Crown in granting monopolies to court favorites in goods or businesses which had long before been enjoyed by the public. *See* Meinhardt, *Inventions, Patents and Monopoly*, pp. 30-35 (London, 1946). The Congress in the exercise of the patent power may not overreach the restraints imposed by the stated constitutional purpose. Nor may it enlarge the patent monopoly without regard to the innovation, advancement, or social benefit gained thereby. Moreover, Congress may not authorize the issuance of patents whose effects are to remove existent knowledge from the public domain, or to restrict free access to materials already available. Innovation, advancement, and things which add to the sum of

---

401. 52 U.S. 248, 267 (1850).
402. 383 U.S. 1, 5-6 (1966).

useful knowledge are inherent requisites in a patent system which by constitutional command must "promote the Progress of * * * useful Arts." This is the standard expressed in the Constitution and it may not be ignored.

11.2 **Jefferson's Perspective**

The early writings of Thomas Jefferson shed light on the foundation of the U.S. patent system. The Supreme Court outlined the history of the U.S. patent system in *Graham v. John Deere Co.*, 383 U.S. 1 (1966), taking care to trace the evolution of Thomas Jefferson's attitude toward patents. "Certainly an inventor ought to be allowed a right to the benefit of his invention for some certain time. . . . Nobody wishes more than I do that ingenuity should receive liberal encouragement." Letter to Oliver Evans, V Writings of Thomas Jefferson, (Washington ed.), at 75 (1807)".[2]

---

2. Additional writings by Jefferson shedding light on his attitude toward patents are maintained at http://etext.virginia.edu/jefferson/quotations/jeff1320.htm (accessed July 4, 2007).

The *Graham* Court succinctly advanced a now-famous three-part test that has become a staple analysis in U.S. patentability determinations:[403]

> While the ultimate question of patent validity is one of law, . . . the § 103 condition, which is but one of the three conditions, each of which must be satisfied, lends itself to several basic factual inquiries. Under § 103, the scope and content of the prior art are to be determined; differences between the prior art and the claims at issue are to be ascertained; and the level of ordinary skill in the pertinent art resolved. Against this background, the obviousness or nonobviousness of the subject matter is determined.

It is seen that the test is contextual; that is, it must be made in context of the sophistication of the skilled artisan and the prior art that existed at the time of the invention. The *Graham* Court actually went further in identifying the contextual nature of an obviousness determination and indicated that it was appropriate in an obviousness analysis to consider what has been called "objective evidence" of nonobviousness or "secondary considerations." The court identified commercial and practical considerations as among the considerations for establishing the context of an obviousness analysis:

> Such secondary considerations as commercial success, long felt but unresolved needs, failure of others, etc., might be utilized to give light to the circumstances

---

403. *Graham*, 383 U.S. at 17 (citations omitted).

surrounding the origin of the subject matter sought to be patented. As indicia of obviousness or nonobviousness, these inquiries may have relevancy.[404]

11.3 **Person of Ordinary Skill in the Art**

The credentials assigned to the hypothetical person of ordinary skill in the art has the potential to swing an outcome from one side to another. Where this has been given attention, it is often the case that the patent owner will urge the level of skill to be relatively low. A patent challenger, on the other hand, will urge a highly educated and experienced skilled artisan. Consider the difference in knowledge that would be imputed to a twenty-year-old undergraduate engineering student (favored as the skilled artisan by the patentee) as compared with an experienced researcher with a doctorate (favored as the skilled artisan by the patent challenger).

A more recent illustration underscoring the distinction between a mere innovation and an invention worthy of a patent monopoly is the Supreme Court decision in the case of *KSR Int'l. Co. v. Teleflex, Inc.*[405] Addressing the U.S. patent law requirement that an invention lack obviousness as compared with the prior art, and in the context of a dispute over the obviousness of an adjustable vehicle gas pedal (whether it was obvious to substitute an electronically adjustable pedal for a mechanically adjustable pedal) the Court attempted to elaborate on the landscape of economic and social considerations:

> We build and create by bringing to the tangible and palpable reality around us new works based on instinct, simple logic, ordinary inferences, extraordinary ideas, and sometimes even genius. These advances, once part of our shared knowledge, define a new threshold from which innovation starts once more. And as progress beginning from higher levels of achievement is expected in the normal course, the results of ordinary innovation are not the subject of exclusive rights under the patent laws. Were it otherwise patents might stifle, rather than promote, the progress of useful arts. See U.S. Const., Art. I, §8, cl. 8. These premises led to the bar on patents claiming obvious subject matter established in *Hotchkiss* and codified in §103.[406]

There is a persistent balancing reflected in the law. Embodied in the limited term of a patent monopoly is the social recognition of a need for incentives to invest in research and development, e.g., in the form of a limited

---

404. *Ibid.* at 17-18.
405. 127 S. Ct. 1727 (2007).
406. *Ibid.* at 1746.

period of exclusivity for their extraordinary innovations. The requirement for invention beyond mere innovation assures that ordinary and common technologies are not appropriated to exclude or stifle development by others.

Harvesting Inventions from within an Organization

Regardless of what they believe, most organizations have some form of proprietary technology. Chapter 3 discusses in detail the process of IP within an organization, including how to go about gathering inventions from within, using a disclosure form and a patent committee or advisor. However, some additional patent-specific topics merit elaboration.

Some organizations are in the business of producing new products. Identifying patent-worthy innovations is relatively straightforward in such organizations. Those in the business of producing staple articles or commodity items, however, often find themselves convinced that because the products they produce are not innovative, they possess no valuable proprietary technology. However, such manufacturers are frequently the subject of downward pricing pressure from their customers. As a result, they have developed efficiencies in the manner of production, from the way they purchase their materials, to the way they operate their plants or equipment, or even how they manage their accounting practices. Intellectual property abounds in even those organizations that would regard themselves as technologically unsophisticated. The challenge they face is developing a disciplined approach to recognizing the occurrence of an innovation and then capturing a written record of the innovation that can be used as a foundation for a patent grant (or in the case of the election to preserve as trade secret), or for otherwise establishing a valuable proprietary right.

A Written Record of the Invention

One object of this book is to sensitize the reader to the benefits of involving an intellectual property advisor at the earliest possible stage. But, given the practical constraints on available resources, that advisor often will not get involved until an innovator has prepared some write-up of an invention disclosure, as discussed in Chapter 2 (See Appendix 4).

The invention disclosure serves primarily as a business document that commonly is prepared by an inventor within a contemporaneous time frame as the invention activities to describe the invention for the business decision-makers within an organization. Most organizations that patent with any regularity will likely have adopted some invention disclosure form document that prompts users to provide relevant information. There is no such thing as

11.4 **Disclosures**

An "invention disclosure" is not the same thing as a "patent disclosure." Unfortunately, in the field of patents, these have become conventional terms that each have unique (albeit potentially overlapping) meaning but are frequently employed loosely or even interchangeably. A patent disclosure is a phrase that has become generally synonymous with the written description portion of a patent application. References to a patent disclosure, thus, have potentially significant legal implications. They refer to the body of a formal legal document that typically has been drafted by a patent attorney or agent. It serves the purpose of patent documents to teach the invention to the other skilled artisans of the world, the essence of the quid pro quo for which a patent monopoly is granted. In contrast, an invention disclosure usually has been employed in the patent field to denote a formal or informal description of an innovation captured in some type of descriptive document or form. Though it may serve to teach others about the invention, it has many other purposes.

a "one size fits all" invention disclosure form that suits the needs of each organization. Before adopting a particular form, each organization should consider the purposes the form is to accomplish, but to establish a written record of invention, the invention disclosure form should:

1. Help to identify the state of the art and the potential scope of a patent;
2. Establish a written record to corroborate invention activities in the event of an invention priority dispute or inventorship; or
3. Preserve records of the organization in the event ever needed to corroborate a prior use.

11.5 **Best Mode**

The U.S. patent laws require disclosure of the "best mode" known to the inventor at time of filing for practicing the subject matter of the claimed invention. It has become a familiar practice in U.S. patent litigation for an accused infringer to challenge a patent because the best mode was a trade secret that was concealed. This is what occurred to the patent owner in the case of *Chemcast Corp. v. Arco Industries Corp.*[3] In that case the court held the patent invalid because the patent failed to disclose the type of material, its hardness, or even its trade name or supplier for a locking portion of a claimed grommet. A sufficient body of case law on both sides of the issue has developed, such that upon being presented with a need to keep certain subject matter trade secret, a patent agent or attorney has various strategies available. To successfully employ such strategies, however, the agent or attorney must be made aware of the issue.

——————

3. *Chemcast Corp. v. Arco Indus. Corp.*, 913 F.2d 923, 930 (Fed. Cir. 1990) ("Whether characterizable as 'manufacturing data,' 'customer requirements,' or even 'trade secrets,' information necessary to practice the best mode simply must be disclosed"); *Cf., Bayer AG v. Schein Pharms., Inc.*, 301 F.3d 1306 (Fed. Cir. 2002).

Another pitfall that commonly occurs in completing invention disclosures, which could result in delay, and for which disclosure is of huge benefit to the drafting agent or attorney, concerns the submission of test data. The perception that data must be fully developed prior to patenting is a myth. Unless and until lawmakers cause actual reduction to practice to be a requirement for patentability, it could be potentially devastating to an innovator to await completion of test data gathering before applying for patent. Already, such delays could jeopardize a party in efforts to obtain rights abroad, where first-to-file systems predominate.

11.6 **Working Models**

The U.S. Patent Act of 1790 included a requirement that models be submitted with patent applications. The working model requirement was abolished by Congress in 1870 and thereafter in 1880 by the Patent Office. The Rothschild Petersen Patent Model Museum presently houses about 4,000 models and related documents.[4]

——————

4. *See* http://www.patentmodel.org/History.aspx (accessed June 25, 2007).

To illustrate how a delay occasioned by awaiting actual reduction to practice before completing an invention disclosure or filing a patent application, consider the following example.

Facts: On January 1, 2007, within the U.S., Innovator A conceives an apparatus for depositing gallium arsenide onto a substrate. One technical problem to be worked out still at the time was optimum temperature of deposition. Innovator A reasonably believed that success was possible in a chamber lined with a metal or a ceramic, at any temperature from room temperature to 1000°C., but she wanted proof before she sought management approval to apply for a patent. From that day forward, with necessary diligence and under strict secrecy, Innovator A actually reduced the apparatus to practice by building and testing it successfully, all before April 1, 2007. Her success also established operability over the entire expected range of temperatures, with optimal performance from 475 to 540°C using a platinum-lined chamber. On April 1, 2007, Innovator A drafted her invention disclosure form proclaiming the preferred range of 475 to 540°C and platinum lining as important features, and submitted it to her patent agent, who promptly filed an application that is filed on April 30, 2007. On January 2, 2007, in Germany, Innovator B conceives of the same apparatus. Instead of trying to build his device, he retains patent counsel, drafts an application to describe it, and files the application with the German Patent Office on April 2, 2007. The application disclosed the use of metal or ceramic linings and the broad range of room temperature to 1000°C.

Outcome: Under first to invent system (e.g., the system in place in the U.S. at the time of the innovations), Innovator A beats Innovator B. Innovator A invented first by both conceiving the innovation and reducing it to practice before Innovator B. Under a first to file system, Innovator B beats Innovator A. Innovator B filed April 2, 2007, before the April 30, 2007, filing date of Innovator B. It is, therefore, seen that even a short delay in filing, while awaiting proof of success, cost Innovator A the opportunity for worldwide rights. To successfully commercialize on a global scale, Innovator A and Innovator B must now find a way to coexist. Indeed, had the U.S. been a first to file country as of April, 2007, Innovator A would have lost there, too.

Suppose that instead of waiting until April 1, 2007, to start preparing her invention disclosure, Innovator A had submitted it on or about January 1, 2007, when she first thought of it, and the attorney instead filed on April 1, 2007. Innovator A would have enjoyed global rights of priority. Another benefit potentially available to Innovator A had she filed before her research was completed is that she would have been less predisposed to emphasize the criticality of the 475 to 540°C temperature range and the platinum lining.

Patent Searching

It is a common practice to conduct a patent search before filing a patent application. However, it is not mandatory in the U.S. unless an applicant is requesting expedited examination.[407] There are many benefits to performing

---

407. *See* 37 C.F.R. § 1. 102.

a search. For example, a search will help to identify potentially relevant prior art. That could be advantageous during the drafting process. That is, if a particular feature in the prior art is known and is perceived as a possible threat to patentability, express wording that distinguishes over the prior art may be added to the original application.[408] This helps to avoid "new matter" rejections and "written description requirement" challenges. This is illustrated in the following example.

Suppose that inventor X invents a new composition that uses a combination of compounds A, B, and C in a water-based solvent. X performs no patent search, instead preparing a patent application that describes and claims A, B, and C in a water-based solvent. After multiple searches, on different occasions, Patent Office discovers a prior art reference that describes A, B, and C in a solvent that contains both water and volatile acetone. To avoid the effect of the reference, X would like to be able to amend her claims to recite that when she said "water-based solvent" she really meant a solvent that was free of any volatile organic compounds. However, under strict applications of the requirements against adding claim requirements that do not have "basis" in the application as originally filed, X could be forbidden from adding a requirement that the solvent be free of any volatile organic compounds. That is, the Examiner may assert a construction of "water-based" that covers more than 50% water. In contrast, had X performed a thorough search and found the prior art, X may have included the language in the application as filed to make it more clear that the composition was free of any volatile organic compounds.

In deciding to search, it is important to formulate a reasonable search scope. Most patent searching, but not all, is conducted by searching with electronic databases. Though databases may be private subscription service databases, free Internet searches of comprehensive patent databases are available, such as patent searching through the USPTO (atwww.uspto.gov), the EPO (atwww.espacenet.com), and WIPO (atwww.wipo.int).[409] These Web sites are relatively intuitive but limited by the range of possible searching. For example, complete document text searching is more limited with some sites.

---

408. Another potential benefit from performing a search is that a search may reveal the existence of patents to competitors that might be infringed by the practice of the technology sought to be patented. It is not required that someone conduct such a search before commercializing a product, but it is recommended as a means to identifying potential risks and addressing those risks at an early stage in the project. At later stages, design changes to address a possible infringement become difficult. It also tends to be less expensive to negotiate a license before commencing an activity that may result in a claim of infringement.

409. The Web site of the Japanese Patent Office is also searchable, with computer "machine" translations available for more recent patent filings. The sophistication of the Japanese Patent Office site requires users to have a basic understanding of the Japanese patent procurement process and the application numbering scheme. Other services are also available for searching, such as www.freepatentsonline.com.

With others, the extent of the searchable text may be temporally limited. For example, the USPTO only enables text searching to patents that date back to the 1970s. Full images of older patents are available, however, a word search would not readily locate the older references. Each one has its benefits and disadvantages, such as described in the following.

11.7 **Searching**			
	uspto.gov	*espacenet.com*	*wipo.int*
Images available	Yes	Yes	Yes
Text searching done on full document	Yes	Limited	Yes
Foreign counterparts identified	No	Yes	Limited
Prosecution files available for published applications	Yes[5]	Yes	Yes
Can directly search patents citing the reference	Yes (U.S. only)	No	No
Can directly search patents cited within the reference	Yes (U.S. only)	Yes	No
Best time of day to access	Before 10 a.m. (EST) and after 5 p.m. (EST)	System is frequently shutdown overnight in Europe and inaccessible	Anytime
Machine translation capable	No	Yes	No

5. Remember that the USPTO did not adopt a practice of publishing pending applications until 2001. Earlier filed applications or applications that are exempt from publication will not be available.

There are different schools of thought concerning who should conduct a search—the client, patent counsel, or both. For most cases, particularly when a person lacks experience in searching or reading patents, the job is probably best left to patent counsel, even though there will be an expense associated with it. For example, according to the American Intellectual Property Law Association, AIPLA Economic Survey for 2007, the median fee for performing a patent novelty search, analyzing the results and preparing a written opinion was $2000.[410]

A person who commissions a search needs to have realistic expectations for the search results. Before the availability of searchable databases, searching was performed only manually. Searchers would load rolling carts with meters of patents and then physically thumb through each one, looking for relevant text and with drawings in plain view. With electronic capabilities now available, searching theoretically has become more straightforward. However, experience shows that it suffers from its own limitations. For example:

1. It is difficult to search patent drawings;
2. It is difficult to search chemical formulae;
3. Patent applicants often define their own terms, which would not show up from a word search of familiar terms and their synonyms;
4. The item originated in another country, and a U.S. equivalent exists, but some of the content or meaning of the item was lost in the translation; and
5. Inherencies of certain of the items were not appreciated immediately from a review of the item.

As can be appreciated, conducting a thorough search will require a continuous assessment of progress and adjustment of strategies. Though such review is subjective, there are some techniques employed by advanced searchers that provide some objective guidance to monitoring progress. For example, one common indicator that a search has progressed successfully is that after several dozen patents have been reviewed, the searcher starts to find that the patents continue to link back to various common patents; that is, the same patents keep getting identified.

Successful database searching will depend upon persistence, familiarity with the operation and limitations of each individual database, and the availability of suitable time and budget. For example, the USPTO database offers a combination of features that allows searchers to locate a target patent, and then access (via a direct link from the text version of the target patent) both the prior art patents or other U.S. patents that are referenced in the target patent, as well as the patents in which the target patent is referenced (e.g., a patent in which the target patent is cited as a prior art document).

Though not always automatic, by accessing a number of these target patents within a related field, and their respective forward and previously cited patents, a searcher can quickly build a history of the art. For evaluating the

---

410. AIPLA *2007 Report of the Economic Survey* at I-83 (2007).

sufficiency of the search for purposes of identifying the scope and content of prior art in contemplation of preparing a patent application, it is probably not warranted or cost-justified to search ad nauseum. Rather, an approach commonly employed is to perform a text search to identify several relevant target patents. These are then searched forward and backward. When searchers find themselves returning full-circle to certain patents, this is often a good objective indicator that the search has been relatively comprehensive.

Throughout the searching process, no matter how much searching is performed, there is always the possibility that further searching would reveal other relevant prior art. To try to exhaust every resource is not practical and would cause such delays that few patents would ever get timely filing. Therefore, it is good to remind oneself of the objective of the search, which is typically to find the glaring prior art that a patent examiner likely would find upon conducting a patent search. Remember though a patent examiner should already have some familiarity with the art to which the invention pertains, the examiner will typically only spend a couple hours with an independent search.

Once the patent grants, in the U.S., it will enjoy a presumption of validity under 35 U.S.C. § 282. Thereafter, the burden is upon a challenger to the validity to prove invalidity by clear and convincing evidence. As part of that challenge, in most instances, the challenger invariably will conduct hundreds of hours attempting to locate prior art and will have access to potential leads, for guiding the search process, obtained through the formal discovery process.

Drafting the Patent Application

To obtain a patent, it will be necessary to submit a written patent application to the Patent Office for examination to determine if it meets the requirements for patentability. It cannot be emphasized enough that some of the best patents result from applications written as a collaboration between attorney or agent and inventor. Not only is the resulting verbiage a more natural description, but the exposure of the inventor to the patenting process goes a long way toward fostering a healthy IP culture, as inventors impressed with the process are almost certain to spread enthusiasm within an organization.

For present discussion purposes, though the U.S. Patent and Trademark Office also grants plant patents to cover certain botanical developments and design patents to cover primarily nonfunctional ornamental features, attention shall be largely directed toward the typical utility application. The patent application fulfills the significant quid pro quo for a patent monopoly—that the invention is taught so that others can use it and benefit from it.[411]

---

411. In the case of *Lizardtech, Inc. v. Earth Resource Mapping, Inc.*, 433 F.3d 1373, 1375 (Fed. Cir. 2006), the Court of Appeals for the Federal Circuit reiterated:

Along these lines, in the U.S., the inventor not only must describe how to practice the inventive technology but must describe that which the inventor knew, upon filing the application, to be the "best mode" for practicing the invention.

There is yet an additional function that is served by the patent application. That function is dictated by the written description requirement of 35 U.S.C. § 112. The purpose of that requirement is to "ensure that the scope of the right to exclude, as set forth in the claims, does not overreach the scope of the inventor's contribution to the field of art as described in the patent specification."[412] What the written description helps to assure is that, after filing a patent application, a patent applicant will not change that which was regarded as the inventive concept.

11.8 **Length of Patent Documents**

Why are patent applications so long? How did my one paragraph invention disclosure summary become a twenty page document? What purpose is served by teaching my competitor all of the different alternatives for practicing my invention?

These are the typical questions that are raised by those who have little experience with filing and prosecuting patent applications, as well as those with experience in filing and prosecuting, but not in enforcing, the patents. They are reasonable questions. Under the law, as it has evolved in the U.S., to believe that a patent will grant on an application much less than about 5 to 8 word-processed pages of written description, is not realistic.

Moreover, in *Sage Products, Inc. v. Devon Indus., Inc.* . 126 F.3d 1420, 1425 (Fed. Cir. 1997), the Court of Appeals for the Federal Circuit has framed the issue of breadth of disclosure and has counseled strongly:

> This court recognizes that such reasoning places a premium on forethought in patent drafting. Indeed this premium may lead to higher costs of patent prosecution. However, the alternative rule—allowing broad play for the doctrine of equivalents to encompass foreseeable variations, not just of a claim element, but of a patent claim—also leads to higher costs. Society at large would bear these latter costs in the form of virtual

---

The policy of the law also supports that interpretation. The whole purpose of a patent specification is to disclose one's invention to the public. It is the quid pro quo for the grant of the period of exclusivity. The need to tell the public what the invention is, in addition to how to make and use it, is self-evident. One should not be able to obtain a patent on what one has not disclosed to the public.

See also Kewanee Oil Co. v. Bicron Corp., 416 U.S. 470 (1974).

412. *Reiffin v. Microsoft Corp.,* 214 F.3d 1342, 1345 (Fed. Cir. 2000).

> foreclosure of competitive activity within the penumbra of each issued patent claim. Because the doctrine of equivalents blurs the line of demarcation between infringing and noninfringing activity, it creates a zone of uncertainty, into which competitors tread only at their peril. *Cf. Markman v. Westview Instruments, Inc.,* 517 U.S. 370, 116 S.Ct. 1384, 1396 [38 U.S.P.Q.2d 1461] (1996) (discussing the importance of certainty in defining the scope of exclusive rights). Given a choice of imposing the higher costs of careful prosecution on patentees, or imposing the costs of foreclosed business activity on the public at large, this court believes the costs are properly imposed on the group best positioned to determine whether or not a particular invention warrants investment at a higher level, that is, the patentees. (citation omitted)

The above requirements are dictated by statutory patent laws. In addition, based upon the "public notice" functions of patents, the courts have defined other uses of patent description. For example, the patent description has been identified as a critical source of information to be employed in an exercise of "claim construction," pursuant to which a judge will determine the meaning and boundary of the patent claims. In recent years, the patent description has been employed also for determining whether a particular equivalent may be employed under the doctrine of equivalents, in an analysis of infringement.

The conventional practice for preparing detailed patent descriptions has been to provide a lengthy verbal description, accompanied by appropriate drawings. In contrast with a copyright application (*see, e.g.,* www.copyright.gov/forms), a patent application is not a mere legal form.[413] Though requiring certain common components, each patent application is a customized document, specific to each invention. The document may be as brief as several pages. More likely, however, the document will be ten, twenty, or even more word-processed pages with one-and-a-half or two-line spacing.

Given all the uses and requirements of the patent specification, the real issue is how such a document can ever be well drafted. Helping to assure the best possible patent coverage for an invention, both attorneys and inventors need to collaborate to understand what any one patent application can cover, or not cover, and hopefully to define a *reasonable* amount of alternatives or variations (an attempt to cover too many creates the risk that the application filing will become delayed). Inventors need to assist the patent attorneys but

---

413. Albeit a form that can be completed on a computer, a copyright application entails the exercise of judgment on some significant issues. Improper completion of the form could jeopardize validity or compromise a claim for certain remedies.

should be prepared to pay for an agent or attorney to spend at least ten hours, and frequently two or four times that or more, for a solid document. Survey data shows that, in recent years, the average cost of a provisional application was $4,384.[414] The average cost for a relatively complex biotechnology or chemical ordinary patent application was $12,393.[415] The average cost for a relatively complex mechanical patent application was $9,412.[416]

Provisional Patent Applications

The provisional patent application is one of the most misunderstood patent application filings, but it does have a significant place in an IP culture. A relatively recent addition to the U.S. Patent Act, the initial perception of provisional patent applications was that they would provide inventors a way to quickly, and possibly without the intervention of a patent agent or attorney, file a description of an invention with the USPTO, and receive a filing date for establishing priority against subsequent junior parties. The laws authorizing provisional applications sought to avoid the potential hardships faced by persons who published or otherwise publicly disclosed their inventions. By affording these persons a mechanism by which their publications or disclosures would not necessarily work a forfeiture of subsequent patent rights (e.g., from the lack of novelty loss of rights provisions of 35 U.S.C. § 102), it was believed that innovators would be less discouraged, and even encouraged, to publish or disclose inventions before enduring the delays commonly occasioned with attorneys and agents inherent in the patent drafting process.

The provisional application laws effectively loosened the formality requirements associated with conventional patent filings. Under the provisional application laws, a document as straightforward as an inventor's manuscript for a trade publication or technical journal might suffice to secure a filing date for the inventor for the subject matter disclosed in the manuscript. Likewise, the laws made it possible to accord a filing date to a document as simple as a hand sketch, a slideshow presentation, a brochure, a Web site, or some other document created by the inventor, without necessarily engaging a patent attorney or agent.

Albeit well-intended, unfortunately, provisional applications may have created a potentially false sense of security for many innovators. Through a small but growing body of case law, it is becoming increasingly apparent that the benefits to be derived from a provisional application filing are commensurate in scope with the quality of the provisional filing. Whether a provisional application is deemed to confer the benefit of a filing date for later claimed subject matter will necessarily be a function of whether the claimed subject

414. AIPLA *Report of the Economic Survey*, at I-72 (2007).

415. *Ibid.*

416. *Ibid.* at I-73.

matter was fully disclosed in the provisional. Consider the following example. Suppose that a university researcher has discovered that a solar panel shaped like a pentagon exhibits surprisingly unexpected energy absorption as compared with prior rectangular panels. Eager to publish the results, but knowing that she also plans to patent her revelation, the researcher files a provisional application that is essentially a manuscript about to publish. The manuscript speaks only of pentagonal panels, mentioning no other alternative geometries. When she files her ordinary application (within one year of her provisional filing date), she includes a claim to a panel having more than five sides. It is likely that the researcher would not be entitled to the provisional filing date for a claim to a panel with more than five sides, because the manuscript did not mention panels having more than five sides.

The U.S. patent laws do not require that provisional applications include any patent claims. By their very nature under the U.S. patent laws, provisional applications are not examined substantively for patentability and will expire after one year. There are many schools of thought as to whether to include claims. Many practitioners favor the inclusion of at least one claim. Usually, the justification is that such provisional application will then more closely resemble the universally accepted standards for according filing dates under the patent laws of most countries. Other practitioners offer a less favorable view towards such claims. It is urged that by including claims, which due to the inherent nature of provisional applications are often drafted in haste and without a complete awareness of the state of the art, any subsequent narrowing of the claims runs the risk of imposing a disclaimer of claim scope or possibly even a restriction on the scope of any equivalents to which the inventor might otherwise be entitled.[417]

11.9 PROVISIONAL vs. NONPROVISIONAL

It is to be expected, particularly when an applicant employs provisional patent applications, that the applicant will encounter the terms utility patent, regular or ordinary patent filing. It is mistaken to use these terms interchangeably. There is an important distinction between a utility application and an ordinary application. In particular, the term "utility" patent ordinarily refers to the class of patents directed to functional combinations. By implication, "utility patent" typically is used to exclude design patents. The latter are not deemed appropriate for protecting nonfunctional features. The expression "ordinary application" or "regular application" generally denotes those nonprovisional applications that are the subject of substantive examination by the USPTO.

---

417. By including claims, there also needs to be an inventorship assessment to help assure the proper inventors are named.

The filing of a provisional application is not the solution for every situation. However, it can be a powerful and effective tool in many instances. For example, the filing of a provisional application is often a good strategy in the following situations:

1. The innovator lacks money to engage an agent or attorney;
2. The innovator is about to make a commercial presentation;
3. The innovator is engaged in ongoing research on the subject matter and seeks to supplement its disclosure based upon subsequent findings;
4. The innovator has been unable to determine whether commercial prospects justify the expense of a comprehensive ordinary patent application;
5. The innovator has not reduced the innovation to practice but wants to corroborate his or her invention activities;
6. The innovator is about to enter a development program with a third party and wants to secure proof of prior inventive activities;
7. The innovator is seeking to establish an early filing date for potential foreign filing or first to file considerations; or
8. The innovator wants to add a year to his or her patent life.[418]

The filing of a provisional application, though potentially quite beneficial in a wide range of scenarios, is not necessarily the best approach for others. For example, it may be in the interest of the innovator to pursue an ordinary filing in lieu of a provisional at a very early stage in the research or development process. In one respect, during early-stage research or development work innovators are more likely to be addressing a wider range of alternative features and have yet to zero in on the specific, most-preferred approach to the technology. By drafting an application at this time, it is quite common for innovators to identify the various alternatives. In contrast, when an innovator awaits reduction to practice or even perfection of the commercial embodiment, typically the innovator will have eliminated many of the alternative technologies from contention. Yet, it is from the eliminated alternatives that competitors will likely direct efforts to design around the resulting patented technology.

Consider a situation in which, at the outset of a project, a researcher for a new metal alloy identifies five different metals (titanium, aluminum, nickel, magnesium, and cobalt) as candidate alloying elements when alloyed in an amount from 10 to 40 weight percent. A patent application drafted at that time would likely disclose each of the metals, as well as the broad range of 10 to 40 weight percent. In contrast, suppose months later the researcher

---

418. According to 35 U.S.C. § 154(a)(3), the year that the provisional application is pending is not counted toward the twenty-year term of the patent.

identifies the use of cobalt in the alloy in an amount of 25 weight percent as providing optimum characteristics. A patent application drafted at that time would offer the benefit of focusing specifically on the 25 weight percent cobalt feature. But it likely will do so to the exclusion of any emphasis on the other elements, the broader concentrations, or both.

The above scenario also addresses another common dilemma encountered under U.S. law, specifically the obligation to disclose the best mode known to the inventor of practicing the claimed invention. Fulfillment of the obligation to disclose the best mode, under 35 U.S.C. § 112, occasionally conflicts with an innovator's desire to conceal trade secret information. For example, an innovator may have a valuable formulation that it has kept secret for a period of years, but for which the innovator recently has identified an improved additive. Depending upon how the innovation is claimed, the innovator may be placed under an obligation to disclose the secret formulation. Similarly, if the innovator knows the best mode to require the additive to be employed at 12.7 percent by weight for achieving optimal results, the best mode obligation may impose upon the innovator the obligation to specify the 12.7 percent value in the written description.

Recall, however, that the time when an innovator has the obligation to disclose the best mode is the filing date of the application. One possible approach to fulfill the best mode requirement, but avoid risking disclosure of what may prove to be a valuable trade secret, is to file before research or development activities have identified the optimal parameters. To illustrate, suppose the above innovator had not yet identified the 12.7 percent value as optimal but rather merely had plans to test the range of 5 to 20 percent. A patent application filed before the testing is done should be able to fulfill the best mode obligation by reciting the range of 5 to 20 percent.

11.10 "But the Invention Has Not Yet Been Built"

While it is a respectable and often prudent practice to await reduction to practice of an invention before filing a patent application, reduction to practice is not requirement. In fact, the filing of an application is regarded as a reduction to practice, albeit a "constructive" reduction to practice. In "first to file" patent systems, awaiting the actual reduction to practice has to potential to work a forfeiture of rights.

Patent Prosecution and Patent Office Rejection

Upon complying with the filing requirements for filing an ordinary or regular, nonprovisional patent application, the USPTO assigns the application to an appropriate examiner. Examiners are grouped into different technologies according to their backgrounds, with examiners looking at the same technologies being in the same art unit (a group within the Office). The Office attempts to identify an examiner who is generally familiar with the subject of the invention.

Patent applications are taken up for examination within each art unit usually in the order they are received. The typical pendency period of an application before the examiner first examines an application will be about 22.6 months and a total average pendency of 31.1 months.[419] The examiner (or an assistant) is supposed to conduct a thorough search of the prior art, as well as considering any prior art that the applicant has submitted, and compare it with the subject of the claims. According to USPTO records, in 2006, a total of 4,883 examiners (4,779 utility/81 design) faced a workload of examining 443,652 newly filed patent applications (utility, design, plant, and reissue), 1,003,884 total pending applications, and 701,147 applications merely awaiting a first action by the Office.[420] In practice, examiners are limited in the amount of time they can spend in their examination, particularly if they aspire to perform a reasonably thorough examination (e.g., search, comparison of the claims and the prior art, review of the written description for compliance with content and formality requirements, and review of any information submitted by an applicant).[421] The examiner then formulates an initial position regarding the patentability of the claims and reduces it to writing in what is referred to as an "Office Action."

11.11 USPTO Quality

The USPTO aspires to issue only patents of the highest quality, which would withstand challenge from the public and judicial scrutiny. The grant of certain patents in recent years has caused the USPTO to intensify its own internal quality review. The Office has established target quality goals, and continues to progress toward achieving the goals.

For example, in 2003, the USPTO established as one of its goals the reduction in its acknowledged error rate in 2000 of 6.6 percent to 3 percent by Fiscal Year 2006. The USPTO defined "error rate" to mean:

At least one claim within the randomly selected allowed application under quality review that would be held invalid in a court of law, if the application

---

419. 2006 USPTO Annual Report, Fiscal Year 2006 USPTO Workload Table 4.

420. 2006 USPTO Annual Report, Fiscal Year 2006 USPTO Workload Tables 2, 3 and 28 (citing preliminary data).

421. In Mark Lemley, "Rational Ignorance at the Patent Office", Berkeley Program in Law & Economics, Working Paper Series, Paper 19 (2000) [http://repositories.cdlib.org/blewp/19], Professor Lemley, of Boalt Hall School of Law, examined the practical difficulties that examiners face with limited amounts of time (he quotes some estimates on the order of about 16 to 18 hours per patent in footnote 20).

were to issue as a patent without the required correction. Some examples of errors include the issuance of a claim notwithstanding the existence of anticipatory prior art under 35 U.S.C. § 102, or relevant prior art under 35 U.S.C. § 103 that would render the allowed claim obvious. Other errors may include lack of compliance of a claim to other statutory requirements (i.e., 35 U.S.C. § 101, 35 U.S.C. § 112) and judicially created doctrines.[6]

Data published by the USPTO for Fiscal Year 2006 shows the PTO to have achieved an error rate of 3.5 percent,[7] which was deemed to have met a target error rate of 4 percent.

---

6. http://www.osec.doc.gov/bmi/budget/03APPRAPP/pto.pdf (accessed July 6, 2007).
7. http://www.uspto.gov/web/offices/com/annual/2006/desc_pat_allow.html (accessed July 6, 2007).

Rarely will an examiner conclude that the claims as filed are all patentable. More typically, examiners will reject the application as unpatentable. The Patent Office has procedures for challenging rejections. For example, applicants can argue against the rejection, amend the claims, or both. This is usually done by filing a document entitled to the effect of "Amendment and Response to Office Action." The filing of such a document frequently, but not always, results in the patent office withdrawing its rejection and allowing the application. Sometimes it becomes necessary to engage in further challenges to the Patent Office decision. For example, it may be possible to appeal the decision (theoretically all the way to the U.S. Supreme Court). Other options include filing a request to continue examination, which involves payment of a fee and completion of a formal request. A continuing application may also be filed. Of course, an applicant can expressly abandon the application and also has the option to do nothing, which would result in an abandonment of the application.

As can be gathered from the above, the process of prosecuting a patent application is potentially, slow, and expensive. Applicants need to prepare to spend thousands of dollars over a period of about two to four years. What results from the transactions before the Patent Office is that a written record is developed that documents the history of the application, including any modifications to application, positions taken by the Office and arguments made by the applicant regarding the scope of any resulting patent grant. The record that is kept for the application by the Patent Office is commonly referred to as the "prosecution history" or by the classic expression "file wrapper." For granted patents, all published patent applications, and certain other unpublished applications, the prosecution history is a public record, which may be relied upon by members of the public to determine the scope of the patent rights.

11.12 **Keeping Good Company**

Some of the most widely regarded inventions have been rejected as unpatentable by the Patent Office along the way to issuance. In 2006, the USPTO allowance rate ("the percentage of applications reviewed by Examiners that are approved") was a mere 54 percent, the "lowest on record," and a sharp decrease from the greater than 70 percent rate of 2000.[8]

---

8. USPTO Press Release (December 22, 2006).

CHAPTER

12

International Flavor

Differences in National Laws, Cultures, and Attitudes

As mentioned from the start, the knowledge economy is global. Cultivating value-driven attitudes about the technological achievements of an organization must therefore be done without necessarily imposing undue geographical boundaries.

Suppose an organization has decided to embark upon a path toward patenting its proprietary technology. Apart from the expected wave of attorney fees within the first year after filing a patent application, it should likely expect to receive from its counsel advice on the proper marking of products with the notation "patent pending," a request for citations of any known prior art or other material information pursuant to 37 C.F.R. 1.56, and a request for a decision about whether to file the patent application in foreign countries. Patent rights are territorial and generally protect only against violations confined to the country of the patent grant. As a result, to receive global protection, or at least protection in countries of interest to an organization, the organization must file separate applications in each country.

For the most part, the patent laws around the world are structured the same. They typically authorize an agency to grant patents or otherwise register inventions. Upon successful registration, the proprietor is conferred an exclusive right for a limited period of time (e.g., twenty years from application date for patents or ten years for utility models). The global patent law uniformly includes standards for patentability against which an innovation described in a patent application is measured. The laws also include a mechanism for enforcement of rights and remedies for addressing violations.

Country to country, the laws diverge relatively little. Certain important differences exist, nonetheless, requiring appropriate maneuvering and planning. For example, perhaps the most familiar of the differences among the international laws is the absolute novelty requirement imposed outside the United States.[422] In the U.S., a patent applicant typically has one year from the date of most public activities to file or risk forfeiture of rights. In contrast, absolute novelty countries require filing to precede commercial activities. To illustrate, suppose that, instead of watching college football, Dr. X presented a paper that describes her innovation on January 1, 2006. On July 12, 2006, she filed a patent application for the innovation. In the U.S., the presentation on January 1, 2006, presents no immediate per se forfeiture of her patent rights. However, the presentation will preclude Dr. X from patenting what she presented in absolute novelty countries.

As a result, though the concept of "prior art" is a universally understood notion, defining what qualifies as "prior art", and what does not, must be

---

422. Another difference, illustrated in Chapter 11 is the "First-to-invent" system in the U.S. that gives the patent right to the first inventor in time, instead of the first person to file a patent application (i.e., the victor in a "first to file" system).

done on a country-by-country basis. For example, a reference that is prior art in the U.S. under 35 U.S.C. § 102(e) because it was filed earlier (e.g., less than a year earlier) than a patent application may be prior art against the application in the European Patent Office, but only for purposes of novelty (and not inventive step or obviousness).

Another significant difference in the U.S. law, as compared with laws of other countries, is the requirement that the inventor disclose the best mode of carrying out the invention, pursuant to 35 U.S.C. § 112. Though other countries generally require sufficient teachings to enable the practice of the technology, the best mode requirement is not present. To illustrate, consider the situation in which a patent claims a "method of making ethanol from used sugar-free chewing gum." At the time of filing the application for the patent, the patent owner knew that the best results were possible by using a chewing gum in which the sweetener included a combination of aspartame, sucralose and potassium acesulfame in equal proportions. The applicant would be obligated under the best mode requirement to describe that in the patent document. In contrast, for countries that have no best mode requirement, the applicant could avoid making such disclosure.

Yet another significant difference among laws of various countries pertains to the burden upon a patent applicant to disclose information to the patent office that may be "material to the patentability" of one or more patent claims.[423] Elsewhere, though disclosure is encouraged, there is typically no such duty, let alone the consequence of rendering a patent unenforceable if the duty is breached. Suppose Dr. X, in the above scenario, had filed her patent application on January 5, 2007. She would have a duty to tell the USPTO about the presentation. However, she has no such obligation to tell the patent offices of other countries where there exists no duty of candor. Dr. X could file a patent application in the U. K., for example, and have no duty to tell the U.K. Patent Office about the January 1, 2006, presentation.[424]

Attitude differences among the various countries are manifested in other ways. For example, the German system is structured to afford patent owners considerable procedural benefits. For example, the law affords liberal enforcement under the doctrine of equivalents. The enforcement function is conducted

---

423. 37 C.F.R. § 1.56(a) states in pertinent part:

A patent by its very nature is affected with a public interest. The public interest is best served, and the most effective patent examination occurs when, at the time an application is being examined, the Office is aware of and evaluates the teachings of all information material to patentability. Each individual associated with the filing and prosecution of a patent application has a duty of candor and good faith in dealing with the Office, which includes a duty to disclose to the Office all information known to that individual to be material to patentability as defined in this section.

424. Though she has no duty, it would be perilous for Dr. X to pursue such a patent in any event. Even if the UK Patent Office was unable to locate the presentation, and the patent granted, a subsequent challenger likely would find the presentation and present it to a court to invalidate the patent. The challenger then also would face a likely recovery of attorney fees.

in the federal courts, the Landgericht. Any challenges to the validity of the patent must be made in a separate Federal Patent Court called the Bundespatentgericht, located in Munich. The Landgericht infringement court does not address validity issues, only the Bundespatentgericht. Moreover, even if an accused infringer challenges the validity of a patent, there is no guarantee that the infringement court will suspend its proceedings before the validity challenge is concluded. Under this scenario, it is possible that a party could lose an infringement lawsuit, be subject to a damages award, and even face an injunction, all while the patent validity challenge remains pending. Though also serving a public notice function, in some respects the laws are more lax in Germany. Statements made during prosecution have little, if any, evidentiary consequence. Further, the laws allow liberal amendment to the claims of a patent, even after the patent has been granted. It is not unusual for a prior art invalidity challenge to succeed, but the patent is reincarnated with another set of claims that still cover the challenger.[425]

12.1 **General practice and laws in the U.S. and Germany**		
	United States	*Germany*
Best Mode Required	yes	no
Grace Period Before Filing	yes	no
Duty of Candor	yes	no
First to File Wins	no	yes
Opposition Proceedings to Challenge Patents	no	yes
Patent Number Marking Required	yes	no
Attorney Fee Awards Automatic to Prevailing Party in Enforcement Suits	no	yes
Patent Prosecution Statements are Used to Limit the Patent Coverage	yes	no

Toward Harmonization

Not surprisingly, as the knowledge economy has expanded globally, patent authorities around the world have made significant advancements toward removing the barriers imposed by patent law differences. The movement toward harmonization of the patent laws around the world has been gradual

---

425. U.S. laws also afford amendments to patent claims but with restrictions. For example, a reissue patent may be sought, and if filed within two years of a patent grant, may even be used for broadening the claims. 35 U.S.C. § 251. In contrast, a reexamination procedure (*see* 35 U.S.C. § 301 et seq.), claims may only be amended by narrowing.

and progressive. Within the past forty years alone, among the significant occurrences has been the implementation in 1970 of a global treaty, the Patent Cooperation Treaty (PCT), creating an "international patent office" affording patent applicants an opportunity to have their examination needs met by a single examining authority.[426] In the 1990s, significant changes were made to the U.S. patent laws in a move toward harmonizing its laws with those of other countries and particularly arising from the North American Free Trade Agreement (NAFTA) and the Agreement on Trade-Related Aspects of Intellectual Property Rights (TRIPs) negotiated in association with the General Agreement on Tariffs and Trade (GATT) Uruguay Round. Prior to this, in challenges to prove invention priority, patent applicants in the U.S. were confined in their proofs solely to evidence of invention within the U.S. Implementing legislation led to changes in the patent laws to afford applicants from outside the U.S. the ability to prove invention priority by reference to activities occurring at home.[427] Perhaps more significant, the 1995

---

426. The notion of affording foreign nationals rights of priority in patent filings elsewhere long preceded the PCT. For instance, the Paris Convention for the Protection of Industrial Property was signed in 1883 and still remains in force, with more than 170 member countries.

427. The legislation specifically arose from the Agreement on Trade-Related Aspects of Intellectual Property Rights (TRIPs), which addressed international standards for governing forms of intellectual property. See generally, http://www.uspto.gov/web/offices/com/doc/uruguay/SUMMARY.html (accessed August 22, 2007); *see also* 35 U.S.C. § 104, which was amended in 1993 and again in 1994 to provide:

(a) IN GENERAL.
(1) PROCEEDINGS. -In proceedings in the Patent and Trademark Office, in the courts, and before any other competent authority, an applicant for a patent, or a patentee, may not establish a date of invention by reference to knowledge or use thereof, or other activity with respect thereto, in a foreign country other than a NAFTA country or a WTO member country, except as provided in sections 119 and 365 of this title.
(2) RIGHTS. -If an invention was made by a person, civil or military-
  (A) while domiciled in the United States, and serving in any other country in connection with operations by or on behalf of the United States,
  (B) while domiciled in a NAFTA country and serving in another country in connection with operations by or on behalf of that NAFTA country, or
  (C) while domiciled in a WTO member country and serving in another country in connection with operations by or on behalf of that WTO member country,
  that person shall be entitled to the same rights of priority in the United States with respect to such invention as if such invention had been made in the United States, that NAFTA country, or that WTO member country, as the case may be.
(3) USE OF INFORMATION. -To the extent that any information in a NAFTA country or a WTO member country concerning knowledge, use, or other activity relevant to proving or disproving a date of invention has not been made available for use in a proceeding in the Patent and Trademark Office, a court, or any other competent authority to the same extent as such information could be made available in the United States, the Director, court, or such other authority shall draw appropriate inferences, or take other action permitted by statute, rule, or regulation, in favor of the party that requested the information in the proceeding.

amendments purported to harmonize the length of a patent term in the U.S. so that U.S. patents would expire substantially contemporaneously with their foreign counterparts.[428]

12.2 **Calculating Patent Terms**

As a result of the adoption of the GATT Uruguay Round implementing legislation amendments of 1994, a complicated and elaborate process became necessary for determining the expiration date of a U.S. patent. The amendments made to 35 U.S.C. § 154 called for any application with an actual (not effective) filing date prior to or on June 8, 1995, to be entitled to the longer of seventeen years from the patent grant date, or twenty years from the earliest effective filing date. Applications with an actual filing date after June 8, 1995, enjoy a term of twenty years from the earliest effective filing date of an original application (which excludes provisional applications and foreign-origin priority applications).

- An application filed June 1, 1995, which grants as a patent on June 1, 2000, would not expire until June 1, 2017.
- An application filed June 10, 1995, which grants as a patent on June 10, 2000, would expire June 10, 2015.

See http://www.uspto.gov/web/offices/dcom/olia/aipa/patent_term_ guarantee.htm (accessed August 22, 2007); *see also* Manual Patent Examining Procedure Section 2700.

In 1999, with the passage of the American Inventors Protection Act, the U.S. took steps to conform its laws with other countries by calling for publication of certain pending patent applications.[429] Under current U.S. law, as is the law generally outside the U.S., a pending patent application will publish, and its application file will become open for public inspection, eighteen months after the effective filing date.[430] Though the publication will afford

---

(b) DEFINITIONS. -As used in this section-
    (1) The term "NAFTA country" has the meaning given that term in section 2(4) of the North American Free Trade Agreement Implementation Act; and
    (2) The term "WTO member country" has the meaning given that term in section 2(10) of the Uruguay Round Agreements Act.

428. The GATT implementing legislation is also the basis for the creation of the Provisional Patent Application in the U.S.
429. 35 U.S.C. § 122(b).
430. 35 U.S.C. § 154, as amended to introduce the publication requirement, allowed applicants who do not file outside the U.S. to request that the application remain secret within the Patent Office.

competitor access to the technology, the laws provide a deterrent from infringing activity. A patent applicant can forward a copy of a published application and, provided that the claimed invention of the patent "is substantially identical to the invention as claimed in the published patent application," a party who receives notice can be liable for a reasonable royalty for preissuance infringement activities.[431]

International Filing Options

In other chapters, the policy considerations underlying patent laws and trade secret laws are explored, and readers learn that in protecting specific innovations by patenting, there is necessarily a tacit waiver of secrecy that occurs at the time the patent application publishes. In the course of deciding to file for a patent, therefore, applicants must balance the consideration of disclosing trade secrets against the possible benefits from a limited monopoly for a period of years. Unless a patent applicant files an application in every country in the world, however, the applicant becomes vulnerable to copying by competitors in unprotected territories. For example, suppose that a company invents a new rubber compound for a vehicle tire and seeks to patent the innovation in the U.S., Europe, and Japan. After eighteen months, the application will publish, and competitors will learn the formulation. The competitors can then commercialize that compound outside of the U.S., Europe, and Japan (e.g., it can make the compound in China for sale of tires in Israel), and unless the applicant has some other dominating intellectual property right, the applicant is without recourse.

In a perfect world, where money is no object, patent applicants would likely elect to file in as many countries as possible. However, the reality is that filing in each country has a cost associated with it, starting with the act of filing the application (which likely will require translations), continuing with the prosecution of the application toward securing its grant (usually done through foreign patent counsel), and even thereafter, with the payment of maintenance fees (also referred to more euphemistically outside the U.S. as "annuities").

Accordingly, the challenge facing every patent applicant who wants protection outside the U.S. is to find the most cost-effective and efficient way to capture the broadest territorial monopoly. There is no simple formula to do this. Every organization must tailor a specific plan for its individual needs. However, understanding the available options will help facilitate the development of such a plan.

---

431. *See* 35 U.S.C. § 154.

National Patent Offices and the National Patent

In order to enforce a patent right in any major industrial country, a national patent for that country (i.e., a patent granted under the laws of that country) is necessary. In general, the courts of different countries will only exercise jurisdiction over patents granted in that country. The U.S. Court of Appeals for the Federal Circuit has expressed that U.S. courts should decline to exercise jurisdiction for the litigation of foreign patents.[432]

Technically, there is no such thing as an "international patent" or "world patent." Such a right does not exist, no matter how badly patent applicants want their competitors to believe so. The closest thing to an "international patent" is a regional European Patent–more on this shortly. But there is such a thing as an "international patent application," which is one of the two most widely used vehicles by which an intellectual property owner can pursue a national patent in a foreign country. Under a procedure authorized by the Patent Cooperation Treaty (PCT), patent applicants can file a single application ("an international patent application" or "world patent application"), prosecute it before one patent examining authority, and use the results of that prosecution before the national patent offices to pursue grant of national patents in member countries.[433]

12.3 **Examples of Countries that Do Not Participate in PCT and for which Direct National Phase Filing Is Necessary**				
Afghanistan	*Argentina*	*Bangladesh*	*Bolivia*	*Cambodia*
Congo	Chile	Ethiopia	Guatemala	Iran
Iraq	Jordan	Kuwait	Lebanon	Libya
Nepal	Nicaragua	Nigeria	Pakistan	Panama
Paraguay	Peru	Rwanda	Saudi Arabia	Somalia
Taiwan	Thailand	Uruguay	Venezuela	Yemen

In some of these countries U.S. citizens or nationals may be precluded from engaging in any commerce.

A second procedure involved the direct filing by an applicant into a foreign country. Under this latter approach, the applicant may have the option

---

432. *Voda v. Cordis Corp.*, 476 F.3d 887 (Fed. Cir. 2007).
433. The operative word here is "application." Until a national patent is granted, these are merely applications and confer no monopoly upon their owners, other than possible provisional remedies, applicable only if a national patent ultimately grants.

to claim priority to an application filed within the previous year, pursuant to the Paris Convention.[434]

Remember when considering the present filing options that inventions first made in the U.S. are subject to a unique national security provision, which effectively requires that the underlying priority application for patent must first be made in the U.S., and a foreign filing license be granted.[435] This often creates logistical challenges to assure a foreign filing license is obtained, particularly when the ultimate demand for the invention is outside the U.S.

Another consideration is the possible need for a foreign filing license for inventors who reside outside of the United States. Some countries, like the U.S., have requirements on filing first in that country for inventor residents, or may grant foreign filing licenses.

Patent Cooperation Treaty[436]

The Patent Cooperation Treat (PCT) was adopted in 1970 in an effort to streamline the process of obtaining foreign patent rights. PCT procedures allow an applicant for patent to make a single application that is examined by a single examining authority for patentability. Upon conclusion of the

---

434. The Paris Convention for the Protection of Industrial Property was adopted in 1883, and since has been revised several times. Article 4 of the Convention confers the right of priority. Section A(1) specifically states:

> (1) Any person who has duly filed an application for a patent, or for the registration of a utility model, or of an industrial design, or of a trademark, in one of the countries of the Union, or his successor in title, shall enjoy, for the purpose of filing in the other countries, a right of priority during the periods hereinafter fixed.

Article 4, Section B provides:

> Consequently, any subsequent filing in any of the other countries of the Union before the expiration of the periods referred to above shall not be invalidated by reason of any acts accomplished in the interval, in particular, another filing, the publication or exploitation of the invention, the putting on sale of copies of the design, or the use of the mark, and such acts cannot give rise to any third–party right or any right of personal possession. Rights acquired by third parties before the date of the first application that serves as the basis for the right of priority are reserved in accordance with the domestic legislation of each country of the Union.

435. *See* 35 U.S.C. §§ 184-186.

436. For easy reference the following three links supply up-to-date electronic versions of the Patent Cooperation Treaty where all of the rules in this section can easily be viewed: http://www.wipo.int/patentscope/en/ (accessed December 11, 2007) (for the World Intellectual Property Web site, which includes links to all of the most recent PCT updates); http://www.wipo.int/pct/guide/en/ (accessed December 11, 2007) (for a listing of participating countries and what phase of the PCT each country participates); and http://www.wipo.int/pct/en/texts/rules/rtoc1.htm (accessed December 11, 2007) (for a table of contents containing all of the PCT rules, including a hyperlink to all of the rules).

examination, and upon entry into respective national patent offices, the PCT examination is supposed to carry significant weight, such that repeat examination by the national patent office can be avoided or minimized. While ordinarily the major countries of interest for most countries are PCT-contracting states, not all countries are contracting states to the PCT. It is important in developing a filing strategy to consider the possibility that direct national phase filings may be needed for certain countries within a year of the priority date, along with attendant fees and translations.[437]

12.4 PCT Search Reports

Various philosophies abound among PCT applicants. Some applicants adopt the approach that if the PCT is filed at an early enough stage, the applicant will quickly have in hand the preliminary search report. He or she, thus, will have important data available for building a strategy to protect the innovation. Further, the early feedback may also afford the applicant time to file additional applications (e.g., before the PCT application publishes and may become prior art against later filings by the applicant).

Procedural Overview

International Phase

Having as a stated objective the avoidance of diminishing rights of applicants under the Paris Convention for the Protection of Industrial Property, PCT contracting states form an International Patent Cooperation Union. For a modest fee (usually about $6,000), Applicants from any of the contracting states are afforded the option to file an international application with a designated receiving office and request to treat the international application according to the treaty.[438] Applicants may claim priority to a prior patent application filing in a Paris Convention country.[439] A properly filed PCT

---

437. Use of the PCT can be an important strategic consideration for most companies. However, many companies end up using it because it is so convenient, by affording a single examination process respecting a large number of national patent offices. Further, it is especially popular because it can delay patent granting in some countries and because it delays filing directly in each country. This may be desired or not. For example, delay is of lesser consequence for technologies having a long life span. Yet, for many products (e.g., consumer electronics, automotive parts, etc.), product life often expires before completion of post-PCT national phase prosecution.
438. Patent Cooperation Treaty art. 4.
439. Patent Cooperation Treaty art. 8.

application request will confer upon the applicant the benefit of the filing date of the PCT application for subsequent applications that are filed into national patent offices.[440]

At the time of filing, the applicant selects an Examining Authority, which is charged with the duty to perform a preliminary examination of the application for patentability, including performing an "international search" for prior art[441] and issuing a search report, the "international preliminary report on patentability."[442] In response to the report, the applicant has an opportunity to make voluntary amendments to the claims of the application.[443] The search report is published, along with the international application after eighteen months from the earliest priority date.[444]

An applicant, who so desires, may pay a fee and request a procedure called International Preliminary Examination.[445] This is what is known as a "Chapter II demand," and (for abiding countries) it generally must be filed within twenty-two months from the earliest priority application date. Upon such request, the applicant shall be entitled a chance to respond, which response may include amendments to the application.[446] Thereafter, the International Preliminary Examination Authority will issue an "International Preliminary Examination Report" (IPER).[447] The IPER then typically will provide the starting point for examination before the national or regional patent offices.[448]

A change in PCT practice in 2002 now extends the Chapter I period and makes the thirty-month deferral automatic, even if a Chapter II demand has not been filed, provided that the country into which an applicant seeks to file has not elected to be bound by Chapter II, per PCT Article 64.[449] Thus, the major remaining benefit from filing a Chapter II demand is that the applicant can preserve the right to continue to amend its claims and engage in dialogue toward obtaining a nonbinding opinion that the claimed subject matter is patentable. For countries that have not modified their Article 22 time limits

---

440. In addition to the right to claim priority to the PCT filing date, it is possible also to claim the benefit of an earlier filed application under the Paris Convention.
441. Patent Cooperation Treaty art. 15.
442. Patent Cooperation Treaty art. 18.
443. Patent Cooperation Treaty art. 19.
444. Patent Cooperation Treaty art. 21. Before publication, the applications and the contents of their respective files are kept confidential. Patent Cooperation Treaty art. 30; *see also* Patent Patent Cooperation Treaty art. 38. (regarding confidentiality of IPER).
445. Patent Cooperation Treaty art. 23.
446. Patent Cooperation Treaty art. 34.
447. Patent Cooperation Treaty art. 49.
448. Until recently, it was required that in order to defer entry into the National Phase for the full thirty months, an applicant must have made the Chapter II demand. If the demand was not timely made, then before the end of twenty months from the earliest effective filing date, the applicant must have filed the national phase application for entry under Chapter I.
449. Patent Cooperation Treaty art. 22.

to conform with the thirty-month period, applicants not pursuing Chapter II must enter the national phase within twenty months.

Most major industrial nations have subscribed to the 2002 Chapter II modifications. Only a small number of countries do not yet participate.[450]

12.5 PCT to Get Allowable Subject Matter v. Buying 30 Months for Decision Making

Universally, one of the most widely accepted benefits of the PCT process is that it allows applicants to postpone making premature bad decisions about countries for foreign filing. The 30-month pendency period, from the earliest priority application, coincides with a couple of pivotal stages in the life of an innovation. First, before the end of 30 months, it is likely that, if prosecution of the underlying patent application is ongoing before a national office, the prospects of obtaining a patent of meaningful scope will be better known. That is, by the end of thirty months, it is likely that patent examination will have commenced, if it already has not been concluded in the priority country. Next, a thirty-month period allows a patent applicant considerable amount of time to ascertain the commercial viability of the innovation. In contrast, if proceeding with national filings merely on the basis of a Paris Convention priority claim, the decision to incur costs by direct national phase filings must be made within twelve months of the priority date. Results from national phase prosecution of the priority application are unlikely, and early stage commercialization feedback is likely to be sparse as well. Recall, too, that though the PCT examination is nonbinding, experience shows that allowable subject matter during the PCT can help expedite national phase prosecution. Therefore, many applicants take the PCT examination process seriously and will attempt to secure allowable subject matter.

PCT National Phase

During the pendency of a PCT application, applicants may enter the national phase from the international phase (usually at the end of the international

---

450. The countries of Luxembourg, Switzerland, Uganda, and United Republic of Tanzania are the only remaining countries that have maintained that the adoption of the modification to PCT Article 22(1) remains incompatible with its national laws. Accordingly, national phase entry into these countries under the PCT should be within 20 months, unless a Chapter II demand is filed. http://www.wipo.int/pct/en/texts/reservations/res_incomp.pdf (accessed August 19, 2007).

phase).[451] The process of entering the national phase involves the filing of certain papers with the national patent office of the desired country or the regional patent office of a certain region, such as the European Patent Office (EPO). Typically, the process involves the submission of formal request paperwork, the payment of a filing fee, and the submission of a translation into the official language recognized by the region or country. These acts are normally performed by an attorney or agent recognized to practice before the regional or national patent office. In contrast, during the International Phase, any attorney or agent licensed before the national office from which the International Application was filed is authorized to practice before the International Bureau and the International Preliminary Examining Authority.[452] Thus, a U.S. attorney or agent who filed a PCT application for an applicant in the U.S. is authorized to conduct prosecution of the international application before the International Preliminary Examining Authority, which may for instance be the European Patent Office.

Upon entry into the national phase, prosecution commences according to the national law of the country.

Direct National Filing

There are three typical situations in which a patent applicant will make a direct national filing into a national patent office:

1. When the country of interest does not participate in the PCT;
2. When the country of interest does participate in the PCT, but the applicant desires to avoid PCT filing, and proceed directly to the national patent office; or
3. The scenario discussed in the immediate preceding section, when the country of interest does participate in the PCT, the applicant has filed an international application under the PCT, and the applicant has decided to enter the national phase on the basis of the international application.

As discussed above, some countries do not participate in the PCT. Accordingly, to secure protection in such a country, a patent applicant has no choice but to file directly into the country, by making a patent application directly to the national patent office of that country. Even if a country is a contracting state to the PCT, a patent applicant is under no obligation to

---

451. If you do not enter the national phase in a country or region, then your application is no longer in effect, and you no longer have a patent application pending in those particular countries or regions.
452. Patent Cooperation Treaty art. 49.

pursue a PCT application to seek protection in the country. Both of these scenarios will typically require engagement of an agent or attorney in the country of interest,[453] along with the payment of fees and the submission of a translation into the official language recognized by the national patent office. A claim of priority to the priority application will be made pursuant to the Paris Convention.

The examination of the patent application will be pursuant to the procedures and substantive requirements set forth by the national law of the respective country. As discussed, this may result in different outcomes, as compared with the outcome of prosecution of the priority application. Unlike the PCT, where the preliminary examination may help influence decisions by the national patent offices, any prosecution that may have occurred before the patent office of the priority country generally will not influence the outcome.[454]

Summary of PCT v. Direct Filing

As seen from the above, a number of considerations weigh into the decision of how international filings are to be made, whether by PCT or by direct national filing. For some countries that are not PCT contracting states, only the direct filing option exists. But for countries that are PCT contracting states, the question is not always clear cut. In general, against a background that must take into account the commercial circumstances surrounding the subject matter sought to be patented, the most important factors that must be addressed in making the decision include:

1. The overall expected costs and when those costs will be incurred;
2. The number of countries that are serious candidates for filing and, of those, their respective official languages,
3. Whether the applicant desires the benefit of preliminary examination; and
4. How quickly the applicant desires its patent.

Suppose, for example, the applicant has a priority application in the U.S. and only plans to market its products in the U.S., Canada, and England.

---

453. It is possible that some attorneys or agents will be licensed to practice in more than one country. However, when attorneys or agents are not licensed in a particular country, such countries generally require that the applicant's representative be licensed. Accordingly, a common practice is for the applicant, counsel who drafted a patent application, or both to engage a "foreign associate," namely, an attorney or agent licensed in the country of interest.

454. It should be borne in mind that applicants making application to the USPTO, from a foreign filed priority application still have a duty of candor under 37 C.F.R. § 1.56, which may require the applicant to share information about foreign prosecution proceedings.

In this situation, the cost of translation is not an influencing consideration. There will be no translation costs. By filing a PCT application to keep its options open for thirty months, the applicant can delay entry into the national phase in Canada and the UK until at least the thirty-month period expires. Unless the applicant has made meaningful prosecution progress, by filing a Chapter II demand and seeking to arrive at patentable claims during Preliminary Examination, the PCT costs of about $5,000-$8,000 (USD) alone may have been better spent by expediting filings in Canada and the UK.

In contrast, suppose that an applicant has no definite commercial plans but has received inquiries about its technology from Europe, Canada, Mexico, Brazil, Japan, Korea, and China. Each such country presents a viable market opportunity. To file into each of these countries within the one-year priority period the applicant will need to prepare Spanish, Portuguese, Japanese, Chinese, and Korean translations. Filing fees will be incurred for the patent offices of each country, as well as service fees from its U.S. counsel and foreign associates for filing and for prosecution. During the first thirty months, under this scenario, the patent applicant is likely to expect the following total costs (in U.S. dollars):

Translations	: $30,000
Patent Office Filing Fees	: $10,000
Attorney Fees	: $20,000
Total	: $60,000

By pursuing the PCT application, the total fees through thirty months likely will be on the order of about $15,000 (USD). At the end of the thirty-month period, the translation costs will need to be incurred, along with the Patent Office filing fees. However, in the interim, the applicant may have determined that the likelihood of commercialization in some of the countries is remote, such that fewer translations are needed. Further, it is possible that the applicant has successfully engaged in international preliminary examination, so that its overall attorney fees for prosecution of the national phase application will be reduced upon entry into the national phase. By and large, significant overall cost savings can be gained from the PCT process.

It should be appreciated that along with the benefits to be obtained by PCT filings, there are also potential disadvantages. The most obvious is the cost potential delay of thirty months, as is illustrated in the above example, in which the applicant ultimately filed only in Canada, the UK and the U.S. Another disadvantage resides in the accessibility of information about the patent application during its pendency. On the one hand, the publication of PCT applications can offer its owners a potential basis for seeking a provisional remedy, in the case of infringement of a subsequently granted patent.[455] It can also, thus, be effective as a vehicle to deter infringement.

Accordingly, many organizations conduct patent watches, particularly if they are known to file patent oppositions in countries that provide such a procedure. PCT applications tend to be among those monitored by watch services because they are accessible in many popular search databases. The fact that the search report is published along with the application makes the job of a competitor comparatively easier to ascertain the likely scope of claim coverage that will be granted and possibly plan for invalidity challenges or even commence early activities to start designing around the patent filing. In contrast, though some organizations monitor national filings in a host of countries, it is possible that they will not monitor the databases of national filings in many countries. As a result, for organizations that would like to "fly under the radar screen" of their competitors, direct national filings offer the possibility that the publication of the filings will not attract attention. Moreover, even if the national filings are monitored, the task of the competitor to obtain the prosecution history to ascertain the prior art being applied, requires additional efforts by the competitor.

12.6 **Summary of Pros and Cons of PCT filings**	
Pros (favoring the use of PCT)	*Cons (against the use of PCT)*
Options kept open for thirty months	Expensive
Preliminary examination increases possibility of early allowed claims	Will likely delay patent grant if preliminary examination not vigorous
Publication can provide possible provisional remedy	PCT applications are popular for competitors to monitor
Multiple dependent claims can be pursued at no surcharge	Upon entry into countries that prohibit or charge for multiple dependent claims, amendments will be needed

---

455. 35 U.S.C. § 154 states, in part: "In addition to other rights provided by this section, a patent shall include the right to obtain a reasonable royalty . . . during the period beginning on the date of publication of the application for such patent under section 122(b), or in the case of an international application filed under the treaty defined in section 351(a) designating the United States under Article 21(2)(a) of such treaty, the date of publication of the application, and ending on the date the patent is issued. . . ."

Costs

The issue of costs has been raised throughout the discussion of foreign filing and is probably the most compelling consideration influencing any foreign filing decision. Under ideal circumstances, when cost is no object, attorneys and agents would recommend to their clients to file in every country having a patent system. After all, while patents in some countries will have some potential extraterritorial effect, that effect is limited and is no guarantee to assure the worldwide right to exploit the invention. In reality, only a few inventions warrant such an investment. Hence, a decision is necessary by which applicants will weigh the potential benefits of a patent grant in a country against the costs. While overall economic costs are difficult to estimate with certainty, there are several components of cost that frequently will be consistent and predictable to a certain degree, specifically counsel fees, translation fees, filing fees, and maintenance fees.

Counsel Fees

Counsel fees are the components of costs that are paid to the attorneys and agents. The fees compensate the attorneys and agents for a host of services, ranging from intensive substantive tasks such as claim drafting, drafting to conform papers to local requirements, reviewing prior art, preparing responsive papers, and drafting appeals. The services also include many less glamorous, but also critical, administrative tasks undertaken for assuring the progression of a patent application through the bureaucracy that defines a typical patent office, such as the preparation of formal papers, the fulfillment of proper filing procedures to assure that a filing date is granted, and even docket maintenance to assure that deadlines are met.[456]

Remember, too, that the processing of foreign applications will involve at least two attorneys, one from the priority filing country and one from the destination filing country. These attorneys frequently collaborate in an effort to keep prosecution consistent among the various countries. By way of illustration, if during prosecution of an application in the U.S., it is rejected on the

---

456. At first blush, many charges billed by attorneys and agents for processing foreign filed patent applications appear disproportionate to the service described. It would be foolish to deny that attorneys and agents view this work as profitable. It can be profitable, but only after the attorneys and agents have invested the resources necessary to administer the practice. This involves intensive training of professionals, personnel dedicated to the function of docket administration, fulfillment of filing requirements, file maintenance, and other very labor-intensive tasks. Additionally, the attorneys and agents engaged in this facet of the practice typically have spent many uncompensated hours themselves in training and in appreciating comparative differences among the laws of different countries.

basis of a patent that would also be prior art against the application in Europe, it is common for the attorney in the U.S. to communicate this information to the attorney prosecuting in Europe.

Many foreign filing tasks are done on a flat fee basis. The American Intellectual Property Law Association publishes survey data every two years that identifies some of the typical costs that are to be expected in filing outside the U.S.

12.7 Examples of Average Attorney Fee Charges (U.S. only)

Filing PCT from previously prepared U.S. Application: $1,285
Filing into U.S. from foreign origin application: $1,443
Filing into National Phase in U.S. Receiving Office: $1,052
Filing Non-PCT Application Abroad: $1,173
*Source: *AIPLA Report of Economic Survey* (2007), I-86; I-87.

It is common for attorneys or agents to engage their own choice of foreign associates. Often, the choice will be based upon an established business (or even personal) relationship the attorney or agent has with the foreign associate. However, most attorneys and agents are not beholden to their foreign associates. Accordingly, it is important that if an organization has a particular preference for choice of counsel that the organization express that to its attorney or agent.

Translation Fees

Translation fees tend to be the single biggest cost of foreign practice, and it is typical to try to delay or limit this cost. The most effective way to manage translation costs is to make timely foreign filing decisions well in advance of filing deadlines. This avoids surcharges that some firms charge for expedited processing. It also avoids surcharges that patent offices will charge for accepting late-filed translations. Advance planning also provides an opportunity to seek competitive bids.

Against all of the above, it is important to remember that with some inexpensive translation services you may "get what you pay for." In the end, patents are all about words. A well-prepared translation, by a professional with technical training, especially in the field to which the patent application pertains, may cost a few extra dollars, euros, or yen. However, the money spent early in the process, could save millions in later litigation expenses.

Machine translations, or translations generated by software, will likely be inadequate, unless circumstances are dire. Many terms used by patent attorneys simply do not translate well. For example, it was observed that an Asian language patent depicting a small structural reinforcement body machine translated as a "reinforcement child."

Another way to manage translation costs is through terse wording. Translation fees are usually on a per-line or per-word basis. More pages mean higher costs. Fulfillment of written description requirements may compel a lengthy write-up of the specification, and short documents may be unavoidable or impractical.

The recent implementation of the London Agreement within the European Patent system is certain to thelp alleviate some costs of translations for obtaining patent protection throughout Europe.[457]

Filing Fees

Filing fees vary from country to country, but are commonly on the order of about $1,000-$2,000 per country. The costs may be higher or lower depending upon the number of patent claims, page count, or other special circumstances. For instance, some countries charge on a per-claim basis.

Maintenance Fees

Often overlooked in the initial decision to file a patent abroad is that, like the U.S., other countries normally require the payment of a maintenance fee ("annuity") throughout the life of the patent filing. The charges vary from country to country. In some countries, like the U.S. the charges progressively increase. Over the life of a patent maintenance fees paid in a single country may approximate $10,000 or more. For a patent having numerous foreign counterparts, maintenance fees alone may be upwards of $100,000.

Making Decisions

There is no one-size-fits-all decision-making process to determine of whether to file in a foreign country and, if so, in which countries to file. Each company

---

457. *See generally*, http://www.epo.org/topics/issues/london-agreement.html (as accessed April 1, 2008) (addressing the simplication of post-grant translation costs under the London Agreement).

must develop its own decision-making guidelines and weigh the benefits of filing against the costs.

To Foreign File or Not

The following questions might be asked when considering the decision to file in a particular country. Yes answers weigh in favor of filing (consider also Appendix 9).

1. Does the foreign country grant patents on the inventions that are the subject of the application?
2. Is the applicant unaware of any public activities by itself or another entity that preceded the priority date, albeit less than one year from the filing date in the U.S., and would constitute an absolute bar to novelty?
3. Does the applicant contemplate significant commercial activities in the foreign country by itself or its licensees?
4. Is the technology a valued technology in the foreign country?[458]
5. Is the applicant under any contractual obligation to pursue foreign patent rights (e.g., per a license or development agreement)?
6. Does the application cover a significant advancement in the technology rather than a mere incremental improvement?
7. Is there a gap in coverage from other patent filings that would preclude coverage of the improvement?
8. Does the applicant have any competitors that reside in the foreign country?
9. If the applicant discovered an infringement in the foreign country, is the applicant prepared to file a lawsuit to enforce the patent in the country, and does the applicant expect to get a fair adjudication in the country?
10. If the purpose of the filing is as a defensive publication, then is the filing of the foreign application the most cost-effective approach to publication?[459]

---

458. For example, in some countries, strict laws may forbid a certain activity (e.g., possession of a firearm). In those countries, an invention of a holster for carrying a firearm may be of relatively little value. By way of further example, the health care system of a particular country may not pay for cosmetic medical procedures. An invention for porcelain dental laminates might be of limited use in that country.
459. In general, for a publication to constitute prior art that is useful to preclude a competitor from patenting in a specific country, the publication need not be in the official language of that country. The publication of the underlying U.S. priority patent application, for instance, can prevent patenting by others under the laws of other countries, much like a foreign language publication can prevent patenting of inventions in the U.S.

11. Will the useful life of the protected technology last for a meaningful time after the patent grants?

PCT or Direct

Once the decision to foreign file is made, the next decision is whether to proceed under the PCT or to file directly into the national patent offices of the respective chosen countries. To guide that decision, consider adapting the following decision-making questionnaire to your organization's needs. Yes answers favor PCT filing.

1. Does there remain uncertainty about the identity of the specific desired countries?
2. Does the applicant desire to keep options open for investigating its market opportunities?
3. Is the number of countries more than a few?
4. Is additional time needed to raise funds for translations and other costs needed for filing into the countries selected?
5. Does the applicant regard it as critical to take advantage of relatively early preliminary search results, the opportunity to pursue preliminary examination pursuant to Chapter II of the PCT, or both?
6. Does the applicant deem it critical to have its application publish under PCT to take advantage of either the greater likelihood the application will be detected by a competitor patent watch or provisional remedies that may be available, and such provisional remedies are not otherwise available?

As with any decision herein, before making any final decision, the applicant must also consider whether there is some special circumstance that compels a different outcome. Also, the decisions to file PCT and directly into a country are not necessarily mutually exclusive. It is possible to do both, if budget permits.

European Patent Office

The European Patent Office (EPO) was created pursuant to the European Patent Convention for the purpose of establishing a system of laws among European states such that patent "protection may be obtained in those States by a single procedure for the grant of patents and by the establishment of certain standard rules governing patents so granted."[460] The EPO is regarded as a "regional patent office."[461] A similar analysis ensues to decide whether to file

---

460. Preamble of European Patent Convention.
461. Other examples of regional patent offices include the ARIPO (African Regional Intellectual Property Organization) Office, the Eurasian Patent Office, and OAPI (African Intellectual Property Organization).

into the EPO or directly into selected countries. However, a couple of other prevalent considerations must be taken into account. First, upon granting as patents, EPO filings are subject to a nine-month period of opposition. Like PCT filings, EPO filings more likely will tend to be monitored and detected by competitors than the direct national filings.[462] While the national laws of many of the European countries authorize oppositions as well, the chances of flying under a competitor's radar screen are greater when direct filing. Second, the EPO tends to give very strict readings to the disclosures in patent specifications, which may be very different from the readings given the exact same patent specifications in the USPTO, German Patent Office and UK Patent Office (just to name a few). Thus, EPO filings tend to produce narrow claims, when filings directly in some European countries may produce patents with broader claims.

Maintaining Patents

Over the lifetime of a patent, the expense to maintain the patent, particularly when multiple foreign countries are selected can often exceed five or ten times the initial investment. This might be acceptable to many organizations, especially when they have relatively few patents. However, for organizations trying to build a portfolio, the maintenance fees accumulate, not just for individual patents, but also across the board to newer filings. Very quickly, an organization unaccustomed to any fees for patents, because they historically did not patent, will start to see maintenance fees become the single largest component of its investment expenditure.

Therefore, it becomes critical for organizations to be selective about the patents they are going to maintain. Such organizations must engage in difficult decisions about letting patent filings lapse. Recall, Chapter 3 illustrates an analysis that might be employed for maintenance decisions.

Three Tips for Managing Investment Expenses

Make Hard Decisions

To successfully enjoy the returns from an investment of a patent portfolio, hard decisions need to be made about abandoning patent filings that no longer have value to an organization. Much like people clean their closets and

---

462. The very fact that in Europe alone the possibility of encountering at least a dozen different languages makes it difficult for many smaller and mid-sized organizations to conduct thorough patent watches.

throw or give away clothes, patents of no use need to be discarded as well, to make resources available for new patents.

Choose Countries Where You Are Willing to Sue and Be Sued

No matter the integrity of its judiciary, a country may be hostile to a foreign patentee seeking to stifle local business. A patent is of no value to a company unless that company is willing to enforce it. If a company has concerns that it will never invoke the legal system of a particular country to enforce patent rights, then patent filings should not be made in those countries.

Choke the Ability to Commercialize

When complete regional exclusion or blanket regional coverage is not possible, pick a country or two in which you can choke the ability of a competitor to commercialize. Consider the issues historically faced by applicants into Europe. Securing the translations (if needed as a result of the London Agreement), paying patent validation fees, and annuities for every European country is simply out of the question for most smaller to mid-sized organizations, and even for most large organizations. Many industries adopt product platforms (e.g., automobiles) that will not necessarily vary from country to country. In those instances, the threat of disruption to a competitor in just one country is often sufficient to deter the competitor from using the patented technology across several countries. For example, a German patent for a bicycle frame might deter an Italian frame-builder from building a frame for sale throughout Europe.

Logistical Issues

Foreign Filing License for U.S.-made Inventions and Vice Versa

U.S. patent laws impose a requirement that generally receives little attention by applicants. However, the failure to abide by it has the potential of invalidating the patent and subjecting the applicant to penalties.[463] Specifically, for patent applications that are based on inventions that are made in the U.S., 35 U.S.C. § 184 requires the applicant to obtain a license from the Commissioner

---

463. *See* 35 U.S.C. §§ 185 and 186.

of Patents before filing an application in any foreign country.[464] The U.S. government has imposed this requirement so that it can determine whether an order of secrecy for the technology is appropriate.

Generally, unless the disclosure of the technology poses a national security concern, a foreign filing license will be granted in due course by the Patent Office, with the license grant normally displayed on the Official Filing Receipt, in which the Patent Office specifies the filing date granted for the application. In some instances, it is possible that a foreign filing is made before a license is granted, or otherwise in the absence of a license. Section 184 allows for retroactive foreign filing licenses, when the filing was made erroneously and without deceptive intent and the subject of the application was outside the scope of 35 U.S.C. § 181.[465]

Occasionally, decisions to file outside the U.S. are made at the last minute and before a foreign filing license is in hand. Procedures are available in such instances for obtaining an expedited foreign filing license. A petition may be

---

464. 35 U.S.C. § 184 provides, in pertinent part:

> Except when authorized by a license obtained from the Commissioner of Patents a person shall not file or cause or authorize to be filed in any foreign country prior to six months after filing in the U.S. an application for patent or for the registration of a utility model, industrial design, or model in respect of an invention made in this country. A license shall not be granted with respect to an invention subject to an order issued by the Commissioner of Patents pursuant to section 181 of this title without the concurrence of the head of the departments and the chief officers of the agencies who caused the order to be issued. The license may be granted retroactively where an application has been filed abroad through error and without deceptive intent and the application does not disclose an invention within the scope of section 181 of this title.
>
> The term "application" when used in this chapter includes applications and any modifications, amendments, or supplements thereto, or divisions thereof.
>
> The scope of a license shall permit subsequent modifications, amendments, and supplements containing additional subject matter if the application upon which the request for the license is based is not, or was not, required to be made available for inspection under section 181 of this title and if such modifications, amendments, and supplements do not change the general nature of the invention in a manner which would require such application to be made available for inspection under such section 181. In any case in which a license is not, or was not, required in order to file an application in any foreign country, such subsequent modifications, amendments, and supplements may be made, without a license, to the application filed in the foreign country if the U.S. application was not required to be made available for inspection under section 181 and if such modifications, amendments, and supplements do not, or did not, change the general nature of the invention in a manner which would require the U.S. application to have been made available for inspection under such section 181.

465. 35 U.S.C. 184. The standard of "detrimental to the national security" typical triggers the requirement for secrecy; see 35 U.S.C. § 181; see also 35 U.S.C. § 122(d), which provides in part: "No application for patent shall be published under subsection (b)(1) if the publication or disclosure of such invention would be detrimental to the national security."

made even when the application has yet to be filed.[466] While these issues of obtaining foreign filing licenses are usually not of grave consequence, they do require time and preparation, further underscoring the need for prompt foreign filing decision making and communications with counsel.

Other countries have similar laws (e.g., China and India), and if you have inventors outside of the U.S. that are planning to file first outside of that country, you should check for the need for a foreign filing license. In those countries, the law may require that any inventions made in the country are filed first in that country. Thus, in building a foreign practice or working with inventors in foreign countries, you need to know the regional laws about where to file.

Filing into the U.S. from Overseas

It is often the case that an organization is based abroad but has substantial commercial activities in the U.S. that warrant the pursuit of patents in the U.S. As has been discussed, there are certain peculiarities in U.S. practice that require attention by applicants. For example, the U.S. imposes a duty of candor.[467] Further, an applicant for a U.S. patent is required to sign a declaration or oath affirming, inter alia, that he believes himself to be the original and first inventor of the process, machine, manufacture, or composition of matter, or improvement thereof, for which he solicits a patent.[468] These are typically matters that are addressed over time, in the course of prosecution, and generally will not impair the grant of a filing date. For instance, applications can be filed in the U.S. without all the required parts and still be afforded a filing date.

What Is Needed for a Filing Date

In order to assure a filing date, all that is required in the U.S. is the filing, in the name of at least one inventor, of a written description, drawings, and at least one claim. The application may even be filed in a foreign language. What is needed to keep the filing date is an oath or declaration pursuant to 35 U.S.C. §§ 111 and 115, and 37 C.F.R. § 1.63, along with the filing fee and a translation. If a claim of priority is made to an earlier application, the claim must be timely made, and a certified copy of the priority application may be required as well. When an application is filed with missing parts, the USPTO will notify the applicant and allow the applicant to file the parts within a certain period of time, accompanied by a surcharge payment.

---

466. *See* 37 C.F.R. § 5. 13.
467. 37 C.F.R. § 1. 56.
468. 35 U.S.C. §§ 111 and 115; 37 C.F.R. § 1. 63.

The Multiple Dependent Claim Dilemma

Another logistical issue faced by applicants filing patent applications into the U.S. is the use of multiple dependent claims. Multiple dependent claiming is very popular in some countries. This practice involves have a dependent claim depend upon more than one preceding claim. It can be recognized from language such as "The article according to any of claims 1 through 8." In the U.S., claims are counted individually by the patent office for fee calculation. The count considers not merely the total number of dependent claims, but also the various intermediate dependencies. Thus, suppose that claim 1 is independent, claim 2 depends upon claim 1, and claim 3 depends upon claim 1 or 2. This would be counted as 4 claims: claim 1, claim 2(1), claim 3(1), and claim 3(2). It is important when entering the U.S. national phase to have a claim set prepared that takes this into account. Otherwise, an applicant can expect that there will be a cost incurred from the USPTO from filing fees or a service charge by the U.S. attorney or agent.

Appendices[468]

Simple Services Agreement (One-Way with Consultant)

Nondisclosure Agreement (One-Way)

Nondisclosure Agreement (Mutual Two-Way)

Invention Disclosure

Simplified Cradle-to-Grave Time Line for Illustrative Non-Pharmaceutical Consumer Product with Moderate Product Life

Sample Claim Chart

Sample Lab Notebook Usage Guidelines

Policy and Form for Review and Approval of Information Prior to Public Disclosure

Categorizations of Inventions for Prioritizing Filings

Sample Intellectual Property Policy

---

468. For the most part, the documents assembled in these Appendices have been synthesized from form documents used within the IP field for many years. Considerable boilerplate provisions will be recognizable, as will be the many adaptations to reflect the use of various suggested practices and philosophies in this book. Please recognize that these documents are examples only. They will not be appropriate in every situation and will need modification (or a complete overhaul) to address the particular needs of an organization.

APPENDIX

1

Services Agreement

(One-Way with Consultant)

This AGREEMENT is effective the date of _____, and confirms the agreement by and between IP Proprietor ("IPP") and John and Jane Consulting, Inc. ("CONSULTANT").

1. CONSULTANT shall render technical, design and manufacturing consulting services ("Services") to IPP at an hourly rate of $_____ per hour, plus reasonable out of pocket expenses approved in advance by IPP, up to a maximum of _____. IPP shall pay CONSULTANT within thirty (30) days of the date of invoice by CONSULTANT. CONSULTANT shall be an independent contractor to IPP, and not an employee. CONSULTANT is not authorized to enter any agreement on behalf of IPP.

2. IPP agrees to disclose to CONSULTANT, and CONSULTANT agrees to receive, valuable Confidential Information, which may include information (whether fixed in a tangible medium, marked as confidential, or neither) about IPP's designs, business plans, formulations, data, business practices, vendors, pricing, costing, margins, customers, drawings, prototypes, manufacturing processes, material samples, product specifications, databases, software, equipment, or otherwise, which IPP uses in connection with his _____(insert technology description).

3. Unless IPP agrees in writing otherwise, for five (5) years from the above Agreement date, CONSULTANT agrees not to use, disclose outside of IPP, reverse engineer or chemically analyze any Confidential Information (or information derived from it) that has been or will be disclosed to CONSULTANT, for any purpose, except such information that CONSULTANT can show by written records, is generally available, as a whole, to the public at the time of the initial disclosure to CONSULTANT by IPP, or becomes publicly available through no fault of CONSULTANT or was in CONSULTANT'S possession, as a whole, at the time of the initial disclosure to CONSULTANT by IPP, having been lawfully and independently obtained by CONSULTANT. CONSULTANT will not copy any

Confidential Information, and will return all Confidential Information to IPP within 24 hours of receiving written request of IPP. Provided, however, CONSULTANT may use Confidential Information for purposes of providing Services to IPP.

4. This Agreement conveys no license or other right to CONSULTANT in any proprietary right of IPP, and does not commit IPP to enter any further agreement with CONSULTANT. All proprietary rights (including but not limited to patent rights, trademarks, trade dress, copyrights, trade secrets and confidential information) in and to the Confidential Information, and modifications or improvements to the Confidential Information or inventions related thereto (including but not limited to any previously or hereafter suggested or made by CONSULTANT, which CONSULTANT shall be obliged to promptly disclose to IPP) shall be the property of IPP as sole owner; and for no additional consideration and upon request of IPP, CONSULTANT hereby transfers and assigns to IPP all right, title and interest in and to any and all such proprietary rights that have inured or may inure in the future to CONSULTANT, and agrees to cooperate with IPP to secure protection (such as, without limitation, patent, trademark or copyright) for such proprietary rights, and to execute all documents necessary to evidence this transfer.

5. The law of the state of _____ governs this Agreement, which is the complete Agreement between the parties, superseding all prior Agreements (oral and written) concerning the same subject matter. If any provision of this Agreement is determined invalid or unenforceable, the remaining provisions shall not be affected, shall be binding upon the parties, and shall be enforceable, as though the invalid or unenforceable provision were not contained in the Agreement. If there is any dispute under this agreement, the parties agree to meet in a good faith effort to resolve it. If that fails to result in resolution, the parties agree to submit the dispute to binding arbitration or to a court, with each party waiving his right to a jury trial. CONSULTANT acknowledges that any breach by it shall constitute irreparable harm to IPP and shall be subject to appropriate injunctive relief. All modifications to the Agreement need to be in writing.

6. Unless terminated earlier (for any reason or no reason and subject to 30 days written notice), this Agreement shall be for a renewable term of one (1) year. The obligations of paragraphs 3 and 4 shall survive termination.

IT IS SO AGREED:

IPP   CONSULTANT

_____   _____

Date: _____   Date: _____

Nondisclosure Agreement

(One-Way)

THIS Confidentiality Agreement ("Agreement") is made effective as of _____ _____ by and between Disclosco, Inc., and its affiliates ("Disclosco") and _____ ("Company"), to protect and pre-serve confidential and proprietary information that Disclosco discloses or makes available to Company.

1. "Information" means all information Disclosco discloses to Company, whether in oral, written, graphic or electronic form, including experimental results, techniques, and applications; Disclosco's compounds, proprietary position, trade secrets, information, processes, techniques, algorithms, programs, designs, drawings, formulas, test data, methods, sequences; and Disclosco's business, budgets, present or future products, sales, suppliers, clients, employees, or investors.

2. Company has no obligation under Paragraph 3 as to Information that Company can show, by documentary evidence: (i) is or becomes generally known to the public, through no fault of Company and without breaching this Agreement; (ii) Company rightfully possessed such materials before Disclosco's disclosure; (iii) Company receives in good faith from a third party with no obligation of confidentiality to Disclosco; or (iv) Disclosco permits (in writing) to be disclosed.

3. Company agrees to maintain Information in trust and confidence and not disclose Information to any third party. Company may use and reproduce Information only to the extent required to accomplish the intent of this Agreement. Disclosco grants no other rights to trademarks, inventions, copyrights, or patents under this Agreement. Company may not use Information for any unauthorized purpose. Company will not violate any laws or regulations, including the export control laws of the United States. Company further agrees that it will not use Information to trade in Disclosco's securities.

4. This Agreement will continue in full force for so long as Company continues to receive Information. Either party may terminate this Agreement upon 30 days' written notice to the other. Company's obligations under this Agreement survive for five (5) years from the date of termination. Upon termination or Disclosco's earlier request, Company will return all media containing or representing Information.

5. This Agreement contains the parties' final, complete and exclusive agreement relating to the subject matter hereof. Only a mutually executed written instrument may modify, amend or supplement this Agreement.

6. Company acknowledges that Information contains Disclosco's trade secrets. If Company breaches or threatens to breach this Agreement, Disclosco will suffer immediate, irreparable injury for which no remedy at law will be adequate. Accordingly, Company agrees that Disclosco is entitled to seek specific performance of Company's obligations, as well as such other relief as a court of competent jurisdiction may grant.

7. If a court of competent jurisdiction declares or adjudges any provision hereof to be illegal, unenforceable or void, this Agreement will continue in full force to the fullest extent permitted by law without said provision.

8. In this Agreement, "including" means "including, without limitation". The laws of the State of ____ govern this Agreement.

9. The parties may execute this Agreement in counterparts and/or by facsimile.

IT IS SO AGREED:

DISCLOSCO   COMPANY

_____   _____

Date: _____   Date: _____

Nondisclosure Agreement

(Mutual Two-Way)

THIS AGREEMENT is effective as of _____, 2007 between RecipDisc, Inc. and its Affiliates (collectively, "RecipDisc") and _____ ("Company"), and protects confidential and proprietary information to be disclosed or made available between the parties. For purposes of this Agreement, "Affiliates" means an individual or entity directly or indirectly controlling, controlled by or under common control with RecipDisc or Company. The direct or indirect ownership of more than fifty percent (50%) of the outstanding voting securities of an entity shall be deemed to constitute control.

1. Company and RecipDisc (each, a "Discloser" or "Recipient" as the case may be) are the disclosers and recipients of confidential information.

2. The confidential information RecipDisc discloses under this Agreement is described as and limited to RecipDisc's technology, proprietary position and business strategy including experimental results, techniques, processes, equipment, drawings, designs, compositions of matter, software and other information RecipDisc discloses. The confidential information Company discloses under this Agreement is described as and limited to its interest in RecipDisc's methods for producing certain products and technical and business information with respect to such methods. The discussions and potential working relationship between Company and RecipDisc are also considered confidential. Confidential information as defined in this paragraph, separately and collectively, as the case may be, is referred to hereunder as "Information."

3. Recipient agrees it will use Information only to evaluate a possible business relationship with the Discloser and agrees not to engineer, construct, purchase, fabricate equipment or utilize the Discloser's Information in any other way without Discloser's prior written consent. Recipient further agrees it will not use Information to trade in Discloser's securities. Recipient assumes all risk associated with any misuse of the Discloser's Information.

4. Recipient shall not disclose Information to any third party and shall protect Information by using the same degree of care, to prevent unauthorized disclosure as Recipient uses to protect its own confidential information of a like nature, but in no event less than a reasonable degree of care.

5. If a judicial or administrative process requires Recipient to disclose Information, Recipient shall promptly notify Discloser and allow Discloser a reasonable time to oppose such process or otherwise seek to safeguard any Information that is subject of disclosure.

6. Either party may terminate this Agreement by giving the other party at least thirty (30) days written notice. Notwithstanding any earlier termination of this Agreement, Recipient's duties under this Agreement expire five (5) years from the date of disclosure of Information.

7. Recipient's duties under this Agreement apply to Information Discloser discloses in writing, orally, visually, in the form of tangible products or otherwise. The Discloser shall conspicuously identify any Information as CONFIDENTIAL. The omission of a CONFIDENTIAL identification shall not constitute a waiver of confidentiality or otherwise relieve a Party of its obligations hereunder as to any Information that is a type of Information ordinarily regarded or treated in the industry as CONFIDENTIAL (e.g., formulae, specific process parameters, or the like).

8. Recipient agrees not to analyze or have a third party analyze any tangible products or materials constituting Information for chemical composition or content.

9. This Agreement imposes no obligation upon Recipient with respect to Information that Recipient can clearly prove by documentary evidence (a) was rightfully in Recipient's possession before receipt from Discloser; (b) is or properly becomes available to the public through no fault of Recipient; (c) Recipient received in good faith from a third party that did not owe an obligation of confidentiality to Discloser; (d) Recipient independently developed without reference to any Discloser Information; or (e) Recipient disclosed with Discloser's prior written approval. Information shall not be considered within the above exceptions merely because the Information is embraced by more general information within the exceptions. The above exceptions relate only to Information as a whole, any combination of features of Information shall not be considered within the above exceptions merely because individual features, as opposed to the combination as a whole itself and its principles of operation, are within the exception.

10. A Recipient agrees to return or destroy all Information (including documents containing Information Recipient generated) upon Discloser's request and in accordance with Discloser's instructions. Recipient may retain in a secure storage environment one archive copy of written information for record purposes only.

11. Discloser warrants it has the right to make disclosures under this Agreement. Except as the parties may otherwise agree in writing, Discloser gives no warranties of any kind, whether express or implied, with respect to any Information or any use thereof. Discloser provides the Information "AS IS."

12. Except for the limited right to use Information as set out in paragraph 3 above, neither party acquires any license to intellectual property rights of the other party under this Agreement.

13. Neither party shall make any application for patent that describes specific Information received from the other party. To the extent that a party makes an application for patent that relates generally to the field of the Information it has received as a Recipient, such party shall notify the other party prior to filing such application and afford the other party a reasonable period within which to provide reasonable objections and suggestions to obviate the objections.

14. The parties do not intend that this Agreement will create any agency or partnership or other relationship between them.

15. This Agreement is the parties' final, complete and exclusive agreement relative to its subject matter and may not be changed, modified, amended or supplemented except by a mutually signed written instrument.

16. This Agreement is made under and shall be construed according to the laws of the State of _____, without regard to conflicts of laws provisions.

17. If any provision of this Agreement becomes or is declared to be illegal, unenforceable or void, this Agreement shall continue in full force and effect to the fullest extent permitted by law without said provision.

18. Each Recipient may disclose Information to its employees or agents ("Representatives") so long as the Representative reasonably requires access thereto and has undertaken a written obligation of confidentiality with respect

to Information entrusted to him or her. Each party agrees to be responsible for any breach of this Agreement by any of its Representatives.

19. This Agreement may be executed in counterparts, each of which shall be deemed an original and all of which taken together shall constitute one and the same instrument and may be executed by facsimile.

Agreed to and accepted:

IT IS SO AGREED:

RECID DISC   COMPANY

_____   _____

Date: _____   Date: _____

APPENDIX

4

Invention Disclosure[469]

TITLE

1. _____ (please provide a brief descriptive title of the subject of the invention)

SUMMARY

2. (a) **Please provide a Short Description (40-60 words) that Summarizes the Invention by referring to key structural features and a statement of any surprising result, benefit or advantage.**

   • _Answer:_ _____

   _____

   _____

   _____

2. (b) **What problem did you identify and/or solve or what improved result were you seeking?**

   • _Answer:_ _____

   _____

   _____

   _____

DETAILS OF THE INVENTION

3. (a) **What elements/ingredients/components/steps (including sequences) do you believe are important in the invention or for the invention to operate?**

   • _Answer:_ _____

   _____

   _____

   _____

---

469. This form is over-inclusive, meaning that it has items that will not be applicable to every organization.

3. (b) What <u>additional</u> elements/ingredients/components/steps (including sequences) do you believe can be added or substituted with those listed above (please include here any candidates with which you experimented but may have ruled out as not optimal)?

   • *Answer:* _____

_____

_____

_____

3. (c) What are the permissible ranges of concentrations of ingredients, processing conditions, resulting properties, dimensions, or other important parameter listed above (please also identify the "sweet spot" ranges under which the invention demonstrates its best utility)?

   • *Answer:* _____

_____

_____

_____

3. (d) What additional research and development do you expect to perform relative to your invention over the next year?

   • *Answer:* _____

_____

_____

_____

3. (e) What modifications to your invention do you think a competitor might attempt to make in order to compete with your invention without copying it? (please also describe the current approach used by competitors to address the problem you have solved)

   • *Answer:* _____

_____

_____

_____

3. (f) **Examples:** Describe at least one detailed example of the invention, and include a comparative example, if available to illustrate improvements relative to the closest known prior art. Please use additional pages as needed and attach any necessary or appropriate diagrams, micrographs, figures, tables, drawings, etc.

   • *Answer or description of attachments:*_____

_____

_____

_____

BACKGROUND AND PRIOR TECHNOLOGY

4. (a) Search & Analysis Details: Please describe any search of prior patents and literature that you conducted, including an identification of the databases searched, when the search was performed, the search strings employed, and who conducted the search.
- *Answer:* _____

_____

_____

_____

4. (b) Other Information: Other than the technology described in the above literature and patent publications, what is the closest technology (e.g., existing publicly used or commercially available technology) of which you are aware that has been employed for this problem/area?
- *Answer:* _____

_____

_____

_____

4. (c) Search & Analysis Results: List the patents, non-patent literature, or other publications or information of which the contributors are aware (whether from the above search or otherwise), which relate to the invention, and explain how each item relates to the invention. If this list includes any non-patent references, please provide a copy.
Keep Your Explanation Factual: Do Not Include Speculations or Opinions.
- *Answer:* _____

_____

_____

_____

4. (d) Differences and advantages: What are the most significant differences and advantages between this invention and the prior art identified? In other words, what makes this invention unique or different from the prior technology; or what was lacking from the prior technology that your invention supplies? Be as specific as possible.
- *Answer:* _____

_____

_____

_____

OTHER ACTIVITY

5. **Disclosures**

    Has the invention or information relating to the invention been disclosed to anyone outside of Organization (even if under a nondisclosure agreement)? __Yes __No

    If so, pl ease describe when, to whom and the circumstances of the disclosure.

    • *Answer:* _____

    _____

    _____

    _____

6. **Commercial Activity: Please identify the circumstances (including dates) concerning any commercial activity or steps toward commercialization that have been made relative to the invention,** including but not limited to sales, offers for sale, prototypes, publicly visible testing, delivery to an outside organization for testing, licensing, advertising, etc.:

    _____

    _____

    _____

    _____

7. **Third Party Cooperation or Contributions:**

    7(a) Was the invention made or completed as part of a development agreement or other contract with a partner? __Yes __No

    Agreement: _____

    7(b) Did any party provide any funding to the Organization that was used to make the invention? __Yes __No

    Name of such funding part: _____

    7(c) Is the Organization under contract with any organization that is otherwise assisting in the testing or development of any aspect of the invention? __Yes __No

    *Name of such other organization:*_____

8. **Test Methods**

    Please specify the test methods employed for any test data that accompanies this Invention Disclosure, including the specific numbers of any standardized test method (e.g., ISO test method, ASTM test method, etc.)

    • *Answer:* _____

    _____

    _____

    _____

9. Documentary Evidence of Invention

Where and how is the invention documented (e.g., lab notebooks, e-mails, slide show presentations, reports, etc.)?

- *Answer*: _____

_____

_____

_____

10. Countries Involved

Was the invention made in whole or in part outside of the United States, and if so, in which countries?

- *Answer*: _____

_____

_____

_____

11. Abbreviations: If you have employed any abbreviations in this document, please provide a definition for the abbreviation below.

- *Answer*: _____

_____

_____

_____

12. Signatures and Information about Participants in the Innovation

(OPTIONAL ASSIGNMENT OBLIGATION:) I acknowledge and agree that, in exchange for consideration paid to me as an employee of the Organization, I am under obligation to transfer any and all rights that may be owned by me in this invention to the Organization, I hereby transfer any and all rights in this invention to the Organization, I will execute all necessary documents to evidence my transfer of rights to the Organization, and I will cooperate in pursuing patent protection for the invention.

Full Name:	Full Name:
Citizenship _____	Citizenship _____
E-mail _____ Phone _____	E-mail _____ Phone _____
Signature:	Signature:

WITNESS: I have read and understood the foregoing Disclosure and any attachments

Printed Name	Date
Signature	

APPENDIX

5

Simplified Cradle-to-Grave Time Line for Illustrative Non-Pharmaceutical Consumer Product with Moderate Product Life

Time	Technology Activity	Patent Activity
0	Conception and steps toward making the idea (reduction to practice)	Submit Invention Disclosure
First year	Ongoing development and steps toward commercialization	File patent application
One year from filing date of patent application	Same; competitor likely now aware of technology	Foreign patent applications filed
Two-four years from filing date of patent application	Commercial activity ongoing; competitor may be trying to enter with similar product; Technology development ongoing; products of Organization covered by any issued patents are marked with numbers of U.S. patent numbers	Patent prosecution commences in first-filed country; claims are reviewed in view of current status of technology (Organization and its competitors); first patents grant; possible continuation applications on-going; Possible early stage prosecution activities for foreign filed applications
Four to eight years from filing date of patent application	Commercial activity ongoing for Organization and competitor; any infringements have started to surface; possible enforcement commenced	Continuation applications may still be in prosecution; foreign prosecution ongoing and mostly completed (at least in Europe); maintenance fee payments starting to be incurred in substantial amounts

Time	Technology Activity	Patent Activity
Eight to twelve years from filing date of patent application	Next generation products entering market	Patent prosecution is mostly complete; may still have pending continuation or foreign application; emphasis has shifted to patenting improvements for next generation technology; substantial maintenance fees incurred annually; patents in some territories may start to become abandoned
Twelve to twenty years from filing date of patent application	Next generation products are established in the market	Patent prosecution is mostly complete; may still have pending continuation or foreign application; emphasis has shifted to patenting improvements for next generation technology; substantial maintenance fees incurred annually; patents in some territories may start to become abandoned as unnecessary, particularly if no longer cover the next generation products

APPENDIX

6

Sample Claim Chart

(Based upon claim 1 of U.S. Patent No. 6,004,596[470])

Claim Element	Interpretation	Correspondence
1. A sealed crustless sandwich, comprising		
—a first bread layer having a first perimeter surface coplanar to a contact surface;		
—at least one filling of an edible food juxtaposed to said contact surface;	Insert interpretation of element, including citations to the specification, file wrapper, and external sources in the boxes of this "Interpretation" column	Insert corresponding element of compared item (.,e.g., prior art, infringing technology, own technology) in the boxes of this "Correspondence" column
—a second bread layer juxtaposed to said at least one filling opposite of said first bread layer, wherein said second bread layer includes a second perimeter surface similar to said first perimeter surface;		
—a crimped edge directly between said first perimeter surface and said second perimeter surface for sealing said at least one filling between said first bread layer and said second bread layer;		
—wherein a crust portion of said first br ead layer and said second bread layer has been removed.		

---

470. This patent gained widespread media attention as the "peanut butter and jelly sand-wich patent". Despite proof of millions of dollars of sales attributable to the invention, the patent was struck down as invalid. See, e.g., "Patent No. 6,004,596: Peanut Butter and Jelly Sandwich", by Sara Schaefer Muñoz (April 5, 2005); http://online.wsj.com/article_email/SB111266108673297874-INjgYNolad4o5uoaXyGb6qGm5.html (accessed December 1, 2007).

Sample Lab Notebook Usage Guidelines

Policy on Use of Research and Development Notebook

(Sample Liner Page)

This notebook, all information recorded in it and all associated intellectual property rights therein are the property of Organization, and must be provided to Organization upon completion of the notebook, upon request by Organization or termination of employment of the employee to whom it was issued, whichever occurs first. Acceptance and use of this notebook by employee constitutes employee's consent to treat as confidential the notebook and the information in it, and to transfer ownership to Organization of all inventions described in the notebook or made by employee in the employment of Organization. This notebook and information in it should not leave the premises of Organization and should not be shared with persons outside of Organization, without written permission.

1. All concepts, ideas, designs, development records, calculations, test data and progress summaries should be recorded in this notebook in a clear and legible manner, whether or not you deem them to be legally, technically or commercially significant. All entries should be made in permanent ink, using a single pen for each entry. There should be no erasures or correction fluid used. If a change is made, the original entry should be crossed out, and the change initialed and dated by the entrant.
2. Each entry should be signed and dated by the person performing the work on the date the work is performed. All notebook entries should be witnessed by at least one witness who you might not considered a contributor to or author of the particular recorded item. The witness should be able to testify that he or she read and understood the notebook entry. Preferably the witness should be one who can testify that he or she saw the work being performed. The witness (es) should record the words "read or witnessed and understood", sign and date each entry.
3. All models, samples, and prototypes should be demonstrated and shown to at least one witness, who will enter in this notebook an entry consistent with the above paragraphs. The location where the model, sample or

prototype is kept for safe-keeping should be identified and a photograph of it included.

4. The information recorded should be factual only and not contain opinions. There should be no characterization of any information as being infringing or noninfringing. Do not use legal terms (or derivatives thereof) believed by you to have any legal meaning; for example, avoid words like "conception", "best mode", "enable", "diligence", "suppression", "abandonment", "invention", "reduction to practice", "infringe", "prior art" or "equivalent".

5. Pages in this notebook are numbered consecutively to help assure reliabilty and trustworthiness of the notebook. Pages should not be removed from this notebook. Any attachments (e.g. photos, data drawings, etc.) to any pages should bear the page number to which it is attached and should be secured to the page using staples, glue, adhesive tape or the like. Please do not leave large blank spaces on any notebook page. Instead, any spaces separating different entries should be filled in with a large "x", signed and dated to make it clear that no after the fact entries were made. Entries for different projects may be recorded in the same notebook.

ORGANIZATION NAME

NOTEBOOK NO. _____

RESEARCH AND DEVELOPMENT NOTEBOOK

FROM: _____, 20_____ TO: _____
_____, 20_____

   (Date First Used)   *(Date Last Used)*

   NAME:
_____
                          (Person To Whom Notebook Issued)

THIS NOTEBOOK IS THE PERMANENT, CONFIDENTIAL
PROPERTY OF ORGANIZATION

THIS NOTEBOOK CONTAINS INFORMATION FOR ORGANIZATION, WHICH IS CONFIDENTIAL AND/OR LEGALLY PRIVILEGED. THE INFORMATION IS INTENDED ONLY FOR THE USE OF THE INDIVIDUAL OR ENTITY NAMED ON THIS NOTEBOOK. IF YOU ARE NOT THE INTENDED RECIPIENT NAMED, YOU ARE HEREBY NOTIFIED THAT ANY DISCLOSURE, COPYING, DISTRIBUTION OR THE TAKING OF ANY ACTION IN RELIANCE ON THE CONTENTS OF THIS INFORMATION IS STRICTLY PROHIBITED, AND THE DOCUMENT (S) SHOULD BE RETURNED TO THIS FIRM IMMEDIATELY. IF YOU HAVE RECEIVED THIS IN ERROR, PLEASE NOTIFY US BY TELEPHONE SO THAT WE CAN ARRANGE FOR THE RETURN OF THE ORIGINAL DOCUMENTS AT NO COST TO YOU

This notebook must be immediately returned to _____
upon completion of the notebook or termination of employment of the
employee whichever event occurs first.
Date Issued: _____ (By _____)
Date Closed: _____ (By _____)

SAMPLE NOTEBOOK PAGE

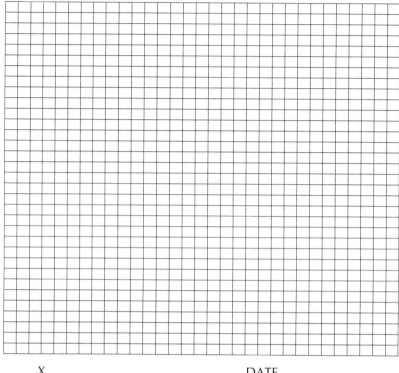

X_____DATE_____
(Signature of Writer)

Witnessed and Understood (Signature of 1st Witness):
X_____DATE_____

Policy and Form for Review and Approval of Information
Prior to Public Disclosure

The Organization maintains a practice and policy that requires review and approval by technical, business and legal personnel of all outside disclosures (presentations, papers, abstracts, posters, etc.), prior to when such disclosures will be made publicly—that is, without having a confidentiality agreement covering the disclosure. The review process has been developed to help ensure that the disclosure is consistent with the strategies (including the IP strategy) of the Organization, and to help ensure that Organization makes consistent records of technical and business information that enters the public domain. The policy requires personnel to:

1. Complete an outside disclosure form entitled "Form—REQUEST FOR APPROVAL FOR OUTSIDE DISCLOSURE OF CONFIDENTIAL OR PROPRIETARY INFORMATION" to provide the detailed information re who, what, where, when . . . *etc.*;
2. Submit a draft of the outside disclosure, together with the completed outside disclosure form to the IP department, at least **two weeks** prior to the required submission date.;
3. Revise the draft, as necessary, to incorporate all suggested changes from the review process;
4. Obtain approval of any 3rd parties (e.g., research partners, contracting organizations, sponsoring organizations, etc.), as necessitated on a case-by-case basis.; and
5. Submit the final, as-disclosed version of the document, as well as the marked-up draft and the fully approved disclosure form, to the IP department for their records.

Form: Request for Approval for Outside Disclosure of Confidential or Proprietary Information

Instructions: Complete form and attach the research article or presentation to be approved for public. Please submit at least [TIME PERIOD] prior to due date of article submission or outside presentation.

Name of all authors or presenters: _____

Please check one to describe intended disclosure:

      Outside Presentation ☐   Research Article ☐   Other ☐

☐ OK to supply presentation to conference or conference attendees (paper or. pdf format only)

Proposed Title: _____

Deadline for submission: _____

Name of Publishing Journal (if applicable): _____

Location and Date of Presentation (if applicable): _____

*If an Abstract will be published in advance of publication or presentation, please attach copy of proposed Abstract

Signature of Reviewer	Comments
IP Department	
Date	
Technology Person	
Date	
Director/Manager	
Date	
Business Unit	
Date	

Categorizations of Inventions for Prioritizing Filings

General Factors for Consideration

1. Any quantifiable amount that measures the size of the business to be protected by the patents and can be weighed against the amount of the patent investment;
2. The availability of alternative measures to protect the technology (e.g., trade secrets);
3. The availability of alternative measures to preserve evidence of invention or commercialization to provide a prior user or prior art defense in the event of future dispute with another patent owner;
4. How readily the technology can be policed for infringement by others;
5. How easy will it be for a competitor to design around the expected patent claim coverage to avoid infringement (or extensibility of the technology);
6. Whether there is a competitive technology (or threat of competitive technology) that a client needs to protect against;
7. Whether any compelling special circumstance warrants a patent filing; or
8. Whether the patent filing would serve some other useful purpose (e.g., potential cross-licensing).

Category Breakout for Facilitating Prioritization

Category I

- <u>Purpose:</u> Mainly defensive, to preserve freedom to practice; create "prior art" to help prevent others patenting. Incidentally will preserve image of Organization as innovative.
- <u>Activity:</u> File and publish patent application in U. S; possible request for expedited publication.
- <u>Cost:</u> The target cost for this option is expected to be on the order of about $10,000 for filing.

Category II

- <u>Purpose:</u> Mainly exclusion, to prevent copying of products or ideas, or be able to select appropriate licensees. Incidentally will serve purpose of category I filings.
- <u>Activity:</u> File in the U.S., in at least one foreign country where the technology is used; possible utility model filing (if appropriate).
- <u>Cost:</u> The target cost for this option is expected to be on the order of about $20,000 for filing.

Category III

- <u>Purpose:</u> Mainly to protect significant new advancements and also to serve purposes of category I and II filings on a broader geographic scale.
- <u>Example:</u> breakthrough developments; commercialization with substantial revenues expected; etc.
- <u>Activity:</u> Possible PCT or direct file in the U.S., EPO (European patent), Asia; possible utility model filing (if appropriate); possible measures to expedite grant of rights.
- <u>Cost:</u> The target cost for this option is expected to be on the order of about $60,000 for filing.

Category IV

- <u>Purpose:</u> Mainly address an extraordinary innovation scenario, a competitive circumstance or both.
- <u>Examples:</u> Career-making inventions (from the inventor's viewpoint); Patenting is governed by an Agreement with another party; a commercial situation arises that necessitates the filing; or a competitor enters the market with an infringing product.
- <u>Activity:</u> File priority application in the U.S.
- <u>Cost:</u> The target cost will depend upon circumstances, but should be planned to be on the order of about $150,000 over the 12-30 months of filing priorities (depending on the filing route).

10

Sample Intellectual Property Policy

I. Statement of Intent and Purpose

ORGANIZATION engages in design and development of proprietary methods, designs, compositions, compounds and other technology resulting in valuable trade secrets or in other intellectual property (IP) rights owned by ORGANIZATION. ORGANIZATION may seek to protect trade secrets or other IP by continuing to hold the technology as trade secrets, by registration of copyrights or by patenting as the law permits. ORGANIZATION expects others to respect its valid and enforceable IP rights and trade secrets. It is likewise the intent of ORGANIZATION to respect the valid and enforceable IP rights and trade secrets of others. In order to carry out this intent, and administer the IP functions of the ORGANIZATION, the ORGANIZATION establishes an Intellectual Property Team ("IP Team") and adopts the following provisions as its policy on IP.

II. IP Team

An IP Team shall exist within ORGANIZATION and shall consist of representatives from the sales, marketing, engineering, and finance functions of ORGANIZATION. The IP Team shall make reasonable efforts to perform the following tasks:

- Developing and overseeing an IP program and processes for administering it;
- Establishing measurable goals for ORGANIZATION's IP Program, and strategies for achieving the goals;
- Monitoring the progress of ORGANIZATION toward achieving the goals and modifying its strategies as needed to achieve the goals;
- Meeting regularly as a Team for administering and assuring compliance with this Policy;
- Educating ORGANIZATION employees and agents about IP issues and apprising the employees and agents about known valid and enforceable IP rights of others;

- Helping to assure ORGANIZATION respects the valid and enforceable IP rights of others of which ORGANIZATION is aware;
- Assisting to preserve records for establishing prior art, a prior user defense, an inventorship contribution, an independent development or other purposes related to helping assure the continued right of ORGANIZATION to conduct its business;
- Helping to assure compliance with marking and notice requirements imposed by the patent and copyright laws;
- Maintaining regular and continuing communications with ORGANIZATION management to apprise of IP issues;
- Reviewing disclosures of inventions and original works and approving or rejecting disclosures for patent and/or copyright registration applications;
- Preparing recommendations to management for enforcement of IP rights;
- Preparing recommendations to management for licensing or other acquisitions of IP rights;
- Identifying trade secrets and develop strategies for maintaining them;
- Maintaining regular and continuing communications with outside IP counsel as appropriate to assist the IP Team in carrying out its purposes and responsibilities; and
- Monitoring the fees incurred by ORGANIZATION in the process of carrying out the purposes and responsibilities of the IP Team and exploring reasonable alternatives to manage the fees.

III. Company Trade Secrets and Confidential Information

ORGANIZATION has enjoyed a valuable commercial advantage due to its trade secrets and confidential information. Examples of said trade secrets or confidential information include (without limitation) formulations, designs, business methods, recordkeeping practices, customer lists, supplier lists, pricing data, profit and costing data, data in the form of flow charts, electronic data, object code, source code, databases, research or experimental results, and the like. ORGANIZATION believes that the protection of its trade secrets and confidential information to be an utmost concern for the company, its employees, and agents.

ORGANIZATION has invested in considerable resources to develop practices for documenting and securing its trade secrets and confidential information. Employees will comply with all such practices.

ORGANIZATION shall take reasonable precautions to preserve and uphold its own trade secrets and confidential information as well as the trade secrets and confidential information of others to which ORGANIZATION lawfully gains access. When the circumstances reasonably permit, such precautions shall preferably include, but shall not be limited to conspicuously marking as "CONFIDENTIAL" any information reasonably believed to contain confidential information or trade secrets. Other precautions may include storing such information in reasonably secure locations; escorting visitors of ORGANIZATION through ORGANIZATION facilities; restricting computer access; requiring suppliers, other third parties and employees to sign a confidentiality agreement before obtaining such information, and the like. It is the policy of ORGANIZATION to consider all trade secrets confidential, regardless of whether they are marked as such.

Any time that anyone enters into any agreement that could impose an obligation of secrecy or confidentiality upon ORGANIZATION, such agreement shall be presented at once to the IP Team. Any information acquired by ORGANIZATION under any such agreement shall be maintained to at least the standards set forth in this policy, if no stricter standards are set forth in the agreement.

If any information reasonably appearing to contain trade secrets or other confidential information of a third party shall come under the control of ORGANIZATION from a person outside of ORGANIZATION, without solicitation by ORGANIZATION and ostensibly without consent of such third party, such information shall not be disseminated. This information shall be reported at once to a member of the IP Team at ORGANIZATION. No copies shall be made, nor shall the information be used. The IP Team shall quarantine such information in a reasonably secure location until it can be evaluated and an appropriate disposition can be determined. If the information originated from an employee, communications with such employee shall be restricted.

IV. Obtaining Patents and Registered Copyrights

It shall be the policy of ORGANIZATION to protect its inventions and original works of authorship in a commercially reasonable manner. ORGANIZATION shall take into account such factors as, without limitation, the likelihood of commercial exploitation of an invention or original work of authorship, the prevalent market considerations, the desire to assure uninterrupted service to ORGANIZATION customers, the preservation of evidence of prior invention, availability of appropriate personnel and/or financial resources, and the like. Such protection may include but is not limited to seeking to obtain patents and/or copyright registration to be owned by ORGANIZATION or an ORGANIZATION designee for inventions that reasonably relate to the fields of business engaged in by ORGANIZATION or in which it is reasonably anticipated that ORGANIZATION may engage.

When an employee, contractor or other agent of ORGANIZATION, participates in the making of any such inventions and/or works of authorship, the employee, contractor or other agent shall notify a member of the IP Team of

ORGANIZATION in writing promptly of such participation. The employee, contractor or other agent shall assist ORGANIZATION (at ORGANIZATION's sole expense) to apply for one or more patents for such inventions and/or one or more copyright registrations for such original works of authorship. The employee, contractor or other agent shall assign or otherwise transfer all right, title, and interest in and to any such inventions to ORGANIZATION. In recognition of the requirements in the U.S. and other countries for novelty, all persons who participate in the making of any inventions at ORGANIZATION shall consult with a member of the IP Team at the earliest practicable time. All persons who participate in the making of any inventions or original works of authorship shall maintain corroborated records made contemporaneously with the invention and/or authorship activities, and shall make those records available upon request to outside counsel for ORGANIZATION. Under any circumstance, work product that results from the use of ORGANIZATION time, materials or equipment belongs to the ORGANIZATION.

V. Enforcement of Rights

ORGANIZATION shall enforce its valid and enforceable IP rights in a manner reasonably consistent with the purpose and intent of this Policy, but with the recognition that the decision to enforce must be made by management of ORGANIZATION and must take into account the entirety of the circumstances surrounding a detected violation of a ORGANIZATION right. Under all circumstances, ORGANIZATION shall employ its IP in a lawful manner, and shall not engage in practices that are likely to expose ORGANIZATION to liability for unlawful anti-competitive conduct. When confronted with the prospect of litigation of IP rights, ORGANIZATION will consider whether the circumstances are appropriate for attempting resolution by litigation in the courts or by an alternative form of dispute resolution. By way of example, ORGANIZATION will consider arbitration, mediation, or the like. In making such decision, ORGANIZATION shall consider such factors as the anticipated cost of the proceeding, the anticipated length of the proceeding, the nature of the remedies available to the prevailing party, or the like.

ORGANIZATION shall have discretion to enter into license agreements (as a licensee or a licensor) or other transfers of interest of IP rights when reasonable to do so under the circumstances. ORGANIZATION shall not be obliged to enter into any licensing relationship that would impose an unreasonable commercial disadvantage upon ORGANIZATION under the circumstances. In all instances when ORGANIZATION licenses its technology to others, or when ORGANIZATION seeks a license from others, ORGANIZATION shall seek to negotiate a reasonable royalty rate for the technology.

By way of illustration, without limitation, ORGANIZATION may, but is under no obligation to, license technology to others in any fields of use not engaged in or reasonably expected to be engaged in by ORGANIZATION. ORGANIZATION may license its technology at the request of a customer that demonstrates a compelling need for the license. ORGANIZATION may license its technology when it is reasonably believed to be necessary for fostering future business relationships. By way of further illustration, without limitation, ORGANIZATION may, but is under no obligation to, seek to obtain a license under someone else's valid rights in instances when reasonably believed necessary to assure continued and uninterrupted service to a customer, and where after it concludes upon reasonable investigation that the circumstances do not warrant the risk, expense and uncertainty of litigation to resolve a dispute and no modifications or design around measures reasonably can be made or taken as to the accused subject matter to further secure a successful outcome if litigated.

VI. Inventions Not Pursued by Company

If ORGANIZATION decides not to file a patent application, maintain as trade secret or publish an invention, in its sole discretion, ORGANIZATION may offer the inventor the right to pursue his or her own patent application (at his or her own expense). The patent shall be owned at least in part by the inventor, subject at a minimum to an automatic nonexclusive royalty free license under any resulting patent grant that shall be granted for such invention, which shall extend to ORGANIZATION and any customers, suppliers of ORGANIZATION, or other persons identified by ORGANIZATION. Any divestiture of a copyright by ORGANIZATION in favor of a ORGANIZATION employee, contractor or other agent shall likewise be subject at a minimum to an automatic nonexclusive royalty free license under any resulting copyright that shall be granted, which shall extend to ORGANIZATION and any customers, suppliers of ORGANIZATION, or other persons identified by ORGANIZATION. Any request for permission to pursue patent or copyright protection under this paragraph must be submitted in writing. Notwithstanding the foregoing, ORGANIZATION shall abide by any and all applicable Inventor Compensation laws.

VII. Publishing

ORGANIZATION recognizes that it may be necessary and desirable for employees or agents of ORGANIZATION to publish or allow to be published written descriptions of ORGANIZATION technology, such as in the form of trade journal publications, press releases or otherwise. Before any such publication or presentation is made, it shall be the responsibility of each employee to seek and obtain approval and guidance from the IP Team for making such publication or presentation and safeguarding any ORGANIZATION proprietary rights associated with the publication or presentation. Such safeguarding may include the requirement that an appropriate notice of ORGANIZATION proprietary rights be included within the published information.

VIII. Trademarks and Tradenames

ORGANIZATION will seek to protect its trademarks and tradenames when commercially reasonable to do so. Names that will be used as trademarks and/ or tradenames and the manner in which these names are used will be determined on a case-by-case basis by ORGANIZATION's IP counsel. ORGANIZATION shall take reasonable measures to respect any trademarks and/or tradenames of third parties, in the selection and/or use of such trademarks or tradenames by ORGANIZATION

IX. Computer Software

It is the policy of the ORGANIZATION to license and use software in compliance with any agreements made when obtaining such software. Any improper or unauthorized use of any software by ORGANIZATION is contrary to this policy. To this end, ORGANIZATION licenses software from outside sources and may not own certain rights in the software. Employees and agents who use such software shall use it only in accordance with any license governing such use. Employees and agents of ORGANIZATION shall not misuse or make any unauthorized copies of any software for use on any ORGANIZATION computer equipment. Employees and agents shall not store on his or her company-provided computer any software that has not been approved by the IP Team or IT.

X. Copyrighted Materials

It is the policy of the ORGANIZATION to properly use copyrighted works. As may be deemed necessary by the IP Team, due to the internal usage of copyrighted materials, ORGANIZATION may obtain one or more licenses from the Copyright Clearance Center ("CCC") or other appropriate clearing house or permissions bureau, and will abide by the terms of the CCC license in using copyrighted material. Employees and agents of ORGANIZATION shall not use any ORGANIZATION resources or equipment to make any unauthorized copies of any copyrighted material.

XI. Developments made under Contract with Others

Any developments made under contract with or in collaboration with anyone outside of ORGANIZATION shall be brought to the attention of a member of the ORGANIZATION IP Team before any patents or other IP rights are sought.

XII. Conflict of Interest

Employees, contractors and agents of ORGANIZATION shall take no action that would be contrary to this policy, including but not limited to seeking to procure any rights in any intellectual property or trade secrets that would be adverse to the conduct of ORGANIZATION's business in any field of business engaged in by ORGANIZATION or in which it is reasonably anticipated that ORGANIZATION may engage.

XIII. Proprietary Rights Designations

Employees and agents of ORGANIZATION should be mindful of designations of claims of ownership of IP such as the phrases "patented," "patent pending," "®," "™," "SM," "©," or the like. It shall be the regular practice of the ORGANIZATION to mark its patent numbers on products sold by the ORGANIZATION under the patents. Any questions or concerns about the use of these or like symbols should be directed to the IP Team or to ORGANIZATION's legal counsel.

XIV. Acknowledgement of IP Policy

I have read and understand ORGANIZATION's IP Policy and, for good and valuable consideration (the receipt of which I hereby acknowledge), I agree to comply with it.

_____

Signature

_____

Printed Name

Dated: _____, 20____.

Index